Safety of Computer Architectures

Safety of Computer Architectures

Edited by
Jean-Louis Boulanger

First published 2010 in Great Britain and the United States by ISTE Ltd and John Wiley & Sons, Inc.
Adapted and updated from *Sécurisation des architectures informatiques* published 2009 in France by Hermes Science/Lavoisier © LAVOISIER 2009

ISTE Ltd
27-37 St George's Road
London SW19 4EU
UK

www.iste.co.uk

John Wiley & Sons, Inc.
111 River Street
Hoboken, NJ 07030
USA

www.wiley.com

Library of Congress Cataloging-in-Publication Data

Sécurisation des architectures informatiques. English
  Safety of computer architectures / edited by Jean-Louis Boulanger.
    p. cm.
  Includes bibliographical references and index.
  ISBN 978-1-84821-197-1
  1. Computer architecture. 2. Computer systems--Reliability. 3. Computer security. 4. Avionics--Safety measures. I. Boulanger, Jean-Louis. II. Title.
  QA76.9.A73S4313 2010
  005.8--dc22
                                                                          2010016489

British Library Cataloguing-in-Publication Data
A CIP record for this book is available from the British Library
ISBN 978-1-84821-197-1

Printed and bound in Great Britain by CPI Antony Rowe, Chippenham and Eastbourne.

MIX
Paper from
responsible sources
FSC® C013604

Table of Contents

Introduction

In recent years, we have experienced an increase in the use of computers and an increase of the inclusion of computers in systems of varying complexity. This evolution affects products of daily life (household appliances, automobiles, etc.) as well as industrial products (industrial control, medical devices, financial transactions, etc.).

The malfunction of systems within these products can have a direct or indirect impact on integrity (injury, pollution, alteration of the environment) and/or on the lives of people (users, population, etc.) or an impact on the functioning of an organization. Processes in industry are becoming increasingly automated. These systems are subject to *dependability* requirements.

Today, dependability has become a *requirement*, not a concern (which was previously the case in high-risk domains such as the nuclear or aerospace industries), in a similar fashion to productivity, which has gradually imposed itself on most industrial and technological sectors.

Dependable systems must protect against certain failures that may have disastrous consequences for people (injury, death), for a company (branding, financial aspects), and/or for the environment.

In the context of systems incorporating "programmed" elements, two types of elements are implemented: hardware elements (computing unit, central processing unit (CPU), memory, bus, field programmable gate array (FPGA), digital signal processor (DSP), programmable logic controller, etc.) and software elements (program, library, operating system, etc.). In this book, we will focus on the safety of the hardware element.

Where the gravity and/or frequency associated with the risks is very important, it is said that the system is "critical". These "critical" systems are subjected to evaluations (assessment of conformity to standards) and/or certifications (evaluation leading to a certificate of conformity to a standard). This work is carried out by teams that are outside of the realization process.

This book aims to present the principles of securing computer architectures through the presentation of tangible examples.

In Chapter 1 the overall set of techniques (diversity, redundancy, recovery, encoding, etc.) for securing the hardware element of an architecture is presented.

For the railway transport field, Chapters 2, 3, 4, 5 and 11 present the applicable standards (CENELEC EN 50126, EN 50128, and EN 50129) as well as tangible examples (SACEM, SAET-METEOR, CSD, PIPC and the DIGISAFE XME architecture).

Chapters 6 and 7 will cover the field of aeronautics and outer space through three known examples, which are the aircraft from the AIRBUS Company, satellites and the ARIANE 5 launcher. The aviation field was one of the first to establish a referential standard that is currently composed of the DO 178 standard for embedded software development aspects, a trade referential consisting of a set of regulations FAR/JAR, applicable to all aircraft manufacturers and a set of methodological guides produced by the aviation community, ARP 45.74 and ARP 47.61. This referential has been recently complemented by the DO 254 standard, which applies to digital component aspects, such as FPGAs and other ASICs. The DO 278 standard applies to ground software aspects.

For automation-based systems, Chapter 8 presents examples of installations in the oil industry. The IEC 61508 standard allows for a definition and control of the safety objectives (SIL). Chapter 8 presents an opportunity to revisit this standard and its use. This chapter is supplemented by Chapter 10, which is a summary of the implementation of safety instrumented systems (SIS) in industry.

It should be noted that Chapter 12 provides an example of the implementation of a rather interesting automation-based system: the Large Hadron Collider (LHC).

Finally, in Chapter 9 we present examples in the automotive field. The automotive field is currently evolving. This development will result in the establishment of a variation of the IEC 61508 standard for the automotive industry called ISO 26262. This standard takes the safety level concept (called here the automotive safety integrity level, or ASIL) and identifies recommendations for activities and methodologies for implementation in order to achieve a given safety objective. The automotive field is driven by different types of objectives (cost, place, weight, volume, delays, safety), which requires the establishment of new solutions (see Chapter 9).

It is hoped that this book will enlighten the reader as to the complexity of the systems that are used everyday and the difficulty in achieving a dependable system. It should be noted that this encompasses the need to produce a dependable system but also the need to guarantee the safety during the operational period, which can range from a few days to over 50 years.

Chapter 1

Principles

1.1. Introduction

The objective of this chapter[1] is to present the different methods for securing the functional safety of hardware architecture. We shall speak of hardware architecture as safety can be based on one or more calculating units. We shall voluntarily leave aside the "software" aspects.

1.2. Presentation of the basic concepts: faults, errors and failures

1.2.1. *Obstruction to functional safety*

As indicated in [LAP 92], the functional safety of a complex system can be compromised by three types of incidents: failures, faults, and errors. The system elements are subjected to failures, which can potentially result in accidents.

DEFINITION 1.1: FAILURE – as indicated in the IEC 61508 [IEC 98] standard: a failure is the suspension of a functional unit's ability to accomplish a specified function. Since the completion of a required function necessarily excludes certain behavior, and certain functions can be specified in terms of behavior to avoid, then the occurrence of a behavior to avoid is a failure.

Chapter written by Jean-Louis BOULANGER.

1. This chapter is based on educational material produced together with M. Walter SCHÖN, Professor at the University of Technology of Compiègne, whom I can never thank enough.

From the previous definition, the need to define the concepts of normal (safe) and abnormal (unsafe) conduct can be removed, with a clear boundary between the two.

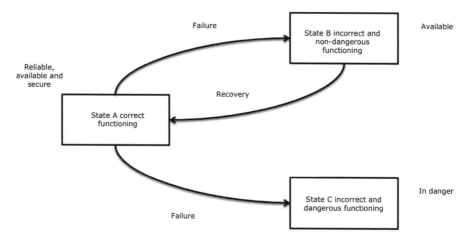

Figure 1.1. *Evolution of the state of the system*

Figure 1.1 shows a representation of the different states of a system (correct, incorrect) and the possible transitions between these states. The system states can be classified into three families:

– correct states: there is no dangerous situation;

– incorrect safe states: a failure was detected and the system is in a safe state;

– incorrect states: this is a dangerous, uncontrolled situation: there are potential accessible accidents.

When the system reaches a fallback state, there may be a partial or complete shutdown of service. The conditions of fallback may allow a return to the correct state after a recovery action.

Failures can be random or systematic. A random failure occurs unpredictably and is the result of damage affecting the hardware aspects of the system. In general, random failure can be quantified because of its nature (wear, aging, etc.).

A systematic failure is linked deterministically to a cause. The cause of the failure can only be eliminated by a reapplication of the production process (design, manufacture, documentation) or by recovery procedures. Given its nature, a systematic failure is not quantifiable.

A failure (definition 1.1) is an external manifestation of an observable error (the IEC 61508 [IEC 98] standard speaks of an *anomaly*).

Despite all the precautions taken during the production of a component, it may be subject to design flaws, verification flaws, usage defects, operational maintenance defects, etc.

DEFINITION 1.2: ERROR – an error is the consequence of an internal defect occurring during the implementation of the product (a variable or an erroneous program condition).

The notion of fault may be derived from the defect, the fault being the cause of the error (e.g. short-circuit, electromagnetic disturbance, design flaw).

DEFINITION 1.3: FAULT – a fault is a non-conformity inserted in the product (for example an erroneous code).

In conclusion, it should be noted that confidence in the functional safety of a system might be compromised by the appearance of obstacles such as faults, errors, and failures.

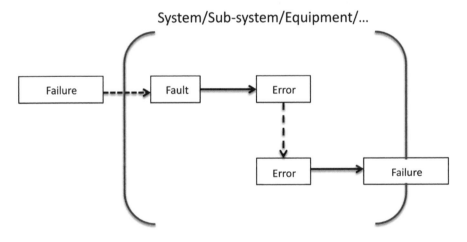

Figure 1.2. *Fundamental chain*

Figure 1.2 shows the fundamental chain linking these obstacles. The onset of a failure may reveal a fault, which in turn will result in one or more errors: this (these) new error(s) may lead to the emergence of a new failure.

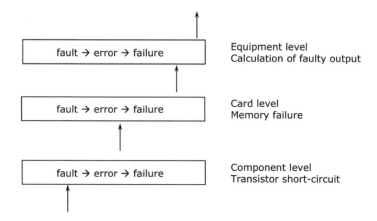

Equipment level
Calculation of faulty output

Card level
Memory failure

Component level
Transistor short-circuit

Figure 1.3. *System propagation*

The link between the obstacles must be viewed throughout the entire system as shown in Figure 1.3.

The fundamental chain (Figure 1.2) can happen in a single system (Figure 1.3), and affect the communication of components (sub-system, equipment, software, hardware), or occur in a system of systems (Figure 1.4), where the failure generates a fault in the next system.

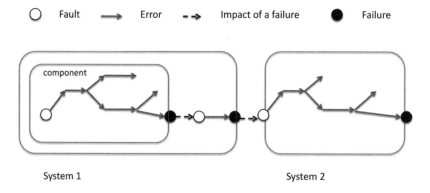

Figure 1.4. *Propagation in a system*

Figure 1.5 provides an example of the implementation of failures. As previously indicated, a failure is detected through the divergent behavior of a system in relation to its specification. This failure occurs within the limits of the system due to the fact that a series of internal system errors has implications for the development of the output. In our case, the source of the errors is a fault in the embedded executable software. These defects can be of three kinds: either they are faults introduced by the programmer (BUG), or they are faults introduced by the tools (generated by the executable, download methods, etc.) or by hardware failure (memory failure, component short-circuit, external disturbance (for example EMC), etc.).

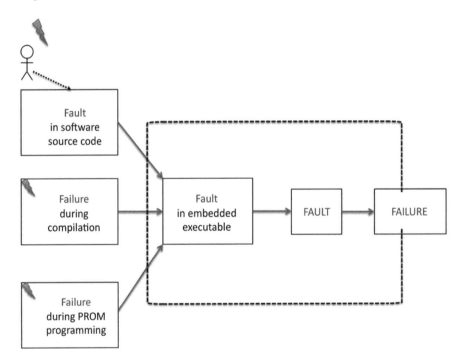

Figure 1.5. *Example of propagation*

It should be noted that faults can be inserted in the design during conception (default in the software, under-sized design of the system, etc.), during production (generation of the executable, manufacturing equipment, etc.), during installation, during use and/or during maintenance. The diagram in Figure 1.5 may well reflect various situations. Figure 1.6 shows the impact of human error.

At this point in the discussion, it is interesting to note that there are two families of failures, systematic failures and random failures. Random failures are due to production processes, aging, wear, deterioration, external phenomena, etc. Systematic failures are reproducible, because they result from design flaws. It is noteworthy that a random failure can occur from a conceptual defect (underestimation of the effect of temperature on the processor). As we shall see later, there are several techniques (diversity, redundancy, etc.) allowing detection and/or control of random failures. For systematic failures, control is more difficult because it relies on quality (predetermined and systematic practice) and activities of verification and validation.

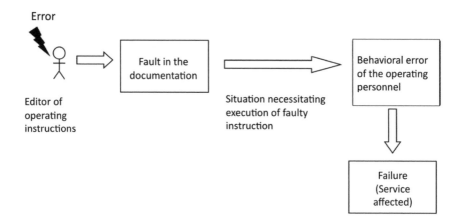

Figure 1.6. *Impact of a human error*

1.2.2. *Safety demonstration studies*

The previous section served to recall some basic concepts (fault, error, and failure), but the systematic research of failures and the analysis of their effects on the system is achieved through activities such as preliminary hazard analysis (PHA), failure modes and effects analysis (FMEA), fault trees analysis (FTA), etc.

Analyses related to dependability are now common (see [VIL 88] for example) and imposed by standards. All of these studies allow a demonstration of safety, which will be formalized through a safety case. The generic standard IEC 61508 [IEC 98], applicable to electronic-based systems and programmable electronics, covers this point and offers a general approach.

1.2.3. *Assessment*

When designing computer architecture, there are three notable types of failure:

– random failures of hardware components;

– systematic design failures: both at the hardware and software level;

– specification "errors" at the system level.

1.3. Safe and/or available architecture

In terms of hardware architecture, the main failure is related to the emission of erroneous output. There are two possibilities:

– emission of an incorrect permissive output, creating a security problem (e.g. a green light allowing the wrongful passage of a vehicle);

– emission of incorrect restrictive output, creating a problem of availability (e.g. trains stopping).

Depending on the impact of the lack of output, it is possible to define two families of systems:

– integrity systems: there should not be any erroneous output (bad data or correct data at a wrong time, etc.). Integrity systems are systems where the process is irreversible (e.g. banking transactions). For such systems, it is preferable to stop all functions rather than to malfunction. The system is called fail-silent (fail-safe, fail-stop);

– persistent systems: non-release of correct data should not occur. Persistent systems are systems with no fallback state, implying that lack of data causes loss of control. For this type of system, it is preferable to have some bad data rather than no data at all. The system is said to be fail-operate.

An integrity system is safe if a fallback state can be achieved passively. For example, in the railway sector, any failure results in cutting off the power supply, and without energy, the train brake is no longer disabled. The train has therefore passively reached a safe state: "stopped train".

1.4. Resetting a processing unit

Section 1.3 served, in the context of the discussion on persistence and integrity, to bring the issue of the necessity, or not, of having a fallback state.

In the case of an integrity system, the transition to a fallback state is final. Within the context of a transient defect, the unavailability induced may be unacceptable from the viewpoint of the client (for example, loss of the anti-lock breaking system (ABS) function in a car). Therefore, it is tempting to go through an intermediate step, which attempts to reset all or part (one processing unit among *n*) of the equipment.

Use of the reset function must be controlled, several problems may appear:

– during start up, reset of a failing processing unit can cause the reset of the requesting unit due to divergent contexts, this can result in an uncontrolled reset loop. A guarantee must ensure that outputs are in a restrictive state during these intermediate states;

– the reset time can be well below the error detection time, and despite requests for reset, the system produces outputs while there is an error. A reset loop can be detected through a reset counter. This reset counter must be controlled. It must also be demonstrated that the reset has an effect *vis-à-vis* the failures that need to be covered;

– etc.

Regarding the reset of equipment, attentiveness is key, and it must be shown that the measure is efficient and there is no risk of hiding an erroneous situation.

1.5. Overview of safety techniques

Securing hardware architecture can be achieved through five main techniques:

– error detection (section 1.5.1);

– the setup of a diversion (section 1.5.2);

– the setup of a redundancy (section 1.5.3);

– the setup of a retrieval (section 1.5.4).

Under this section, we shall present these different techniques and discuss their implementation.

1.5.1. *Error detection*

1.5.1.1. *Concepts*

As shown in Figure 1.7, this technique is intended to complement the hardware architecture with an element for detecting errors: in the case of error detection, different solutions may be envisaged, such as restart or cutting off output.

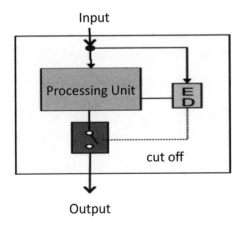

Output

Figure 1.7. *The principle of error detection*

The architecture in Figure 1.7 is an integrity architecture: the output is cut off in cases of error detection.

The implementation of error detection is based on three techniques:

– detection of temporal coherence: this is done through the establishment of a "watchdog" that is able to detect the temporal drift of the application, infinite loops or non-compliance with a due time. The "watchdog" may be a hardware or software element;

– detection of hardware defects: this is done through the establishment of self-tests. These self-tests allow for a more or less complete test of a piece of hardware (ALU (Arithmatic and Logic Unit), memory, voter, etc.). Self-tests can be held fully or partially during initialization, at the end of a mission, during each cycle and/or during certain periods. The main difficulty of this technique lies in the relevance of the tests (coverage and sufficiency) at the time of their execution;

– detection of an execution defect: this is implemented through the verification of different consistencies in the application behavior. It is possible to have an analysis of the consistency of inputs (input correlation, input redundancy, etc.), the consistency of outputs (one output cannot change randomly from one cycle to another), the consistency of behavior (management of the "flag" in the code allows verification of the execution path), the correction of the execution path ("offline" calculation of all the paths and "online" comparison of the execution path).

1.5.1.2. *Watchdog*

Simple and inexpensive, the watchdog is used to detect errors (frequent and not always acceptable) leading to inactivity ("crash") of a central unit. More generally, it can detect a temporal drift.

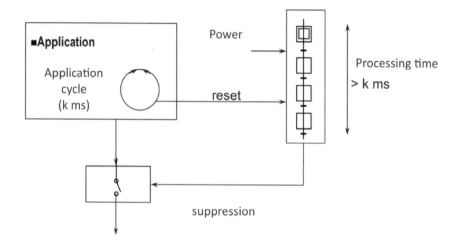

Figure 1.8. *Watchdog*

The temporal drift of an architecture can be induced by different types of failures: failure of the clock or timers, failure of the software application (infinite loop, blocking, expiry of cycle processing time, etc.), failure at resource levels, etc.

In the context of Figure 1.8, the watchdog is a hardware device, periodically refreshed (or reset) by the processor (for example, at the beginning of each application cycle), which has the ability to cut off output. Note that the watchdog can also be a software application.

There is no general rule, but if a refresh is not undertaken after a fixed period, the watchdog generates an error signal that can be used, for example, to perform:

– a restart: reset of the processor;

– output suppression: system fail-silent;

– a change of unit: setup of another unit;

– etc.

1.5.1.3. *Self-tests*

1.5.1.3.1. Presentation

After detecting temporal drifts, it is possible to detect a second source of failure, related to "hardware": memory failure, failure of processing units, etc.

Element	Type of tests
ALU and/or instruction set	Specific tests to detect errors in instruction and in addressing modes
RAM	Writing/reading test, e.g. the 55/AA type
ROM, FLASH	Checksum or 16 bit CRC^2 protection
EEPROM	Checksum or 16 bit CRC protection
I/O	Hardware provided to test inputs and outputs
Clock/timer	Exchange and comparison of signals between two microcontrollers each with own clock

Table 1.1. *Families of tests*

To detect hardware failures, it is possible to put tests in place. These tests aim to verify that a piece of hardware is able to render the expected service. Table 1.1 presents the type of tests that may be associated with different elements of a computer's architecture.

1.5.1.3.2. Example

Table 1.1 summarizes the type of tests that can be implemented to detect different types of hardware failures. We will take as an example the detection of failures in the RAM (random access memory).

The simplest technique, and the most time-consuming in terms of processing, is the implementation of writing tests with proofreading. This test can be random (the memory cell tested and/or the writing value are not predetermined) or predefined. The writing test with proofreading can be done on all or parts of the memory.

This type of check involves saving the memory contents to be tested and implementing the writing test with proofreading. In general, the test aims to write a value (e.g. 55 and/or AA, these values being able to complement each other) and verify by proofreading that the writings have been successfully completed. The main interest lies in the simplicity and effectiveness of the technique; however, the main problem lies in the link between memory size and execution time.

---

2. The notion of a CRC (cyclic redundancy check) will be presented later, see section 1.5.3.2.4.

An evolution of this test consists of selecting a pattern (circle, square, cross, etc.), reproducing it in the memory, and calculating the checksum of the whole memory. There is a significant gain in processing time and this allows for further detection of failures in the ALU, which is used to perform the checksum calculation.

Finally, it may be necessary to focus control on a data set considered "critical" to the analyzed system. It is then possible to write each of these critical data in two areas of the RAM (two different areas, two different memory banks, etc.) and to perform a consistency check between the two copies of the data. The copies may be identical or not. For example, if we choose to write the value and its counterpart, verification of consistency can be achieved through a sum and a comparison with 0. This technique improves the execution time of the check and uses the ALU, but its main disadvantage is an excessive use of memory.

1.5.1.3.3. Implementation strategy

These tests (called self-tests) can be associated with different strategies:

– execution during initialization: the objective is to verify that the system is able to complete its mission;

– execution at the end of the mission: the objective is to have an assessment of the status of the system;

– cyclic execution: the objective is to detect failures during the mission.

Cyclic execution requires cessation (suspension) of the other processes, including the main task, and even of a backup of the context (all memory used). For this reason, cyclic execution may be complete (all tests were conducted), partial (a subset of the test is conducted), or distributed (all tests are conducted over several cycles).

In any case, this mechanism can only detect temporary failures if they occur during the test period.

The main difficulty of these tests lies in the selection of an area with good coverage of the failures and optimization of the frequency of these tests.

1.5.1.4. *Consistency checks*

A consistency check does not attempt to detect all failures but seeks to ensure that the state of the system is consistent with regards to a specific criterion. To conclude, it is not meant to verify the correction. It is possible to detect errors by checking:

– consistency between input data;

– consistency of output data *vis-à-vis* input data;

– consistency of performance by setting up checkpoints to check execution traces;

– etc.

It is not possible to present all types of checks, so we will only detail three different types hereafter.

1.5.1.4.1. Consistency between input data

The consistency of input data is based on the fact that in all inputs, a redundancy exists:

– two separate acquisitions, for example the same channel or two separate channels;

– a unique acquisition of several data to data, for example, speed is measured through two cogwheels;

– information can be sent encrypted (the notion of code introduces redundancy);

– two opposing inputs are made available;

– etc.

1.5.1.4.2. Consistency between outputs and inputs

For some systems, there are post-conditions that allow verification of the consistency of processing. These post-conditions establish a link between the calculated outputs and the inputs.

Some post-conditions address a particular aspect (e.g. the measurement of an angle) and are related to physical phenomena (maximum acceleration), to implementation choices (the last element of a list is always null), etc.

For example, in the context of measuring the angle of the steering wheel of a car, the angle cannot evolve beyond 90° with regards to the cycle time.

1.5.1.4.3. Consistency of execution

Consistency of performance allows us to gage whether a software application is following the paths that have been previously validated. To do this, we must be able to trace the execution of the software application. The execution of the software application is broken down into a set of traces. Each trace is a sequence of crossing points (execution path).

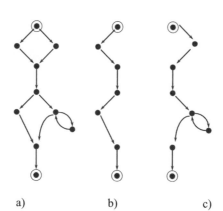

Figure 1.9. *Execution trace*

The part a) in Figure 1.9 is a representation of a program with two consecutive IF instructions and a WHILE instruction. An analysis of the execution paths in operation may lead to the selection of two execution traces. The characterization of these tracks is revealed by crossing points. The crossing points may be local (several pieces of information are stored) or global (a single variable is manipulated) indicators.

For example (Figure 1.10), it is possible to have a variable reset to 0, which when passing through a THEN branch is incremented by 1; which when passing through an ELSE branch is decremented by 1, and which, at the end of the execution, must be either 2 or −2.

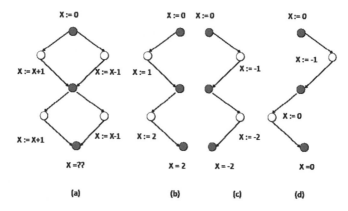

Figure 1.10. *Example of flag calculation*

In some systems with high levels of criticality, the crossing points are numerous and can allow a good control of the execution.

The more numerous and/or complex the traces are, the more important the number of crossing points; consequently, this affects the memory space (memorization of traces and of the current trace), the execution time (complementary processes), and code complexity (adding processes unrelated to the functional makes the code and associated analysis more complex).

1.5.1.5. *Assessment*

The mechanisms of error detection are relatively simple to implement and can take into account the occurrence of failures in hardware which could induce changes in the behavior of the equipment (hardware + software).

Error detection secures the execution of an application when faced with certain types of failures (temporal drift, failure of the means, failure of the process).

It enables the construction of a fail-silent system, with no output upon detection of errors, but it is also the basis of fault tolerance. In the case of detection of an anomaly, it is possible to switch to an alternative computer if there is a redundancy.

1.5.2. *Diversity*

Diversity aims to create a single component (that is to say the same function) using several different methods. The idea is that these components are not subject to the same environmental constraints, and therefore, the failures are different.

Among these diversity techniques, there are:

– ecological (or architectural) diversification: some elements (computing unit, software, operating system, etc.) are different, therefore errors impacting each element will be different;

– geographic diversification: the elements are positioned in different places, therefore the environmental constraints are different;

– spatial diversification: different versions of the same software are deployed on different machines. The idea is that each version of the software has its own defects. This technique is also used in the context of the implementation of "shelf components" (COTS: Commercial Off-The-Shelf), different versions of COTS are used;

– temporal diversification: establishment of a steady evolution of the application to be run (evolution of delays, of settings and/or of the application);

– modal diversification: the system can acquire, in different ways, the same data (network, modem, wired connection, satellite access, etc.), the power supply, etc.

Ecological/architectural diversification is the most common. When it is applied to the software, it is important that the diversification of architecture is evident, ensuring that different software will not have the same defects.

1.5.3. *Redundancy*

Redundancy is a technique that aims to provide an excess of resources to maintain proper functioning. In general, redundancy is available in three settings:

– time: it will take more time than necessary to complete the process. The application will run at least twice on the same computing unit. This simple technique requires some means of comparison of the results (voting) that is secure (self-test, etc.);

– information: there are more data than necessary, resulting in an encoding of information (bit parity, checksums, cyclic redundancy check (CRC), Hamming code, etc.). This encoding can be performed to detect errors but also for correction purposes;

– hardware: there is more equipment than necessary. Redundancy of equipment is the basic technique for nOOm architectures (*m* greater than *n*). Within this type of architecture, we may find the 2oo2 or 2oo3 architecture (*x* processing units perform the calculation and a voter shows if the result is correct). 2oo2 architecture is fail-safe, while 2oo3 architecture is available and fail-safe. Hardware redundancy can be passive (allows for emergency equipment) or active. It is not possible to list all nOOm architectures in this chapter, therefore we will present some representative examples.

The importance of redundancy is that it enables detection of random failures that occur punctually. In the context of systematic failures, redundancy will only detect the presence of a defect in the software application (for example, the unit of calculation does not know/cannot undertake more additions). Therefore, redundancy is generally enhanced by the use of diversity.

1.5.3.1. *Execution redundancy*

1.5.3.1.1. Presentation

Execution redundancy consists of running the same application twice using the same processing unit (processor, etc.). The results are usually compared by a device external to the processor, with any discord causing a fallback of the computing unit (fail-stop behavior). This technique is often used in programmable logic controllers.

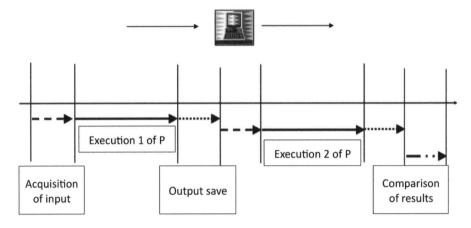

Figure 1.11. *Principle of execution redundancy*

Figure 1.11 shows the temporal pattern of an execution redundancy. We can see that the triplet "acquisition, execution, save" appears twice, and there is ultimately a comparison of the saved results.

The first use of an execution redundancy can be used to detect memory failures. To do this, one program is loaded into two different memory areas (two different addressing areas of the memory, two different memory media, etc.). Therefore, memory failure (RAM, ROM (read-only memory), EPROM (erasable programmable ROM), EEPROM (electrically erasable programmable ROM), etc.) can be detected alongside intermittent failures of the processing unit.

It should be noted that certain failures of shared hardware devices (comparison unit, processing unit) are not detected and thus remain hidden. Indeed, there are two possibilities for masking errors:

– the result of the comparison of results can always be positive regardless of the input (failure of the comparison means is the common failure mode);

– subtle failures (e.g. A–B is routinely done instead of A+B) of the ALU part of the processing unit can give the same erroneous result for each execution (the processing unit is the common failure mode).

One solution is to introduce self-testing within the execution, a comparison of discordant data (in general without going into fallback), comprehensive functional testing of the processing unit. To have effective detection, the test coverage must be adequate (coverage of the application instructions, etc.) and must be executed at the right time (initialization, during each cycle, regularly, at the end of the mission, etc.). This solution has the main disadvantage of performance costs (related to the size of self-tests and their frequency).

A second solution is to introduce a diversification of the code. This diversification may be "light" and in this case, we speak of voluntary asymmetry of the code of both applications. It is possible to force the application to use two different sets of instructions for programming, with one program using A+B and the second using –(–A–B).

An asymmetry of data (different memory allocation) can be introduced for all objects (variables, constants, parameters, functions, and procedures) in memory for both programs. Note that these voluntary asymmetries can be introduced automatically within a single program. For both types of asymmetry, the compilation phase should be carefully inspected and asymmetry must always present in the final executable.

In general, redundancy should be complete (the entire application is executed twice), but a partial redundancy may be sufficient (Figure 1.12b).

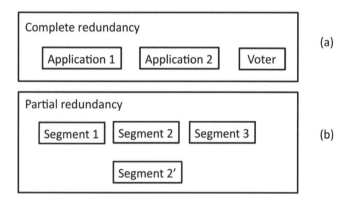

Figure 1.12. *a) Complete redundancy and b) partial redundancy*

The establishment of a floating-point computation in a security function requires the implementation of a security technique. The introduction of a partial redundancy of the floating-point computation requires a diversity, which might, for example, use different libraries. Therefore, it is necessary to accept certain errors during comparison.

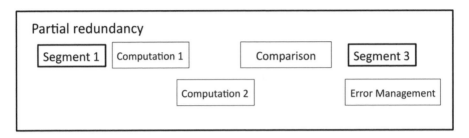

Figure 1.13. *Partial redundancy*

Software diversity can be accompanied by hardware diversity. As in [LEA 05], it is possible to have a hardware architecture offering the FPU of the main processor and an annex unit to perform the computations. The diversification of the code is a little higher because we will use two sets of instructions. The concept of error acceptance here will be essential.

1.5.3.1.2. Example 1

The introduction of a partial asymmetry has the advantage of being relatively simple to implement, but has the main drawback of having a fairly low ability to detect failure. It is then possible to generalize this solution through the establishment of a diversification of the application to be executed. There are then several options: have two production teams, have two different code generators, etc.

For example, Figure 1.14 shows how EBICAB 900 works. There is a diversification of the application developed under application A and B. Application A is divided into F1, F2, F3, and application B into F1', F2', F3'.

Three development teams are then required, two independent teams are responsible for the implementation of two applications, the third team is in charge of the specification (which is shared) and of synchronization. As there is only one acquisition phase, the data are protected (CRC, etc.). The data handled by application A is varied (stored differently in the memory, bit to bit mirror, etc.) with regards to application B.

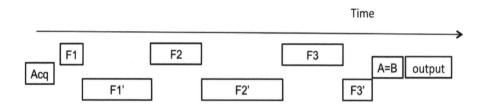

Figure 1.14. *Principle of EBICAB temporal execution*

1.5.3.1.3. Example 2

As a second example, we introduce campaign equipment, which links a central terminal to the tags (element allowing orders to be given to the train). In this application, a single software application is formally developed using method B [ABR 96] and a processing unit.

B is a formal method which guarantees (through mathematical proof) that the software is correct *vis-à-vis* the attributes. This guarantee is interesting, but it does not cover the code generator, the chain generating the executable (compiler, linker, etc.) and the loading means.

In the context of this application, there are two code generators and two channels of generation of the executable (two compilers). This allows for two different versions of the code, and it is shown that the address table (variables, constants, functions, parameters, etc.) of the two executables are effectively different. The loading of each version of the application is made in different memory spaces.

1.5.3.1.4. Assessment

Execution redundancy is a rather simple technique with the main advantage of the use of a single processing unit. The major drawback is the execution time, running double processing with voting and self-test takes at least 2.5 to 3.5 times the duration of a single process. Therefore, this type of solution is used for systems where processing time is not critical.

The implementation of partial or total diversity of the code allows a good detection rate of random and systematic errors (depending on the degree of diversification), but increases the cost (maintenance of two software programs, etc.).

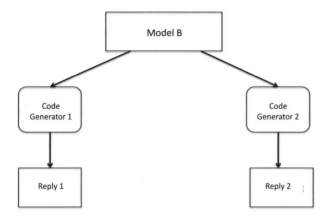

Figure 1.15. *Diversification*

As shown in Figure 1.15, in the context of this application, there are two code generators and two channels of generation of the executable (two compilers). This allows for two different versions of the executable. It is thus possible to show that the address table (variables, constants, functions, parameters, etc.) of the two executables are actually different. The loading of each version of the application is made in different memory spaces.

1.5.3.2. *Informational redundancy*

1.5.3.2.1. Presentation

Informational redundancy is a major fault-tolerance technique. Informational redundancy consists of handling additional information (called control or redundancy) that can detect, and even correct, errors.

Under this section, we will discuss:

– parity check;

– cyclical redundancy code;

– Hamming code;

– arithmetic code.

In general, informational redundancy is used to detect failures related to stored (memory, etc.) and/or transmitted (data bus, network, etc.) data, but it can also be used (more difficult) to detect failures of calculation and/or control (self-checking) units.

Given that a network(s) of critical communication systems is (are) considered closed, the codes used are essentially separable (control bits distinct from the main information bits).

Note that this is still evolving, and with the implementation of "open" networks (wireless network, traveler network connected to a control network, etc.), it will be necessary to implement non-separable codes (where extraction of the useful part is more complex). This section is a presentation and not a course in cryptography, therefore we will not delve further into the topic (see for example [LIN 99]).

1.5.3.2.2. Parity check

Parity check is a very old technique that was used in modem transmissions. It is the simplest of techniques for detecting errors, a single control bit (called parity bit) is added per word. The additional bit is calculated so that the sum of the bits of the word (*modulo* 2) is null (even parity convention) or equal to 1 (odd parity convention).

A parity check detects an error (or errors in odd numbers). It does not detect double errors (or in even numbers). Upon detection of errors, there can be no correction.

A parity check can be extended to the processing of a block of words, in this case we speak of cross-parity check.

1.5.3.2.3. Checksum and process check

In the context of an executable, rather than adding an information bit related to a word or to several words, it is common to have a checksum corresponding to the sum of words that make up the application. A checksum can also be applied to a series of words, such as a column in the memory.

A checksum can be easily calculated and it is possible to quickly verify that the program loaded into the memory is that which was expected: in the railway sector the checksum is stored in a stub, which is read during initialization. An evolution in the application involves a change of stub.

In the field of networks, it may be necessary to distinguish frames of information from "life index" frames. Indeed, some systems may require that subscribers report through frames that have no functional need. This applies to the automobile sector, certain computers emit frames containing no information, but as there is a principle of persistence of information, these frames have a long lifetime on the network. A piece of information allows dating and thus excludes the use of frames.

The implementation of these techniques is not a problem, but they cover only certain very specific errors.

1.5.3.2.4. Cyclic redundancy check

The CRC is a powerful and easy to implement means of controlling the integrity of data. It is the primary method of error detection used in telecommunications.

The principle of a CRC is to treat binary sequences as binary polynomials, that is to say, polynomials whose coefficients correspond to the binary sequence. Therefore, the binary sequence $M=u_{n-1}u_{n-2}...u_1u_0$ can be considered as polynomial $M(x)=u_{n-1}x^{n-1}+u_{n-2}x^{n-2}+...u_1x+u_0$.

In this error detection mechanism, a predefined polynomial (called the polynomial generator), denoted $G(x)$ is known to the transmitter and to the receiver. The $G(x)$ degree is k. For the transmitter, error detection consists of implementing an algorithm on the frame bits in order to generate a CRC, and to transmit these two elements to the receiver. The receiver then needs to perform the same calculation to verify that the CRC is valid.

In practice, M is the message corresponding to the frame bits to be sent and $M(x)$ corresponds to the associated polynomial. We call M' (Figure 1.16) the transmitted message, that is to say, the original message to which the CRC of k bits was appended.

The CRC is such that $M'(x)/G(x)=0$. The code part of the CRC ($R(x)$) is thus equal to the rest of the polynomial division $x^k.M(x)$ by $G(x)$ ($M(x)$, to which we appended k bit null, corresponds to the length of the CRC).

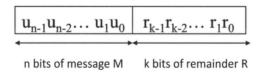

n bits of message M   k bits of remainder R

Figure 1.16. *Format of message M' with the CRC*

The transmission aims to deliver the message $x^k.M(x)+R(x)$. It is therefore a separable code. When received, if $M'(x)$ is not divisible by $G(x)$, there is an error. If $M'(X)$ is divisible by $G(x)$, it is likely (depending on the choice of the polynomial $G(x)$) that there is no error.

1.5.3.2.5. The Hamming code

The Hamming code consists of injecting the set of messages (source vocabulary over k bits: generally consisting of 2^k possible words) within a larger space (n bits n>k) so that the coded words corresponding to the messages are sufficiently different.

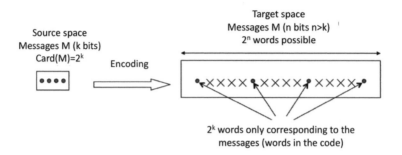

Figure 1.17. *Hamming code principle*

The difference between two coded messages (words corresponding to messages form the source vocabulary: words said to be in the code) is measured by the Hamming distance, which is the number of different bits. The Hamming distance (d) of a code for a given source vocabulary is the lower value of the distance between two words in the code. The words not corresponding to the coded messages are said to be outside of the code. A Hamming code is characterized by the triplet [k, n, d].

A code whose Hamming distance is d can detect up to d–1 errors. A code whose Hamming distance is d=2D+1 is capable of correcting up to D errors, by bringing the erroneous word (outside of the code) to the word in the closest code.

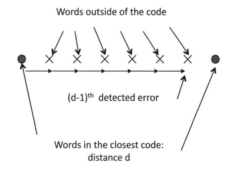

Figure 1.18. *Hamming distance*

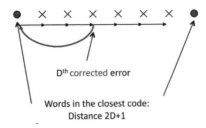

Figure 1.19. *Error correction*

In order to make the Hamming code more tangible, we will describe a Hamming code characterized by the triplet [4, 7, 3]. Source messages are of a $M_4M_3M_2M_1$ form, we require three control bits C_1, C_2, C_3 (which brings the target space to seven bits) with a Hamming distance of three, allowing for detection of two errors and the correction of one.

The basic principle of our code is as follows: M_4 intervenes in the calculation of the three C_j and each M_i is used by two different C_j on three.

The message emitted takes the shape of $E_7\ E_6\ E_5\ E_4\ E_3\ E_2\ E_1 = M_4\ M_3\ M_2\ C_3\ M_1\ C_2\ C_1$; based on the choices listed above and the fact that the number 7 encodes itself over three bits and that there is only one breakdown with three bits to the value one.

The expression of the relationship between the elements of the message and the breakdown of position j of the associated element E_j allows construction of the following equations:

– M_4 corresponds to E_7 that is k=111, therefore M_4 intervenes in C_1, C_2, C_3;

– M_3 corresponds to E_6 that is k=110, therefore M_3 intervenes in C_2, C_3;

– M_2 corresponds to E_5 that is k=101, therefore M_2 intervenes in C_1, C_3;

– C_3 corresponds to E_4 that is k=100, therefore C_3 intervenes in C_3;

– M_1 corresponds to E_3 that is k=011, therefore M_2 intervenes in C_1, C_2;

– C_2 corresponds to E_2 that is k=010, therefore C_2 intervenes in C_2;

– C_1 corresponds to E_1 that is k=001, therefore C_1 intervenes in C_1.

C_j can be constructed through equations (+ for XOR):

– $C_1 = M_1 + M_2 + M_4$;

$$- C_2 = M_1 + M_3 + M_4;$$

$$- C_3 = M_2 + M_3 + M_4.$$

The Hamming distance is three because the two source messages, differing by M_i result in two coded messages of which the control part differs by at least two C_j.

The construction of the message poses no problem. The code developed is a separable code (we know the position of the control elements). Upon receiving the message, a calculation of C_j with the M_i received allows detection and correction:

– if a single equation is wrong, the false bit is the C_j bit of the equation in question;

– if two equations are wrong, the false bit is the M_i bit common to both equations;

– if the three equations are wrong, the false bit is M_4.

Based on this principle, on receipt of the message $m_7 m_6 m_5 m_4 m_3 m_2 m_1$, it is possible to calculate three n_j so that $n_3 n_2 n_1$ gives the number of the erroneous bit in binary. If it is 0, the transfer occurred without error, otherwise a simple error is detected and corrected, or if a simple error is detected but corrected improperly, the triple error may not be detected.

The n_j are calculated using equations (+ for XOR):

$$- n_1 = m_2 + m_3 + m_6 + m_7;$$

$$- n_1 = m_4 + m_5 + m_6 + m_7;$$

$$- n_1 = m_4 + m_5 + m_6 + m_7.$$

To conclude this section, the Hamming code, once constructed, can quickly and easily detect errors. The main difficulty lies in the development of this code (for a larger space) and in demonstrating that the Hamming distance is required throughout the development of the application that has been encoded (addition of variable, changing functional areas, etc.).

1.5.3.2.6. Arithmetic code

An arithmetic code replaces the data with coded data containing two fields: the data value ("functional" part) and a coded part containing redundancy information with regards to the functional part whose consistency is preserved by arithmetic operations.

The coded part implies that the arithmetic operations be replaced by specific operations manipulating the two parts.

The coded part is constructed so that it can detect three types of errors:

– operational (and/or alteration) errors of the data; for this to happen redundant information is stored as $-2^k.x$. This information applies the principle of proof by nine, but nine is replaced here by A, which is a large number;

– processing errors (applying a plus instead of a minus) when establishing B_x. B_x is a signature associated with each variable X. This signature is predetermined (OFFLINE process) in a pseudo-random manner. For each variable result of a calculation, it is possible determine the expected B_x OFFLINE. The calculation of B_x should consider the processing of alternatives and loops. The B_x calculated OFFLINE is stored in a programmable ROM (PROM) and the execution of the program with different values for the input variables always leads to the same evolution of signatures;

– handling errors of obsolete data in the form of date D.

The encoding put into place is again a separable code.

The use of this particular encoding and associated operations allows the detection of several types of errors with a single processor, but at the cost of a processing blow, which is induced by the checks to be undertaken, as these checks highly increase the processing time.

This technique [BIE 99; MAR 90] has been developed through the introduction of SACEM[3] [GEO 90] in the 1980s and its use will be detailed in Chapter 2 of this book.

1.5.3.2.7. Assessment

The implementation of information redundancy is an interesting technique that can detect several families of errors and even make corrections. The few examples presented show that the implementation of the code is relatively easy and can affect the overall running time.

___

3. SACEM (*système d'aide à la conduite, à l'exploitation et à la maintenance*) equips line A of the RER of the Parisian subway.

1.5.3.3. *Hardware redundancy*

1.5.3.3.1. Presentation

As shown in Figure 1.20, a redundant system is a processing unit set that must be seen as a single entity. In this chapter, it is not possible to present all combinations, but we will present the most significant.

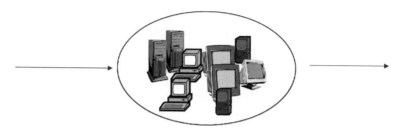

Figure 1.20. *Hardware redundancy*

Regarding the processing units used, two cases can be reported:

– either they are identical and we speak of homogenous architecture;

– or they are different and we have a heterogenous architecture, the difference being the introduction of diversity:

- processing units may be different,

- processing units may be identical but with different operating systems and the same application,

- processing units and operating system are identical but the application is different,

- all elements are different, etc.

Regarding redundancy, there are two forms:

– redundancy without voter: one unit is responsible for preparing the outputs;

– redundancy with voter: several units carry out processing and an additional element selects the output.

There is already a wide field of possibilities. In the following sections, we will present them in more detail but this will serve as an overview only.

1.5.3.3.2. Master/slave architecture

As shown in Figure 1.21, the master/slave architecture is composed of two identical processing units. The "master" unit is responsible for all processing. It triggers the sequence of activity for the "slave" unit, executing the processes and selecting the output based on its own results and those of the "slave" unit.

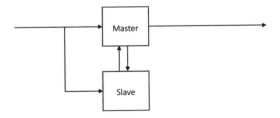

Figure 1.21. *Master/slave architecture*

One of the finer points of this architecture lies in the synchronization of the processes. As the processing units and applications (*modulo* the control of the master) are identical, there are a number of common failures (processor failure, software defect, etc.), which will not be detected.

As the units and the applications are identical, the maintenance costs are controlled. The presence of a master unit ensures output checks. The main drawback of this architecture lies in the absolute control of the master unit; it alone selects the value of outputs without consulting the slave unit.

The architecture presented previously (Figure 1.21) can be improved to better control failures. The introduction of a bilateral exchange between the two processing units and the introduction of decision making (triggering a reset, cutting off outputs, correction indicator, etc.) for the slave unit in case of divergence can correct the main defect of the first architecture, as shown in Figure 1.22.

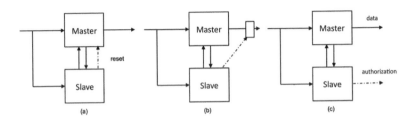

Figure 1.22. *Three variants*

This supplemented architecture remains sensitive to the shared mode (hardware failure, software failure, etc.), but can handle random failures.

Regarding Figure 1.22, case (b) is an integrity architecture and case (c) is a persistent architecture. For case (a), the slave unit can reset the master unit, introducing a latency period and the impact on output must be analyzed.

A double reset (each unit, upon detection of a divergence, may trigger the reset of the other unit) can introduce endless reset loops, see the discussion in section 1.4 concerning reset of a processing unit.

This architecture will of course be supplemented by self-tests guaranteeing the detection of hardware defects, data protection, and the program. The establishment of a dual acquisition channel allows the detection of defects during acquisition. This architecture can be supplemented by application asymmetry or by diversity (hardware or software).

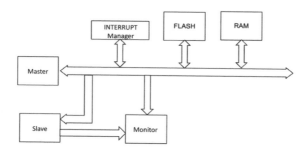

Figure 1.23. *Lock-step dual processor architecture*

Figure 1.23 (see [BAL 03]) presents an architecture proposed by the automobile sector, where two identical processing units perform the same process and share common hardware components (memory, bus, interrupt manager, etc.).

Each instruction is sent to two processing units, each performing the process and making requests for reading, writing and/or access to the next instruction. The "master" processing unit controls the bus while the slave unit is connected to a monitor. This same monitor is listening to the bus (and therefore the master unit). If a divergence arises over a request for access to a variable, writing a variable or access to the next instruction, the monitor secures the system.

The monitor's role is to verify the process consistency of a processing unit, but not failures of the bus, memory, or interrupt manager. The bus and the memory can be protected by an integrity check. The interrupt manager, which is of low complexity, must be tolerant to faults.

A variant of this architecture called "orthogonal redundancy" [LEA 05] uses two different processing units to perform floating-point computations, for example.

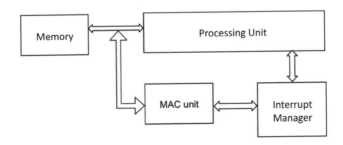

Figure 1.24. *"Orthogonal redundancy" architecture*

This architecture is based on an asymmetry of hardware resources (processing unit, memory, etc.). The main interest is to have two different computation units (ALU and DSP (Digital Signal Processing) for example).

For example, Figure 1.24 presents an implementation of the ST10 processor from ST Microelectronics. This processor contains an ALU internally and can be interfaced to a MAC (Multiply and ACcumulate) is a DSP. The ALU and MAC each have a set of specific instructions for mathematical operations. The MAC optimizes computations of the product, accumulation and operations of digital filtering type.

As shown in Figure 1.25, in the context of the brake function, floating-point computations are made by both computation units. The results of both calculations are compared and must be equivalent. The equivalence should be defined (problem of accuracy and acceptability of results).

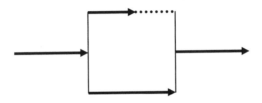

Figure 1.25. *Temporal aspects*

Orthogonal redundancy mainly allows detection of failures at the ALU level when handling floating-points for example.

1.5.3.3.3. Worker/checker architecture

An evolution of the master/slave architecture consists of separating the role of each unit. One of the processing units is dedicated to completing the process while the second unit is designed to control processing.

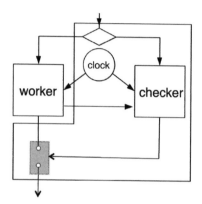

Figure 1.26. *Worker/checker*

As shown in Figure 1.26, a processing unit (worker) is dedicated to elaborating outputs, while the second processing unit (checker) is dedicated to elaborating the authorization of outputs. The checker can undertake the same process and carry out a comparison, an approximate calculation, or verification of outputs produced by the first processing unit. The approximate calculation and verification of the outputs produced does not verify the correction but the plausibility of the results.

The processing units must be synchronized in order to come to a decision. This architecture introduces diversity at the software application level. The greater the diversification, the lower the impact of shared modes of failures induced by the presence of identical hardware.

Maintenance costs for this type of architecture are somewhat higher, due to the management of both software applications, the main difficulty being to ensure that it is always possible to decide the plausibility of the output calculated during the life of system.

1.5.3.3.4. nOOm Architecture

2oo2 architecture uses two identical processing units and a voter. Both units carry out the same processes, and the results are submitted to a vote. If the results are identical, the output is delivered. In case of divergence, the system can (a) stop (integral system) or (b) indicate the anomaly (persistent system).

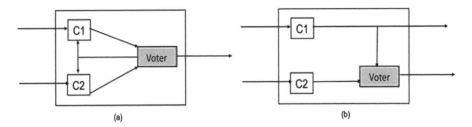

(a)   (b)

Figure 1.27. *2oo2 architecture*

This architecture allows the detection of faults but it is not fault tolerant. It should also be noted that there are shared failure modes associated with the processing units and the software. Regarding the software, it should be developed with an adequate level of security. For hardware defects, there should be an introduction of self-tests at least for the memory and processor.

The voter is a unique element, but the safety justification is based on the fact that the voting hardware is of a small size and can be fully analyzed.

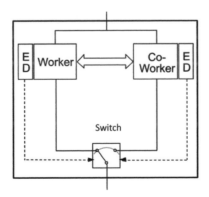

Figure 1.28. *1oo2D architecture*

A variant (see Figure 1.28) of the 2oo2 architecture is called 1oo2D. Both processing units are active, but each unit is controlled by a mechanism of error detection. The mechanisms of error detection control a switch that allows the choice of authorized output.

The 1oo2D architecture is a persistent architecture. In case of failure on both processing units (shared mode or not), the switch will oscillate without the possibility of stabilization.

The 2oo2 architecture can be extended to three processing units as shown in Figure 1.29. This is known as 2oo3 architecture.

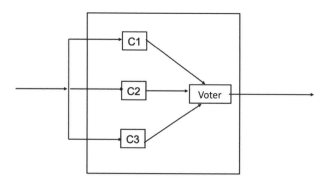

Figure 1.29. *2oo3 architecture*

The processing units simultaneously execute the same application with identical or differentiated inputs. Their results are compared by a voter (hardware and/or software) or through a pilot process. The results should be identical.

During a process cycle, if the voter confirms that the results of the three units are consistent, they are all considered functional. If there is convergence of the vote but that unit is not in phase, it is considered faulty and removed from the cycle. At this moment there is transition from a 2oo3 architecture to a 2oo2 architecture. The system is therefore tolerant to failure. Working in 2oo2 mode, the operating system places the system in fallback mode at the next divergence.

In practice, due to synchronization problems, the results may be different; for this reason the result is formed by consensus. If there is consensus, the result is considered correct.

Regarding synchronization, it is possible to establish a shared physical clock, which becomes a critical point of the architecture. The other most common solution consists of performing asynchronous processing, but this requires that the software application be robust *vis-à-vis* delays and that the voter agrees to deal with temporal windows.

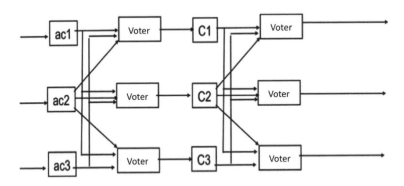

Figure 1.30. *Triple modular redundancy (TMR)*

To avoid failure of input acquisition and of the voter, TMR (triple modular redundancy) architecture triples the entire chain as shown in Figure 1.30.

In the context of 2oo3 architecture, having identical processing units and software results in the presence of a shared failure mode. This problem can be addressed through the quality control of software development and selection of a processing unit with great return of experience (the railway sector have used 68,020, 68,030 and 68,040 processors since the 1980s).

It is currently very difficult to define the behavior of new processors (pre-empting calculations, pseudo-parallelism, gambling on the execution path, use of internal cache, use of multicore processor, etc.) and to obtain effective "feedback", hence the establishment of a diversification of processing units and/or of applications (diversification of sources, compilers, teams, temporal behavior, etc.).

The voter is a delicate issue and the current trend is to incorporate software voters. Control of a hardware voter is a feasible task, and the deployment of a software voter is risky.

The main interest in using a software voter is its flexibility and lack of supplementary hardware. However, the execution time is greater.

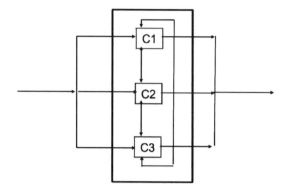

Figure 1.31. *2oo3 architecture with a software voter*

As shown in Figure 1.31, in the context of the implementation of a software voter, it is necessary to define a voting strategy. There are several possibilities:

– one of the processing units is chosen as the master, which is not realistic if a failure emerges in that unit;

– one of the units is elected during each cycle with respect to a defined process;

– predetermination of the voting cycle is already in place;

– each unit carries out the vote and produces a half-output, two half-outputs are then necessary to have one effective output;

– etc.

2oo3 architecture can be generalized as a *nOOm* architecture. Generally, we use odd K in order to achieve the vote, although in some areas such as nuclear power, we find K=4 ([ESS 00], section 3.2) or more.

The establishment of a *nOOm* architecture allows the development of more complex software voter strategies such as:

– majority vote: in *nOOm* architecture, *n* values must be identical to have a vote;

– vote by consensus: the results *m* are compared and each different value is associated to a score. The value with the highest score is chosen. If two values have the same high score, choice is not possible;

– vote by confidence: this takes into account the reliability of the software in the voting;

– etc.

nOOm architecture thus detects the failure of a unit and disables it. This disabling is generally definitive (fuse principle), but some architectures provide a learning mechanism that allows, after failure, the reset of the faulty unit and the sharing of the common context to the other units.

To give an example of *nOOm* architecture, we will briefly present the architectural development in the Boeing 777. As shown in Figure 1.32 (for more details see [YEH 96]), the overall "Primary Flight Computer" (PFC) is broken down into three PFCs. The PFCs communicate through a network composed of three identical channels. Each line is self-powered and has a computer and a communication block ARINC 629.

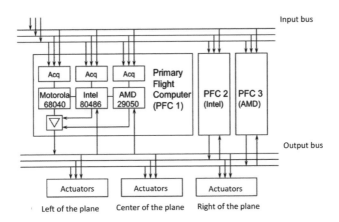

Figure 1.32. *Architecture of Boeing 777*

Each line of a PFC has a different processor, the three chosen processors are: the Intel 80486, Motorola 68040, and the AMD 29050. Each PFC uses the three processors differently.

We recall some facts:

– the three channels each have a role: control, standby, and monitor;

– the control channel has a complementary role of selecting the output;

– selection of the output is done through the choice of an intermediate value;

– synchronous acquisition of the three PFCs, thus requiring a synchronization mechanism;

– for critical variables, a consolidation of the results is implemented;

– 99% of software is written in Ada and uses three different compilers.

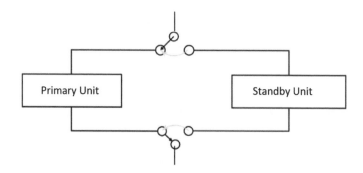

Figure 1.33. *Passive redundancy*

Up until this moment, we have dealt with passive redundancy, with the set of processing units carrying out their processes. Certain types of architecture use passive redundancy.

In the context of passive redundancy, the passive unit is generally on standby, but it is possible to have the unit undertake additional functions (Figure 1.33).

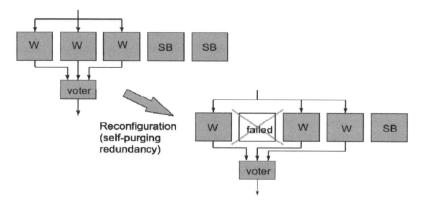

Figure 1.34. *Passive redundancy and active redundancy*

Active redundancy (W) and passive redundancy (SB) can be combined to increase the availability of the system (see Figure 1.34). In case of failure of a processing unit, the unit is put out of service and a reserve unit is inserted in the loop. This type of architecture is often put into place for systems with difficult access.

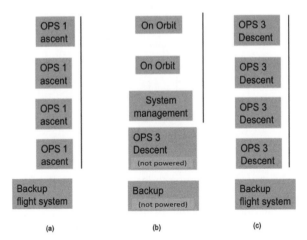

Figure 1.35. *Reconfiguration of the architecture*

Implementation of active and passive redundancy can be dynamic. Notably in the case of a space shuttle, flight hazards can be controlled by rapidly changing the mission, as shown in Figure 1.35. The five processing units linked to the flight functions can be reconfigured.

For the ascending phase (Figure 1.35a), four units are configured in the ascending mode and one of the units is in saved mode. For the orbital flight phase (Figure 1.35b), two processing units are configured to manage flight, one unit manages the whole system, one unit is inactive and configured with the descent management application, and the last unit remains in saved mode. The descent phase (Figure 1.35c) is similar to the ascending phase (Figure 1.35a).

1.5.3.3.5. Asymmetric architecture

The preceding section showed the *nOOm* architectures, their main fault residing in cost (implementation and maintenance costs), but as shown in [DUF 05], the automobile sector is subject to other constraints, which are just as important: weight, bulk, energy consumption, etc.

For this reason, there are proposals for optimization of the worker/checker architecture (section 1.5.3.3.3). An initial idea is the possibility of giving different objectives to each processing unit. The "functional" unit will have the role of deploying its own function F. The second unit ("checker") checks the first unit.

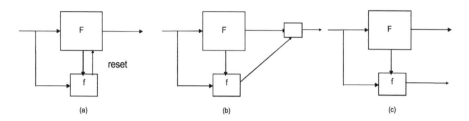

Figure 1.36. *Functional/check*

More precisely, unit F, in addition to the functional, undertakes the deployment of a set of self-tests. The results of these self-tests are transmitted to a unit f, which decides on the state of functioning of the first unit. Depending on the final architecture, unit f can (a) ask for a reset, (b) cut off output, and (c) indicate if there is a malfunction. With regards to the proper functioning of unit f, specific self-testing is done. These self-tests concern only necessary functions.

This architecture imposes at least two constraints:

– self-tests must be chosen with care in order to effectively detect unit F problems;

– the software executed by unit F is "classified" as secure and requires the utmost care.

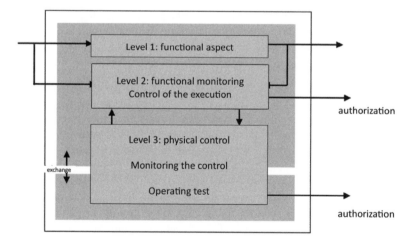

Figure 1.37. *Asymmetric architecture*

This type of architecture has a main advantage of reducing bulk, weight, energy consumption, and cost (unit f being cheaper).

The automobile sector (see Chapter 9) goes even further in implementing an asymmetric, three-layer software architecture.

Figure 1.37 presents an asymmetric architecture with two connected processing units of different sizes.

The software is broken down into three layers:

– level 1: this level deals with "functional" aspects through acquisition, execution of functions and output generation;

– level 2: this level controls functional processing. It aims to detect level 1 processing errors and control reactions in case of error detection;

– level 3: this level checks that there is no malfunction of the hardware resources. This level is independent of level 2, broken down over the two processing units and providing an audit based on a question/answer game.

Level 2 is usually based on dual acquisition of inputs, functional redundancy, verification of temporal constraints and data controls. For level 3, the question/answer game is available in ROM and the main unit provides incorrect answers in order to verify that the control unit can detect errors, the main unit undertaking several trials.

This architecture has several advantages:

– it offers a clear separation between the functional and the safe mode;

– it offers a break down that can be generalized to a domain (e.g. automobile), to an employment standard (regarding both the software and hardware);

– it offers cost control (financial, energy and bulk) linked to hardware means.

1.5.3.3.6. Assessment

This section presents a substantial number of redundant architectures. The possible combinations are quite numerous, but some architectures become classic.

A small list of redundant architectures of the (*nOOm*: *N out of K*) type:

– 1oo1: simplex system;

– 1oo2: duplicated system, one unit is sufficient to undertake a function;

– 2oo2: duplicated system, all units must be operational (*fail-safe*);

– 1oo2D: duplicated system with error detection (*fail-operational*);

– 2oo3: two units must be functional (*masking*);

– *nOOm*: architecture with any N and K.

1.5.4. *Error recovery and retrieval*

nOOm architecture allows for error compensation. If the level of redundancy is sufficient (N>2), the erroneous state of a unit has no impact on the outputs of the system. In this case, caution is necessary regarding automatic and systematic compensation (error concealment) that might affect the observability of the system; reporting the defect is necessary.

Error compensation can be achieved by establishing a mechanism for recovery:

– error recovery by retrieval: the state of the system is periodically saved and allows us to return to the previous saved mode in case of error;

– error recovery by continuation: in case of error, a new acceptable state is sought but it is generally damaged. Continuation can be achieved only if we have a list of errors to address.

1.5.4.1. *Retrieval*

Retrieval (back recovery of errors) consists of restoring the system to a previous secure state. To do this, regular backups of the system must be undertaken and one of the backups must be able to be charged. Upon detection of an erroneous situation, it is possible to reload a previous situation and restart the execution. If the error comes from the environment or from a transient failure, the system should resume proper operation. If this is a systematic failure (hardware or software), the system will return to an erroneous state. Some systems also dispose of several software application alternatives and can activate another replica of the application during retrieval.

The main advantage lies in the fact that the erroneous state is deleted and that this deletion is not based on finding the location of the fault or the cause. The back recovery of errors can be used to recover unanticipated faults, including design errors.

Retrieval can be either of high or low grain. The recovery by high grain restores the last overall correct condition and reruns the same software application completely. Recovery by low grain is a finer recovery strategy with the restoration of a local correct state (confined to a function, for example), alternative execution, etc.

High-grained recovery has the advantage of setting up a single point of recovery and remains suitable for systems subjected only to hardware failures.

1.5.4.2. *Continuation*

Continuation (forward recovery of errors) consists of continuing to run the application from the erroneous state by making selective adjustments to the state of the system. This includes making the controlled environment "safe", as it may have been damaged by the failure.

Continuation is therefore an activity specific to each system and depends on accurate predictions of the locations and causes of errors (that is to say, identifying damage).

1.5.4.3. *Assessment*

Retrieval is generally used in practice (data backup of the banking system, etc.). It may be purely composed of hardware or software.

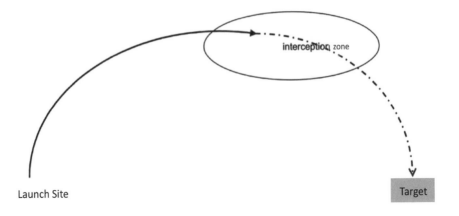

Figure 1.38. *Example of retrieval-based system*

Figure 1.38 shows an example of a missile aiming at a target and which must pass through a "turbulent" interception zone (wind, temperature, EM fields, explosion, radiation, etc.). The system periodically saves its state and in case of an untimely reboot, the previous state can be restored to continue the mission. For this type of system, it is not necessary to have an alternative and recovery by high grain is enough.

1.5.5. *Partitioning*

Partitioning is a security technique that is highly recommended by the automobile sector. The current version (not finalized) of standard ISO 26262 [ISO 09] introduced the basic operation of this technique (see Figure 1.39).

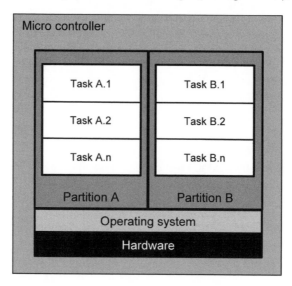

Figure 1.39. *Partitioning within a processing unit*

The partitioning software must be specified during the architectural phase at the equipment level (to establish protection mechanisms) and/or during the software architecture.

The sharing of resources cannot be done unless it can be demonstrated that there is no interference between the partitions. Either there is no interaction between the different partitions and safeguards must ensure the tasks are sealed against each other, or there are interactions between tasks and it must be demonstrated (in addition to being sealed off) that exchanges between tasks are consistent with their respective security level.

In the context of a high security level application (SIL 3-SIL4), partitioning can be implemented only through a dedicated architecture. Note that the "software" elements that manage partitioning have the same level of security as the software partitioned.

1.6. Conclusion

In the context of computer architectures, there are techniques to detect and even correct errors produced by random and even systematic errors. These techniques are very common in different sectors (rail, aviation, energy, process control, automobile, etc.).

This chapter has provided an opportunity to present these techniques and some significant examples, but the number of possibilities does not allow an exhaustive list. Therefore, it seemed necessary to present the implementation of these techniques in specific cases which is the objective of the subsequent chapters.

1.7. Bibliography

[ABR 96] ABRIAL JR., *The B Book - Assigning Programs to Meanings*, Cambridge University Press, Cambridge, August 1996.

[BAL 03] BALEANI M., FERRARI A., MANGERUCA L., PERI M., PEZZINI S., "Fault-tolerant platforms for automotive safety critical applications", *Proceedings of the 2003 International Conference on Compilers, Architecture and Synthesis for Embedded Systems*, p. 170-177, 2003.

[BIE 99] BIED-CHARRETON D., "Concepts de mise en sécurité des architectures informatiques", *Recherche Transports Sécurité*, vol. 64, p. 21-36, 1999.

[DUF 05] DUFOUR J.L., "Automotive safety concepts: 10-9/h for less than 100E a piece", *Automation, Assistance and Embedded Real Time Platforms for Transportation*, AAET, Braunschweig, Germany, 16-17 February 2005.

[ESS 00] ESSAME D., ARLAT J., POWELL D., Tolérance aux fautes dans les systèmes critiques, LAAS, n° 151, March 2000.

[GEO 90] GEORGES J.P., "Principes et fonctionnement du Système d'Aide à la Conduite, à l'Exploitation et à la Maintenance (SACEM). Application à la ligne A du RER", *Revue Générale des Chemins de Fer*, vol. 6, n° 6, p. 23-28, 1990.

[IEC 98] IEC, IEC 61508: Sécurité fonctionnelle des systèmes électriques électroniques programmables relatifs à la sécurité, International Standard, 1998.

[ISO 09] ISO, ISO/CD-26262, Road vehicles – functional safety.

[LAP 92] LAPRIE J.C., AVIZIENIS A., KOPETZ H. (EDS), "Dependability: basic concepts and terminology", in *Dependable Computing and Fault-Tolerant System*, vol. 5, Springer, New York, 1992.

[LEA 05] LEAPHART E.G., CZERNY B.J., D'AMBROSIO J.G., DENLINGER C.L., LITTLEJOHN D., "Survey of software failsafe techniques for safety-critical automotive applications", Delphi Corporation, SAE, reference 2005-01-0779, 2005.

[LIN 99] VAN LINT J.H., *Introduction to Coding Theory*, Springer, Berlin, 1999.

[MAR 90] MARTIN J., GALIVEL C., "Le processeur codé: un nouveau concept appliqué à la sécurité des systèmes de transport", *Revue Générale des Chemins de Fer*, vol. 6, p. 29-35, 1990.

[VIL 88] VILLEMEUR A., *Sûreté de fonctionnement des systèmes industriels*, Eyrolles, Paris, 1988.

[YEH 98] YEH Y.C., "Triple redundant 777 primary flight computer", *Proceedings of the 1996 IEEE Aerospace Applications Conference*, vol. 1, p. 293-307, 1998.

Chapter 2

Railway Safety Architecture

2.1. Introduction

In this chapter[1], we will present the first implementation of a processor and software-based application in the field of railway transport. This application is known as the "safety-coded processor" (SCP).

This chapter presents the normative and legal constraints that were subsequently imposed.

2.2. Coded secure processor

2.2.1. *Basic principle*

In the early 1980s, the establishment of a driving assistance system for the RER A (*Réseaux Express Régional*/Parisian Regional Express Network) was used to introduce microprocessors in trains. This system of driving assistance is called SACEM [GEO 90; HEN 94; MAR 90] (*Système d'Aide à la Conduite, à l'Exploitation et à la Maintenance*), meaning system for assisting driving, operation and maintenance.

At that time, safety was based on redundant systems (2 of 2 or 2 of 3). The duration of operation (40 to 50 years) is a strong constraint, which led to the

Chapter written by Jean-Louis BOULANGER.

1. This chapter is based on educational material produced together with M. Walter SCHÖN, Professor at the University of Technology of Compiègne, whom I can never thank enough.

selection of another type of safety process. Indeed, securing a redundant architecture (against shared failure modes) requires the establishment of controls that are dependent on implemented components. In view of the lifespan of railway systems, it was considered preferable to put into place safety principles that were independent of the hardware components.

Therefore, encoding information [FOR 89] replaced hardware redundancy as the method to ensure safety. A single processor is used. The technique of a "coded uniprocessor" is based on a probabilistic approach developed in the 1980s. It is noteworthy that during the initial implementation stages of SACEM, two models were developed and compared: a prototype based on dual redundancy and a uniprocessor architecture based on (arithmetic) encoding.

As all internal data are encoded, data manipulation can only be achieved through elementary operations named OPEL that preserve the encoding characteristics.

The implementation of arithmetic encoding is done through three encoding techniques:

– an arithmetic code, which aims to detect errors in data manipulation (memory failure, communications failure, failures in the handling of data, etc.);

– a signature that can detect errors in program execution (wrong instruction, wrong calculation, wrong connection, etc.);

– dating data, in order to avoid using outdated data.

2.2.2. Encoding

This section complements section 1.5.3.2.6. To ensure the safety of the system, all malfunctions and errors that may occur, from writing the software source code to running the software in the equipment, must be detected.

These failures always result from a combination of the following three cases, whether they occur during compilations or during execution of the program:

– operand error (wrong address or no refresh: a calculation is made using incorrect starting values);

– operator error (wrong address or wrong decoding: for example, an addition is made instead of a multiplication);

– operation error (wrong value, the calculation data were correct, but the result is false).

2.2.2.1. *Arithmetic encoding*

In order to deal with operation errors (wrong operator, etc.) and/or data alteration, redundant information is stored as $-2^k.x$. This information uses the principle of proof by nine, but nine is here replaced by A which is a large number.

Figure 2.1 shows a simplified example of the implementation of arithmetic encoding. We chose A=9 and k=4, so then we have 2^k=16 and -2^k[A]=2. After encoding, the data X=5 becomes 81, and for Y=7, we have an encoded value of 117. The addition of X and Y results in an encoded data of 198. As encoding is separable, the decoding of Z is done by extracting the most significant bits, resulting in Z=12. Verification of the absence of an execution error is done by checking that 198[A]=0.

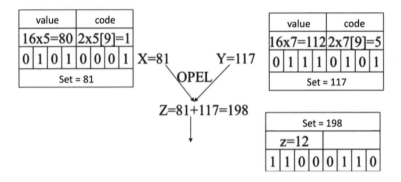

Figure 2.1. *Arithmetic encoding*

The principle of arithmetic encoding protects against all corruption of data value, with a probability of 1/A.

2.2.2.2. *Signature*

Arithmetic encoding does not, however, protect against the permutations of operands or operators (for example X+X or X–Y may be performed instead of X+Y). These errors being possible (address and/or operand code errors), we must find a way to cover them.

To manage this type of error, it is possible to add a signature noted B_X to any coded variable X. The input signatures are constants (integers *modulo* A) predetermined in a pseudo-random manner. The signatures of the calculated variables can be predetermined if the operand signatures are known.

$$X = \left(5; -2^k.5 + 3[A]\right) \qquad\qquad B_X = 3$$

$$Y = \left(7; -2^k.7 + 5[A]\right) \qquad\qquad B_Y = 5$$

$$Z := X + Y = \left(12; -2^k.12 + 8[A]\right) \quad B_Z = B_X + B_Y$$

$$X := Z \qquad\qquad\qquad\qquad B_X = B_Z = 8$$

Figure 2.2. *Example of signature determination*

Figure 2.2 shows that from the combination of a signature composed of input data ($B_x=3$ and $B_y=5$), the evolution of the signatures of the internal variable Z can be determined independently of the X and Y values.

The permutation of operands is now detected (unless the two operands have the same signature, which has a probability of $1/A$ of occurring). The permutation of operators is also detected because the evolution of signatures depends on it: $B_{X+Y}=B_X+B_Y$ or $B_{X-Y}=B_X-B_Y$.

Figure 2.3 shows the mechanism of generation of the executable with the predetermination of signatures phase. The OFFLINE phase is predominant here for the safety of the application.

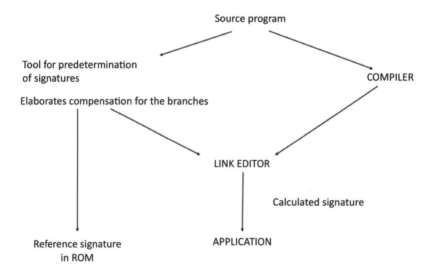

Figure 2.3. *Example of signature determination*

We presented the management of operators + and –; this principle is widespread but for the other operators (*, /, etc.) it is more complex. Regarding connections, the evolution of signatures is different for each branch, thus the need to establish convergence, and for loops, the number of iterations is not necessarily predetermined, consequently there is a need to realign the signature during each iteration.

2.2.2.3. *Dating*

In order to avoid problems following the use of obsolete data, the encoding used contains a dating mechanism D.

2.2.2.4. *Synthesis*

The encoding put into place within the SCP is $-2^k.x + B_x + D$. The code is a separable code and a specific instruction set named OPEL is used.

This encoding and the use of OPEL show that all the errors of the processing unit and of the memory are propagated to the signature provided at the end of each cycle. Therefore, the software is executed by a processing unit that has no safety characteristics and does not require periodic testing. For this reason we speak of probabilistic safety.

2.2.3. *Hardware architecture*

As mentioned previously, the SCP principles are independent of the hardware architecture and safety does not depend on the processing unit in charge of running the application. In the context of Figure 2.4, we present the hardware architecture of the SCP. It is broken down into several parts:

– a safe input acquisition card, providing encoded data;

– the processing unit that performs the processes;

– the dynamic controller, which is responsible for validating processes through the verification of signatures produced ONLINE with regards to the signatures calculated OFFLINE;

– the manager of safe outputs, which, based on requests from the processing unit and verification by the dynamic controller, will produce and control their outputs;

– the safe clock, which paces the whole set, participating in the dating, and which is also a shared failure mode.

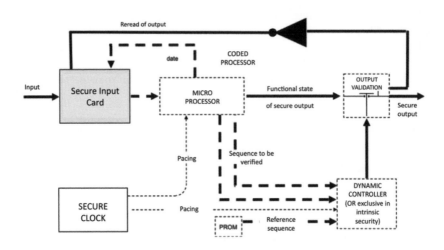

Figure 2.4. *Hardware architecture of the SCP*

In the context of the SCP architecture, two types of safety can be implemented[2]:

– probabilistic safety: for a system, safety objectives are awarded, expressed in the number of victims (or accidents) per year, and these are demonstrated by calculations of probability that the system meets its objectives;

– intrinsic safety: a system is said to be safe if any failure of one or more components does not let the system convert to a less permissive state (*vis-à-vis* safety) than the situation in which it was in at the time of failure, so that the result is a safe configuration.

The safe input acquisition card, the safe clock, the dynamic controller, and the safe output manager depend on intrinsic safety. The completion of a process (processing unit) depends on probabilistic safety.

2.2.4. *Assessment*

From the application's source code, the encoding put into place can detect failures in all the tools (Figure 2.3) of the generation chain (compiler, assembler, etc.), in download processes (handling, programming memories, etc.), and in

---

2. The objective of this chapter is not to lecture on the notion of safety, but as the principle characteristic of the SCP is linked to the duality between probabilistic/intrinsic safety, it is difficult not to cover this aspect. We encourage the interested reader to read the summary report [BIE 98], which delves further into these two notions.

hardware components (processor, memory, etc.). The implemented safety is independent of the technology used, but remains linked to the efficiency of the encoding (number of bits, Hamming distance, etc.).

Code manipulation significantly increases processing time. Therefore, for the following systems, coprocessors and field programmable gate arrays (FPGAs) have been implemented to alleviate the processor. In view of the effectiveness of these new processors, execution time should not be a problem.

Regarding the software, the first used was based on the language MODULA 2, for the following uses, the language of reference is Ada 83 [ANS 83].

2.3. Other applications

After successful implementation within the SACEM context [GEO 90; HEN 94; MAR 90], the coded safe processor was considered by all stakeholders in the field as an architecture ensuring safety of a software-based system. The principles implemented are independent of hardware architecture.

For this reason, in addition to the SACEM project, this architecture has been deployed on many railway projects such as the POMA 2000 in Laon, Maggaly in Lyon [MAI 93], the automatic light vehicle (VAL: *véhicule automatique léger*) in Chicago O'Hare, the TVM 430 of the North TGV, the SAET from METEOR or the two VAL lines from Charles de Gaulle airport (inaugurated in 2007).

2.3.1. *TVM 430*

The TVM (Train Vital Management) 430 is a signaling and speed control system in use on certain French high-speed railway lines. TVM 430 is an ATC (Automatic Train Control) system of the continuous type. TVM 430 is a system split between the ground and on board.

TVM 430 can continuously transmit to the train all the information necessary for its movement and allows continuous monitoring so that the train remains within its assigned safety envelope.

Figure 2.5 shows the architecture of ground equipment. This hardware architecture implements four types of safety: dual redundancy with dial indicator, controlled safety (in case of detection of a defect, stopping can be commanded), safety by output reread, and intrinsic safety (dynamic dial indicator for example).

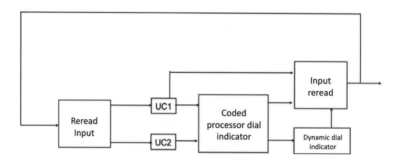

Figure 2.5. *Architecture of TVM 430 ground equipment*

Dual redundancy is homogenous (same processing unit and same application) but there are asymmetries: temporal lag, additional data involving the use of additional Boolean operators. It should be noted that the dial indicator is not a hardware vote but a SCP carrying out a software vote. The binary input/output cards are of the same technology as those used in the SACEM context (intrinsic safety and SCP encoding management).

2.3.2. *SAET-METEOR*

2.3.2.1. *Presentation*

In the early 1990s, the RATP (Régie Autonome des Transports Parisiens/Autonomous Operator of Parisian Transports) decided to implement a new system to alleviate the exploitation of the RER A and open up certain areas (south of Paris and the 13th *arrondissement*). This new system [MAT 98] has been used, since October 1998, on line 14 of the Parisian underground railway, and was named SAET-METEOR (*Système d'Automatisation de l'Exploitation des Trains – Métro Est Ouest Rapide*), meaning automation system of train operation – East West rapid underground.

Line 14 is a distributed real-time complex system, the main function of which is to transport passengers, while guaranteeing high safety for travelers. The system needs to ensure that it meets certain functional constraints said to be *safe* [CHA 96]. The real-time character reflects the fact that the railway system interacts with its physical environment, the behavior of which is *uninterruptible* and *irreversible* in nature.

Regarding technical aspects, the service is currently provided by 19 trains, each composed of six cars (an extension is planned to eight) with a service speed of 40 km/hour and an interval between trains of 85 seconds in full automatic driving.

This underground railway line has the peculiarity of being driverless. All movement of the trains is handled by computer calculations, with supervision remaining under human control through a centralized control station (CCS). SAET-METEOR is not the first driverless underground railway, but it has two particularities: the safety functions are performed by computers (as opposed to the VAL[3] system where they are undertaken by electronics) and it allows for mixed trains. Indeed, it is possible to run a train without equipment (with drivers) on the line managed by SAET-METEOR.

One of the characteristics of line 14 is that it allows the movement of non-equipped trains with a driver and equipped trains with or without a driver allowing for automatic driving. In the case of equipped trains, there are two operating modes: manual steering and automatic integrated driving.

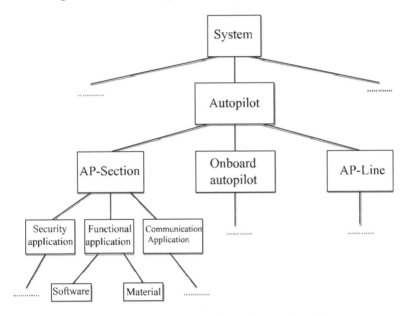

Figure 2.6. *From the system to the software and hardware*

---

3. The VAL is a light underground railway running on several sites in France (for example: Lille, Toulouse, Orly-Val and CdG-Val) and abroad (for example: Chicago, Taipei and Turin).

The breakdown of the SAET-METEOR system into sub-systems, equipment, software and hardware is presented in Figure 2.6

To this complexity must be added objectives for safety engineering, such as failure rates, contrary to the safety for equipment ranging from 10^{-7} to 10^{-9} per hour and which are reflected by the fact that:

– all instances of hardware failure leads to the activation of the emergency break and if necessary, to cutting off the traction power;

– no fault with regards to safety can subsist within the software.

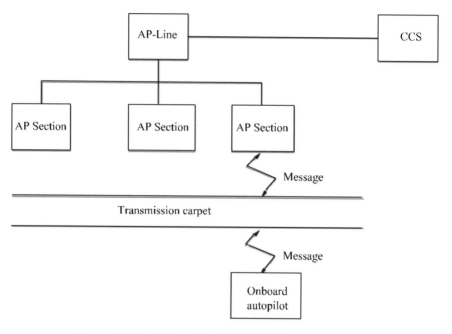

Figure 2.7. *Breakdown of the SAET-METEOR automatic pilot*

The management of the line is performed by the *autopilot* sub-system (see Figure 2.7), which is distributed along the line and in equipped trains. The line is managed by the autopilot line (AP-Line) and is divided into automation sections [LEC 96]. Each section is managed by a computer called autopilot ground (*PA-Sol*). Equipped trains have an onboard computer called onboard autopilot which, among other things, regularly sends a tracking message to the autopilot ground supporting it. Computer processes are undertaken cyclically and are uninterruptible.

2.3.2.2. *Elements concerning "hardware" aspects*

As indicated by [FOR 96], the equipment of the SAET-METEOR is structured around the coded safe processor. This combines arithmetic encoding and signature verification in the context of processes said to be safe.

The demonstration of the effectiveness of the coded safe processor has been made in the context of the implementation of several automatic and semi-automatic railways (SACEM [FOR 89], MAGGALY [MAI 93], etc.). As the SCP was lacking in performance, SAET-METEOR was an opportunity to add a *coprocessor*.

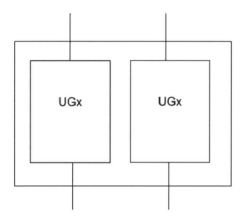

Figure 2.8. *Autopilot architecture*

There are three types of autopilot (PA), but they are all composed of two "management units" (UGx). The UG all have the same architecture but may differ on the means of acquiring inputs (the *PA-Section* uses ground interfaces for example) and the application software that is on board. The redundancy level of a PA is homogenous (same hardware and software). Both UG are active (acquisition and processing), but at time *t* only one unit is capable of applying its output, this is sometimes referred to as a *semi-active* replication.

Upon detection of a defect, the unit taking care of outputs goes into an output restrictive mode and, if possible, a switch of unit management is implemented.

As the principles are the same for all other PAs, we present the architecture of the *PA-Section* as an example.

Each *PA-Section* consists of two units in cold redundancy named UGS, which ensure the availability of the equipment (see Figure 2.9). The UG-Section are designed to operate safely. In conjunction with its environment, the *PA-Section* has:

– binary functional and safe inputs acquired by each unit;

– binary functional and safe outputs wired "or permissive".

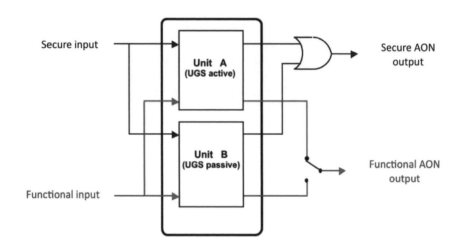

Figure 2.9. *PA-Section architecture*

Only the "active" UG-Section unit controls functional and safe binary outputs, those of the "passive" UG-Section not being powered.

Each UG-Section is made up of a rack, therefore, there are two racks for each piece of *PA-Section* equipment. A UG-Section is comprised of several trays containing different types of cards:

– CUCV card (VME central unit card): this supports non-safety related applications, based on MOTOROLA 68020;

– CUCM card (modular central unit card): this supports safe applications (MOTOROLA 68020 + coprocessors) and has a real-time monitor that is used to manage exchanges between processors;

– input/output cards: several cards dedicated to different families (safe input, unsafe inputs, safe outputs, and unsafe outputs).

Safe input and output cards are made following the coded processor principle: aside form the input/output ground value, they furnish encoded and dated data, which protects the values of inputs/outputs.

The software operating on the CUCM allows the acquisition of inputs (functional and safe) and activation of outputs (functional and safe) via a network manager that guarantees management of safe emissions.

When safe processes are undertaken on the CUCM, the absence of error is guaranteed by the dynamic controller, which controls:

– the smooth implementation of the application by verifying output codes;

– maintaining a restrictive state for previous restrictive outputs;

– the increment of the safe cycle date during each application cycle;

– the smooth functioning of the safe input cards.

In addition to the above aspects, there is a constraint on the software "to be without defect", because the safety mechanisms of the SCP do not detect systematic defects of the processing unit. For such systems, the software is generally classified as Safety Integrated Level (SIL) 3-SIL 4, as defined in the CENELEC EN 50128 [CEN 01a] standard.

But there are still some additional checks:

– the monitor allows checksum verification of the program memory as well as the reset of the RAM;

– the central unit cards are equipped with a watchdog software;

– the additional services provided by the coprocessor allow the verification of RAM type local memory as well as the checksum of stored safety data.

Safe inputs are acquired over two redundant paths, which allows detection of discrepancies. The safe outputs dispose of a functional reread, aside from the safe reread.

On the rack, there is an encoding stub that has a dual role: the first is to provide safe information, concerning the identity of the *PA-Section* of the unit, to the software applications of the UG-Section. The information also concerns the version of the secure software. Its second role is to enable the physical configuration of input/output networks where the *PA-Section* has several input/output trays.

2.3.2.3. *Elements concerning the "software" aspects*

Under SACEM [GEO 90], the RATP commissioned a proof of Hoare [HOA 69] to demonstrate the inclusion of requirements (for more information see [GUI 90]). From a program P and a set of preconditions C, the proof of Hoare highlights all post conditions. The proof of Hoare, which was conducted in the SACEM context, has helped to show a number of code properties but it was not possible to link it with safety requirements (for example, the requirement for non-collision).

In the French railway field, the use of formal methods, including the use of method B [ABR 96], is increasingly common in the development of critical systems. The software of these safety systems (railway signaling, automatic driving) must meet strict criteria for quality, reliability, and robustness. One of the first applications of these formal methods was done retrospectively on SACEM [GUI 90]. More recent projects, such as CTDC, KVS or SAET-METEOR [BEH 93; BEH 96], used method B throughout the development process (from the specifications to the code).

To learn more about the implementation of method B on the SAET-METEOR project, the interested reader is referred to [BOU 06], which presents both the work of the industry and the RATP.

2.3.2.4. *Adjoining work*

In view of the principles of safety, of redundancy and semi-active replication implemented within SAET-METEOR, work has been undertaken to optimize the process of commutation failure.

The Protocol for Asymmetric Duplex Redundancy (PADRE [ESS 99]) is a protocol for asymmetric management of duplex redundancies, which augments availability without compromising safety.

[ESS 98] presents a realistic implementation of the PADRE protocol on the SAET-METEOR example, but requires a real experiment.

2.4. Regulatory and normative context

2.4.1. *Introduction*

Critical and safe operating systems (air and railway transport, nuclear power plants, etc.) are characterized by the fact that failures can have serious consequences both on the lives of people and from an economic and/or environmental viewpoint. In several sectors, including the railway sector, there are normative references that require the demonstration of the achievement of a safe system.

These references recommend a separation of roles and responsibilities. One team will be responsible for the implementation of the system (development, verification, and validation), while another will be responsible for demonstrating the safety of the system (safety studies, safety case, and analysis of work completeness).

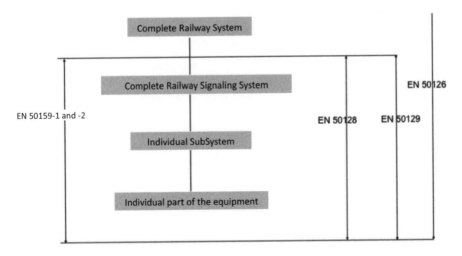

Figure 2.10. *Standards applicable to railway systems*

In the railway sector, the normative reference is composed of standards:

– the CENELEC EN 50126 [CEN 00] standard, which describes the methods for specifying and demonstrating reliability, availability, maintainability, and safety;

– the CENELEC EN 50128 [CEN 01a] standard, which describes actions to undertaken in order to demonstrate the safety of the software;

– the CENELEC EN 50129 [CEN 03] standard, which describes the structure of the safety case.

These standards are complemented by a standard related to the "transmission" aspects. CENELEC EN 50159 is divided into two parts, one part [CEN 01b] is dedicated to closed networks and the other [CEN 01c] to open networks and processing of confidentiality safety.

The objective of the CENELEC reference is to:

– provide a common reference in Europe to promote the expansion of markets for railway system elements and interoperability, interchangeability, and cross-acceptance of railway components;

– respond to the specificities of the railway sector.

According to the CENELEC EN 50129 standard, the requirements are divided into two categories: those related to system safety and those not related to safety.

The CENELEC EN 50126 standard proposes the following steps (we consider only the implementation aspects) to specify and demonstrate the safety of a system:

– system definition and applicability conditions: mission profile, system description, operating strategy and maintenance, and identification of constraints generated by existing elements (other systems or other lines previously developed);

– risk analysis;

– system requirements: requirements analysis, system and environmental specification, defining the criteria for demonstration and acceptance of the system;

– allocation of system requirements: specifying sub-system, equipment and/or components requirements and defining the criteria for acceptance of these elements;

– design and implementation: realizing the design, development, and conducting verifications and validations.

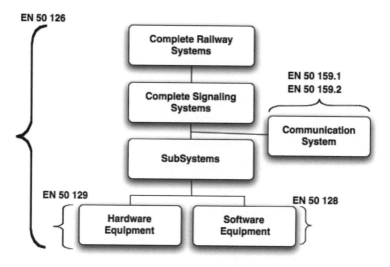

Figure 2.11. *Standards applicable to railway systems*

The EN 50128 [CEN 01a] standard is specifically dedicated to aspects of software development for the railway sector. Regarding software, the defined SSIL (Software SIL) allows the definition of the different levels of criticality – 0 (no danger) to 4 (critical).

While the safety requirements have always been taken into account in complex systems (railway and aviation transport, nuclear power plants, etc.), contractual obligations on performance allows railway industries, for example, total control of the parameters related to reliability, availability, and maintainability. The choice of norms and standards is the responsibility of the designer and/or the manufacturer.

2.4.2. CENELEC and IEC history

Electrical/electronic systems have been used for years to perform functions related to safety in most industrial sectors. The IEC 61508 [IEC 98] standard presents a generic approach for all activities related to the safety lifecycle of electrical/electronic/programmable electronics (E/E/PES), which are used to perform safety functions.

In most cases, safety is achieved through several systems of various technologies (mechanical, hydraulic, pneumatic, electrical, electronic, programmable electronic). A safety policy must take into account all factors contributing to safety. Thus, IEC 61508 [IEC 98] provides an analytical framework that applies to systems related to safety based on other technologies, and specifically deals with systems based on electronics.

Because of the wide variety of electrical/electronic/programmable electronics and the very different degrees of complexity, the exact nature of safety measures to be implemented depends on factors specific to the application; for this reason there are no general rules in the IEC 61508 standard, but only recommendations on analytical methods to be implemented.

In the field of complex systems based on electronic and/or programmed systems, IEC 61508 ([4]) defines the concept of SIL. SIL is used to quantify the level of system safety. It evolves from 0 (no danger, destruction of equipment), 1 (minor injury), 2 (serious injury), 3 (one death) to 4 (multiple deaths).

As shown in Figure 2.12, the railway reference CENELEC EN 5012x is a variation of the generic standard IEC 61508, which takes into account the specificities of the railway sector and of various success stories (SACEM, TVM, SAET-METEOR, etc.).

The railway reference CENELEC EN 5012x is equally applicable to railway applications of the "urban" type (underground railway, RER, etc.) and conventional railway applications (high-speed lines, conventional trains, freight).

One of the restrictions of the railway reference CENELEC EN 5012x is related to the scope of standards EN 50128 and EN 50129, which are normally limited to signaling sub-systems (see Figure 2.10). For the hardware architectures used in other sub-systems, there are older standards that are still applicable (NF F 00-101, etc.). Work is underway within certification groups to extend and generalize these two standards to the railway system as a whole.

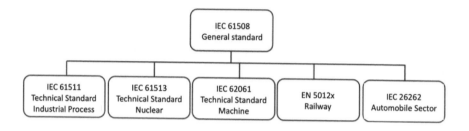

Figure 2.12. *IEC 61508 and its variations*[4]

Furthermore, we indicate that in addition to these standards related to equipment architecture (hardware + software), there are additional standards regulating interactions with the environment, such as the CENELEC EN 50121 standard (the latest version dates back to 2006) which deals with EMC problems, in transmission of railway systems *vis-à-vis* the outside world and from an environmental viewpoint of the railway system (train and fixed equipment).

2.4.3. *Commissioning evaluation, certification, and authorization*

The existence of these standards enables the assessment of the compliance of the developmental process of a product *vis-à-vis* a reference. This assessment can even result in being awarded a certificate. Several agencies may issue such a certificate through their EN 45011 accreditation.

Regarding the European railway network and compliance *vis-à-vis* the technical specifications for interoperability (TSI), Europe only recognizes apprised bodies (at least one per country) that are accredited through the EN ISO/IEC 17025 standard.

---

4. The ISO 26262 standard is not yet available, but automobile industrials are currently preparing implementation, as shown in Chapter 9.

Each country must have at least one apprised body; for France the apprised agency is CERTIFER[5].

The authorization of a railway system is made through a state agency that is responsible for reviewing the safety case:

– for the urban area: STRMTG (Service Technique des Remontées Mécaniques et des Transports Guidés)[6];

– for the railway sector: EPSF (Etablissement Public de Sécurité Ferroviaire)[7].

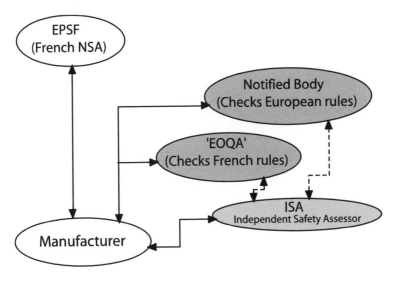

Figure 2.13. *Authorization process*

In both cases, the safety case contains a description of the system and its implementation, the safety features of the operator and an opinion on the safety system provided by an independent party appointed EOQA (expert or approved qualified organization). For the urban area, the mission of the EOQA is defined by note [STR 06].

---

5. Further information regarding the CERTIFIER association and its activities can be obtained at http://www.certifer.asso.fr/.

6. Further information regarding STRMTG can be obtained at http://www.strmtg. equipement.gouv.fr/.

7. Further information regarding EPSF can be obtained at http://www.securite-ferroviaire.fr/fr/.

Further information regarding the implementation of this regulation can be obtained in [BOU 07].

2.5. Conclusion

This chapter has provided an opportunity to present the first architecture implemented in the context of railway systems: the coded safe processor. Several systems have been constructed based on this system (SACEM, TVM, MAGGALY, SAET-METEOR, etc.). Since then, industries have implemented 2oo3-type architectures in addition to the SCP. Chapters 3, 4 and 5 will present some examples of this evolution.

2.6. Bibliography

[ABR 96] ABRIAL JR., *The B Book - Assigning Programs to Meanings*, Cambridge University Press, Cambridge, August 1996.

[ANS 83] ANSI, Norm ANSI/MIL-STD-1815A-1983, Langage de programmation Ada, 1983.

[BEH 93] BEHM P., "Application d'une méthode formelle aux logiciels sécuritaires ferroviaires", in H. HABRIAS, *Atelier Logiciel Temps Réel, 6es Journées Internationales du Génie Logiciel*, Nantes, 1993.

[BEH 96] BEHM P., "Développement formel des logiciels sécuritaires de METEOR", in H. HABRIAS, *Proceedings of 1st Conference on the B Method, Putting into Practice Methods and Tools for Information System Design*, IRIN Institut de recherche en informatique de Nantes, pp. 3-10, November 1996.

[BIE 98] BIED-CHARRETON D., "Sécurité intrinsèque et sécurité probabiliste dans les transports terrestres", *Synthèse INRETS*, vol. 31, 1998.

[BIE 99] BIED-CHARRETON D., "Concepts de mise en sécurité des architectures informatiques", *Recherche Transports Sécurité*, vol. 64, pp. 21-36, 1999.

[BOU 06] BOULANGER J.L., Expression et validation des propriétés de sécurité logique et physique pour les systèmes informatiques critiques, PhD thesis, Compiègne University of Technology , 2006.

[BOU 07] BOULANGER J.L., SCHÖN W., "Reference systems and standards for safety assessment of railway applications", *ESREL 2007*, Stavanger, Norway, 25-27 June 2007, pp. 2247-2253.

[CEN 00] CENELEC, NF EN 50126, Railway applications – the specification and demonstration of reliability, availability, maintainability and safety, January 2000.

[CEN 01a] CENELEC, NF EN 50128, Railway applications – communications, signalling and processing systems – software for railway control and protection systems, July 2001.

[CEN 01b] CENELEC, EN 50159-1, European standard. Railway applications – communication, signalling and processing systems. Part 1: safety-related communication in closed transmission systems, March 2001.

[CEN 01c] CENELEC, EN 50159-2, European standard. Railway applications – communication, signalling and processing systems. Part 2: safety-related communication in open transmission systems, March 2001.

[CEN 03] CENNELEC, NF EN 50129, European standard. Railway applications – communication, signalling and processing systems – safety-related communication in transmission systems, 2003.

[CHA 96] CHAUMETTE A.M., LE FÈVRE L., "Système d'automatisation de l'exploitation des trains de la ligne METEOR", *REE*, September 8 1996.

[DAV 88] DAVID Y., "L'évolution des méthodes de certification de la sécurité face au développement des applications de la micro informatique dans les transports terrestres", *Annales des Ponts et Chaussées*, 1st trimester 1988.

[ESS 98] ESSAMÉ S.D., Tolérance aux fautes dans les systèmes critiques – application au pilotage des lignes de métro automatisé, PhD thesis, LAAS-CNRS, 1998.

[ESS 99] ESSAME S.D., ARLAT J., POWELL D., PADRE: un protocole pour une gestion sure des redondance duplex, LAAS, n° 99105, March 1999.

[FOR 89] FORIN P., "Vital coded microprocessor principles and application for various transit systems", *IFAC - Control, Computers, Communications in Transportation*, p. 137-142, 1989.

[FOR 96] FORIN P., "Une nouvelle génération du processeur sécuritaire codé", *Revue Générale des Chemins de Fer*, vol. 6, pp. 38-41, 1996.

[GEO 90] GEORGES J.P., "Principes et fonctionnement du Système d'Aide à la Conduite, à l'Exploitation et à la Maintenance (SACEM). Application à la ligne A du RER", *Revue Générale des Chemins de Fer*, vol. 6, 1990.

[GUI 90] GUIHOT G., HENNEBERT C., "SACEM software validation", *ICSE*, p. 186-191, March 26-30 1990.

[HEN 94] HENNEBERT C., "Transports ferroviaires: Le SACEM et ses dérivés", *ARAGO 15, Informatique Tolérante aux Fautes*, Masson, Paris, 1994, pp. 141-149.

[HOA 89] HOARE C.A.R., An axiomatic basis for computer programming, Communication of the ACM, vol. 12, p. 576-583, October 1969.

[IEC 98] IEC, IEC 61508: Functional safety of electrical/electronic/programmable electronic safety-related systems, International standard, 1998.

[LEC 96] LECOMPTE P., BEAURENT P.J., "Le système d'automatisation de l'exploitation des trains (SAET) de METEOR", *Revue Générale des Chemins de Fer*, vol. 6, p. 31-34, 1996.

[MAI 93] MAIRE A., "Présentation du système MAGGALY", *Symposium International sur l'Innovation Technologique dans les Transports Guidés*, ITIG'93, Lille, September 1993.

[MAR 90] MARTIN J., WARTSKI S., GALIVEL C., "Le processeur codé: un nouveau concept appliqué à la sécurité des systèmes de transports", *Revue Générale des Chemins de Fer*, vol. 6, p. 29-35, 1990.

[MAT 98] MATRA, RATP, "Naissance d'un Métro. Sur la nouvelle ligne 14, les rames METEOR entrent en scène. PARIS découvre son premier métro automatique", *La Vie du Rail & des Transports*, vol. 1076, special issue, October 1998.

[STR 06] STRMTG, Mission de l'Expert ou Organisme Qualifié Agrée (EOQA) pour l'évaluation de la sécurité des projets, version 1, March 27, 2006.

Chapter 3

From the Coded
Uniprocessor to 2oo3

3.1. Introduction

In this chapter, we describe the architectural evolution of safety computers in the railway signaling sector, namely at Ansaldo STS. CSEE-Transport, a company established in 1902 to work the underground railway signals in Paris, became Ansaldo STS in July 2007. However, CSEE-Transport is better known as a world leader in high-speed signaling.

CSEE-Transport developed the signaling for the high-speed Paris-Lyon train line in 1981. The company is the supplier of all high-speed train line signaling in France. The Ansaldo STS group is also responsible for developing the new European signaling system (ERTMS: European Railway Traffic in Management System, [COM 06]) for LGVEE (Paris-Strasburg), in addition to several train lines in Europe, namely Madrid-Lerida in Spain and Rome-Naples in Italy.

Railway signaling is characterized by a high level of safety, the objective being to demonstrate an error rate against safety less than 10^{-9}/hour. In the railway field, it is certainly possible to halt the train with the emergency break as a last resort, but with increased traffic, the availability requirements become ever higher.

Chapter written by Gilles LEGOFF and Christophe GIRARD.

Table 3.1 indicates the relationship between the Safety Integrated Level (SIL) defined by the EN 50129 [CEN 00] standard and the description generally used in the railway field.

Acceptable occurrence rate of an adverse event (THR) (by hour and function)	Safety Integrity Level (SIL)	Usual description
$10^{-9} \leq$ THR $< 10^{-8}$	4	CRITICAL
$10^{-8} \leq$ THR $< 10^{-7}$	3	
$10^{-7} \leq$ THR $< 10^{-6}$	2	ESSENTIAL
$10^{-6} \leq$ THR $< 10^{-5}$	1	
/	0	NON ESSENTIAL

Table 3.1. *THR and SIL*

Ansaldo STS is also the supplier of underground railway signaling systems (Copenhagen, Paris, Shenyang, Milan, etc.), which use the same technology.

The first safety computer in the French railway field was developed within the SACEM [GEO 90; MAR 90] context: the A line of the Parisian Regional Express Network (RER: *Réseaux Express Régional*), which started operating in August 1989. This technology, the coded uniprocessor (MPC: *Monoprocesseur Codé*), was also used for the large-sized automatic underground railway for the Lyon conurbation (MAGGALY: *Métro Automatique à Grand Gabarit de l'Agglomération Lyonnaise* [MAI 93]), which started operating in 1992. CSEE-Transport was a partner on these two projects and is therefore the owner of the technology.

CSEE-Transport developed its own technology in response to the needs of TVM 430 ground signaling equipment, used since 1993 for cabin signaling and speed control for the Paris-Lille high-speed railway line (LGV: *Ligne à Grande Vitesse*) [GUI 92]. This equipment has been in commercial use since 1993 in the Channel Tunnel.

For the Mediterranean LGV, Valencia-Marseille, which has been in operation since 2001, CSEE-Transport integrated the interlocking (route management) and the spacing function (TVM 430) together within the same safety computer. This architecture, called the available safety computer (CSD: *Calculateur de Sécurité Disponible*) is used in Spain on the high-speed railway Madrid-Lerida line, in England on the CTRL (Channel Tunnel Rail Link) arriving at St Pancras, in China and also on the Paris-Strasburg LGV.

To conclude the chapter, we will mention the characteristics pertaining to the DIVA (Dynamic Integrated Vital and Available system) architecture, which allows for technological integration and performance improvement of ERTMS equipment, as well as potential evolutions.

3.2. From the uniprocessor to the dual processor with voter

On the Paris-Lyon route, the LGV signaling consists of controlling maximum speed over one section: the TVM 300. This means that the information is simple (one frequency of 18) and the equipment is based on analog technology, which is currently being used on the Paris-Lyon and Paris-Tours lines.

3.2.1. *North LGV requirements and the Channel Tunnel*

From an operational perspective, the North LGV requires higher-performance signaling requirements in comparison to other existing lines as a result of the following factors:

– train spacing of 3 minutes (as opposed to 5 minutes for the Paris-Lyon line);

– increase in the operating speed from 270 km/hour to 300 km/hour;

– distance/target type signaling for better speed control.

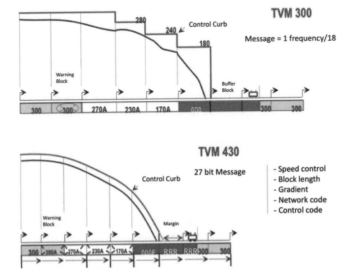

Figure 3.1. *Comparison between TVM 300/TVM 430*

This last point requires additional explanation. On high-speed railway lines in France, lateral signaling does not exist (signal lights on the side of the railway). Signaling happens in the cabin through an authorized speed rate display. The speed limit is calculated on the ground according to the state of traffic on the line, and then transmitted on board the train.

This transmission is achieved through the rails. The train has sensors on the front of the first axle, which enables it to capture information from the ground. On board, the safety computer calculates and then displays the speed limit to the conductor, using the emergency break if the conductor does not respect the authorized limit.

Figure 3.2. *An example of a TVM 430 display cab used on trains in China (DMI)*

The North LGV, operating since 1993, required the application of a distance/target type signal, the TVM 430. This means that the information transmitted on board is a lot more complex: speed input and output, and length and slope for each section. Consequently, the move to digital technology for all ground equipment became necessary. Additionally, the idea of having identical generic equipment adjusted differently for the different posts was introduced.

The [MOE 07] setting corresponded to the need for speed tables (input/output block, different for the North LGV and for the Channel Tunnel). The configuration of the input/output has to be adapted to the geographic configuration of the lines and signaling posts.

Ground signaling equipment is characterized by a great number of inputs/outputs (a safety input and a message for each signaling section, in addition to all the commands and controls for the pointers). Due to the different characteristics of the application, coded processor technology was rapidly proving to be very complex to operate: for this reason Ansaldo STS France, together with the SNCF, advanced development in this technology.

3.2.2. *The principles of the dual processor with voter by coded uniprocessor*

For on-board equipment TVM 430, coded uniprocessor technology was retained.

For ground equipment TVM 430, and to meet the above constraints, the coded uniprocessor technology was modified and the ground safety computer TVM 430 divided into four blocks supported by four electronic cards.

The basic idea of the architecture is to acquire the input, followed by the calculations and the development of the output messages through a dual processor-type architecture, with the objective of using coded uniprocessor technology to vote on the output results. Each element of the dual processor structure elaborates a "result", which is in fact a safety message with SACEM coding and dating representative of the output conditions.

The "voter" in coded uniprocessor technology compares the safety between two messages and, in case of discord, emits a non-compliant sequence towards the dynamic controller (CKD), which in turn secures the ground sub-system.

The strict computing section is composed (in a two out of two setup) of:

– two application blocks with microprocessor and standard software (safety functions);

– a block in charge of dual processor voting with coded uniprocessor technology software;

– a dynamic controller block (CKD) with inbuilt analog technology safety.

The CKD allows for restrictions on the physical outputs of the system (a restrictive state is achieved by securely cutting off the power), which will cut off the rail transmission and consequently halt the train securely, after on board trigger of the emergency break.

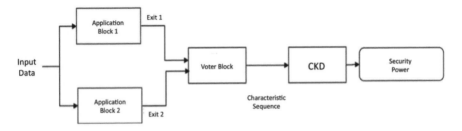

Figure 3.3. *The principle of the dual processor with voter by coded uniprocessor*

Description of the mechanism as shown in the diagram above:

– the input data are supplied to two application blocks working in parallel with each other (uniprocessor technique);

– each application block calculates an output-type sequence from the shared input data and supplies it to a voter;

– the voter compares the two application block outputs and if these are coherent, the voter issues a coded and dated sequence that is transmitted to the CKD, which allows for maintenance of the safety power;

– the CKD deploys the safety power and authorizes the physical outputs;

– the dual processor is synchronized by the input, placed on one card and then distributed to the other card;

– the execution of the second card software is slightly delayed in order to avoid disturbances to the shared mode.

The execution of the physical outputs is undertaken in a similar manner to SACEM-coded uniprocessor technology: the physical output is performed functionally first and then reread securely. If the ordered value is restrictive, in the case of divergence between the ordered value and the reread value, the elaborated sequence is false; the CKD crashes and the sub-system goes into a restrictive state (absence of power).

In terms of technology:

– the CKD TVM 430 card is directly derived from the CKD card used on SACEM (SNCF standards);

– the card in charge of "voting" uses a 68020 processor. This solution allows conservation of the OPEL library (elementary operations of SACEM coded uniprocessor);

– the dual processor application card may use any technology, but the 68020 or the 68040 processors were retained. The TVM 430 generic application code required 15,000 lines of Ada 83 [ANS 83] code outside of setup.

TVM 430 ground equipment has been used in France since 1993. The TVM 430 is also used in Belgium and Korea.

3.2.3. Architecture characteristics

Among the advantages of this solution is a greater facility for the application setup, enabling the development of shared generic software for TVM 430 ground equipment and shared voting software associated with the different system parameters (signaling rules) for tunnel signaling posts of the North LGV and other lines in the world.

In addition, the geographic setup of TVM 430 ground equipment is undertaken uniquely on block 1 and block 2 application software. The coded uniprocessor software is limited to safety comparison functions and algorithms, developed only once and easy to operate and transmit to uniprocessor technology.

It should be noted that in this architecture, safety is completely controlled by the software, and no other hardware elements, other than the dynamic controller (CKD), use analog technology with inbuilt safety.

The main characteristics are as follows:

– the software of both applications must receive the same input data, necessitating input synchronization (one card supplying the other card under the dual processor method);

– the applied software is developed using Ada under specific programming rules, but without the constraints usually linked to coded uniprocessor software development (MPC).

The input data are protected by a SACEM type code (arithmetic code with dating control), verified by the two dual processor cards:

– the output data are SACEM coded and dated by each dual processor card before being sent to the voter for comparison and validation;

– where there is no link with the other channel, all memorized information is lost (hard reset after CKD crash);

– the availability of the system is secured after complete duplication of all elements;

– transmission of the shutting down message to the rail is done by cutting off the safety power, through a safety relay, rendering this solution costly.

This architecture is subject to constraints:

– as for coded uniprocessor technology, output is issued functionally and reread securely;

– in the case of divergence between the reread outputs and the ordered outputs, a false sequence is emitted to the CKD resulting in a restrictive output state;

– safety rereads of functional outputs are difficult to operate and result in damaged modes, which need to be studied minutely;

– for example, a reread of a TVM 430 safety message emitted from the rails is subject to a 4 second reread time lapse before a comparison between the ordered value and the reread value can be made;

– this architecture is centralized within the signaling posts and it is difficult to export the physical outputs, due to the direct link they have with the CKD safety power output.

3.2.4. Requirements for the Mediterranean LGV

Under the Mediterranean LGV project, preliminary studies have shown the benefits of integrating interlocking and signaling functions into a single safety computer in order to significantly reduce the number of safety relays necessary to set up a signaling terminal.

To meet the needs of the Mediterranean LGV, Ansaldo STS France designed and implemented the CSD. The CSD is characterized by two major changes compared to the TVM 430 dual processor architecture:

– the safe storage of information between two application cycles;

– the offset of the safety power cut off (CKD function).

The principle of the safety computer (outside availability) of the Mediterranean LGV is composed of five blocks supported by standard microprocessor cards. In fact, the only safety constraint weighing on CSD equipment is the implementation of two independent clocks: the safety of the computer is entirely ensured by the software.

The safety computing function consists of:

– two application blocks with a standard microprocessor and software;

– a block in charge of the dual processor voting with coded uniprocessor technology;

– a memory block that allows exchanges between the application blocks;

– a coupler block, which allows interface with the physical input/output controllers.

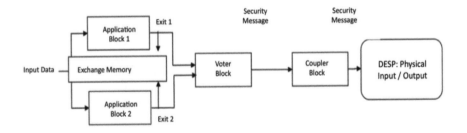

Figure 3.4. *Two out of two CSD operating principle*

The CKD dynamic controller has been removed and, strictly speaking, is no longer part of the computer. The coupler formats the data (either through a series connection, or through a transmission network) and supplies them to the physical input/output device (DESP: *dispositif d'entrée sortie physique*). The DESP does not form part of the CSD.

The DESP ensures the physical input and output. In the Mediterranean LGV application, the DESP was implemented in an input/output basket with a coded uniprocessor computer, a CKD and output cards (CSS: *cartes de sorties*), and safety input cards (CES: *cartes d'entrée de securité*). In recent applications (Spain LGV), the DESP is implemented using MTOR cards (processor card with encoded COLDFIRE and CKD integration), handling 48 inputs/outputs on a single card.

The operating principles of the CSD are described below:

– input data are provided to two separate identical application blocks that work in parallel (dual processor technique);

– a memory exchange block allows synchronization between the two applications and the secure storage of information;

– the voter is master and provides synchronization between the applications;

– each application block calculates the output from the shared input data and supplies it to the voter. The voter compares the two sets of output from the application blocks and, if they are consistent, the voter sends it to the coupler.

The information from the "voter" output is not a typical CKD sequence but SACEM coded, and dated messages sent through unmarked routes to the DESP, which then carries out the physical input/output of the safety equipment. The input and output operations (rereading and securing) are then carried to the nearest ordered output in a minimum amount of time.

The reread of the output and the occurrence of a restrictive state happen at the DESP level. The CSD merely generates safety messages.

The CSD is therefore a safety computer (or PU: processing unit) that receives and sends out safety messages. It acts as safety server with the application (the cyclic safety software developed by the CSD user), receiving and cyclically delivering SACEM-coded and dated messages.

The safety principles of this architecture are complemented by various protections:

– undertaking self-tests as background tasks to guard against latent failures. Self-testing protects program memory and data storage memory, the processor (all instructions and all types of address) as well as the calculation of a "magic" number (predefined and dated) to be transmitted to the voter for validation of the dual processor;

– slight desynchronization of the applications (between block 1 and 2) in order to protect against external interference that could affect simultaneously applications 1 and 2 (protection against the shared modes, e.g. electromagnetic interference). The voter, by way of an interruption, starts the execution of the two programs and imposes a slight lag;

– diversification of physical address memory location on electronic cards (protection against shared mode). The programs are physically implanted in different memory addresses and can access data that are also at different physical addresses;

– safety rests entirely on the cyclic CSD software, which ensures safekeeping in case of failure of the hardware or the card interface layer software (BSP: Board Support Package) or OS (Operating System). This software can be standard commercially available software;

– received and transmitted messages (data managed by the application are protected by a SACEM code that guarantees the safety of the message through arithmetic coding):

   - identification of the transmitter,

   - identification of the receiver,

   - functional value of the data,

   - information refresh (dating),

   - order of receipt of messages.

In the CSD, each functional safety link between the transmitter and the receiver is decided by a logical path (VL), and is uniquely identified in the system.

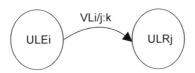

Figure 3.5. *Logical path (VL)*

DEFINITION OF A LOGICAL PATH – a logical path is an oriented connection allowing the exchange of safety information (maximum 256 safety information, using SACEM coding as protection) between a logical unit transmitter ULEi and a logical unit receptor ULRj.

The format of the data transmitted over logical paths is given in Table 3.2.

2 bytes	IDULE: identifier for the logical unit transmitter (*identifiant de l'unité logique émettrice*)
2 bytes	IDULR: identifier for the logical unit receptor (*identifiant de l'unité logique réceptrice*)
2 bytes	TRBINDS: size of the binary representation of non-safety-related information (word count below 32 bits) (*taille de la représentation binaire des informations non de sécurité*)
2 bytes	TRBIDS: size of the binary representation of safety-related information (word count of 32 bits) (*taille de la représentation binaire des informations de sécurité*)
(4 × TRBINDS) bytes	RBINDS: binary representation of non-safety-related information (*représentation binaire des informations non de sécurité*)
(4 × TRBIDS) bytes	RBIDS: binary representation of safety-related information (*représentation binaire des informations de sécurité*)
8 bytes	SC: sum of the SACEM-controlled safety-related information (*somme de contrôle SACEM des informations de sécurité*)

Table 3.2. *Data format*

The CSD logical paths ensure the safety of the information. A protective code (CRC 16 for example) or a self-correcting code can be added at the coupler level to guard against transmission errors over telecommunication networks.

The CSD has been the subject of a presentation [CSE 97] and a research project supported by PREDIT[1].

---

1. http://www.predit.prd.fr/predit3/.

3.3. CSD: available safety computer

3.3.1. *Background*

Under the SII (System of Integrated Interlocking) project for the Mediterranean LGV, the CSD is an integral part of the processing unit. The diagram below shows the position of the PU within the SII signaling equipment that performs the interlocking (command and control pointers, and route management) and spacing (TVM 430 transmission for spacing and control of train speed) functions. These facilities are in continuous operation 24 hours a day, every day of the year on the Mediterranean LGV.

The CSD provides a level of safety of 2×10^{-10}/hour. In terms of availability, the CSD is capable of supporting a first breakdown without any functional damage. If a processing channel fails, the card can be exchanged with the operational computer (dual processor 2oo2). After repairing and repowering the broken channel, it is automatically reinstated by the CSD in the updated context and the computer can run again in two by three.

The processing unit integrates the CSD and the application software, which is configured according to the geographical layout of the track associated with each SII GROUND equipment.

The processing unit consists of three electronic baskets in 6U format (basket application PAP: *panier applicatif*) and integrates the CSD. The processor cards are the 68020 and 68040 type with a VME bus for communication between cards.

The meaning of acronyms is as follows:

– BSP (*boucle à saut de phase*): phase shift loop (timely transfer to the train);

– PEP (*panier émission ponctuelle*): timely emission basket (e.g. pantograph management);

– CdV (*circuit de voie*): track circuit (supports continuous TVM 430 transmission);

– PIV (*panier interface voie*): track interface basket. It manages the circuit track;

– PIP (*panier interface poste*): terminal interface basket. It manages the physical inputs and outputs;

– SAM (*système d'aide à la maintenance*): maintenance support system;

– PAP (*panier applicatif*): basket application (integrates the CSD software);

– PCD (*poste de commande à distance*): remote command terminal. It controls the interlocking system remotely;

– LIM (*module d'interface exploitant en local*): local interface module. It controls the interlocking system locally.

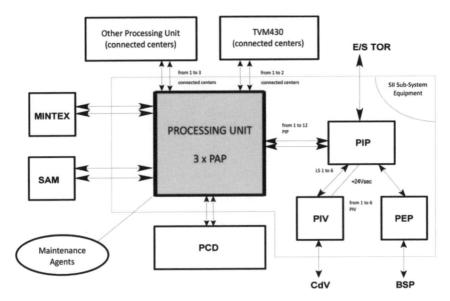

Figure 3.6. *Mediterranean SII LGV (PU environment)*

The PIP corresponds to the DESP as described in the schematic diagram of the preceding section and will not be further detailed. The PIP safely controls the physical inputs/outputs and the messages issued by the PIV. The PIP uses coded uniprocessor technology and has a CKD capable of cutting off the safety power and, therefore, placing the outputs in a restrictive state.

Figure 3.7 shows a ground PU whose characteristics are:

– three 6U baskets;

– VME bus;

– 680×0 technology;

– two complete baskets with:

  - coupler card,

  - voter card (mono),

- application card;

– an under-equipped basket:

- application card;

– basket exchange;

- fiber optic,

- exchange memory card.

Figure 3.7. *Ground SII – PU*

3.3.2. *Functional architecture*

Figure 3.8 describes the functional architecture of the CSD. The memory copies are depicted by the bold double arrows, and the internal data transit by the double arrows.

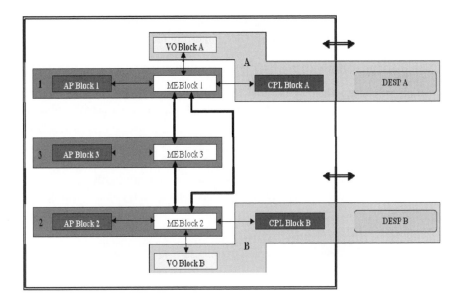

Figure 3.8. *CSD functional architecture*

The previous diagram shows that the CSD is made up of:

– three processing channels performed by the application cards CAP1, CAP2, and CAP3;

– two input/output channels A and B in direct liaison with the CVOA and the CVOB cards, in charge of supporting the dual processor vote.

The safety of the CSD is therefore based on the existence of two independent processing channels (CAP1 and CAP3 cards in the diagram above) each supporting the application. Together, both processing channels form a dual processor, which is controlled by a coded processor called a voter (CVOA card). To ensure a high level of availability and tolerance in the case of a simple failure, it is necessary to add a third physical unit supporting the application (CAP2 card) and a second hot redundancy voter (CVOB card). In this case, the voter(s) determines the valid dual processor(s), issuing the outputs of the validated dual processor.

The CSD is a cyclical and synchronous computer. The temporal characteristics (cycle time, frequency of self-tests) are adjusted by the user and performed by software interrupt mechanisms.

At initialization, the CAP (VME bus master) transmits these characteristics (cycle time and frequency of self-tests) to the voter in its basket.

The voter plays the role of the "conductor": the starting voter signals the beginning of the cycle by a sign of life (SoL) interrupt message.

This message is absorbed by:

– each processing channel, in order to determine the type of operation required: reset, restart wait, restart without valid dual processor, restart with valid dual processor, cycle;

– the second voter, in order to retrieve the context of the first voter.

The voter of channel A starts off the initialization arbitrarily. In case of a breakdown of the first voter, the second voter takes up the relay automatically.

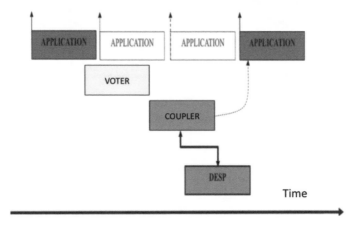

Figure 3.9. *The cyclic process of the CSD*

During each cycle, the processing channels acquire the input message from the couplers and the sign of life message. Then, if ordered by the CVO, they process the application and generate invalidated output messages (SNV: *sorties non validées*) and a message containing the self-test results, destined for the "voters" (AT: self-test results message).

During each cycle, the voter acquires SNV messages from each CAP and a sign of life message from the other voter. Then, it validates the dual processors based on the self-test messages, and generates a validated output message (SV: *sortie validée*) towards the couplers and a message of sign of life to each processing channel and to the other voter. As shown in Figure 3.9, the full process is performed over three cycles.

The CSD inputs/outputs are messages sent from or to the peripherals. These messages are SACEM encoded and securely date messages. The transmission of messages between CSD and DESP is asynchronous.

These messages may transit over open or closed networks, provided they meet the safety requirements of the CENELEC EN 50159 [CEN 01] standard. Part 1 of this standard applies to "closed" networks. The CSD does not handle analog inputs/outputs: these analog inputs/outputs are also deported by mail service to the autonomous peripheral devices called DESP.

Typically, the SII CSD (Mediterranean LGV configuration) can support applications like ATP (automatic train protection) TVM 430 and route management, integrated with the following characteristics:

– 50,000 lines of Ada generic code, without geographic parameters;

– application cycle time: 448 milliseconds.

3.3.3. *Software architecture*

CSD software is distributed throughout each of the processing channels and the voters. All software located on the voter, called CSD-LCVO or LCVO, belongs to the CSD. In contrast, only part of the software in a processing channel, the LCAP, belongs to the CSD: this part is called the "CSD software layer" of LCAP.

3.3.3.1. *LCVO software*

LCVO software is independent of the application and ensures output vote. Figure 3.10 shows the architecture of CVO card software.

If we look closely at LCVO software, we can distinguish the lowest software layers from the highest layers, i.e. from the center to the exterior of the circle:

– the CST interface library: written in the Ada (95) language and with the MC680x0 system integrator, is made up of reusable software components interfacing with the BSP (Board Support Package) card;

– the OPEL interface library: written with the MC680x0 system integrator, has an interface in the Ada (95) language. This library is necessary for all software that uses coded uniprocessor technology;

– the CSD interface library: written in the Ada (95) language, is made up of reusable software components developed by CSEE Transport and specific to the CSD. This library relies on the CST interface library;

– CSD-CVO software provides a comparison of two out of two dual processors. This software and its associated compensation tables (see coded uniprocessor technology) are written in the Ada (95) language. It relies on the OPEL interface library (elementary operations of coded uniprocessor);

– the center is the hardware, not the software, and consists of standard 680x0 hardware technology.

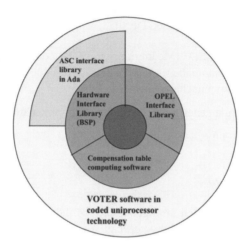

Figure 3.10. *Architecture of voter software*

CVO card software is the same *for all CVO cards* (*CVOA and CVOB*) *in all CSDs*. Thus, the CVO card and its software can be assimilated to an invariant set. A stub associated with a basket rather than a card allows for one-to-one identification of the logical paths (VL) of each CSD.

3.3.3.2. *LCAP software*

The functional operations are supported by LCAP software. Figure 3.11 shows the software architecture of CAP cards. LCAP software is developed in Ada standard (example of application: TVM 430, SII).

LCAP software is composed from the lowest software layers to the highest layers, i.e. from the center towards the exterior of the circle, of:

– standard hardware without technological impediments;

– the CST interface library: see section 3.3.3.1;

– the self-tests from the CAP cards: a software component written largely with a system integrator. It is specific to the hardware used on CAP cards: self-testing of ROM (read-only memory; the program), RAM (random access memory; data), instructions from the microprocessor;

– a CSD-CAP layer: written in Ada (95), is the basic CSD software specific to CAP cards. It relies on the CST and CSD interface libraries. Some modules from the CSD-CAP software are specific to each CAP card (CAP1, CAP2, or CAP3);

– the "configuration" layer establishes the interface between the CSD layer and the application software and ensures the independence of these two layers. It is written in Ada (95) by the CSD user;

– the "application" layer: written in Ada (95) by the CSD user. It uses services offered by CSD-CAP software and must provide the software with a certain number of configuration settings. These parameters are essentially temporal constants matching the real-time behavior of the CSD to performance of the equipment being used ("software control knobs").

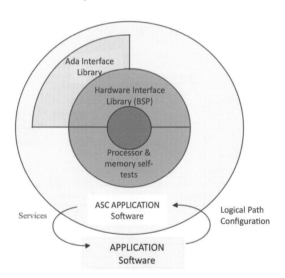

Figure 3.11. *Application software architecture*

The application software of CAP cards is *the same for the application cards* (CAP1, CAP2, and CAP3). Thus, the user need only write a single software application that is then instantiated for the three application cards.

This generation process, originating from the application software provided by the user and the libraries associated with the basic CSD software for application cards, develops three separate executables, one for each application card CAP1, CAP2, and CAP3. The three executables are differentiated by:

– a spatial diversification: each address of each CAP software instruction differs according to card CAP1, CAP2 or CAP3;

– a temporal diversification: the execution timing of each microprocessor instruction differs from one card to another.

Temporal diversification is managed by the "voter" through the interrupt mechanism software and the synchronization signals. Diversification is intended to protect the shared modes as all three applications use the same microprocessor and the same software.

3.3.4. *Synchronization signals*

Figure 3.12 shows the CSD principles for synchronization. The IT_AP signal prompts the start of the unsynchronized applications. The IT_VO signal allows synchronization of voters and the IT_CPL signal is related to the authorization of voted outputs.

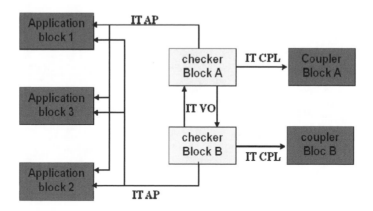

Figure 3.12. *Synchronization signals*

3.3.4.1. *Synchronization between two voters*

The synchronization signals (IT_VO) exchanged between the voter cards have a dual role:

– they allow an initializing voter card to synchronize with another voter card that is already operational. If an initializing voter card cannot synchronize with another voter card, it continues its cyclic operation without delay. This allows the CSD to start where one voter card is present or one of two voter cards is inoperative;

– they allow the two voter cards, which are already operational and synchronized to remain synchronous. However, during each CSD cycle, a voter card may decide to abandon this synchronization, if it considers that the period of signal synchronization from another voter card is not within a predetermined window. Thus, the failure of a voter card does not halt the CSD, which may continue operations with the other voter.

3.3.4.2. *Synchronization between a voter and an application card*

The synchronization signals (IT_AP) broadcast from the voter cards to the application cards allow synchronization of the operations of the application cards.

Three cases may arise:

– the application card is synchronized with the two voter cards, CVOA and CVOB: this is the normal operational mode of the available CSD in which the two voter cards are synchronized;

– the application card is synchronized with one of two voter cards, CVOA or CVOB: this is the normal operational mode of an unavailable CSD (only one voter card is present) or a damaged mode of operation of an available CSD (one voter card is down or the two voter cards are out of sync). In the case where the two voter cards are out of sync, each application card randomly chooses to synchronize with the voter card of its choice, CVOA or CVOB. This is not a problem as there will always be at least two application cards out of three that will make an identical choice: in the worst case, a desynchronization of the two voter cards will result in the loss of a voter card and an application card, but the CSD will continue to operate normally with the remaining voter card and the two application cards;

– the application card is no longer synchronized: this is a damaged mode of operation of the CSD. In this case, the application card that can no longer synchronize triggers an auto-reset procedure. Thus, if this loss of synchronization was originally due to an exterior disturbance, the application card may, after reset, resume operations without the need for a maintenance procedure.

3.3.4.3. *Global synchronization*

The synchronization signals ensure that the outputs will not be emitted before the end of voting. These internal CSD mechanisms replace the basic mechanisms of the operating system (OS). The cyclical process, the control of the clocks and the "voters" ensure safety independently from the OS. There is no particular constraint on the OS at the CSD level and a commercial VRTX core may be used.

Figure 3.13 describes the global synchronization between the various entities of the CSD.

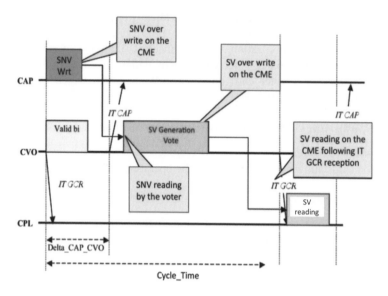

Figure 3.13. *Synchronization signals*

The voter is master and triggers the start of the CAP application cycle through the IT_CAP, as well as authorizing the physical outputs and, therefore, the transfer to the coupler through a priority hardware interrupt (IT_GCR).

3.3.5. *The CSD mail system*

3.3.5.1. *Basics of the mail system*

In principle, the CSD exchanges safety messages with other safety computers, which may be CSDs or other types of computers (the latter must know the characteristics of encoding exchanged messages).

The CSD communicates with the outside world through physical links. A physical connection can support multiple logical paths within the meaning of the CSD. Each VL is protected by a safety coding.

The CSD has several safety protocols. As a standard, there is a double dating protocol with data protection through SACEM encoding. The CSD also offers the ERTMS Euroradio protocols with double dating and protection of data by a cryptographic DES type code with private keys. However, the CSD user application can define its own protocol provided it respects the abovementioned rules. Protecting external messages *vis-à-vis* transmission faults is the responsibility of the application (standard services are offered).

3.3.5.1.1. CSD internal exchanges

All exchanges internal to the CSD are undertaken by SACEM formatted messages (except for internal messages related to synchronization signals exchanged between the CAP and the CVO). The SC control sum of a message transmitted over a logical path VLi/j:k internal to the CSD is calculated as follows (SACEM encoding):

$$(1) \quad SC = \left[\sum_{n=0}^{255} \left(-rk * IDSn * \theta^n \right) \right] + SVLi/j:k$$

All calculations are performed *modulo* the key code (large number) and where:

– IDSn (signed integer over 32 bit) represents the safety information of rank n;

– SVLi/j:k is the signature of the logical path used;

– rk and θ are predefined constants over 48 bit.

3.3.5.1.2. Exchanges outside of the CSD

The safety code used for safety input/output messages is a maximum 64-bit safety code defined by the CSD user. However, as a standard, the CSD includes the SACEM code and the Euroradio ERTMS code.

The communication medium used to transmit (non-safety related) messages is the application software, which must ensure the safety of transmitted information, based on a number of services offered by the basic CSD software.

The safety protocol to be implemented should allow a receiver to detect the following errors:

– the receipt of erroneous data (integrity);

– the receipt of data from the wrong sender or destined for another receiver (identity);

– loss of data or receipt of obsolete data (temporal validity);

– the reception of off-sequence data (temporal coherence).

3.3.5.2. *Messages linked to self-tests*

Self-tests can detect latent and transient failures. In order to avoid penalizing the cycle time of the application, most of these tests are performed over several application cycles. The tests, conducted during time Td, are:

– program memory test, AT_PROM;

– volatile memory test, AT_RAM;

– constants test in RAM and AT_CTE;

– microprocessor test, AT_CPU.

Some tests are performed during each application cycle (Ta period). These tests include:

– time unit and time lag test, AT_UTDT;

– stored variable context test, AT_VMC.

The self-test results are coded over 32 bit words and time Td is adjusted to meet the protection for an overall safety of 10^{-9}/hour for the equipment (usually a few minutes).

In order to detect whether self-test results have not refreshed, they are energized as follows:

(2) Signature_autotest n = Date_start_cycle_AT + K_n

or:

– Date_start_cycle_AT: represents the cycle date commencement of self-tests. This date is equal to the current date of the voter (date_voter) during the first cycle of the self-test;

– K_n: predefined constant for self-test *n*. To avoid the risk of confusion between two self-test results, the constants K_n were chosen so that they have a Hamming distance of 16.

The self-test results of each CAP card are transmitted, during each application cycle, to the voter via the self-test message (AT message internal to the CSD).

3.3.5.3. *Technical functions related to context memory*

A context variable is a variable whose current state depends not only on the current cycle but also on the precedent cycle(s). The computer needs to know the existence of context memory variables (VMC) for two reasons:

– during the powering of a CAP card when the voter has a valid dual processor, the CAP card must retrieve all the variables stored to get back on the same level as the other two CAPs. This mechanism is called the context recovery mechanism. To avoid disrupting the operation, the CAP card must retrieve all the stored variables (critical or not);

– the application software must provide a picture of all critical variables stored in each cycle.

The CSD offers a service that allows a stored context variable to be taken into account by the software services of the CSD: AT_REF _VMC and AT_VMC.

The definition of context variables is the responsibility of the user, hence the following constraint for the application software: "the CSD user must define stored context variables using the proper CSD service and their initial respective value".

Note that this constraint also constitutes an availability constraint for the CSD. Indeed, context is necessary for the nominal operation of the card.

3.4. DIVA evolutions

The ERTMS system is the new European signaling system that is currently being deployed on various high-speed and conventional railway lines. Ansaldo STS was selected for the high-speed Madrid-Lerida railway line in Spain, for Rome-Naples in Italy and also for Paris-Strasburg in France.

This system is characterized by the implementation of the onboard Eurocab computer, which is able to travel on different ground signaling equipment:

– ground with lateral signaling and EUROBALISE: ERTMS Level 1;

– ground without lateral signaling and GSM-R radiocommunication: ERTMS Level 2;

– ground with existing signaling systems, such as TVM 430, KVB, or LZB.

In principle, the maximum number of functions and operations are undertaken on board the train; Eurocab equipment must, therefore, be capable of securely storing a large amount of information and have a high computing power.

3.4.1. ERTMS equipment requirements

Currently over 1,000 ONBOARD TVM 430 devices are in operation. These devices use coded uniprocessor technology. The ONBOARD TVM 430 computer ensures that during every cycle the message issued by TVM 430 ground equipment in the rail is read through the track circuit. It reads the message from the ground and after calculating the speed control curve, displays the directions for the driver or applies the emergency brake if necessary. The software uses coded uniprocessor technology (MPC) and stores only a minimum amount of information between two cycles.

The ONBOARD ERTMS equipment receives messages from beacons on the track and radio messages in a completely asynchronous way. The devices store these messages containing a large amount of information (track profile over several kilometers) in order to continuously and securely control the movement of the train.

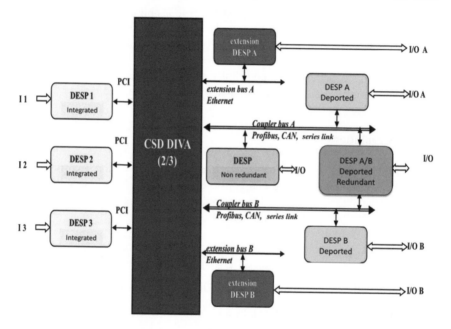

Figure 3.14. *CSD DIVA environment*

The evolution of the EUROCAB onboard equipment to a CSD-type architecture, therefore, proved fairly obvious to Ansaldo STS France.

Note, however, the specific constraints that have led to significant architectural improvements in the context of the evolution of the CSD to the DIVA: Dynamic Integrated Vital and Available system.

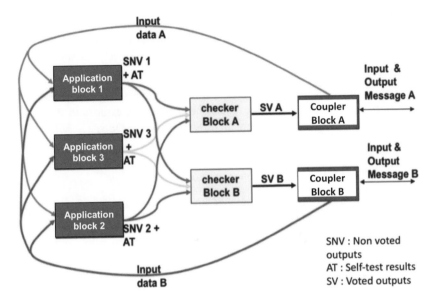

Figure 3.15. *Internal mailing system of the CSD DIVA*

DIVA is primarily a technological evolution: the integration on a single card of four basic CSD functions and four microprocessors (coupler, application, voter, and memory exchange). DIVA is also accompanied by a number of CSD improvements but as with the CSD, DIVA safety is based entirely on software and, therefore, the hardware has no specific safety constraints:

– on the ground, the cycle times are of the order of 500 milliseconds, which is quite acceptable in terms of the actual time it takes to move a pointer or release a track circuit. Onboard, these times are not sufficient to control the speed of a high-speed train at 320 km/hour and 50 milliseconds is a preferable target;

– on the ground, the equipment is in air-conditioned compartments, distributed every 15 km along high-speed lines. The establishment of an electronic bay with three baskets, which operates 24 hours a day, does not pose any particular problem. Onboard the train, size and price are key factors and technological change was necessary;

– onboard, a speed control function measures the real-time speed of the train and also carries out a precise localization of the train when passing a beacon. This is a complex function that requires the minute synchronization of different events from multiple sensors. Therefore, the implementation of an accurate clock at the CSD level became necessary. A software mechanism allows a guaranteed accuracy of 10^{-3};

– additionally, the constraints of availability and maintenance are not the same on the ground as onboard. Onboard, the mission needs to be pursued, ensuring a standard rapid depot exchange, while the continuity of service is paramount on the ground;

– the messaging service has also been improved to make the passage through the coupler systematic, through both the input and output of messages to the deported DESP. The CSD DIVA can interface with different types of DESP.

3.4.2. *Functional evolution*

The "availability of anticipated outputs" (MADAS: *mise à disposition anticipée des sorties*) allows the coupler software to access the voted output (SV) written by the voter as soon as possible.

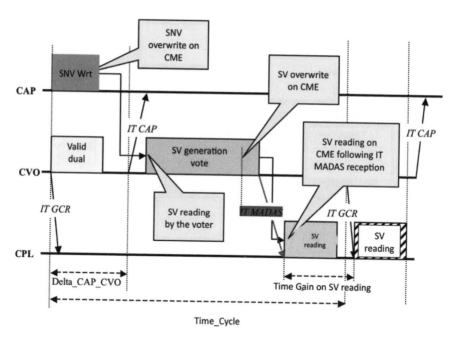

Figure 3.16. *CSD DIVA synchronization*

During the CSD authorization operations, the coupler could only read the SV during "IT GCR reception".

The addition of an extra signal emitted by the voter to the coupler at the end of the vote allows the coupler to save time and access the SV.

3.4.3. *Technological evolution*

The CSD DIVA has been developed to meet the specific needs of onboard equipment:

– integration of the various CSD blocks into a single card;

– ease of implementation and programming for various targeted applications;

– significant increase in performance to meet the different short and long-term needs (CPU load, reduced cycle time, memory size, speed of internal/external communications);

– acceptance of different bus types (PCI and Ethernet) in order to interface with different sensors or external CSD devices, specific to train interfaces (braking, circuit breakers, etc.).

3.4.3.1. *Presentation of the CCTE card*

The CSD DIVA is based on the CCTE card, which integrates the four basic functions of an onboard CSD onto a single card:

– a memory block architected around a Coldfire microprocessor: MP_ME;

– an application block architected around a Coldfire microprocessor: MP_AP;

– a voter block architected around a Coldfire microprocessor: MP_VO;

– a coupler block architected around a Coldfire microprocessor: MP_CPL.

These four microprocessors are connected together by a PCI bus, which allows the exchange of data and a set of IT buses that enables the synchronization of the whole.

Furthermore, the CCTE offers the possibility of adding extensions called daughter cards:

– a tachometry extension, which communicates and synchronizes the MP_AP *via* a proprietary bus TACHY;

– a PMC extension, which communicates *via* the PCI with other MPs and which synchronizes with them *through* a set of configurable IT.

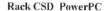

Rack CSD PowerPC

Figure 3.17. *CCTE DIVA and CSD PPC card*

3.4.3.2. *CSD DIVA implementation*

The CSD DIVA is made up of three CCTE (CCTE1, CCTE2, and CCTE3), each containing a power card (ACSDV); there is no shared mode between the different CCTE cards:

– each CCTE card supports a processing chain consisting of a Coldfire application-type microprocessor (MP_AP);

– CCTE1 and CCTE2 cards support coupler (MP_CPL) and voter (MP_VO) functions as well as Coldfire technology.

Figure 3.18. *EUROCAP basket computer and ERTMS agent conductor interface*

The three cards are interconnected by means of an exchange memory microprocessor (MP_ME) and an Ethernet link. The PMC extension and the tachometry card are optional blocks (it is possible to use an external tachometry).

An identification stub (different on each of the three processing chains) is associated with each CCTE card to ensure uniqueness of the logical path identifiers.

3.5. New needs and possible solutions

Ansaldo STS France's CSD DIVA computer continues to evolve and improve. It will be interesting to follow microprocessor technology and rapid communication between processors.

Ansaldo STS France is currently studying different developments:

– a new CCTE card based on a more powerful microprocessor;

– improved memory exchange between the three processors;

– fast Ethernet links for connection between blocks.

These technological developments are needed in order to remain competitive in the railway signaling market, but are they sufficient to meet the needs of future guided transport applications that require high levels of safety and availability?

ERTMS is a European standard, which is currently being deployed, whilst applications for automatic underground railways are spreading around the world. The evolution of safety platforms will continue in order to meet the needs of these new applications, which often exceed 100,000 lines of Ada code. Increasing the size of the software will also lead to increased complexity and hence new requirements for the CSD.

In the following sections we discuss two potential improvements of the CSD operating principles.

3.5.1. *Management of the partitions*

Increasingly, in conjunction with the generalization of the EN 50128 [CEN 01a] standard in the railway sector, we can classify the applications according to three levels of safety requirements. The discussion is about the SSIL (Software Safety Integrity Level). This applies to system-level hardware and software, but for the current and future applications, the development of critical software is particularly important.

Therefore we may distinguish:

– SIL level 0 corresponds to software without specific safety constraints, this may be commercially available software or graphics libraries, for example. These programs provide safe functions in all cases where rail traffic safety is not essential;

– SIL level 2 corresponds to functions that participate significantly to the safety of the application but where false results are not directly dangerous. These functions implement safeguards and mechanisms that are often linked to the overall system availability. For example, SIL 2 software can be in charge of displaying the set speed to the driver. The display of a higher value can cause incorrect behavior on behalf of the driver but this will be overridden by the speed control of SIL 4;

– SIL level 4 corresponds to safety software (that is to say, zero defects). The software accomplishes set tasks and nothing else. False results can cause dangerous situations. The methodology of monitored development (strict compliance with standards) must ensure proper functioning or the initiation of a restrictive state of the output. For railway applications, this means triggering the emergency brakes and stopping the train.

The CSD is obviously a SIL 4 software, but today the application software (developed by the CSD user) is considered as the only software. The notion of SIL level partition covers the notion of isolating mechanisms between software partitions.

The services offered by the CSD will be twofold:

– safeguard mechanisms ensuring that SIL 0 software does not disrupt the functioning of SIL 2 or 4 software; in addition, the loss of a SIL 2 software function must not disrupt the smooth functioning of SIL 4 software;

– mechanisms for the transfer and storage of information between partitions (refresh function and protection of shared data).

These developments are being analyzed and will very probably undergo substantial change: replacing the real-time core (using an INTEGRITY or RAVENSCAR solution) in conjunction with an adaptation of the principle of logical paths internal to the CSD.

3.5.2. *Multicycle services*

Currently the CSD DIVA supports a cyclic application, the cycle time can be set and adjusted by the user, but within certain limits; it is necessary for the cycle time of the application to be consistent with the voting time (validation of at least one dual processor and control of self-testing and preparation of outputs). One can certainly increase the computing power of a microprocessor ensuring the vote but again it cannot fall below a certain limit without impacting costs.

Conversely by analyzing the functions performed by our applications, we can see that all functions do not have the same requirements in terms of response time. For example, the functions carried out onboard for an automatic underground railway application, which communicates with the ground using the radio. This application is under consideration for the MODURBAN[2] European project, which Ansaldo STS France is participating in, alongside leading European manufacturers and operators. Operational implementation is currently underway.

We can take three examples of functions:

– update of the maximum speed allowed on a new route. The change of route requires the physical movement of pointers, resulting in a recalculation of a track area: this can take hundreds of milliseconds;

– control of the train's position must be done permanently; when the train is going fast, it is normally far away from a danger point and speed accuracy is more important than location. Conversely, when the train approaches a station, the accuracy of location is paramount. In both cases, a cycle time of about 10 milliseconds is required;

– the emergency shutdown signal following an incident, such as a pointer that is out of control: the information should be addressed as soon as possible.

These three functions obviously contribute to traffic safety. They have different requirements in terms of performance response time and to process them within a single application cycle involves complex software, which could be avoided.

We may consider incorporating complementary mechanisms within the CSD to provide trigger and task sequence services (cyclic tasks with minimum redundancy). The validity of the results of each task (compared with its counterpart executed on another processor) will then be validated by a vote using coded uniprocessor technology.

Based on standard multicyclic mechanisms, validated once and for all, the coding application can be simplified and, therefore, the development and validation effort reduced. This should also facilitate the safety analysis and minimize the delays and costs of certification. It should be noted that rail operators increasingly require reliance on standard products already in operation, necessitating minimal changes to meet their operational needs.

3.6. Conclusion

This chapter presented the original architecture of the coded uniprocessor technology and dual processor architectures. The evolution towards a two of three-type computer (2oo3) was made in order to ensure the storage of safety information and hot recovery after a breakdown (application context recovery).

---

2. MODURBAN: European project, see www.modurban.org.

This architecture can also be easily used in a two of two configuration. This is the case for EUROCAB ONBOARD equipment for ERTMS level 1 projects circulating on conventional lines with lateral signaling (e.g. in India and Sweden). The loss of the computer does not bring the mission to a halt because the driver can continue using lateral signaling. This is not the case for applications onboard the TGV along high-speed lines. The absence of lateral signaling involves a high level of safety and availability.

In the field of guided transport, applications concerning automatic underground railways have, of course, similar requirements. They often demand more stringent performance than for high-speed trains. Improved performance is a result of technological change, but improvements in the architecture principles are also essential.

The comparison with other areas of activities can be useful.

3.7. Assessment of installations

Table 3.3 represents equipment sets installed onboard trains.

Application	Trains	Technology	Number
TVM 300	Paris Lyon in 1981 LGV Atlantic (Paris-Le Mans 1989, Paris-Tours 1990)	Analog	300
TVM 430	TGV Trains - Network and TGV Duplex	Coded uniprocessor	1200
TVM 430	Eurostar, Shuttle, and Class 92 Trains	Coded uniprocessor	-
TVM 430	Korea and China	Coded uniprocessor	76
EUROCAB ERTMS N1 & N2	CAF ATPRD Trains for Madrid-Lerida	CSD	69
BI-STANDARD TVM + ERTMS N2 + STM	POS: for Paris-Strasburg THALYS: Paris-Brussels-Amsterdam	CSD DIVA	152
EUROCAB ERTMS N1	India and Korea	CSD DIVA (two of two)	158
ATP 200	China: large passenger lines	CSD DIVA	120

Table 3.3. *Equipment sets installed on board trains*

Table 3.4 represents ground equipment sets.

Application	Lines	Technology	Number
TVM 430	North LGV and Rhône-Alpes LGV	Dual with MPC vote	54
TVM 430	Europe: Belgium (LN1) and tunnel	Dual with MPC vote	24
TVM 430	Korea	Dual with MPC vote	31
SII /TVM 430	Mediterranean LGV	CSD	32
SII/TVM 430	China: QINSHEN	CSD	34
SII	Interlocking on Madrid-Lerida	CSD	13
SII	Interlocking on Figueras-Perpignan	CSD	1
SII / TVM 430	LGVEE: Paris-Strasburg	CSD	37
SII / TVM 430	CTRL: London Channel Tunnel	CSD	17
SII / TVM 300	SHITAI Line in China	CSD	17
RBC ERTMS	France LGVEE	CSD PPC	7
RBC ERTMS	Spain Madrid-Lerida	CSD PPC	5
RBC ERTMS	Spain/France: Figueras-Perpignan	CSD PPC	1
CSD / PAS	OURAGAN Line 3 PARIS underground	CSD PPC	3
CSD / PAS	SHENYANG underground China	CSD PPC	2

Table 3.4. *Ground equipment sets*

3.8. Bibliography

[ANS 83] ANSI, Standard ANSI/MIL-STD-1815A-1983, Ada Programming Language, 1983.

[CEN 00] CENELEC, NF EN 50126, Railway applications. The specification and demonstration of reliability, availability, maintainability and safety (RAMS), January 2000.

[CEN 01] CENELEC, EN 50159-1, Railway applications – communication, signalling, and processing systems. Part 1: safety-related communication in closed transmission systems, March 2001.

[CEN 01a] CENELEC, NF EN 50128, Railway applications – communications, signalling and processing systems – software for railway control and protection systems, July 2001.

[COM 06] EUROPEAN COMMISSION, ERTMS – delivering flexible and reliable rail traffic, 2006.

[CSE 97] CSEE-Transport, PREDIT Presentation, CSD, June 1997.

[GEO 90] GEORGES J.P., "Principes et fonctionnement du Système d'Aide à la Conduite, à l'Exploitation et à la Maintenance (SACEM). Application à la ligne a du RER", *Revue Générale des Chemins de Fer*, n° 6, p. 23-28, 1990.

[GUI 92] GUILLEUX B., "Signalling on new lines, The transition to the TVM 430 System", *Revue Générale des Chemins de Fer*, pp. 59-65, 1992.

[MAI 93] MAIRE A., "Présentation du système MAGGALY", *Symposium international sur l'innovation technologique dans les transports guidés, ITIG '93*, Lille, September 1993.

[MAR 90] MARTIN J., WARTSKI S., GALIVEL C., "Le processeur codé: un nouveau concept appliqué à la sécurité des systèmes de transports", *Revue Générale des Chemins de Fer*, n° 6, pp. 29-35, 1990.

[MOE 07] MOENS G., "Le système de signalisation", *Revue Générale des Chemins de Fer*, pp. 29-39, 2007.

Chapter 4

Designing a Computerized Interlocking Module: a Key Component of Computer-Based Signal Boxes Designed by the SNCF

4.1. Introduction

The history of transport, irrespective of the type, is full of dramatic stories of accidents and disasters of all kinds. For this reason, over time, various principles and procedures for design and operation have appeared, with the purpose of reducing and preventing the risk of accident. These provisions have led to spectacular progress. Developments in computer science and automation have been the source of new and more effective solutions, but they have also resulted in new complexities, further complicating the sustainable design, evaluation, measurement, and prediction of the dependability of equipment and transportation systems.

With its extensive experience in the railway and signaling domain, SNCF developed (1993-1995) *a concept of high-level safety generic automation*. This initially led to the SYMEL[1] system of single-track rail management, and then to the

Chapter written by Marc ANTONI.

1. SYMEL: modular line system management (*Système Modulaire d'Equipment des Lignes*). This system, originally devised by Mr François Van Deth, allows the management of a single-track line using a safety automation in each railway station, the latter being controlled via a remote PC; the first use was in June 1995 on the Limoges-Ussel line.

development of a computer-based signal box, PIPC[2]; currently, the most commonly used in the modern national rail network. Today more than 150 such boxes are in operation worldwide. Three factors were particularly considered during development: the assessment of dependability; design; and the consideration of human and cognitive factors.

Figure 4.1. *Computerized interlocking module (MEI: module d'enclenchement informatique) and remote control post (PCD: poste de commande distant)*[3]

The aim of this chapter is to describe the prevailing thoughts leading to the development of high-level safety generic automation and the interpretable specifications executed in real-time. Note that, contrary to standards, the systematic stopping of the installation of all or part of an automated rail system, in the case of a "safe" failure, is not a solution without consequences because it leads to other safety problems (traffic management during failure, risks related to restart, interference with automation interfaces, risk management procedures by the operators, etc.), without considering the impact on production, which can be considerable. It follows that beyond the Safety Integrated Level (SIL), the probability of untimely failure

2. PIPC: computer-based post (*poste informatique à technologie PC*) using SYMEL safety automata to manage signal boxes.
3. Photos from Mr. Marc Antoni.

and the repair time are also important design criteria to be taken into account from the conception stage, in order to achieve the safety level required in a railway system.

Beyond the main features of safety automation, we will discuss the approach retained for its definition to the extent that a number of principles are innovative in their implementation but conventional in their issues. In line with proven trade practices, the basic idea was to develop a "unified" automated safety system that could be formally validated[4], was easy to maintain under continuous-use operational conditions, and had a functionally that was simple to edit.

We will study this predicament in the following sections.

4.2. Issues

How can high-level safety computer systems with increasing complexity be made while at the same time controlling costs? This is a problem that concerns all industrial designers and managers of such computer-based systems. Experience has shown that as computer systems become more complex, time and cost constraints increase, their production is more difficult, and tasks related to integration testing and validation are increasingly complicated.

4.2.1. *Persistent bias*

To balance the equation, the pressures exerted on infrastructure managers are such that there is a risk of the safety level becoming the adjustment variable. They may lead to certain common prejudices: as safety is expensive, safety constraints are the arguments of protectionists; the safety of computer systems is a matter for computer experts, etc., despite the fact that certain experiences invalidating this argument appear less and less marginal [EIS 07]. It seems that some operators of critical industrial systems, in view of past experience (published or not), have opted[5] not to use computer systems for safety functions of the highest level.

---

4. Formal validation: the possibility accorded to trade operators to obtain formal proof that the safety automation respects, within the context of the operating premise, all the safety attributes required by the track plan. It should be noted that this type of proof is done after all technical or functional modifications to the signal box are made, which is customary for mechanical signal boxes.

5. For two main reasons: inability to guarantee that the functional application is 100% correct and reduction of the operational availability of the functions.

4.2.2. *Challenges for tomorrow*

These challenges appear clearer in the following contexts:

– industrial computer facilities are becoming more complex;

– development costs increase alongside system size and the possibility of centralization;

– the stakes of development projects are economic before being safety-related;

– the move to integrated automation leads to increased requirements, and loss of trade knowledge;

– incidents or accidents can have incalculable media-related consequences if repeated; the standards acceptable to the population are increasing;

– growth of traffic makes maintenance and modification operations more complex, in order to avoid reducing production capacity etc.

The endemic weakness of computer systems relies on the fact that at the functional level, the level of safety is actually based on *quality assurance* implemented during its development. The constraints imposed by standards [CEN 00; CEN 01a; CEN 03] are mainly based on the hardware architecture (probabilistic approach) and on software quality assurance. It is particularly difficult to quantify the level of safety functions transcoded by a computer system, especially if it is required to be installed at different locations, while the occurrence of accidents will be more expensive due to the media, the Internet, and the high expectations of Western societies.

Dealing with safety at the design level is a more economical approach in the long run, as opposed to development economies that lead to less safe and less profitable systems. The industry should move towards the economic rationalization of task specification and final validation, while improving the control level of risks inherent to these new systems. We must find a path that can address economic constraints while preserving the current safety levels.

Let us take the example of proven past experience: the safest, the most reliable, and the most durable installations are simplest when they are designed in line with their environment and conditions of use. This path is accessible if we go back to the fundamentals of the required functions and not to the choice of technical implementation.

Note that the electromechanical and mechanical posts have undergone many years of formal validation of their interlocking tables, more than 100 years in fact, and well before this terminology appeared in modern computer science. The application of formal methods is based on the full expression by trade experts on expected functionalities, conditions of use and environment, safety properties, all in connection with past fundamentals: a necessary evil in a way. We will propose a method to apply them practically in order to act effectively on the development cycle of critical computer systems.

4.2.3. Probability and computer safety

The operational reliability and safety of computer and computer-based systems cannot be estimated using probabilistic approaches, at least when the targeted level is industrial. It is commonly accepted that so-called "reliability growth" approaches are unhelpful. For hardware, it is not reasonable to give by analogy a reliability rate for a software component (indiscriminately regrouping software and functional application systems).

The operational reliability and safety of computer systems, in an environmental context and given purpose, must be regarded as deterministic in terms of functionality. Indeed, if there is an "interlocking gap", in a case not covered by functional specifications, each time the unforeseen input configuration occurs, the functional will "deterministically" lead to an unsafe system state, regardless of its hardware architecture and its safety level under the current standards (SIL).

Moreover, in some cases, it is sufficient for this feared combination to occur only once for the functional to present multiple dangerous weaknesses.

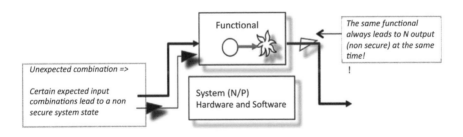

Figure 4.2. *Application software defects deterministically lead to non-safe outputs of the computer system, whatever the level of reliability of the hardware/software support*

Test generators are tools that generate test sequences that conform to specifications. They ensure that the actual system conforms to the original specifications. This technique involves the actual system. It does not guarantee the completeness of the tests undertaken. The coverage is limited due to:

– temporal (or technical) inability to perform all of the anticipated situations (due mainly to time constraints);

– the difficulty in creating tests to verify functional compliance (or input fields) that were not considered during the creation of the original specifications (it is uncommon to remember to test something that was earlier forgotten).

Consequently, the option chosen was to distinguish the functional software from all the basic hardware and software at the design stage, so that the industrial application of a formal method could be subsequently considered.

4.2.4. *Maintainability and modifiability*

The modifiability of a computer application is its ability to be updated, refined, and revised by trade experts, without having to continually consult computer experts. The maintainability of a computer application is its ability to be modified and tested quickly without incurring high economic costs and time delays (delay in operational condition recovery).

Maintainability and modifiability of computer-based functional systems rely primarily on:

– the expression of functionalities using a professional language, which is graphic and intuitive enough to be discussed calmly by trade experts. Experience has shown that modeling trade functionalities in an analytical language has either not been successful or has not allowed for the performed modeling to persist within a time frame;

– the strict separation of, on the one hand, hardware and software aspects providing functions independently of the application and, on the other hand, the functional aspects of the application independently of other computer-based aspects. In this context, a change in functional software has no impact on software managing the hardware and the safety and *vice versa*;

– the demonstration of safety inherent to any modification of the hardware and software system must be independent of hardware technology (processor type, etc.). This is a key point for maintenance; it allows replacement without questioning the demonstration of target achievement (non-regression) required under existing standards and an important cost-saving for the maintenance of the systems in operational conditions.

4.2.4.1. *Error correction and organization*

Complex software is divided into subsets, subprograms, modules or objects according to the type of programming adopted. These are functional units that can reach a level of complexity sufficient to mobilize a team of programmers. Eventually, a team can be entrusted with the programming of several modules or objects. It is common for the development of some modules to be assigned to a subcontractor.

Let us consider the handling of an anomaly discovered at an advanced state of deployment of the software:

– the *first phase* of the process is to identify the cause. A common cause of an anomaly is what is known as a side effect, that is to say an unexpected outcome resulting from a function when an input parameter reaches or exceeds a value limit. For example, a coded value over 1 byte: it should normally only take values between 0 and 255, but because the team responsible for developing the module ignored the hypothesis that the value generated may exceed 255, they forgot to include an output test. Consequently, an input sequence appears leading to the module passing on other values, i.e. "…, 255, 0, …"; instead of "…, 255, 256, …," in other words a discontinuity. The value 256 was capped by the physical limit of the machine when asked to store a value within a byte. Note that we have here a seemingly chaotic phenomenon – a sharp divergence between the expected and the actual in a machine that is not usually chaotic. The modules using the outputs from the first module will be more or less accommodating. For example, a module that is only interested in the parity of the result is not affected by this abnormal value. In contrast, a module that will integrate the result in another calculation or test is likely to produce an absurd result, or enter an infinite loop;

– the *second phase* of the anomaly process is to find a solution. The difficulty is greater than it appears. Not because of the technical choices to be performed – change the type of the variable, add an output test, add input tests, what to do with the test result – but because of the work it represents. At what level should the anomaly be corrected?

- should the user module systematically test the variables passed on to it?

- should the producer module test them before passing them on to others?

- which must be regarded as the true original, the first anomaly?

- who should do this work?

– nonetheless, the rationality that governs the choice must take into account an element that is outside of computer science: what resources are available to solve the problem at the time of presentation? If the origin of the "internal" software anomaly is a module developed by a team that no longer exists, or by a subcontractor who is no longer available or requesting an excessive price to make the change, the most rational choice may be to apply a corrective patch in another place, or even within the organization.

This method of correcting computer anomalies, which has been deliberately simplified, can be found in more complex forms in the design of safety installations. In such a way that even if the technique is not always computer-based, the same questions apply. Generally, it is important not to *jump* immediately to solutions that appear obvious. On identification of a weak link or error, the solution should be carefully examined to ensure that the solution fits the entire system. How many defensive levels are needed to achieve a reasonably safe system? How can they be tested?

A safe system is essentially a simple system, well designed and exhaustively validated. It also seems necessary to create the conditions for a formal validation of the features of the functional software.

4.2.4.2. *Testing before commissioning*

Testing of critical computer systems is not exhaustive, whatever the time allotted to them. Even if a majority of tests can be realized on platform (off-site), the combination is such that only a tiny part can actually be tested. These include negative tests[6], unpredicted commands or those initiated in specific time windows that cannot be tested as well as concomitants of external events, etc., but in practice, it is in these scenarios in which systems present the greatest weaknesses.

The increased capability of industrial computing produces a complicated validation process, requiring a comprehensive and automatic verification of the safety conditions necessary for the environment and operational conditions. The teams in charge of testing before commissioning are challenged when running the tests due to:

– the increasing difficulty of meeting customer requirements in terms of costs and delays;

– the high turnover of staff;

– the increasing difficulty in maintaining the skills required;

– the increasing complexity of the studies of new systems;

– the use of many tools and methods, unwarranted consistency, etc.;

– the misperception that computer systems are easily modifiable;

– the potential omission by developers that the computer system fits into an overall system with men, with procedures for managing degraded modes.

---

6. Tests aiming to verify functional independence and/or implicitly accepted techniques.

A safe system is a system with trade tools for setting functional parameters and exhaustive validation of the system in a given industrial context. Also, it appears necessary to create the conditions for a formal validation of the features of the functional software.

4.2.4.3. *Modifiability of computer systems*

Programmable systems are not as adaptable as we think. Dematerialization does not mean simplification (on the contrary), nor the disappearance of the design work; quite the contrary (centralization makes it even more complex). The adaptation of a poorly designed system is expensive when software must be corrected or hardware modified. The reason is simple: it represents just as much work. Programmable software systems are as rigid as their mechanical ancestors, without the life span.

A poorly designed system, programmable or not, is a permanent poorly designed system. It will require remedial operations.

Similarly, the use of new technologies will not miraculously resolve the functional problems of a system. The risk of overriding safety principles that have proven themselves over many years is high.

The maintenance of safety installations is not only primarily preventive, but is also based on a correct representation of *system philosophy*. Some preventive maintenance interventions are actions normally considered remedial because they are undertaken on latent defects, not on failures. These actions are preventive in the sense that they must be done even if the defects have no effect. As well as reducing the likelihood of a second defect, this prevention has an unnamed function, which is to avoid the establishment of a "habitual offence". Indeed, there is risk in allowing smooth functioning with persistent, "non-serious" defects. Nevertheless, the development of automation (substitution of humans by technical objects) tends to temporarily erase those risks and make them forgotten.

4.2.5. *Specific problems of critical systems*

Technology systems, presenting important stakes in dependability, are now designed, manufactured and operated in varying ways by different sectors (nuclear, aviation, rail, automotive industry), but still fundamentally represent a combination of certain principles such as:

– redundancy: the critical elements are multiplied, so that no random failure of a single element can cause system failure;

– in depth defense: a critical accidental path should be covered by several successive and independent barriers;

– diversification: two redundant channels must employ different technologies;

– segregation: anomalies should be detected and contained, to avoid an error being spread to the whole system and causing it to fail;

– predictability: the same causes must produce the same effects, so that the functioning is deterministic;

– robustness: the system must withstand exceptional environmental pressures.

Applying these principles, adapted to computer technology, to the challenges of dependability, to economic constraints and regulations, to history and to the experience of each professional sector, forms a "state of the art" enabling the design, build, and operation of a safe systems, i.e. with a level of risk tolerated by society.

Given this *state of the art*, much of the risk of a safe system does not come from random failures, but from "systemic failures", affecting an entire system, such as common cause failures simultaneously impacting all the hardware of a redundant system, systematic software failures due to design errors, failures associated with a domino effect, failures due to bad supervision or natural disasters, simultaneously affecting initiating events and barriers, etc.

Systemic risk can thus be defined as the potential for systemic failure. Systemic approaches have been, or are being, implemented to control complexity, particularly through the creation of global installation models designed to study important properties such as safety or availability. These quantitative RAMS (Reliabilty, Availability, Maintainability and Safety) models, based on probabilistic approaches, are fairly well accepted for their representation of pure hardware elements (random failures) and human factors. They are much less so for their representation of deterministic aspects of computer systems (systemic or systematic failures).

It is increasingly difficult to find unprogrammed technical equipment on the market. This is a general trend in almost every industry and consumer market. This omnipresence is justified by the benefits brought by programmed techniques. In particular, they can perform advanced functions that are not possible with more conventional techniques. Features like self-monitoring, self-calibration, online monitoring, the fine control of electromechanical equipment, the installation of sensors without additional wiring, can significantly improve reliability, availability, and safety. Moreover, the increasing integration of electronic components reduces very significantly the number of elementary components and mobile parts, thus reducing the risk of hardware failures.

However, programmed techniques do not only have benefits. Other than a short shelf-life and rapid aging of many programmed equipment, the main difficulties come from the introduction of new failure modes and aging and from a significant increase in complexity. Greater complexity in turn leads to a higher risk of mis-specification and design errors, and a greater difficulty in demonstrating the components of dependability [VIL 88].

In fact, in programmed equipment, it is virtually impossible to guarantee the absence of specification and design defects, namely within the software. In high-quality and high-reliability programmed equipment, these residual errors generally correspond to what was not thought of. It is therefore extremely difficult, sometimes even impossible, to determine the nature, the impact, and the number of residual errors.

In digital technology, having a strongly deterministic and repeatable character (the same behavior will be obtained each time the equipment is put under the same conditions), these residual design errors can pose a risk of common cause failure, where multiple devices share the same error and are subject to the same conditions, failing simultaneously.

Unlike failures due to hardware defects that appear randomly (excluding common mode), the misdeeds of residual design errors may not always be prevented by redundancy. In fact, an "unsafe" specification error can be "awakened" by a particular combination of inputs, which will irreversibly affect the output regardless of the number of redundant units.

4.2.6. *Towards a targeted architecture for safety automatons*

For all these reasons, the work presented will be based on hardware and software architecture as shown in Figure 4.3.

This centers on designing a safety automaton that can easily separate the hardware aspects and the basic software (λ_{PD}, λ_{PNS} for hardware) from those of the application software (λ_{PD} and λ_{PNS} for functional software based on an exhaustive list of accessible states).

In fact, it means returning to a *fail safe*[7] approach, existing in France since the days of mechanical signal boxes and electro-mechanical switches, extending the functionalities that have proven themselves through past experience, as well as the associated regulations, to obtain adaptive, maintainable, safe and economically sensible systems.

---

7. Safety logic where any failure, external perturbation, or incorrect pressures leads to a safe positioning (safe degraded mode) usually by way of a physical law (gravity, Lenz law, etc.).

We will consider all these teachings and findings throughout the definition of our high-level safety generic automaton.

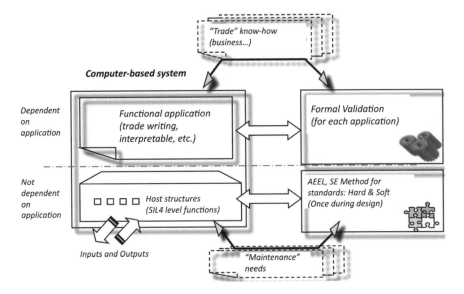

Figure 4.3. *Theoretical vision of the system's targeted architecture*

4.3. Railway safety: fundamental notions

Demonstrating the safety of a technical system, in this case computer-based, can take place without taking into account integration in its environment, within the participating system.

4.3.1. *Safety and availability*

The concept of safety has different practical implications depending on the nature of the activity. The safety of railway traffic is particularly – and even primarily – about the capability of stopping it. When there are no trains running, the danger associated with circulation is in itself removed.

Hence the basic equation system:

– stopped train = safety (non-availability);

– moving train = danger (availability).

There is also an emergency procedure, the warning radio signal, which orders all trains in the area to stop where the signal is emitted.

The literature rarely distinguishes between safety and reliability. This close relationship, not to say causal, between the two is almost never questioned. *Reliability ensures safety; the danger comes from failures.*

What is quietly put aside with the concept of reliability, is that all events that we call failures are not equally undesirable. However, are some failures more desirable than others? The problem is immediately transferred to safety as absolute reliability cannot be achieved.

Engineers are always faced with unreliable machines. Whatever the reasons, it is a fact. In 1949, the famous Murphy's Law was laid down: "*anything that can go wrong will go wrong*". This law turns probability into certainty. It poses the equation: the probability of an adverse event is equal to 1. The time of occurrence is irrelevant: the number of events is sufficiently large that the probability of adverse events happening within a limited time is actually very high.

Safety must be ensured, but what do we do when machines suffer from a lack of reliability? In France, some well-established principles, physical laws (gravity, Lenz, etc.) that are considered reliable, were employed, and thus it is tempting to depend on a certain local reliability of components. For example, a body, which is subjected to no mechanical action other than its weight, falls. The important point is that the designed safety is not based on the reliability of the device, but on the reliability of some physical laws and on an "oriented" conception of machines. Oriented in the sense that all possible evolutions of the mechanism are not equivalent.

They are organized and operated according to the following principles:

– some are more stable than others;

– "spontaneous" evolution of the sub-system is always done in the direction of the most stable state;

– it is possible to make the most stable state correspond to the safest situation.

The "system" combining technical systems was designed so that none of the operational test results ends in an event "contrary to safety".

However, this concept of safety, which is distinct from reliability, has a counterpart that is not free: a rigorous preventive maintenance. Because it is not sufficient to have an installation put itself in a "safe" state when it fails for safety to be ensured. It is also necessary that the operators, under the constraint of production, not be pushed to use an installation that is defective! This safety model does not only rely on technique, despite appearances[8]. *Thus, man, in the context of procedures, plays the lead role in the railway system!*

Safety in the French railway sector is historically based on determinism. Every effect has a cause and if an effect is undesirable, removing the causes should help to avoid it! Deterministic reasoning requires finding an explanation for everything and, in particular, to what seems initially inexplicable. Above all, it must be ensured that the event does not happen again.

This goal can be very close to "zero risk", even if everyone agrees that it does not exist. After all, the perfect circle does not exist either. It does, however, remain a very fruitful idea...

The system is designed respecting the following practical design rules:

– a single cause cannot lead to an accident;

– any failures of the components (whatever happens) will lead to a safe state of the system (directed failures);

– limiting actions (including resilience effects) of man, procedures, and tools;

– a precise definition of the role each safety participant and adapted training;

– recovery loops as independent as possible between the different participants, procedures, and tools;

– control, permanent if possible, of men, procedures and tools;

– a permanent improvement based on past feedback.

The overall reliability of operation has a direct impact on system safety. The signaling installations must be safe and quickly repaired in order to ensure the safety level required: the two critical paths must have an equivalent rate of occurrence (see Figure 4.4). *Operational reliability affects system safety.* If delays and incidents are limited, fewer operators and procedures will be required and the risks will similarly decrease.

---

8. Past experience and feedback on electro-mechanical safety relays confirm this reasoning: a relay that remains in a raised position, despite an interruption of power, occurring, on average, several billion times more often than not. And it is man, in this case a maintenance agent, who preventively or remedially forces the automation, constituted by a signaling installation, to stay within its area of operation.

Note (*) that the error rate in the application of an "unpredicted" procedure in the context of a degraded mode is significantly higher than the same rate in the application of a procedure in a normal operating environment.

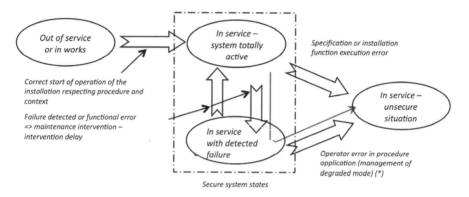

Figure 4.4. *The impact of unavailability on the global safety level of the computer-based signal box*

The history of human factors in the French railway sector is long, even if it clearly remains within the deterministic paradigm. The addition of a safety installation increases the level of system safety only if the "safe" and "unsafe" failure rates are sufficiently low to compensate for the reduced reliability of the human operator in the application of procedures. This finding is particularly important in that such an addition is considered useful only when the increase in traffic overloads the operator whose error rate in *applying the procedures is then judged unacceptable.*

4.3.2. *Intrinsic safety and closed railway world*

This deterministic reasoning is only possible in a *closed world*. The closure principle permeates every thought concerning industrial safety. *The safety of an automated system is possible only in the case of a closed system; whenever there is interaction, there are unpredictable risks.*

It is not so much that interaction with the outside world brings chaos, but that the form of the system (technical installations, etc.), and, subsequently, what this interaction may have on it. Thus, the principle of an organization isolated from its environment is the basis for safety design. A law passed in 1846 imposed the same principle of closing the railway domain, including crossings. This quickly posed organizational and financial problems.

Therefore, for the development of a railway system, the boundaries must be clearly functional, regulatory and physical.

Three types of properties must be imperatively and formally defined:

– those directly guaranteeing the "safety" of the system, with regards to interactions with the environment;

– those guaranteeing the operational availability of the system, with regards to and through its interactions;

– those defining the rules of interaction with its environment.

Moreover, such a system should, in our context, have at least one safe state. It is a state in which the risk has no effect, we talk about a safe fallback position. It is agreed that the system is in a safe state when operated within the operating rules. The safe state is generally a state of lowest energy, consistent with the operating rules. The safe fallback position should be accessible in a short time and while disabling system functions.

4.3.3. *Processing safety*

The technical characteristics of the railway allow identification and anticipation of potential conflicts and impose safety at the center of all actions and of all participants. Overall, the synthesis of all these elements has helped to build a very safe system.

Given their technical characteristics and the actionable levers available, we can traditionally distinguish:

– traffic safety concerning the interaction of traffic between them or the processing of unexpected changes in the environment interfering with traffic. It depends on the operators (the managers) who act on their respective instruments by applying procedures;

– technical safety designed to allow the conservation of dimensional and functional characteristics enabling a train to travel on an infrastructure. It relies on the maintenance operators of fixed installations and maintenance operators of running equipment, whose interventions concerning traffic officers and drivers are undertaken within the procedural context.

Any modification of a system component is likely to affect another component, and thus jeopardizing the balance of the safety of the system itself. It is therefore necessary to supervise all phases of the system's lifespan.

French railways have from the outset pursued a deterministic approach, known as intrinsic safety, which requires comprehensive knowledge of failure modes of the components, this being possible as long as:

– failure modes are determined by physical characteristics (universal gravitation, failure mode of the component, etc.);

– the combination of failures remains accessible to human analysis;

– the (first) failure is detected by setting the system to default.

With the development of computer systems, systems subject to multiple failures do not systematically lead to the default setting of the system, the probabilistic approaches and quality assurance were preferred. It is impossible to identify and address all possible causes of unsafe failure.

The probabilistic approach consists of quantifying the probability of occurrence and assessing the potential impact of an undesirable event.

This approach needs to be handled with care because:

– the calculation includes, generally, important simplifications – rates of forecasted failure of components are not well known and the number of events resulting from past experience is very low;

– the independence of events, often admitted to facilitate the calculation, is in reality rarely checked, as shown by numerous disasters.

It is noteworthy that a probabilistic approach can be applied to software errors, including errors resulting from formalization errors of the functional application and its translations. Thus, for critical computer systems, neither a probabilistic approach nor a quality assurance approach is acceptable. Therefore, it is necessary for infrastructure managers to find a methodological approach to comprehensively ensure the correction of functional applications brought about by computer systems and thus to return to the case of deterministic failures.

4.3.4. *Provability of the safety of computerized equipment*

Thus, the following lessons for developing such a system appear to include:

– the behavior of the automation must be deterministic, in both normal and degraded operating modes;

– three kinds of properties should be formalized without ambiguity:

- safety predicates,

- functional predicates (on abundant),

- interaction with environment postulates;

– the behavior of automation in these conditions is exhaustively verified.

This can be summarized in a diagram as shown in Figure 4.5.

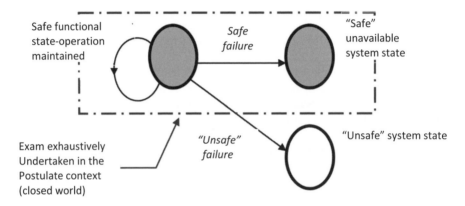

Figure 4.5. *Model of available system states: system safety*

4.3.5. *The signal box*

A signal box is an infrastructure allowing control of the various railway switches and protection signals with the purpose of management of railway traffic within a geographically delimited rail track.

The management of traffic consists of:

– preparing the routes that trains must travel on;

– giving each train present in a station instructions on movement, taking into account the state of planned routes and the positions of other trains.

These actions are broken down into elementary operations that must be undertaken "safely", to avoid collisions and derailments. The signal box allows an operator to perform all these operations.

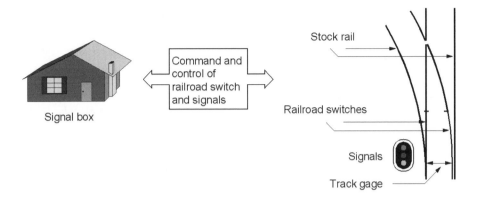

Figure 4.6. *Signal box*

Since the advent of relay and flexible transit signal boxes (PRS: *postes d'aiguillage à relais et à transit souple*), the operating phases of the posts are such that:

– there is one command (button or computerized messages) per route and an independent display unit for optical control;

– it is possible to record a route before the formation requirements are met and to have permanent plotted routes (some preferred routes remain plotted for the passage of several trains, following the block system conditions), in addition its operation is easy to "read" and fully deterministic;

– the regulations specify the methods for processing failures involving, where appropriate, each stage of a route's management.

The operation is done in successive stages, reflecting the successive positions of switches and zones (track circuit); see Table 4.1.

The control phase can be centralized and carried out by an unsafe sub-system. Other stages depend on the highest level of safety and require controlled and monitored execution of the installations. It is the role of the computerized interlocking module that we will now describe further.

Phase	Action	PRS translation	Result
Command	Pushing the command button	Raises the route control relay (CIt). Flashes the command button	Closes relay control pointer circuits (CAg)
Preparation	Positioning of the route pointers and protection pointers provided they are not triggered by another route (transit not taken) or occupied by traffic	The relay control pointers (CAg) switch provided that the transit relays of the route are raised and the relay track circuit is free	The positioning of all relay control pointers (CAg) of the route switches to an open position of the interlocking route relay of the concerned input signal (EIt)
Formation and interlocking	Ensures the immobilization of the route Denies the formation of incompatible routes	Cuts off power of the transit relays, which ensure transit interlocking Raises the route repeater relay (Rit), which ensures permanent control of he position of the CAg and the EIt	Turns on the control button permanently, closes route control circuits
Control (organization)	Ensures the effective execution of the route and opens the protection signal	Imperative control of the pointers is ensured after being put into place by the KAg relays Raises the route control relay of the protection signal (Kit)	Opening of the input signal Extinction of input signal closure light control

Table 4.1. *Functional states for route execution*

4.4. Development of the computerized interlocking module (MEI: *module d'enclenchement informatique)*

The SYMEL or PIPC computerized interlocking module has been developed to control the level of safety and reduce the costs of maintenance in operational condition. To do this, we defined a specification interpretation language, the deterministic finite state automaton (AEFD: *Automate à Etats Finis Déterministe*) language.

We will present:

– the development methodology of safety systems using the writing workshop of the functional application (ASIFER) associated with the safety automaton developed by the interlocking module (MEI);

– the characteristics of the safety automaton recalling the approach that we used in the development of the MEI.

We will present the development methodology of the computerized interlocking module (MEI) and its characteristics adapted for the railway environment. We will try to advance some implemented principles, innovative in their implementation but conventional in their problems. In response to the expectations set forth in the preceding sections, the main idea was to develop an industrial safety automaton having a low-cost, reusable development chain, which behaves like an abstract machine (a factual automaton with zero transition time) in order to allow for subsequent formal validation.

4.4.1. *Development methodology of safety systems*

The development of conventional software performing safety functions for real-time systems in the railway sector includes:

– developing unique software specific to an application and to a hardware structure;

– undergoing a complete safety study as soon as a system is modified (new feature, component obsolescence, new application, etc.);

Faced with the development of a computerized safety system with a strong cost constraint, the approach taken by Alten Industries takes into account the desire:

– for cost reduction of studies, development, installation, operation, maintenance;

– to ensure real sustainability;

– to build a product meeting the industrial needs of customers and thereby to integrate their constraints;

– to propose an industrial development approach directly usable by customers;

– to ensure and demonstrate the level of safety required by the system.

Taking into account the upstream system design phase of these constraints has led to the development of the MEI and of its writing workshop for the AEFD functional language.

The main characteristics of the MEI are:

– SIL level 4 of the standard EN 50129 [CEN 03]: $\lambda_{PND} < 10^{-9}$/hour;

– level of reliability (automaton, inputs, outputs, etc.): $\lambda_{PD} < 10^{-4}$/hour;

– level of protection against electromagnetic interference, according to class 4 of the international standard IEC 1004.4;

– principles of safe transmissions in accordance with the European standard EN 50159-1 [CEN 01] applicable to closed networks.

The writing workshop of the functional graphs is aimed at people with professional competence but without any specific knowledge of computers. The workshop allows customers to specify, at all levels, their needs in unambiguous language.

4.4.1.1. *Choice of MEI techniques*

The hardware and software architecture of the MEIs addresses the following concerns:

– the desire to reduce development costs. This is achieved by defining, on one hand, a specific application software for a given application, which is reusable on multiple hardware platforms (safety is independent of hardware); and, on the other hand, a host structure, approved once, which is reusable on several hardware platforms and for several applications. No new safety study of the host structure for the various applications is necessary;

– the desire to reduce the costs of safety studies. This is achieved by uncomplicating the demonstration of the level of safety by clearly separating, and separately studying, the risks of a deterministic nature and those of a probabilistic nature;

– the desire to reduce maintenance and operational costs in order to ensure the continuity of the safety software when faced with functional and hardware changes.

These are the terms of the scalability of the product, of the durability of the product as well as of the cost control of study and development.

4.4.1.2. *Description of the safety study of an application developed with the workshop*

The study of the safety of the system starts off with a preliminary risk analysis of the system, allowing identification of the system's functional risks. To safeguard and ensure the safety of the functionality of the system carried out in a software manner, the potential risks studied include:

– *risks of a deterministic nature.* This is the behavior of the system when it is subjected to any adverse operating conditions (internal or external). The origin of such risks can be found within the specifications of the system: do the specifications contain all three phases of the system (initial, nominal, degraded)? Do the specifications lead, in a given configuration, to an adverse event in the absence of failures? Are the specifications complete, sufficient, and consistent with each other? In this case, we are interested in the existence of critical paths leading to the realization of these risks;

– *risks of a probabilistic nature.* This is the behavior of the system when it is subjected to external disturbances (electromagnetic interference, weather conditions etc.), or to internal failures (component failure, software anomaly, etc.): are any hardware or software failures detected, leading the system to a restrictive, fallback position, and not to an adverse event? In this case, we are interested in the probability of occurrence of these risks. To protect against such risks, a number of precautions are defined upstream of the design phase in order to improve robustness and to define the system's behavior in such situations.

In any event, the standards primarily address the probabilistic aspects related to basic hardware and software, and not really the deterministic aspects related to non-adjustment and/or incompleteness of the encoded functional in the target machine.

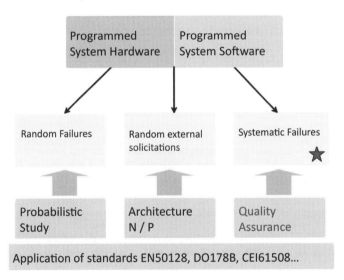

Figure 4.7. *Relation to standards*

To this end, mention is made only of recommendations for the organization and quality-assurance procedures of the software charged with covering any gaps in high-level formalization, specification, and computerized translation.

Thus, developing an application using the workshop associated with the MEI can provide:

– formal validation of interpretable specifications (functional graphs) to cover deterministic risks;

– evidence of transformation to cover risks related to the development chain;

– evidence of covering risks of a probabilistic nature (approved safety automaton – SIL 4).

4.4.1.3. *Writing workshop for functional graphs*

This section will present how the development methodology of safety systems based on MEI and its programming workshop can significantly reduce the costs of study and system development. Reducing the cost of application development is undertaken as follows:

– use of the host structure. It has been approved once. No additional safety study is required;

– seizure of functional generic executable graphs in the form of finite state automata defined or established for each signaling function based on current principles (relay schemes, GRAFCET, etc.). Generic graphs written in AEFD language are chronological, not timed, communicating, etc. Their writing is based on a thorough knowledge of the signaling functions, operating rules, management rules of degraded modes, operation postulates of the railway environment of the signal box;

– seizure of configuration parameters specific to a site that allows instantiation of generic functional graphs in order to obtain the file that will actually be interpreted by the host structure of the target machine.

The generation of an interpretable functional is given by (Figure 4.8):

– association of instantiated generic graphs based on the topology of a track plan, on information arising naturally from it and on those additional ones acquired manually;

– translation of these graphs into a text file that is interpreted by the host structure of the targeted interlocking module;

– reverse translation of this interpretable file and comparison of all of the data extracted with those considered at input (information generated automatically and manually).

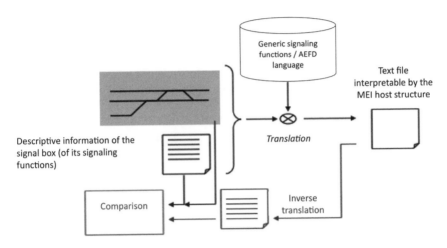

Figure 4.8. *Development process of the interpretable functional file*

The translator ensures processing of the seized networks from the publisher in a data structure interpretable by the host structure of the basic software of the targeted MEI.

The inverse translator can generate, from the previous file:

– the source code of the data structure (graphs);

– the functional information extracted for comparison with the published functional.

This process can cover the risks of translation errors of the information issued by the study agent from the signal post program, from the technical plan and finally the file interpreted by the MEI target.

4.4.1.4. *Formal validation of functional graphs workshop*

An additional validation is necessary to ensure that the functional thus obtained covers the inherent risks in terms of track plan and signaling functions previously described. It is the role of formal validation that then develops:

– an analysis of the existence of certain automata properties (vivacity of the network, etc.);

– a demonstration of the conservation of the safety properties of a system (safety invariants) in a framework defined by lemmas and operating and environmental postulates;

– a demonstration of the absence of any overabundant condition that would erroneously result in a too restrictive behavior (safe degraded mode) and hence the frequent use by the switch operator of risky regulatory procedures.

The SNCF has developed and introduced the tools and methods to achieve these processes industrially during the tests before putting it into operation.

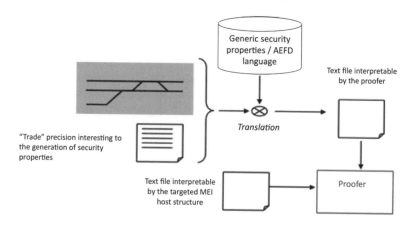

Figure 4.9. *Formal validation process*

4.4.2. *Technical architecture of the system*

4.4.2.1. *General architecture*

The computerized interlocking module (MEI) is a safety automaton behaving like a competing automaton with constraints. It can constitute the basic element of a centralized command and control system ensuring local safety and availability (centralized management of multiple signal boxes providing, for example, the management of the stations on a line).

It should be noted that the MEI modules are duplicated through "hot redundancy". This provision was adopted to simplify to a minimum (therefore to render more reliable) the management structure of the commutation. Also for this reason:

– the deported "input/output" option was rejected;

– the digital connections with the framing modules are managed with a specific SNCF protocol including two CRC16, dating, etc. The transmission functions of the variables are SIL 4 and much less complex than many common protocols, including the Protocol UNISIG;

– the digital connections are managed in a ring in order to manage redundancy, and the sharing of the load (to reduce the repatriation time of the PCD optical controls).

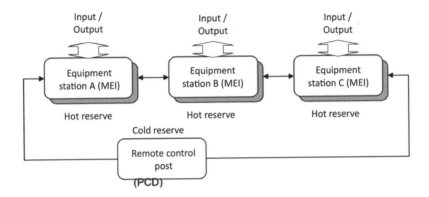

Figure 4.10. *General architecture: PCD and MEI*

4.4.2.2. *Remote control post*

The PCD is a remote command and control system, the availability of communications is guaranteed by the existence of a communication ring (direct link and link loopback).

All safety equipment (MEI) located on different command and control sites are supervised from a remote command and control center. This requires the presence of a single operating agent.

The flow of information between the remote command and control station and the equipment on site is, on one hand, a return flow of the overall condition of the field equipment (field control). This information constitutes the field vision of the operator and, on the other hand, a command flow (operator dialogs) in order to call upon the functionalities of the system. The display function is performed with a SIL 3 (alternating graphics plan, refresh time of less than 6 seconds, etc.).

It consists of standard equipment (IBM/PC). It is a system doubled up with a cold reserve for availability reasons.

4.4.2.3. *Means of communication*

The communication means are modular. This module is interchangeable. The MEI safety automaton does not require specialized communication means. It uses indifferently all types of physical media existing (cable, overhead line, fiber optics, telephone line, etc.). To improve system availability, a connection ring exists between the different equipment.

The communication functions between MEI modules are SIL 4, those between MEI and PCD modules are SIL 4. The ring provides redundancy in case of disruption of communications, thus ensuring transmission delays and facilitating switching and/or maintenance operations.

4.4.2.4. *Site, post, or station equipment*

The equipment of a site consists of an MEI. It manages all site functionalities and the safety system at the site level. Each function is safely managed locally by each site's MEI.

4.4.2.4.1. MEIS hardware architecture

Given the level of safety required for the system and technical choices, a redundant structure of second order was chosen. The MEIS is formed from dual processor architecture. From the acquisition of field entries to the generation of outputs, all the elements involved in the processing chain performed by the safety automaton are redundant. The minimal cuts associated with this architecture are the common modes and the voter.

We will try to show how the construction of the MEIS safety automaton meets the safety requirements of the system.

Reduction of common mode against disturbances external to the system

Efforts to achieve this objective include:

– research of equipment supporting EMC constraints for protection against electromagnetic interference. Moreover, the choice of the industrial "PC" material has been guided by the following general considerations:

- ensure hardware durability. Indeed, the PCI is a "set standard" with regards to the global PC market; the provision of PCI is multisource,

- using the power gains ensures the safety of information handled by a suitable encoding without penalizing the real-time performance of the systems. In this way, the type of microprocessor equipping the units has no influence on safety self-testing. For the record, the MEI spends 80% of its time performing self-tests while ensuring an execution cycle of 100 milliseconds,

- avoid reworking critical software due to a change of microprocessor type. It enables the advantage of backward compatibility between INTEL processors to be employed, without having to rework the basic software of the system and revalidate it. For the memory, the MEIS works interchangeably on processors 286, 386, or 486, with different clock frequencies,

- reduce the overall costs of a computer system with a high-safety level without restriction on this level. The demonstration of the level of safety, taking into account the worst-case reliability theory, shows that the required level is reached,

- takes advantage of the series effect and of its drive to improve performance of the quality of the PC. The current level of hardware reliability is the same as that of the best "professional" UC cards while providing a multisource supply. The average monthly failure in the early days of PCs has gone down to a failure average calculable over 10 years. The PCI option seems to offer the best compromise in terms of performance, cost, EMC, durability of hardware and software;

– the implementation of massive heterogeneity (hardware, software and time): different processor, different clock, different compiler, different manufacturer, partially different software. It is noteworthy that the temporal heterogeneity is complete between the "master" and "slave" processing units. This guarantees processing independently of external disturbances;

– the MEI is a computerized module with the highest level of safety required in the railway environment, respecting the international standard IEC 1004.4 (class 4). This makes it immune to electromagnetic interference and significantly improves availability.

Reduction of common modes associated to the voter

Given cost constraints, an intrinsic safety voter was not retained. The MEIS voter consists of:

– a static voter: the electronic trail between the two elementary outputs is developed and independently controlled on each processing channel;

– a dynamic voter: active crossover control between the two processing channels.

Sanction and automatic reset device

Any failure (master/slave synchrony not respected, or the erroneous signature of a self-test or erroneous control of a gate), even fleeting, results in: stopping the activation of the watchdog (safety relay), an irreversible fallback of the sub-systems (power of safety relay output is cut off after a fixed time), then a reset of the MEI by restoring its power after 5 seconds (lost control).

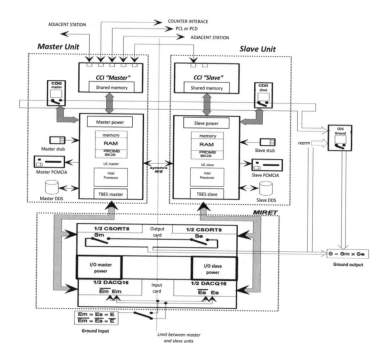

Figure 4.11. *Architecture of half a MEI in 2/2 assembly*

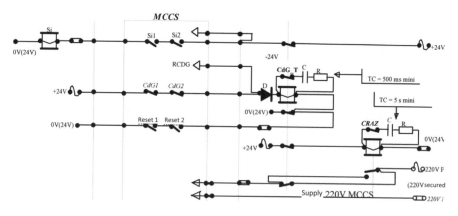

Figure 4.12. *Automatic reset by lost control*

4.4.2.4.2. MEIS software architecture

The MEIS software architecture is characterized by:

– the existence of a software application modeling, as finite state automata, the functional specifications for the three modes of operation (initial, nominal, degraded). The execution of these functionalities is ensured by the host structure (single algorithm with deterministic resolution for the AEFD graphs). A formal proof is directly provided for the specifications in order to highlight any shortcomings, ambiguities, and inconsistencies as well as the retention of certain critical properties;

– the existence of a structure for ensuring the safe management of resources (input, output, communication, processing, etc.), offering the application safe services (timing, etc.). The host structure is independent of the application and of the hardware (in a variety of products). It supports indiscriminately various applications and hardware. The level of safety is ensured by safety control functions. The host structure is studied, developed, validated, and approved once. It is reusable for multiple applications without modification and for different hardware supports;

– the existence of a configuration parameter file for input and output of the site. It is composed of binary information reflecting the presence or absence of field equipment. The configuration parameter file instantiates the application software. The latter describes the maximum capabilities of the system for all possible site configurations.

Therefore the host structure is generic. Only the configuration parameters and the software applications are specific. The software is developed in standard language (C) based on standard hardware (PCI).

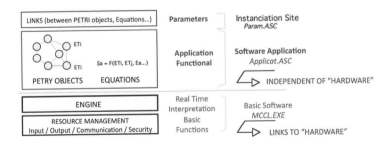

Figure 4.13. *Software architecture*

As part of a development based on MEI, developing a new system comes down to a detailed description of the specifications of the system and defining the configuration of each site. There exists today a library of elementary actions for automata. This library can be completed on a case-by-case basis in order to take into account specific situations.

4.4.3. *MEI safety*

We will now present how MEI safety is constructed.

4.4.3.1. *The host structure*

The primary mission of the host structure is to manage the hardware interface and machine resources, at the level of safety required by the system. This consists of:

– a management module for inter-unit synchrony. It is a mechanism of active consistency cross-checking between the two processing units. It enables the exchange of information flows between the two processing chains. Thus the coherence between the states of the two processing units is controlled during each execution cycle. The two processing units are jointly controlled (cross-checking of execution context);

– a management module for field input. Each acquisition is preceded by a test of the input cards. Each processing chain performs an acquisition of field entries (direct state, complemented state) independently for each execution cycle of the system. It allows the distribution of the field equipment's status to the application software after a formal agreement between the two processing units;

– a management module for field output. Each processing unit independently performs the control of outputs. Each output development-processing step is cross-checked between the two processing units (consistency of the logic control, positioning control by crossed proofreading). The elementary outputs of each processing unit are put in series. This ensures the absence of a control or the maintenance of an untimely output in a raised state;

– a management module for communication means. The messages sent and received by the two processing units are checked for consistency between the two units through the synchronization mechanism. Moreover, a control of the interchanged transmission by the master unit and by the slave unit is performed within the recipient of the message;

– a module for application resolution (development and stabilization of finite state automata (PETRI model) on one hand; of binary equations on the other). This allows execution of the detailed specifications of the system. It ensures a deterministic behavior of the system by guaranteeing that during each execution cycle there is distribution of inputs to all modules of the system;

– a module for resource management. It allows management of the processor, of time, dynamic management of memory, memorization of safety information (cyclic protection code 16, address code, identification code), management of self-tests, management of process sequencing;

– a module for archive management. The system has an integrated storage module. It can monitor the real-time evolution of the system. A selection filter is used to define the storage elements (all events taking place in the system, events concerning the operation of the system, events concerning maintenance, various information for statistical analysis). It is possible to have an execution trace and a trace of defects occurring in the system: feedback and analysis of the causes of defects, etc.

A remote maintenance system allows it to download (periodically or on demand) all information necessary for maintenance interventions.

Therefore, the host structure offers safe services for the application software.

4.4.3.2. *The functional software*

Based on the principles defined indifferently in the form of diode diagrams, relay diagrams, or equations, GRAFCET, Block Diagram, a transcript as finite state automata (AEFD model) is performed. The initialization phase and degraded modes are taken into account by successive refinement. We thus have an unambiguous description of processes to be done under the control of the host structure, a library of standard actions and a principle of unique resolution: the runtime of finite state automata.

The model of specifications used (finite state automaton) requires the definition of a graphical representation of automata and operation for the runtime system (algorithm for resolution and stabilization). For this, we use a drawing tool coupled with a database.

This allows:

– the dictionary definition of functional entities common to all elements of the software (application, host structure and parameter file: input, action, etc.);

– seizure of executable functional models: graphs of states (places, transitions, crossover conditions, marking, actions).

The functional software (text file) and documentation relating thereto are made directly from the database containing the description of automata (detailed executable specifications). Thus, the functional software comprises:

– functional processing modeled as PETRI networks;

– software translation of actions and controls specific to the application developed;

– the implementation of the dynamic initialization phase of the system.

4.4.3.3. *Approach for implementation and validation of the host's structural safety*

The approach taken to achieve the level of safety required for the host structure is as follows. We defined the "principles" to be met throughout the design, implementation, integration and validation phase of the safety automaton in order to reduce the risks at the level of safety required for the system.

4.4.3.3.1. The plan for risk reduction

For this, we have implemented safety control functions (FCS: *fonctions de contrôle de la sécurité*) on the hardware, software, organizational, functional, human, etc.

We have thus developed a list of recommendations, together with development teams, associated with a potential risk. These are measurable characteristics of the system. In parallel, we defined the test plan for controlling safety.

We will describe some examples of how, using a principle necessary for reducing risk or allowing to reduce risks, the necessity of this principle has been taken into account by the development team, how this principle has resulted at the software level, and how this principle has been validated.

4.4.3.3.2. The out-of-phase execution mechanism

This is to ensure temporal heterogeneity between the two processing units in order to prevent the risks associated with the common mode. It allows for a fixed structural shift, guaranteed during each execution cycle of the system. Thus, the two processing units never undergo the same process at the same time (processing of a different nature: self-tests, application processing).

4.4.3.3.3. Inter-unit synchrony

This involves a dynamic 2/2 vote between the two processing units. The inter-unit synchrony mechanism performs an active consistency cross-check. This ensures that during each execution cycle of the system, the execution context is the same for the two processing units: field state input, penetrable transitions of automata, output commands, received messages, and functional signature. The flow of information between the two processing units is structured (at least 128 control bits without application information during each execution cycle).

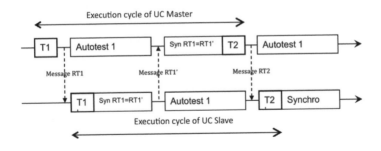

Figure 4.14. *Inter-unit synchrony and temporal heterogenity*

4.4.3.3.4. Maintainability

The principle of the automatic reset is an innovative solution in the field of railway safety automata. This is an example of the implemented principle, defined at the upstream phase of the project, which enables improvement of the overall system characteristics:

– beneficial effect on system safety by reducing the downtime of the system in degraded mode. Downtime is a source of insafety. Any improvement in the availability of the system contributes to improved system safety;

– beneficial effect on maintenance actions. The system's ability to distinguish fleeting failures from permanent failures allows us:

- to act on actionable means available to the maintenance operator. Before moving to the site, the operator is already informed of the nature of the failure by the repatriation of maintenance alarms in real time to the PCD. The modular architecture of the system allows maintenance at the first level;

- to act on the motivation of maintenance operator. Their intervention is necessary only when the system is subject to a permanent failure;

- to reduce maintenance costs. A maintenance operator going to the site is motivated by the need to replace the faulty equipment;

– through the execution trace of the system (events occurring before the onset of a defect), it is possible to reconstruct the sequence that brought on the failure.

4.4.3.3.5. The watchdog and the fallback position

Each processing unit has a watchdog that it remains active as long as no local or dual malfunction is detected (self-tests performed satisfactorily, consistent with the context of the effective dual unit, etc.). The smooth running of the program is reflected by the ability of each processing unit to create and manage a certain complexity. This complexity is controlled locally and/or dually. The watchdog is an electronic device that must be reset at each execution cycle of the system. The watchdog ensures passage of the equipment to a fallback position.

This fallback position is triggered by the unit failure (if the failure does not affect its ability to fallback) or by the dual unit. *It is fallback positioning by collective suicide.* For this, the watchdogs of each processing unit are put in series. Their activation allows the control of a field watchdog (irreversible lock in the form of NS1 relays).

The field watchdog is an irreversible device for ensuring the maintenance of the system in a fallback position in case of a permanent failure. These actions are to ensure that the system is not in a more permissive state than in the absence of failure. For this, the equipment power (all components) is cut off. This lack of power ensures the positioning of output in a restrictive state. This watchdog is periodically self-tested. This device detects, in the course of a program, a defect due to a temporary failure or random characteristic of the hardware or software equipment, and initiates the necessary actions.

4.4.3.3.6. Self-tests

This is to guard against hardware failures or perturbations external to the system while maintaining total independence *vis-à-vis* the processor to the extent that the durability of the hardware requires supporting different hardware in the same product range (Intel 286, 386, 486, etc.).

The self-tests essentially comprise:

– control of the state of input cards (dynamics and control of complementarities);

– control of the consistency between the physical position of the field outputs and the logic control of field outputs in each processing unit by crossed proofreading;

– control by stimulating the relay watchdog of each processing unit;

– control of the integrity of the memory zones, of safety information stored in each processing unit (protection against viruses, safety variables, program, configuration parameters). All these data are protected by a cyclic redundancy code CRC16.

Self-tests create, throughout their execution, an execution signature involved in resetting the watchdog. Thus, a failure to execute the self-tests does not reset the watchdog and leads to a fallback positioning of the system.

The processing units spend 80% of their time checking protection codes! The duration of self-testing is 1 second in the worst case (from 286 to 25 MHz).

4.4.3.3.7. Processing controls

The validation process of the host structure can be broken down into:

– tests for measuring the robustness of the safety control functions of the system. This is to ensure the proper software implementation of the principles defined for quantifying the safety level of system requirements. The method involves deliberately degrading the resources in a controlled and random order (random pollution: memories, inputs, outputs, data, safety variables, etc.) by injecting a controlled failure. This is to verify the effectiveness of the safety monitoring functions. These barriers are defined in terms of risk reduction so that the probability of occurrence of risks is reduced to the level of safety required for the system. Moreover, in a degraded mode, we have verified the efficacy rate of these barriers, making the fallback position of the system effective;

– static and dynamic verification of the specifications;

– platform self-tests at the SNCF laboratory;

– a traditional method of software validation (unit testing, integration testing, validation testing: it is false because it is not true, there is no code developed, the specifications are executable and the structure of the host is already approved). There eventually remains the unit testing of automata actions, which are typically functions without any algorithm. At this stage, the validation in terms of configuration files at the test site level and validation tests in terms of functionality of the system remain to be performed, but it is the simulator that undertakes this so this is different from the classical approach. It is especially important to clearly distinguish validation of the safety automaton from validation of the application developed using ASIFER. This is where the effort, and therefore the gain, in terms of cost and time, is critical;

– complementary approach at the safety level: code proofreading, AEEL.

These are methods of dynamic testing. The statistical methods were intended to ensure the integrity of the control of safety functions, especially for AEEL, the non-pollution of critical functions by non-critical software. This allowed a strengthening of defensive programming and improved functional execution signatures.

4.4.3.3.8. Availability

Any situation not corresponding to a nominal system behavior (triggering control of safety functions and implementation of defensive programming) leads the system to a restrictive fallback position. This provision or principle is not fully verified for the field input. A non-blocking fallback position for field input is defined.

The MEI safety automaton is able to manage combinatorial and sequential applications. The fallback position corresponding to a restrictive behavior of the system results in a lack of power.

For example, for the first installations:

– the acquisition period of the input field is an execution cycle of 100 milliseconds;

– an execution cycle lasts 100 milliseconds of inter-unit synchrony;

– repatriation of field inspections is carried out in a maximum of 7 seconds;

– the ability to archive locally is 2.5 to 4 MB;

– the development time of an output cycle is about three synchronization cycles;

– the maximum capacity is 256 inputs/outputs.

4.4.4. *Modeling the PETRI network type*

The modeling of system specifications of the PETRI network type enables the following to be obtained:

– a *detailed* description of three modes of operation (initialization, nominal, degraded);

– a *hierarchical* description (can specify the functional behavior of the system up to the lowest level) and unambiguous specifications of the system leading to better communication and understanding between the contractor and the owner on one hand, and between the designers on the other;

– an *interpretable* description of the system specifications: generating a database containing the model specifications as PETRI networks. This database is implemented on the host structure of the MEIS (target machine) showing point-by-point specifications. It is not necessary to program specifications;

– a *provable* description of the system specifications. The formalism used is powerful and presents the mathematical properties needed to provide proof of ownership. It is not necessary to have a Boolean abstraction of the program or a model of the automation and its environment. The method used is to demonstrate the adequacy and completeness of the specifications of a system with regards to one or more system risks, based on the description of unambiguous system specifications (for the three operating modes: initial, nominal, degraded) in the form of PETRI networks. The formalism of the model used can develop a proof of ownership.

The prerequisite is identification of system risks (APRS[9] conventional method). This evidence provides assurance that the specifications do not contribute significantly to the development of an identified risk in the system.

The interests of this approach are:

– a *simulative* description of the system specifications: there is a simulator with the same runtime as the host structure (the target machine). This validates the system without needing a validation test on the target machine;

– a design phase limited to the development of an actions library;

– no need to possess skills in computer science: the effort of the user (client) is limited to the functionality of the system rather than to the mechanisms for implementation (detailed specifications are executable).

This modeling relies on the existence of a runtime system whose behavior is known. The response time of the system is guaranteed by the functioning of the host structure. At the onset of an external event, the reaction time of the system (execution cycle of the runtime) and the spread to all modules in all levels of the system are determined. The introduction of an additional synchronization constraint between processes or the taking into account of the process execution time or communication time between modules is unnecessary. The operation of the runtime ensures that the output calculations are carried out before the arrival of new input. *The operation is cyclic and deterministic.*

The host structure is not multitasking. We used PETRI networks (AEFD) as a complete formal model. They effectively allow us:

– to specify and analyze (through simulation of the functioning of the functions and analysis of the completed functions present in the module) the dynamic behavior and to achieve simulation of parallel systems with discrete time;

– to provide a structuring and breakdown role (to the lowest level) for the specification and description of parallel systems;

– to monitor the liveliness of the software (control of the absence of "dead specification": blocking the activity of all or part of the transitions of a network);

– to guarantee a deterministic behavior: the definition of the execution cycle of the runtime system defines the operating rule of PETRI networks. The duration of the examination of transitions is short compared to the changing environment. That is to say that the duration of a cycle is negligible *vis-à-vis* the time constants of the controllable system. No unresolved conflicts remain;

---

9. Preliminary system risk analysis.

– to provide proof of completeness and adequacy of the specifications with regards to one (or more) functional risk(s) (preservation of property).

The various functions of the basic software and of the functional software are illustrated in Figure 4.15.

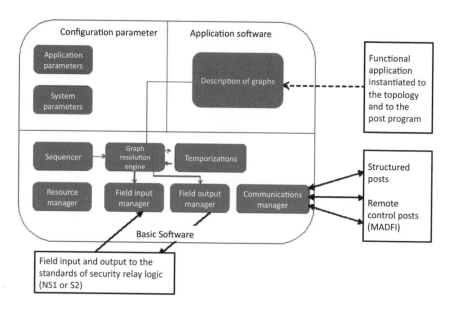

Figure 4.15. *Software architecture of the MEI*

Railway applications are characterized by a set of asynchronous sequential processes and communicate through variables specialized to achieve a common goal. A state machine models each sequential process. Applications (256 inputs/outputs maximum) create networks containing in the order of several hundred states and transitions. The places correspond to the variables of system states. The occurrence of an event reflects a change of system state and a transition. The variables are Boolean (with some exceptions). They are updated during every elementary system cycle (execution cycle 100 milliseconds).

The order in which actions are performed depends on the order in which the automata transitions are crossed. However, this order is important as the automata network may behave differently depending on that order. In fact, in a machine, the interpreter treats automata in a well-defined order, set out at the time of implementation of the automata network. In our case, it is to be noted that this crossing order (writing and evaluation of conditions) has no effect on the operation of the automaton. *Indeed, the order in which the automata are processed is defined during the implementation of the parametered automata network for a given site.*

Also, one of the design constraints of these graphs is that the evaluation order of the automata, in order to find the transitions to the potential occurrence of an event, is not known[10] *a priori* when writing the generic graphs!

The current characteristics of the basic software are the following:

– refresh period of TOR outputs: $\tau_{SORT} \leq 100\,\text{ms}$;

– master-slave synchrony period: $\tau_{SYNC} \leq 100\,\text{ms}$;

– maximum period for self-test crossing: $\tau_{AT} \leq 1\text{s}$;

– maximum period for periodic CdG testing: $\tau_{TP} \leq 10\,\text{mn}$.

4.5. Conclusion

Our development shows that, in general, for a real-time system equipped with computers, it is necessary to differentiate the various aspects:

– functionalities that the system must achieve. In this case, the main problem is the following: are the specifications and their transformation into the final acquired code 100% correct?

– all basic hardware and software perform real-time functionalities of the system. In this case, the main problem is the following: can the hourly rate of unsafe targeted residual failure be guaranteed by the architecture in terms of actual use?

Concerning the first aspect, it is clear that a process of "quality development" cannot effectively respond to our problem: are the functionalities "correct"? *A priori* a formal approach covering the entire development cycle may respond favorably (from the upstream functional program specifications all the way to the code interpreted by the target machine). It is in this spirit that the MEI module was designed in 1993.

Our development has shown that it is possible to achieve automation at the highest level of safety with controlled costs. The PIPC post is the cheapest computer-based French signal box, and the most appreciated by operators

---

10. Note that the tools of interpretation of the commercial PETRI networks are generally dependent on the writing order and therefore on the evaluation of the graphs.

responsible for its maintenance. The cost-reduction effect has been studied for each stage of its life span:

– for studies, software architecture can reduce the cost of a study of a new site at the development of functional software with the help of "trade" workshops that do not require computer knowledge;

– for obsolescence of materials, the demonstration of safety does not rest on the hardware characteristic; in fact, unambiguously formalizing the functional interface – the host structure – can preserve the functional MEI of different manufacturers;

– for safety studies, the host structure (basic hardware and software) is approved irreversibly and constitutes the safety automaton, the conditions are satisfied so that the functional interpretation can be proved formally, thus reducing the proportion of trials before putting into operation;

– for installation costs: the use of connectors in the bottom cabinet and on cards reduces the wiring time and related implementation, and the use of common industrial materials;

– for maintenance: the conservation of signaling functions and naming rules with older sets, remote maintenance, archiving processes for fleeting or permanent failures, internal or external to the MEI, a $2 \times 2/2$ architecture in order to allow rapid changes of functional software, etc.

Note that this architecture has been in operation since 1995, with now over 150 signal boxes running 24 hours a day, and has never defaulted, and never given rise to real obsolescence issues.

The general principles adopted for this development can be carried over to other applications with high safety levels in order to reduce development costs without dropping the actual level of safety. It is possible to achieve safety, reliability, and inexpensiveness! Among these principles:

– a clear distinction of "trade" aspects (the manufacturers do not generally know, or know little about, the business domain of their client) and "technical information" (the client does not generally have the required skills in software design), with all the advantages previously listed;

– a functional common to all the MEI units, written in a formal language understandable by people of the "trade" and "formally verifiable" by the same operators, reducing manual testing before commissioning;

– a functional written in the form of graphs can be generated automatically from the description of the track plan, by association of the generic graphs in functional layers;

– a functional on which a formal proof can be easily performed, with the passage of a means obligation (SIL, DAL), based on quality procedures, to a results obligation in safety system;

– a demonstration of the SIL level of the safety automaton independently from the hardware, with all the advantages useful for obsolescence management, etc.

In simplified terms, the functional model becomes an "executionable specification" (or to be executed) in order to undertake, at the earliest, test scenarios or the analysis of structures at the model level. This is to recognize that current methods of software development can generate specification errors, design faults, or implementation faults (high level) that should be identified at the earliest so that they can be treated inexpensively.

Reasoning with input models is undoubtedly a step forward, only if designers take into account all aspects of the railway context and the environment of the future system. However, the pragmatic proposition described previously makes it possible to describe the functional that will be executed on it in real time and in safety by the module. We have shown that our combined "hardware and software" approach can address these risks effectively, in practical and economical terms. In simplified terms, the model becomes the "executable specification" so that the correct functioning, which will be executed deterministically, of the application is evident.

The interested reader is invited to read the following publications, which offer a more in-depth understanding of certain aspects of this general presentation [ANT 05; ANT 06; ANT 07; ANT 08a; ANT 08b].

4.6. Bibliography

[ANT 05] ANTONI M., VAN DETH F., "Modular Line Management System – SYMEL", *IRSE*, London, June 2005.

[ANT 06] ANTONI M., "Conception d'automatismes informatiques de sécurité, pérennes et économiques", *NTIC*, CNAM, Paris, 18 May 2006.

[ANT 07] ANTONI M., AMMAD N., "Feasibility study for the implementation of a formal proof of interpretable specification (for an interlocking system)", in G. TARNAI and E. Schnieder, FORMS/FORMAT 2007, *Proceedings of Formal Methods for Automation and Safety in Railway and Automotive Systems*, Braunschweig, Germany, 2007.

[ANT 08a] ANTONI M., AMMAD N., "Formal validation method and tools for computerized railway interlocking systems", *WCRR08 Congress, Formal Validation of Computerised Signal Boxes at the SNCF*, Seoul, Korea, 21 May 2008.

[ANT 08b] Antoni M., Ammad N., "Une méthode de validation formelle des systèmes informatiques de sécurité/A method of definite validation of the computer systems of safety", *Congrès Lambda-mu*, Avignon, France, 16 October 2008.

[BIE 93] Bielinski P., Méthode de validation formelle, implantation VLSI d'un algorithme de code correcteur d'erreur et validation formelle de la réalisation, PhD thesis, University of Paris 6, 1993.

[CEN 00] CENELEC, NF EN 50126, Railway applications. The specification and demonstration of reliability, availability, maintainability and safety (RAMS), January 2000.

[CEN 01] CENELEC, EN 50159– 1, Railway Applications – communication, signalling, and processing systems. Part 1: safety-related communication in closed transmission systems, March 2001.

[CEN 01a] CENELEC, NF EN 50128, Railway applications – communications, signalling and processing systems – software for railway control and protection systems, July 2001.

[CEN 03] CENELEC, NF EN 50129, European standard, railway applications communication, signalling and processing systems – safety-related communication in transmission systems, 2003.

[EIS 07] "Incident in the Lötschberg tunnel in November 2007"– Umfall für ERTMS "Lötschberg-Basislinie". *Eisenbahn Revue*, December 2007.

[IEC 98] IEC, IEC 61508: Functional safety of electrical/electronic/programmable electronic safety-related systems, International standard, 1998.

[RAIL 08] "ETCS software error led to derailment", *Railway Gazette International*, January 2008.

[VIL 88] Villemeur A., *Sûreté de fonctionnement des systèmes industriels*, Eyrolles, Paris, 1988.

Chapter 5

Command Control of Railway Signaling Safety: Safety at Lower Cost

5.1. Introduction

The industrialists of the railway world are developing microcomputing architectures, all of which are in response to the same safety needs, but which often use different technological solutions and safety concepts.

This chapter presents the main production concept ideas and safety demonstrations of the computerized interlocking post-PIPC developed by Thales for the management of the signaling lights and switches of railway infrastructures.

5.2. A safety coffee machine

Interlocking stations are designed to cope with feared events identified by a functional analysis of system safety and are defined as "failed route interlocking", "wrongful authorization of incompatible route", "unlocking a pointer engaged by a route", "wrongful command of a permissive signal".

It is at this point that the work of the safety architect begins. He must imagine a generic software and hardware architecture (known as a generic platform) that can support the development and implementation of a railway application. A bit like a

Chapter written by Daniel DRAGO.

coffee machine, which has generic properties such as: "make the mixture of ingredients selected by the consumer", "do not pour the mixture out if a cup has not dropped", "return money if the service is not carried out", etc. The generic safety platform must have the safety attributes: "carry out the functional process in accordance with the settings", "do not carry out wrongful permissive output" or "complete the acquisition, process and outputs in a limited timeframe".

Like an artist, the architect must imagine, design, and constantly challenge these choices so that the platform concepts securely provide the necessary requirements and properties.

The concepts and safety principles are viewed as barriers allowing the execution of algorithms related to the functional of the scope of the application, thus avoiding the occurrence of a feared event.

The analysis of barriers should take into account the duality availability/safety. In view of the complexity and of system automation, availability becomes a sizeable criterion when designing and implementing reliable and secure concepts. The system must be tolerated by normal and/or transient variations (noise transmission, delays in switching network, etc.).

All the technological and methodological barriers aim to:

– reduce the gravity (consequence) of a failure;

– significantly reduce the probability of occurrence of a failure scenario.

"Systematic" failures are covered by a more rigorous development process, while safety barriers can control the effects of random hardware failures.

Thus, this chapter summarizes the safety barriers of the PIPC platform architecture. The detailed arguments in this demonstration are included in the safety dossier (DS) submitted to the French Railway Safety Authority (EPSF: *Etablissement Public de Sécurité Ferroviaire*). The safety dossier should be compliant with the CENELEC EN 50129 [CEN 03] standard.

5.3. History of the PIPC

The PIPC was developed to meet the market for renewals of SNCF signaling posts – to replace aging interlocking relay logic chassis, parts of which were sometimes more than 40 years old! It was developed by a handful of enthusiasts between 1993 and 1999, in close collaboration with specialists from the SNCF, and was for a long time the only electronic interlocking "made in France".

In 1995, a first validated prototype (known as SYMEL) of six stations was installed on a track with little traffic between Meymac and the Palace in the Limousin. After finding success with operators, improvements concerning the industrialization of the solution and of the parameter principles led to the first generation PIPC in June 1999, commissioned on a line between Moirans and St Marcelin.

Following the transfer of activity between industrial groups, the PIPC was then deployed by Alcatel until late 2007. It has since been deployed by Thales.

The crucial choice was brought about by the use of commercially available technology and industrial Intel CPU cards (said to be "off the shelf", we speak of COTS) and by minimizing the design of specific electronic cards. The safety computer then reproduces the Boolean logic interlocking functions (formerly achieved with relays – of the VG type, then more broadly PRCI), while maintaining the principle of relay interface of existing track equipment (no change in the "campaign").

A graphic interface allows an operator to "follow" the interlocking behavior over several stations and to place orders to establish routes (via a simple keyboard). It has a support system for local maintenance (single PC) and can be interfaced with a system of regional supervision (MISTRAL) and remote surveillance.

By design, the PIPC allows the transparency of maintenance interventions *vis-à-vis* the operation of the post, which is not true of competing products.

The mantra that guided the design of the PIPC was "safety at lower cost". The cost must be assessed in its entirety over the lifespan of the product (cost of ownership): purchasing the equipment, its installation, its configuration, its validation, and its maintenance. The PIPC is a challenge.

In the optimization of ownership costs of the signaling infrastructure, the RFF (*Réseau Ferré de France*) and SNCF have since decided to generalize, beyond 2009, the intermediary relay interface principle between the track equipment (switch and signals, etc.) and the heart of the computerized interlocking logic. This decouples the regeneration cycles, limiting the technological constraints of interfacing. Track equipment generally has a lifespan that is much longer (more than 30 years) than that of safety computers, while it is considered reasonable to manage obsolescent computer technology solutions over a maximum of 25 years.

The acronym "PIPC" corresponds to a computerized post with PC technology (*postinformatique à technologie PC*) – some would say it has a "small capacity" and this remains true for the first generation when the stations had approximately three to 15 switches; the new generation (PIPC G2 called PIPC 2006 by SNCF) exceeds a capacity of command of 200 switches pursuant to recent RFF regeneration contracts, the PIPC 2006 will be deployed on at least 75% of upgrading stations.

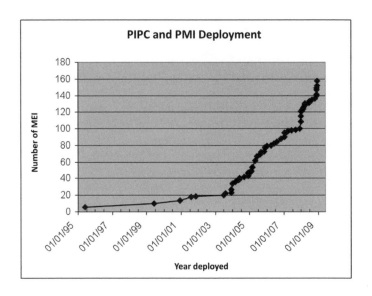

Figure 5.1. *PMI and PIPC deployment*

Line	Number of MEI	Deployed	PIPC type	Line type	Operators/client
Le Palais - Meymac	6	Jun-1995	SYMEL	CCVIG	Head of series SYMEL
Moirans - Saint Marcellin	4	Jun-1999	V0	CCVU	Head of series PIPC_V0
Lutterbach - Kruth	4	Dec-2000	V0	CCVU	SNCF - head of series MTK
Malaunay - Dieppe	4	Aug-2001	V0	CCVU	SNCF
Haguenau	1	Nov-2001	V0	Post	SNCF
Epinal	1	Jul-2003	V0	Post	SNCF
Saint Cyprien - Colomiers	2	Aug-2003	V0	DV	SNCF - RER line C Toulouse
Pagny	1	Dec-2003	V1	Post	Head of series PIPC_V1

Line (cont.)	Number of MEI	Deployed	PIPC type	Line type	Operators/client
Bordeaux tramway	4	Dec-2003	Tramway	Tramway	CUB Bordeaux
Tunes - Lagos (Algarve)	7	Jan-2004	PIPC-V1 P	CCVU	REFER PIPC-P Portugal
Masseret - Allasac	2	Mar-2004	V1	IPCS	SNCF
Rivesaltes - Salses	2	May-2004	V1	IPCS	SNCF
Lizy sur Ourq	1	Jun-2004	V1	Post	SNCF - basis for East LGV works
Athus	1	Jun-2004	V1	Post	SNCF
Dôl - Montreuil sur Ile	2	Sep-2004	V1	DV	SNCF - head of services for Mistral
Muret	1	Dec-2004	V1	Post	SNCF
GCO	3	Dec-2004	V1	DV	SNCF
Beauvoir sur Niort	1	Dec-2004	V1	Post	SNCF
Saint Mâlo (Saint Mâlo - Montreuil)	1	Feb-2005	V1	DV	SNCF
Saint Lô	1	Feb-2005	V1	Post	SNCF
Cannes - Grasse	4	Mar-2005	V1	DV	SNCF
Portet	1	Mar-2005	V1	Post	SNCF
Mouriscas - Castelo Branco (Beira Baixa)	8	May-2005	PIPC-V1 P	CCVU	REFER PIPC-P Portugal
Libourne - Bergerac	5	Jun-2005	V1	CCVU	SNCF
Colmar - Metzeral	2	Aug-2005	V1	CCVU	SNCF
Arras - Saint Pôl	3	Sep-2005	V1	CCVU	SNCF
Station Lilas L11	1	Nov-2005	PMI	Metro	RATP - head of Metro PMI
Tours - Vierzon	4	Dec-2005	V1	IPCS	SNCF
Plaisir Grignon	1	Dec-2005	V1	Post	SNCF
Gruissan	1	Jan-2006	V1	Post	SNCF
Saint Hilaire au Temple	1	Apr-2006	V1	Post	SNCF
Lauterbourg - Strasburg	2	Jun-2006	V1	DV	SNCF
Argenteuil - Ermont	2	Aug-2006	V1	DV	SNCF
Reding - Metz Ville (Baudrecourt)	4	Nov-2006	V1	IPCS	SNCF

Line (cont.)	Number of MEI	Deployed	PIPC type	Line type	Operators/client
M'Saken	2	Jan-2007	V1	Post	SNTF - Tunisia - COGIFER
Annemasse - Evian (phase 1)	5	Jan-2007	V1	DV	SNCF
Montlaur	1	Mar-2007	V1	IPCS	SNCF
Momenheim	1	Apr-2007	V1	Post	SNCF
Kalaa	1	Jun-2007	V1	Post	SNTF - Tunisia - COGIFER
Chaulnes	1	Sep-2007	V1	Post	SNCF
Port Leucate	1	Dec-2007	V1	IPCS	SNCF
Line 6	9	Dec-2007	PMI	Metro	Shanghai Metro - PMI
Line 8 (phase 1)	6	Dec-2007	PMI	Metro	Shanghai Metro - PMI
Line 9 (phase 1)	6	Dec-2007	PMI	Metro	Shanghai Metro - PMI
Marchandise	1	Jan-2008	V1	Post	SNTF - Tunisia - COGIFER
La Roche sur Yon	1	Jan-2008	V1	Post	SNCF
Station Gambetta L3bis	1	Feb-2008	PMI	Metro	RATP
Station Lilas L3bis	1	Feb-2008	PMI	Metro	RATP
Triangle de Sousse	3	Mar-2008	V1	Post	SNTF - Tunisia - COGIFER
Buchy	1	Mar-2008	V1	Post	SNCF
Pau	1	Mar-2008	V1	Post	SNCF
Villefranche - Montlaur	1	Jun-2008	V1	IPCS	SNCF
Coutance	1	Jun-2008	V1	Post	SNCF
Don Sainghain	1	Jul-2008	V1	Post	SNCF
Bourg - Sathonay	2	Aug-2008	V1	DV	SNCF
Ussel	1	Oct-2008	V1	Post	SNCF
Le Havre	4	Nov-2008	V1	DV	SNCF
Le Havre	1	Nov-2008	V1	VS	SNCF – Post S
Aix - Marseille	6	Nov-2008	V1	CCVU	SNCF

Line (cont.)	Number of MEI	Deployed	PIPC type	Line type	Operators/client
Obernai - Rosheim (Saverne - Selestat)	2	Nov-2008	V1	CCVU	SNCF
Lyon La Guillotière	3	Dec-2008	PIVOS	VS	SNCF - head of series, service paths
Nice - Digne	6	Dec-2008	V1	CCVU	SYMA/Veolia

Table 5.1. *List of installations*

At the end of 2008, the PIPC had been deployed over 150 stations (France, China, Portugal, Tunisia, Algeria, Morocco, etc.) and controlled more than 2,900 signals or switches[1] corresponding to an accumulation of over 65 million hours of operation by command control of the elementary function of switches or signals.

In 2009, over 96 PIPC were to be commercially commissioned, representing two-sixths of the park already in operation at the end of 2008.

Table 5.1 and Figure 5.1 represent the progression of deployment since the design of the computer. The different variants and clients are listed.

5.4. The concept basis

The use of "commercial products" (COTS) does not always allow for an architecture with a small bulk. However, highly integrated computerized solutions are not always necessary because there is often room on the ground, within the railway's technical premises: either on those left by the huge signaling relay logic chassis (which are deposited during upgrades of the posts), or during construction of new lines where the premises and buildings (or booths, shelters) can be defined accordingly.

The complexity (and therefore the costs) of railway safety architectures are generally much smaller than for nuclear or aerospace. Perhaps because an aircraft can not have an emergency brake! The availability of the flight control functions is a safety necessity. Architectural solutions naturally have a degree of additional complexity.

---

1. A signal is composed of several colored lamps with command (fixed or flashing aspect) and control (state of filaments) functions. A switch is composed of a motorization command and a control of the stopping position of railway blades.

In most simple railway applications, the state of lowest energy (train stopped) is a secure state. However, the management of safety in railway tunnels requires more "available" architectures: stopping a train on fire in a tunnel is more dangerous than letting it run on to the exit. Beyond this need, there are increasing demands for operational safety, including in major stations, which involves availability constraints in technological solutions integral to the quality of operation of the railway network.

The original safety concept retained for the PIPC was that of probabilistic controlled safety for all acquisition, processing and output channels: in other words: 2 x 2. Each independent channel mutually compares itself to a set of internal and external state variables, therefore ensuring consistency of behavioral performances in processing and outputs. Each channel can be placed in fallback position by an internal defect or an inconsistency in the vote/synchronization of the state variables.

To this, complete hot redundancy is added when necessary, a redundant (for availability) dual (for safety) processor; this is called "2oo2 × 2". Redundancy is designed to make maintenance actions transparent regarding operation (no system shutdown, hot swap, etc.). Redundancy is "optional" and can be implemented retrospectively without affecting the operation of the existing installation.

The choice was also retained for an architecture where each 2oo2 replica has a quasi-single-task cyclic behavior: one safety software process, cyclic, per processor, thus ensuring the determinism of execution.

The demonstration of the level of safety using a probabilistic approach requires safety concepts whose effectiveness "is irrefutable". The demonstration of the effectiveness of a simple concept (but not necessarily easy to implement) allowing the persuasion of a panel of experts and external evaluators, is more compelling than that of a complicated concept. We must be wary of numbers. Probabilities are manipulated with hypotheses (failure models, etc.) that have often been deliberately forgotten. Exponential models of failure rates of electronic components provide only average values (which are frequently "too optimistic"!). Uncertain calculations are difficult to realize. It is difficult to justify the probabilistic safety margins without the "subjective" judgment of an expert.

In "probabilistic safety", the main risk remains the latent failure scenario (undetected failure). It is therefore necessary to put in place fleets of self-testing mechanisms to track this type of failure and prevent a possible spread once activated. These detection mechanisms must themselves be reliable, even "secure". Therefore, latent failure scenarios or those which incur a negligible probability of non-detection of failure must be minimized.

Using a 2oo2 dual processor architecture raises the question of common mode failure, either on the command channels or on the control channels and self-tests. In what circumstances should we consider a common mode of failure of components performing identical functions on different replicas? The simple components (resistors, capacitors, quartz, etc.), as well as the complexes ones (CPLD, CPU, etc.) may be from the same production batch with the same latent defects appearing simultaneously. Here the "safety culture" effect comes into play that can be understood by observing the different companies in the same sector, and from one technological domain to another within the same company. Quality assurance, tests, and checks during the manufacturing of computers bring some solutions for simple discrete components (capacitor, resistor, optocoupler). This is not the case for more complex components (FPGA, CPLD, etc.) whose exhaustive testing is often impossible to complete both in the factory and once implanted on the card. The scenarios of undetected failures must be considered in the combinatorial analysis of failures, with a probabilistic assessment over a horizon encompassing the theoretical lifespan of the product (i.e. 25-30 years).

The safety barriers implemented in the PIPC take these considerations into account.

Beyond the detection of a latent failure, there must be a sanction whose performance must be based on simple concepts (and therefore easily demonstrable). The "sanction" can be viewed in two stages: "immediate safety" (instantaneous behavior of the architecture) and "securely maintaining" the fallback position. Immediate safety limits the spread of crash scenarios. This action can be ensured by "probabilistic safety", as is the detection of the failure. In contrast, the "maintenance in a secure condition" can only be guaranteed by the principles of intrinsic safety. The PIPC cuts off the output power supply with an intrinsic safety watchdog mechanism, based on safety relays (using gravity).

5.5. Postulates for safety requirements

The engineering work of the architect consists of identifying a coherent and comprehensive list of properties ensuring dependability [VIL 88] of the PIPC generic platform.

The resulting safety concepts are defined with regards to the following safety requirements:

– requirement 1: a hardware failure should never generate a more permissive output than if there had not been a failure;

– requirement 2: all simple failures must be detected and sanctioned by the voting and synchronization mechanism in a short enough time, allowing for a level of probabilistic safety of 10^{-11}/hour (failure rate contrary to safety);

– requirement 3: all hardware failures simultaneously affecting the two replicas with homologous effects must be prevented by the design of safety barriers;

– requirement 4: the software source code, common to the two replicas, must be developed using a rigorous process to ensure the absence of defects[2];

– requirement 5: if redundancy is deployed, a "hot redundancy" control mechanism should ensure, at all times, the coherence between each dual processor output, whatever the input values;

– requirement 6: an intrinsic safety mechanism must ensure the persistence of the fallback position of electric outputs.

These safety requirements conceptually have two strong limitations:

– the safety architecture does not guarantee safety when homologous effect failures (possibly of common cause) simultaneously affect both channels working in 2 x 2. This type of "conceptual failure" renders the voting and synchronization mechanism irrelevant;

– the software remains a common cause of failure for the two replicas. Solutions with massive implementation diversification (design and development) reduce the "software risk"; these principles are more expensive and are generally used for applications considered "bulkier" than railway computers. The volume of the PIPC platform software should be as small as possible. This will facilitate testability and maintenance and, thus, the demonstration of its safety level[3].

Obviously, there is another demonstrable limit of a safety level. This limit depends on the "devil's hand". This is not a philosophical approach but a matter of "safety culture". Some believe that if a failure scenario (failure mode) cannot be proven not to occur, then by hypothesis, it will certainly occur (with a probability equal to 1). Others believe the opposite: it is pointless to consider a failure scenario (failure mode) whose existence cannot even be technically proven.

---

2. In the railway domain, the development of the software must conform to the European standard CENELEC 50128 [CEN 01]. For the most critical software, the developmental, validation and verification process is of SIL 4 level.

3 Similarly, concurring applications run with 20,000 to 100,000 instruction lines. The PIPC possesses, depending on various systems, between 15,000 and 50,000 lines of instruction.

Up to what point must complex and combinatorial scenarios be considered in the case of a failure?

There are many technological rules (failure mode and protection mode hypothesis), but although normative, these railway environment rules are not applied equally between the north and south of Europe or even across the Atlantic[4]. Consequently, an architecture whose safety level is accepted in Germany, will not necessarily be accepted in France, and a product developed according to safety rules for the French market will require one or more modifications to meet North American standards. I can assure you there is also inconsistency in the opposite direction. "Cross-acceptance"[5] by the authorities of technological benchmarks specific to each country is pitted against safety culture dogma.

European legislation provides a legal and technical framework for "mutual recognition" in the field of automation protection (ERTMS [COM 06]) of mainline trains. In practice, at the very bottom of "the technical scale", profound differences remain.

5.6. Description of the PIPC architecture7

The PIPC consists of two strictly redundant cabinets (in other words, a single cabinet is sufficient to ensure the safety functions) called the command-control safety module (MCCS: *module de contrôle-commande de sécurité*). Each MCCS is composed of two voted (synchronized) replica units corresponding to the 2oo2 concept (master unit and slave unit) called MEI (computerized interlocking module) and one to six field relay interface modules (MIRET: *module d'interface du relayage terrain*) racks containing digital I/O cards.

The MIRETS racks can be populated with input or output cards, depending on the field configuration.

Each MCCS safely performs input functions, calculation of interlocking and signaling conditions and output functions. MCCS redundancy ensures the full availability of MCCS functions when a module fails or is being repaired. Some railway applications are made without full redundancy whereby the installation has

---

4. I do not think that this can be considered as protectionism, but is rather a matter of *safety culture*.

5. Cross-acceptance is a process that is only starting to be applied between the main railway operators, but powerful clique wars still persist in the matter of rules for the fabrication of electronic cards, the failure modes of components, the design criteria for printed circuits, or common mode failures.

only one MCCS; the risk of operating degradation is considered to be low enough not to require total redundancy.

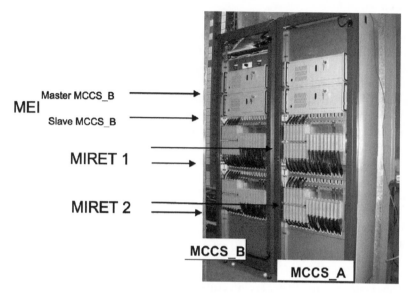

Figure 5.2. *PIPC cabinet with two MIRETS*

5.6.1. *MCCS architecture*

The MEI consists of two COTS industrial PCs (CPU card + PCI motherboard + power supply + rack). On the motherboard are plugged:

– a specific watchdog "WD" card;

– "CCIP" cards managing the communications resources, internal PC "master-slave", "inter-MCCS" and "inter-MEI" (MEI external network);

– "TBES" (head of bus) card: parallel proprietary bus allowing direct access to the records of I/O cards located in the MIRETS.

Industrial PCs are named "master or slave" by the choice of physical cyclic sequencing that drives them; there is no underlying masochism.

The industrial CPU card has dynamic memory RAM modules, a connection to the PCMCIA or USB (for loading data) card readers and a static hard drive (*post-mortem* recording).

The "watchdog" cards of each unit determine an external watchdog based on intrinsic safety relays (using gravity). The relay contacts on the "watchdog" card are placed in series with those of the watchdog of the dual unit, in order to operate the safety relay that disconnects all internal power supply and especially towards the external safety interfaces (relay signaling).

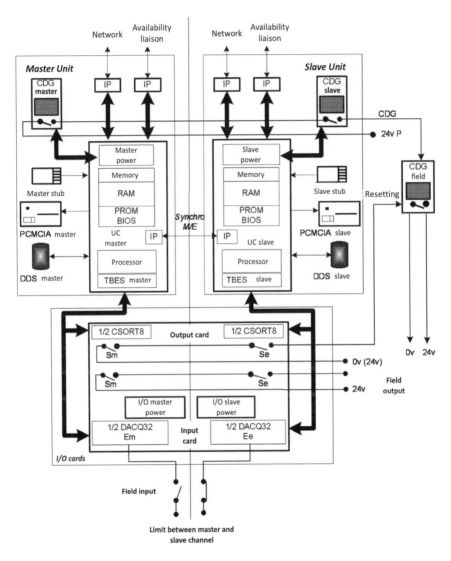

Figure 5.3. *MCCS architecture block diagram*

One processing unit can have two TBES cards. The MCCS can therefore have up to six MIRETS.

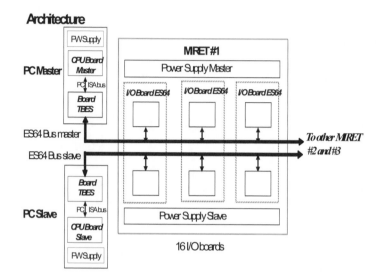

Figure 5.4. *MIRETS architecture*

5.6.2. *Input and output cards*

The input and output cards are designed in two distinct parts, which are isolated one from the other and associated either with the master or with the slave unit.

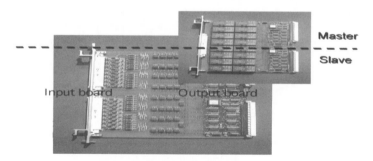

Figure 5.5. *Input/output cards*

5.6.2.1. *Input cards*

The input card works with antivalent signals (electrically complementary) issued by the rest and work contacts of a signaling interface relay. This signaling relay distributes securely and simultaneously the electrical states of both MCCS (Figure 5.6).

Antivalent Input Principle
Redundant configuration

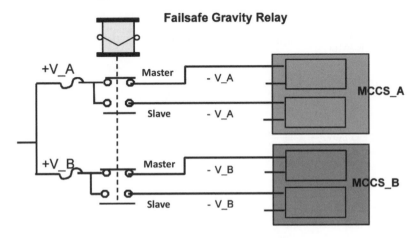

Figure 5.6. *Distribution of complemented states*

Every MCCS half-card performs the same processing, but the electronic information has additional semantics (see Figure 5.7). This creates dissimilarity in the digital processing performed at the card level, thus reducing the activation risk in common mode of a homologous effect between the two half-cards (which are identical in composition). There is a processing dissimilarity on a similar architecture. The central unit's software (master and slave) will verify the logical consistency between the complementary logic states.

A "zero test" can periodically verify the absence of bonding at state 1 in a digital half-channel. However, this test does not cover the cells interfacing with the external environment, which define the limits of the current/voltage analog detection of the logic 0-1 transition.

Input state	Voltage (V)	or	Current (mA)
Restrictive State: "0" logic	<11		<7
Permissive State: "1" logic	>13		>8

Only the "restrictive" electrical threshold is considered in the safety design of the acquisition chain. Any undetected drift of the threshold towards lower values may mask a restrictive state, misinterpreted by a "permissive" value.

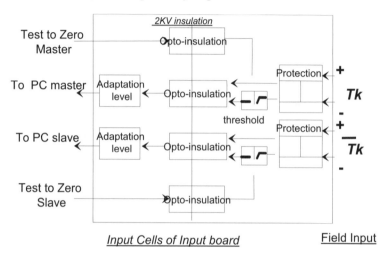

Figure 5.7. *Interface input card level*

Behind the galvanic isolation (optoelectronic), Boolean information is placed on memory registers directly accessible by the master or slave unit.

By default, the master channel reads normal states (powered = permissive) and the slave channel reads antivalent states (powered = restrictive).

The processing units exchange the values and compare them. Inputs that are not antivalent or have a non-compliant zero test are immediately placed in the irreversible restrictive logic state. The Boolean functional value consequently becomes restrictive and an anomaly is then reported allowing the management of the MCCS redundancy.

5.6.2.2. *Output cards*

The safety outputs are carried through the "dry contacts" series of two relays (implanted on the card) and controlled respectively by each master/slave channel (see wiring diagrams in single and double cut, Figures 5.10 and 5.11).

The polarized monostable relay is soldered to the output cards (Figure 5.8). It may fail and have bonded contacts; however, it offers mechanically guaranteed non-overlapping contacts (standard EN 50205-class A, [CEN 02]). The readback of the non-overlapping contacts informs of the power state of the coil relay.

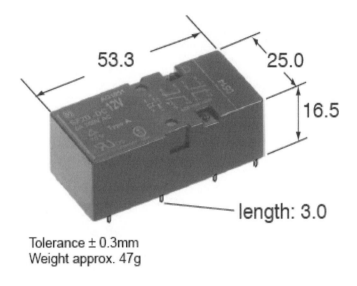

Tolerance ± 0.3mm
Weight approx. 47g

Figure 5.8. *Polarized relay with forced maneuver contacts*

Readback is done multiple times and is crossed; therefore, the master channel directly links the states (normal and complemented) of the relay controlled by the slave channel, and *vice versa* (see Figure 5.9).

We could imagine a common mode affecting the closed contacts of the two relays in series (on a short-circuit current, for example, on external wiring). To this there is only one answer: a current bonding the oversized contacts (>×20) with regards to the fast fuses protecting the external wiring.

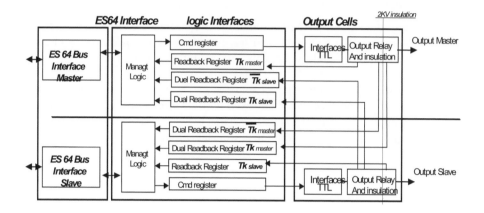

Figure 5.9. *Output card functional block*

Antivalent and crossed readback (the master reads the output of the slave and vice versa) can diversify functional information (on the same architecture) in order to reduce the risk of common mode failure between the master and slave channels.

The natural dynamics of an application aids in the detection of latent failure. Unfortunately in railway signaling, the outputs are feebly boosted (they can stay for days without moving).

The multiple readbacks of work and rest contacts on both channels (six readbacks in all) greatly reduce the likelihood of the accumulation of multiple latent failures not detecting internal card defects (leading to a dreaded event: activation of a wrongly permissive output).

We could periodically test each of the channels by enabling or disabling them, but the changeover time of non-overlapping contacts of the output cell relay would require an activation time longer than 10 milliseconds. This time is considered unacceptable because if the other channel is simultaneously faulty, there is a risk of incorrectly generating a permissive pulse.

The transition to solid state relay (SSR) technology is feasible, but the gains in terms of integration are balanced out by the complexity of the electronic card (and the cost) that would provide readback isolated by voltage bridges. In addition, we are limited by production constraints of the printed circuit that must comply with the routing distances between the tracks. Similarly, the routing placement constraints of connectors ensuring separation distances between tracks (distance ensuring the absence of current leaks between equipotentials) limits the usefulness of SSR technology to applications requiring very few outputs (in the case of an embedded computer in the rolling hardware).

The signaling relay (intrinsic safety) is controlled through a power supply galvanically isolated from the rest of the installation. This insulation helps to reduce the risk of wrongly recharging and activating in the case of a cable rupture.

A common concern in railway signaling is the short circuit. Safety analysis must assess the risk of short circuit on the cables, in order to reduce the risk of fire of a post and to avoid loss of integrity of the safety architecture (a short-circuit always stresses the output cards).

In our case, if a short circuit occurs on the cables, there will be an overcurrent that could "bond" the contacts in the relay together. There are two possibilities to reduce the risk:

– fast fuses (the case of the PIPC). Fast fuses are necessary, with a value providing a "safety" margin with regards to the bonding current of the relay embedded on the cards of at least a factor of 10 (or > 5 A/24 V DC), while the nominal current remains at 40 mA. Often a second fuse (or thermal circuit breaker) is placed upstream of a group of fast fuses whose performance here is to protect against the risk of fire;

– a source of current regulated by intrinsic safety: an intrinsic safety current limiter. If consumption is not too strong, the current limiter can also serve as a watchdog (often the case in the embedded safety architecture on rolling hardware).

The "all or nothing" outputs can activate the relays depending on two types of connections:

– single cut;

– double cut.

5.6.2.2.1. Single cut

The single cut (Figure 5.10) is used as part of the implementation of a short distance relay interface, ideally a distance of a few meters between the post and the command to be executed.

This solution has the advantage of using very little copper cable, but the downside is the risk of recharging the relay upon simple breaking of the hot wire connected to the external wiring.

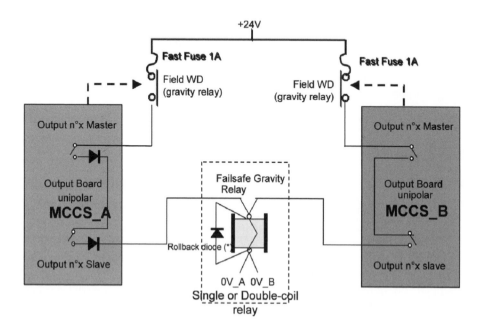

Figure 5.10. *Connection of an output in single cut*

5.6.2.2.2. Double cut

The double cut (Figure 5.11) is used as part of the powering of the remote relay said to be "in campaign". The main benefit is that it reduces the risk of wrongly recharging the remote relay that provides power directly to the field equipment. The main disadvantage is that it uses a lot of (×2) contacts on the "field watchdog" relay.

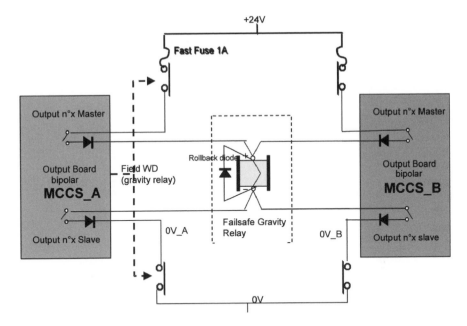

Figure 5.11. *Connection of an output in double cut*

5.6.3. *Watchdog card internal to the processing unit*

Each processing unit has a watchdog card that ensures the fallback position of the unit. The card communicates with the CPU card through a bus backplane (mixed ISA and PCI bus). The internal counter is periodically reset by applying the CPU card.

The principle of the card is to measure a predetermined dynamic processing of the CPU unit and to generate a negative power supply (diode pump) to activate the polarized relay located on the card.

This card is designed so that no single failure:

– can generate oscillations powering the diode pump;

– can generate a negative power supply (negative potential difference).

This relay is similar to those in the output cards. It is periodically self-tested. Self-testing of this relay ensures its availability to solicitation.

The period of self-test is justified by a classical probabilistic approach ($\lambda^2 T$). But the frequency must not render the electrical contact of the relay unreliable by excessive solicitation, so a period of less than 10 minutes is chosen.

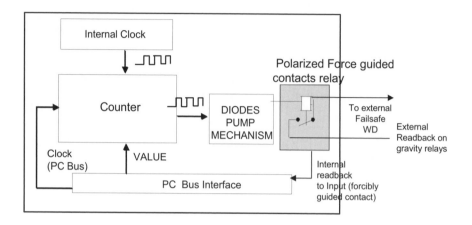

Figure 5.12. *Internal watchdog card*

Self-testing is done by two readback means:

– state of the internal relay: this readback immediately follows the command, but it is confirmed by the readback of the field state;

– external readback of the field state of the watchdog (see dedicated section and Figure 5.16).

5.6.4. *Head of bus input/output card*

This card is a bridge between the bus of the CPU card (usually ISA or PCI) and the registers of the I/O cards. The TBES card allows parallel access, for writing or reading, to all records of a card plugged into one of the six MIRETS.

Communications use a proprietary protocol that ensures authentication of exchanges (coded address of the recipient and respondent) as well as in cases of collision (multiple cards satisfying a query). The integrity of the data on the bus is provided by multiple readings using different and dissimilar channels.

This high-speed bus allows access, in a few milliseconds, to all the input and output cards (for reading and writing). It securely ensures access time and thus the refresh of inputs and outputs. This bus does not require a complex computing unit. This was not the case with the series bus (like a CAN bus) where, on each side of the transmission channel, we would have had to design processing units performing complex encapsulation protocol messages for secure transmission (dating, integrity, etc.).

5.6.5. *Field watchdog*

The field watchdog provides an electric fallback position using intrinsic safety. The fallback position is controlled with a probabilistic level of safety (a concept of 2002 on the organ commands); however, the failure of a channel (commanding the fallback position), could result in multiple failure scenarios that would annihilate (offset) the order to the fallback position. Considering the temporal aspect of these scenarios, it is necessary to "lock" the fallback state. This lock can be effective (and its efficiency easy to prove) only if executed with the concepts of intrinsic safety.

In railway engineering, the fallback state is generally achieved by a power cut, causing, for example, the emergency brake of rolling hardware, or extinction of permissive green signals. Therefore, its execution must ensure and maintain the ability to cut off power. Usually two technological solutions exist:

– either a gravity relay with contacts having sufficient current breaking capacity. The gravity (weight) ensures that the contacts are never continuous while the coil is not powered (for example: in France, the NS1 relay; in England/India, the BR Q-type relay);

– or a power supply whose current is conducted in intrinsic safety; consequently, providing a limitation (risk of short-circuit mentioned on the output cards) and power cut.

The coil of the safety signaling relay Si to be commanded is powered by 24 V that can be cut off (double cut upstream and downstream on the diagram of Figure 5.14) by the Cde Si commands issued from the output cards of the master and slave channels.

Each channel has a watchdog card where the contacts of a relay are put in series in order to power the field watchdog, and to set it up with a secure gravity relay. As soon as one of the units "fails", the field watchdog cuts off the power supply of the signaling relays, thus securing the state.

Figure 5.13. *Field watchdog*

In the French configuration, the gravity relays used are of the NS1 type (see Figure 5.13).

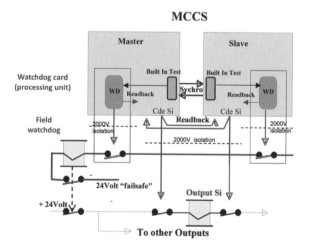

Figure 5.14. *Command and output safety channel*

5.7. Description of availability principles

5.7.1. Redundancy

The management of redundancy is certainly one of the most complex functions of the system. The mechanisms producing the attributes of availability and safety are closely linked.

Basically, it must be remembered that each MCCS securely undertakes the acquisitions, and the functional processing and finally generates the output. The MCCS processing units A and B communicate with each other to determine which one is the "most available".

The physical and logical state of an MCCS must be distinguished. For example, a MCCS named "A" is a hardware configuration, while it may be either in a primary or secondary state.

Physical Status	Logical Status	
MCCS_A	Primary	Secondary
MCCS_B	Secondary	Primary

Figure 5.15. *Redundancy*

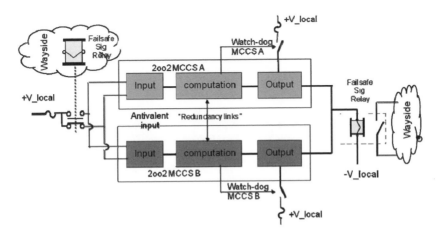

Figure 5.16. *Concept of placing in redundancy*

The logic state of a MCCS evolves in the wake of solicitation of redundancy (in case of failure or reboot of a MCCS). The secondary MCCS is always the last to be awakened or aligned with the other.

Hot redundancy is ensured by:

– Boolean or digital information acquired simultaneously by both MCCS (based on multiple contacts of the signaling relay);

– the permissive logic state commanded in output corresponds to a "powered" electric state; the restrictive state being the power cut;

– each MCCS can switch to a fallback position through its field watchdog;

– electrical states commanded by output by each MCCS converge either on a "wired or" (see Figure 5.16, SNCF type) or on a double coil relay (English, Chinese, relays, etc.). The combination of logic states by a double coil relay reduces the risk of repowering the safety output via the defaulting output circuits of the redundant MCCS.

The "wired or" on the outputs ensures the absence of switching time (no transition of the electric state).

To meet safety requirement number 5, any divergence between the two MCCS must be detected and a fallback strategy must be considered. Indeed, each MCCS performs safety calculations; therefore, a divergence of output can only come from divergent inputs.

Digital links between the MCCS processing units establish a "cross-check" of MCCS alignment thereby optimizing the management of the availability of the redundant architecture.

The information exchanged enables algorithms to locate the differences in behavior (internal state) to a lack of acquisitions (local acquisition or digital link).

Several cases are considered:

– in case of defect on a processing unit or output card, the MCCS goes into a mandatory fallback position (watchdog of the field watchdog);

– if the defect (at the origin of the divergence) is unique and remains localized on an input card (the coverage of self-testing is a safety requirement) then an acquisition channel is declared faulty and the MCCS continues operations considering only the data acquired by the other MCCS (switching the acquisition channel and exchange by "cross-check");

– if the defects (at the origin of the divergence) are multiple (simultaneous loss of multiple inputs) then the MCCS acquisition channel with the most inputs is declared faulty and goes entirely into a fallback position. Indeed, it can be estimated that several cards are already failing (whose inputs are treated as restrictive). The discrimination algorithm preserves the MCCS acquisition channel, which "seems the least defective" (switching the acquisition channel and exchange by "cross-check");

– unfortunately though, if an acquisition divergence is not associated with an internal defect then it means that the defect responsible for the divergence is outside the architecture (relay contacts, fuses, cut cable, etc.). A dilemma arises: which of the MCCS is correct? This enduring situation is potentially dangerous. The proposed strategy is then limited to maintaining the level of safety at the expense of availability: an MCCS goes into fallback position, by default always the channel said to be secondary, but without knowing whether it functionally provides the greatest functional availability. We could keep the acquisition channel that delivers the most permissive information (as every MCSS is making acquisitions that cannot be wrongly permissive). Currently, this discrimination is not implemented on the PIPC.

5.7.2. *Automatic reset*

To improve the availability performance of the architecture when faced with an inevitable fleeting defect, the PIPC performs an automatic external reset.

As soon as it is in the fallback position (field watchdog), the external power supply of the MCCS is cut for at least 5 seconds, the MCCS then restarts (by setting the outputs in restrictive mode, the watchdog is disabled). The power cut will remove potential residual erraticon on silicon junctions.

Once the internal self-tests have been performed and the acquisition and alignment of functional contexts is made with the other MCCS (education phase and total transfer of the functional context of one MCCS to another), the watchdog is rearmed, thereby activating the electric outputs.

The automatic reset capability is limited in number and time. Beyond that, we judge that the hypothesis of the fleeting character of the failure is not verified and the risk of a "warning behavior" is detrimental to the overall level of operational safety.

The reset principle constitutes a "theoretical weakness" in the demonstration of safety, but it is indispensable for the availability of the architecture.

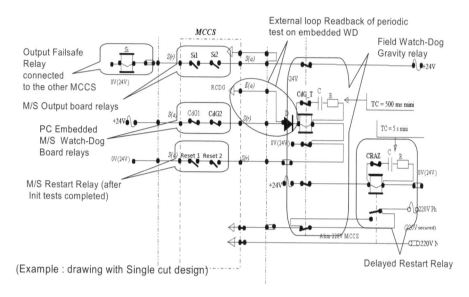

Figure 5.17. *Watchdog wiring and resetting*

5.8. Software architecture

5.8.1. *Constitution of the kernel*

The software architecture of the PIPC, developed in C, has a layered structure in order to benefit from the hierarchical approach of safety dossiers as advocated by the standard CENELEC EN 50129 [CEN 03].

The "safety kernel" hardware and software architecture constitutes the generic product.

The low-level software interface module (middleware) managing the cards on the CPU bus, are proprietary and optimized in order to avoid the use of external libraries.

To this is added a software layer that is more or less bulky depending on its generic functional application (depending on each client).

The safety kernel ensures the deterministic execution of the applicative layers through exported, traced, and then validated constraints in the safety demonstration dossier.

We will come back later to the generic application constituted by part C software and part "customized" graphset.

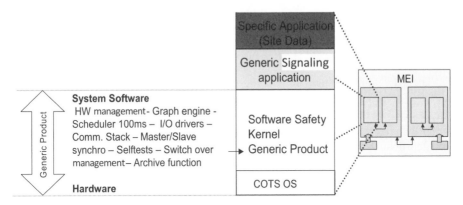

Figure 5.18. *Software architecture in layers*

5.8.2. *The language and the compilers*

The development language is C, limited by a programming guide. The application of encoding constraints, identified in the programming guide, is verified by tools such as Purifier, Polyspace and/or C++Test (for some automatable rules) and during the code review by peers.

For the C toolchain, we chose not to use a "certified" compiler for the simple reason that it does not yet exist. The safety of the generation is paramount.

We will use the following arguments:

– the dissimilarity of compilation: use of two different compilers for the master and slave: WATCOM and VISUAL. The dissimilarity of compilers is our response against the common modes for generating executable;

– these compilers have been used for a long time and have been "proven through experience". Moreover, the history of bugs has been the object of impact analysis on our applications. It is thus considered that these compilers are "qualified" by use, by all justification elements (list of bugs, analysis of bugs, list of uses, etc.) forming the qualification record;

– all phases of validation (hardware software integration and sub-system validation) are undertaken on targeted equipment.

These standard compilers enable us to easily consider the qualifications of new CPU cards (which was already the case, as the result of over 10 years of feedback). Of course, the compilation scripts do not contain any optimization options.

5.8.3. *The operating system (OS)*

The PIPC software uses simple and affordable generic components (COTS) for its OS. The processor being X86 compatible (the most common family), the PIPC uses as an OS the DOS complemented by a DOS-Extender, allowing access to a larger memory area. As we speak here of COTS, and not having the source code and detailed documentation of these two software components, they are not unitarily "valid".

We will advance the following strategy with regards to safety:

– each master and slave channel has a dissimilar "DOS - DOS Extender" couple; several vendors have versions considered sufficiently dissimilar to allow us to reject the hypothesis of the common mode;

– each software component is known to the public market and reflects a high usage history (followed by bug reports of supplier and user communities);

– all phases of validation (integrated hardware and software sub-system validation) are realized with the target computers and their OS (validation of internal function calls of the OS and low-level interfaces);

– the few instructions used by the kernel are trivial and limited. They are subject to an interface validation.

DOS only serves to load the program memory and the instructions used are IN, OUT, and Printf for archiving (non-safety-related). Although DOS functions are simple, even simplistic (naturally secure), the management of the addressing is more problematic. Indeed, the "DOS Extender" allows extended addressing through swap and management unknown by memory cells during calls by functions or processing interruption. "Memory gardening" is generally "not good for safety"!

Thus we can summarize the risk for both failure modes:

– the "no-call" or "failure to return" of the functions;

– the undesired modification of data.

The PIPC offers safety barriers against these risks through the control of the integrity of the execution and of the data (section 5.8.4) and through the segregation of resources (section 5.8.5).

5.8.4. *The integrity of execution and of data*

The segregation of memory zones is usually the hardest part of the safety demonstration of architectures.

To further reduce risk (beyond the argument of dissimilarities of DOS-Extenders), the software design of the PIPC incorporates additional constraints:

– a single-task software, interruptible only twice: once to control the resetting of the watchdog, another to control the temporal drift. It also imposes a cyclical behavior of the main application;

– robust programming of the software must be able to detect anomalies on the parameters and data exchanged during function calls;

– the analysis of software safety must identify safety data to protect them against all undesirable modifications (a symptom of "memory gardening") from incorrect processing of the memory cells;

– the software design must establish a "no call" or "no return" mechanism of control of critical functions (robustness of coding and execution signature).

The definition of data safety meets two criteria:

– protection against "memory gardening" of the OS;

– protection from loss of integrity: random memory component defect (bonding or flip bit, etc.).

Risk reduction involves two requirements. The first requirement is intended to address a systematic defect in software execution (possibly covered by tests on the targets), the second responds to a probabilistic approach of the failure mode.

In the latter case, we consider that data are critical if their corruption (glitch) on one of the two channels cannot be detected immediately by the master/slave voting and synchronization mechanism.

The software error effect analysis (SEEA[6] type) verifies the completeness of the dictionary of critical data (a datum is not critical if the spread of a defect on its output value is detectable by the synchronization; no latent effect); the data thus identified are protected by a semantic ensuring their identity (type, functional nature) and the integrity of its value (CRC code). Before each reading use, identity

---

6. SEEA: analysis of the effects of software error (*analyse des effets des erreurs du logiciel*), it is a type of failure mode analysis (AMDE: *analyse des mode de defaillanc*) applied to the software.

and integrity are verified, as well as during each writing, the integrity code is recalculated (this method of protection is similar to that used in coded uniprocessor technology). The set of functional signaling data, which is naturally critical, adds certain data specific to the Safety Kernel.

The "no call" or "no return" of the critical function is treated by the principle of execution signature. The software being cyclical, the scheduling function is predetermined. The PIPC implements a signature of each of the critical functions ensuring the full execution of all calls. The signature is the result of a calculation made during each call. The complexity of the semantics of the signature and its operating procedure reduces the risk of "wrongful correct calculation".

This signature is verified during the master-slave synchronization at the end of each cycle. This signature also ensures dynamic acquisition and processing. The tasks involved in signature execution are mainly:

– acquisition: input readings (so that the passage into each input reading loop is controlled);

– processing the generic application (graphset);

– management of MCCS A/B crossed control and of availability;

– management of synchronization between the master and the slave;

– management of outputs of message and/or "all or nothing" type;

– completeness of self-tests, those executed during each cycle and those executed periodically (distributed over several cycles).

5.8.5. *Segregation of resources of different safety level processes*

Using a cyclic single-task OS does not allow easy management of non-secure functions on the same CPU resource or of external communications with the best reaction time performance.

The segregation of data and program memory is problematic with a single memory address field seen by the CPU (no memory access protection). Moreover, low-level communications media (IP protocol layer and management of communication cells, or other features of non-secure archival) are generally very resource intensive.

The choice of implementation of the PIPC can achieve, at best, a physical segregation of resources by allocating and realizing these processes on annex CPU cards (called "CCIP"). This card is a buffer between the external world, which is asynchronous, and the internal world of the PIPC, which is cyclic and synchronous. It has many serial ports (IP or RS) dedicated to external communication. The exchanges between the CPU and the CCIP are accomplished through a shared memory (DMA) on the CCIP card.

All encapsulation processing of the safety protocols of messages to be emitted externally (according to the CENELEC EN 50159 standard, part 1 and/or 2, see [CEN 01a; CEN 01b]) are performed by the master or slave processing unit.

This card is a "gray channel" for safety messaging. It supports exchanges between master/slave voting/synchronization. These are dated by the CPU cards and of predetermined format.

The CCIP card realizes many non-secure or just SSIL 2 functions not requiring master/slave synchronization and vote.

5.8.6. *Execution cycle and vote and synchronization mechanism*

The voting and synchronization mechanism of the master-slave processing units constitutes the core of the safety demonstration, since it corresponds to a 2oo2 dual processor mechanism.

Each unit calculates and compares its results with those of its counterpart; the principle of mutual vote. If one unit does not agree with the expected results, it autosanctions itself by going into fallback position: it orders the outputs to a restrictive state, interrupts messaging, orders the fall of the watchdog.

On failing to receiving any more synchronization messages, the other unit also commits suicide in the same way.

The master unit maintains the pace of the cycles. Based on a cyclic interruption, it generates a "top synchro" to the other MCCS Master, a "top synchro" delayed by a few milliseconds towards the slave unit.

Both units perform their processing and then mutually compare each other before "allowing time" for self-testing as "background tasks". The duration of a processing task may increase at the expense of time allocated to self-testing. In any event, the cycle time for each unit shall not exceed a terminal securely controlled by a double clock mechanism.

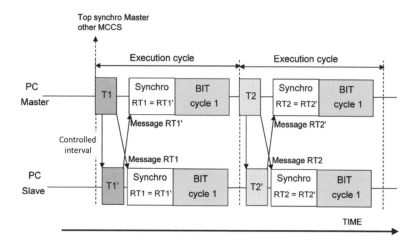

Figure 5.19. *Vote and synchronization mechanism*

From an internal quartz, the TBES card generates a millisecond tick of the clock resulting in an interruption handled with priority by the safe kernel.

This interruption microtask causes increments to a global counter, which is cyclically compared to the theoretical value based on the cycle time generated by the master CPU clock. A drift beyond tolerance is immediately sanctioned.

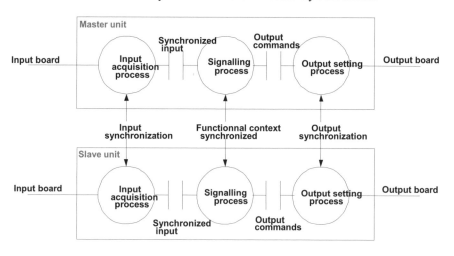

Figure 5.20. *Synchronization and vote sequence*

This time control mechanism allows the control of the overall reaction time of an architecture. These reaction times are generally cumulative as a result of all processing and communication stages, considering worst-case values. The accumulation of worst-case values is associated with a clock drift scenario within the limits of tolerance. Usually, we assume a maximum theoretical drift of 10% of the cycle time.

The master-slave synchronization allows the vote of information at all stages of processing. Thus, the data acquired are mutually compared, then the state variables of functional processing and finally the pile of controlled outputs and messages.

A current output commanded by a unit is the subject of at least three phases of synchronization:

– data input must be identical;

– processing results must be identical;

– the piles of command and output messages must be identical.

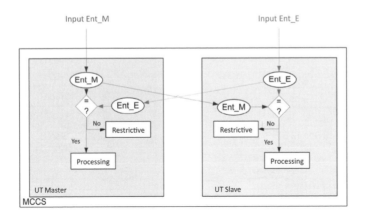

Figure 5.21. *Input vote*

The vote in three steps may seem too rich for some. Note that the computerized interlockings generate a lot of Boolean information which is not very dynamic; there is little change in the controlled outputs during each cycle. If the ordered outputs were voted in isolation, this would not ensure the detection of latent failures in the processes (change of inputs, new processes, and internal state, but no new outputs).

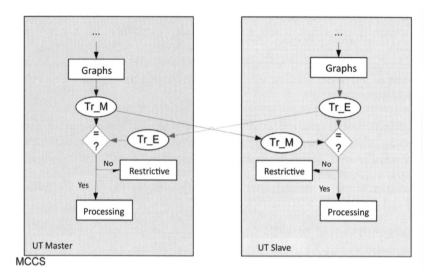

Figure 5.22. *Graph vote*

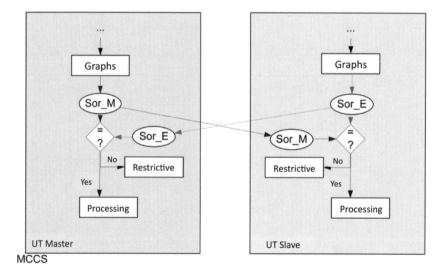

Figure 5.23. *Output vote*

In fact, a railway signaling function generally uses many Boolean inputs to generate a single output. Comparing only these Boolean outputs would not detect all anomalies that may have intervened in the processing (latent or compensatory failure scenario).

The vote of a Boolean abnormally reduces the complexity of the function that generates it. We must therefore create a vote on interim information. This is called the principle of a "tracing algorithm", which retains the complexity level of the original function, and thus, does not reduce the power of the Boolean comparer to a simple game of "chance".

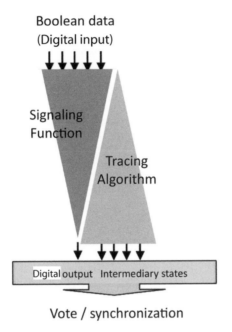

Figure 5.24. *Tracing algorithm*

In the context of the PIPC, the principle of the tracing algorithm results in the voting/synchronization of all graphset transitions of interlocking signaling functions carried out during the cycle. The concept of a tracing algorithm should be brought closer to the protection needs of safety data. Both concepts have the same origin which is a precaution against latent failures.

Thus for the analysis of the software, the SEEA helps "break the output data" of the functions and then propagates them to synchronization. If the broken data result in a change of state that is detected by the vote, then we can say it is part of the tracing, otherwise it must be protected (type and integrity).

5.9. Protection against causes of common failure

The risk of common mode failure is generally due to a natural weakness of 2oo2 architectures. As previously presented, the PIPC certainly implements the best protection imaginable.

Each of these protective mechanisms taken individually may not mathematically 100% guarantee the absence of common mode. In fact, a set of means should be considered, such as "using many belts and suspenders to hold up loose pants"!

5.9.1. *Technological dissimilarities of computers*

The "commercial" CPU cards (of industrial range) are as dissimilar as possible (also known as technological diversification):

– CPU core (i.e. via or AMD on one side and Intel on the other, or two Intel of very different generation): the CPU frequencies are naturally different;

– BIOS: BIOS diversification may remain problematic, but analyzable;

– the makers of Chipsets;

– the makers of RAM modules.

It must also involve the integration of processing units in analyzing common failure modes:

– different PC power supply blocks for each processing unit (of the industrial range);

– temperature monitoring;

– EMC packaging/rack of the processing units.

The dissimilarity of CPU cores is verified with the technical notes of suppliers, but there is no guarantee of their accuracy; we have no way to verify this. Moreover, we do not really know how to measure a dissimilarity; how far should we go?

The dissimilarity of the CPU cores remains an almost subjective "soft argument" for the safety demonstration. Discussions are on-going!

So far, the technical arguments have been in our favor: different makers, different technology; however, in the future, how can we continue to provide this dissimilarity with the monopolies of Intel or AMD?

Fortunately, the flexibility of the software architecture allows us to consider a transfer to a new core in the future.

5.9.2. *Time lag during process execution*

The lag of the master-slave processing cycle is part of the protections of the common mode against an external disturbance (EMC) or electromagnetic pulse (EMI) affecting both computers simultaneously.

With a lag of a few milliseconds, the instructions affected by the disruption will not have the same failure mode and, therefore, different effects on the algorithmic processing and detected by synchronization.

This barrier is difficult to test; however, the concept remains attractive!

5.9.3. *Diversification of the compilers and the executables*

The dissimilarity of compilers is a solution against the common modes for generating an executable.

To test the hypothesis of dissimilarity compilers, we evaluated the executable code generated by both compilers.

The dissimilarity is effective for 80% of cases (different operand and register). In the remaining 20%, C instructions being trivial, compilation naturally gives the same result.

Thus our choice to use different compilers for reasons of lack of qualification of a single C compiler, allows us, to some extent, to ensure a relatively diversified machine code.

However, the complexity of the recent internal CPU architectures does not allow us to provide different execution paths for the two executables on the same target CPU core. For this reason, we prefer the dissimilarity of CPU cores.

5.9.4. *Antivalent acquisitions and outputs*

Digital acquisition information is antivalent, as well as the control of digital outputs.

Each half-card performs the same processing, but the electrical information is complemented. This creates a certain dissimilarity in the digital processing carried out on the cards, thus reducing the risk of activation in homologous effect mode between the two half-cards (which are identical in composition); diversification of the process on a similar architecture.

5.9.5. *Galvanic isolation*

Galvanic isolation between units ensures a reciprocal immunity *vis-à-vis* power supply disruptions; the only existing connections are basic Ethernet links isolated at 1,500 Vac.

	Master unit	Slave unit	Track equipment	Mass
Master unit	-	500 Vac	2,000 Vac	500 Vac
Slave unit		-	2,000 Vac	500 Vac
Line equipment: power supply relay signaling				2,000 Vac

Mechanisms and filters and fuses at the cable passage level in the station building provide some protection against lightning hitting the wire along the path. However, a residual transient can always reach the safety equipment in the post.

Insulation usually required in the railway environment is of at least 2,000 Vac. Beyond that, the secure behavior of the architecture is not assured.

5.10. Probabilistic modeling

5.10.1. *Objective and hypothesis*

The objective of probabilistic modeling is to evaluate the performance of the architecture *vis-à-vis* an hourly unsecure behavioral rate (contrary to safety). The rate objective of the PIPC solution is 10^{-11}/hour.

As there are multiple methods of probabilistic safety demonstration, we have selected one that highlights the depth of the architecture and the temporal behavior.

Markov stochastic models allow us to have a representative modeling of the safety mechanisms.

Thus, when a failure occurs in an element of the MCCS, two cases may arise:

– the failure is detected by inter-unit synchronization: maximum safety is ensured beyond the duration of a nominal execution cycle *Tsynchro* (the system goes into fallback position). The detection usually occurs within the dual processing unit due to its synchronous nature;

– the failure is detected by the self-tests: maximum safety is ensured beyond the duration of a cycle of self-tests *Tselftests*. The detection usually occurs within the processing unit by nature of the implemented self-test.

These two means of detection do not cover the same types of failures. Self-tests concern hardware failures relative to each processing unit (program memory, data memory (graphs and parameters), backreading of output contacts, safety variables, 1 millisecond interruption, watchdog) while the dephased execution synchrony corresponds to a test of consistency of the operating environment and of the data between the two processing units (outputs to be ordered, state change of field input, crossed transitions of the graphs, messages received).

5.10.2. *Global model*

The generic model is a translation of the behavioral representation of the system.

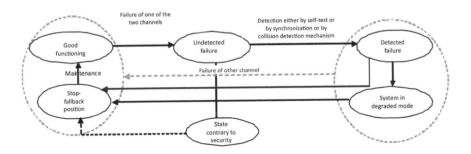

Figure 5.25. *Representation of the behavior of the system*

The state of good working order is a secure system state. The state "undetected failure" is the state where one of the two channels has a latent undetected failure. The failure may be detected by three different mechanisms. Depending on the sub-system, the detection means vary. After the failure is detected, the action phase seeks to remedy the failure. Depending on the sub-system and the type of failure, the sub-system is put into a degraded state or a fallback state. The unsecure state is a state in which the two channels each have an undetected failure.

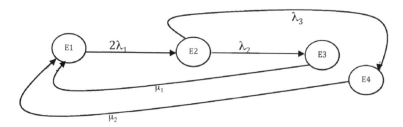

Figure 5.26. *Generic model*

The model of a generic Markov chain is given in Figure 5.26 and has four states:

– state E1 represents a secure system state (state of good working order; in some cases this may represent two states considered secure: a state of good working order and a system in fallback state);

– state E2 is a state of undetected failure (failure on one of the two channels);

– state E3 represents a state of detected failure (corresponds indirectly to the degraded or fallback state depending on the system);

– state E4 is a unsecure state (or an undesired state).

The transition rates are the values of transition from one system state to another:

– λ_1: hourly rate (failure rate) of transition from good working order of an undetected failure (that is to say: failure rate of a channel);

– λ_2: hourly rate describing a failure detected either by self-test, synchronization or a mechanism of collision detection;

– λ_3: hourly rate (failure rate) where the remaining channel also fails. The system is then in a state contrary to safety;

– μ_1: hourly rate of transition of a detected failure to a secure state, either by reparation in the case of a permanent failure or reset in the case of a fleeting failure;

– μ_2: hourly rate of transition of the state contrary to the safety, to a secure state (E1), either by reparation in the case of a permanent failure or reset in the case of a fleeting failure.

The MCCS elements follow an exponential probability law, that is to say that each element i has a failure rate λ_i, the probability of failure of the element i is: $p(t) = 1 - e^{-\lambda_i t}$.

To assess the probability of the system being in a state of good working order E_i (knowing that $i \in \{1,2,3\}$), this amounts to studying the Markov chain in a symptotic regime (permanent regime).

Therefore, the probability of being in a state of good working order (E1, E2, or E3) is given by:

$$P_1 = \frac{\lambda_3 + \lambda_2}{2\lambda_1} P_2$$

$$P_2 = \frac{1}{\frac{(\lambda_3 + \lambda_2)}{2\lambda_1} + 1 + \frac{\lambda_2}{\mu_1} + \frac{\lambda_3}{\mu_2}}$$

$$P_3 = \frac{\lambda_2}{\mu_1} P_2$$

The safety study comes down to rendering the "unsecure state (E4)" absorbent (return of E4 to deleted E1 - µ2). The failure rate of the generic model representing the reliability of the system is equal to:

$$\lambda = \frac{2\lambda_1\lambda_3}{(\lambda_3 + \lambda_2)}$$

This equation expresses the system's failure rate of going from a secure state to a state contrary to its safety.

The literal expression of the failure rate values remains complex and is subject to specific analysis that are not disclosed in this document.

5.10.3. *"Simplistic" quantitative evaluation*

Another approach is to assess the failure rate of a "worst case" system, by modeling the complete system by a "simple" Markov graph.

When a failure occurs on a particular element of an MCCS, two means of detection exist:

– the failure is detected by the inter-unit synchronization ($T_{synchro}$): the system goes into fallback position, through the dual unit (loss of synchronization), after a maximum of two processing cycles (200 milliseconds for the MEI);

– the failure is detected by the self-test $T_{self-test}$: the system goes into fallback position on detection of the defect (failing unit orders fallback). The self-test cycle is performed every 2.5 seconds.

The worst case of failure detection is a failure detected at the end of a self-test cycle. Therefore, the rate of passage from a state of failure of one of the two units in good working order is equal to:

$$\lambda_{self-test} = \frac{P_{self-test}}{T_{self-test}}$$

$P_{self-test}$ represents the probability of detecting a failure by self-test (coverage rate). The probability of detection by synchronization is $(1-P_{self-test})$. The nominal time between two self-tests is of a few seconds.

The time between two self-tests of the local watchdog (several minutes) is not retained as a pessimistic value of the duration between two self-tests. Indeed, the probability of not detecting a failure on the local watchdog is considered low compared to the safety objective.

The operation of the system can be modeled by three states:

– state E1 represents the good working order of the system (master and slave channel in nominal operation – secure state);

– state E2 represents the failure state of one of the two units (master or slave failure);

– state E3 represents the failure state of both master and slave channels, that is to say a failure contrary to safety.

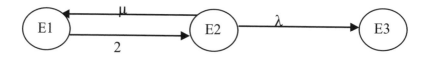

Figure 5.27. *Markov chain of the system (modeling the reliability) – worst case*

When the system is in a secure condition (E1), the master and slave channels are in their nominal operating conditions.

The transition rates (failure rate) of state E1 to E2 reflects the possibility that either the master *or* the slave unit is defective. The transition from state E2 to E3 expresses the failure rate of the remaining unit, i.e. that both the master *and* slave units are down.

The transition from state E2 to E1 reflects the possibility that the failure of the master unit (or slave unit) was detected by a self-test (worst case).

In order to resolve the Markov chain of the system, we used the state sequencing method, we have:

$\lambda = \lambda_{master} = \lambda_{slave}$.

The failure rate of the system (state sequencing method) is expressed by:

$$\Lambda = \frac{2\lambda^2}{\mu + \lambda} \, .$$

This equation reflects the failure rate of a system passing from a secure state (E1) to a state contrary to safety (E3).

$\lambda = 4.47 \times 10^{-4}$/hour (failure rate of a dual channel, considering the system is managing 300 objects, only one processing channel is considered):

$\mu = (P_{selftest}/2.5 \text{ s})$.

$P_{self-test} = 80\%$: given the different self-tests performed, and the synchronized data, the rate is assessed by expert opinion at 80%. Indeed, it is estimated that no failure remains undetected by self-testing or synchronization. Any failure results either in detection of inconsistency in the synchronization, or in detection of malfunction in the execution of self-tests, leading in both cases to a fallback position.

The failure rate obtained is: $\Lambda = 3.5 \times 10^{-10}$/hour.

The curve in Figure 5.28 shows the evolution of the probability of being in a situation contrary to safety with regards to the coverage rate. This curve shows that the objective is met with a coverage rate below 40%.

The safety objective is respected in the "worst case" conditions:

– detection of all failures by self-tests (detection by synchronization in conjunction with that for self-testing);

– maximum duration of self-tests including cycle time drifts;

– failure rate of equipment allowing for the management of 300 objects to the track.

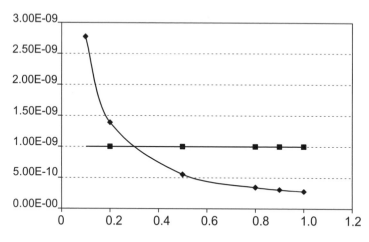

Figure 5.28. *Evolution of probability*

5.11. Summary of safety concepts

In conclusion, the safety analysis of the architecture allowed us to formalize the safety concepts of the PIPC, which are:

– concept 1: 2oo2 architecture;

– concept 2: protection against common modes;

– concept 3: self-tests;

– concept 4: watchdog;

– concept 5: protection of safety-related data.

5.11.1. *Concept 1: 2oo2 architecture*

One of the concepts ensuring the desired safety level is based on a 2oo2 architecture. Two independent processing channels acquire input data and process them. The result of the acquisition of inputs, of the processing of the inputs and of the actions retained following this process must be mutually compared. This comparison is called synchronization. The actions retained following the input process are only effective if both processing channels are agreed.

This concept allows for the following safety principles:

– C1_P1: synchronization of digital inputs: digital inputs acquired are mutually compared between each dual unit and put into restrictive state by the input unit in case of inconsistency on the state of this input between the two processing channels;

– C1_P2: synchronization of messages coming in through the external link: all incoming messages are mutually compared between the dual units. On divergence or absence of a message on a channel, the MCCS ignores the message;

– C1_P3: graph of crossed transition synchronization: all crossed transitions graphs done over a cycle are compared. On divergence between the two channels, the MCCS goes into fallback position;

– C1_P4: synchronization of request for commands of field output: the command requests of field output over a cycle are compared. On divergence between the two channels, the MCCS goes into fallback position;

– C1_P5: vote of the messages going out through external links: the outgoing messages are voted by the dual units;

– C1_P6: crossed backreading of the output state: after ordering a local output, each channel connects the state of the local output and also the state of the output of the associated dual channel. On divergence between the two channels, the MCCS goes into fallback position;

– C1_P7: double development of outputs: each channel commands a local output that is wired in ET logic with the local output of the associated dual channel. A field command may be in a permissive state only if both channels have ordered their local output in a permissive state.

5.11.2. *Concept 2: protection against common modes*

For concept 1 to be effective, it is necessary to guard against common causes. For this, the MCCS has a diversification, between the two channels of dual processing, the principles being the following:

– C2_P1: complement to field inputs: the acquisition of field input is complemented between the two dual channels (complement done on the slave unit);

– C2_P2: complemented backreading of field output: backreading of local output is made in addition to the direct local output and is complemented for local outputs of the dual channel. On divergence between the value read and ordered, the MCCS goes into fallback position;

– C2_P3: temporal lag: the processes performed on the dual channels are temporarily dephased in every cycle;

– C2_P4: hardware dissimilarity: microprocessors and frequency rhythm of the microprocessors of the dual channel processing units are diverse;

– C2_P5: software dissimilarity: compilers and link editors used for the generation of executable software are created by different publishers.

In addition, galvanic isolation is maintained between the master and slave units:

– C2_P6: galvanic isolation between the dual channels at the inputs and outputs level (I/O of the master unit galvanically isolated from I/O of the slave unit);

– C2_P7: different power supply between the dual channels.

5.11.3. *Concept 3: self-tests*

To detect possible latent failures, self-tests are implemented in each processing unit. Such tests implement the following principles:

– C3_P1: periodic self-test: process allowing full execution of each main software task (for example, acquisition of inputs, processing graphs, positioning of output, etc.) in order to ensure that processes are fully carried out (control by a digital signature);

– C3_P2: periodic self-test: control of clock drift by comparison with a secondary clock based on a different crystal;

– C3_P3: periodic self-test: test to zero on each digital input after acquisition and before any processing of acquired states;

– C3_P4: periodic self-test of the integrity of residual safety data;

– C3_P5: periodic self-test of the integrity of the executable;

– C3_P6: periodic self-test: each channel connects the state of its local output and also the state of the local outputs of the dual channel. On divergence between the two channels, the MCCS goes into fallback position;

– C3_P7: periodic self-test of the watchdog of each processing unit.

5.11.4. *Concept 4: watchdog*

The safety architecture is also ensured by an external watchdog controlled by the two watchdogs of the dual processing units. The fall of the watchdog causes the fall of the field watchdog. This watchdog protects against the diversion of the software and stops the MCCS upon detection of a defect:

– C4_P1: fall of the watchdog: the fall of the field watchdog causes the power cut of the processing units and of the MIRET racks, but cuts the 24 V "field output post". The fall of the field watchdog puts the MCCS in a restrictive state;

– C4_P2: watchdog: during normal operation, the software asks to periodically reset the local watchdog. During software diversion after a failure, the local watchdog is not reset causing the opening of the field watchdog relay (fall of field watchdog);

– C4_P3: detection of a defect: on detection of a defect, the software can force the opening of the local watchdog relay to bring down the field watchdog relay.

5.11.5. *Concept 5: protection of safety-related data*

The protection of safety-related data is achieved at different levels:

– C5_P1: protection of residual safety data (integrity and dynamism). The data are checked before modification or use;

– C5_P2: protection of settings (integrity of graphs and parameters).

5.12. Conclusion

The robustness and efficiency of the safety concepts of the PIPC have been proven. These concepts have been the subject of numerous external evaluations either by railway authorities or by technical experts assessing safety or by university laboratories. None could reasonably find a flaw.

It was the first signaling safety computer "made in France" put in service at the SNCF in 1995 then at the RATP in 2005 (see [GAL 08] which presents an overview of the safety demonstration conducted as part of the commissioning of the PMI line 3 bis of the Parisian underground system).

Of course, the execution methods of these concepts have many subtleties that remain in the domain of industrial confidentiality.

Beyond the simple architecture of this "coffee machine", the strength of the PIPC lies in the principles of design and execution of signaling functions and tools for generating signaling functions and implementation of their settings.

The signaling functions are carried out by graphs (with proprietary semantics between the grafcet and the Petri networks). They are executed in the targeted PIPC by a motor providing a deterministic and factual behavior. This minimizes the computational load of the processing units (only a subset of Boolean equations is recalculated at each cycle depending on external events). To this is added the process of validation by a formal method of the signaling safety properties, demonstrating that PIPC is certainly one of the "machines" making the "best coffee".

5.13. Bibliography

[CEN 00] CENELEC, NF EN 50126, Railway applications. The specification and demonstration of reliability, availability, maintainability and safety (RAMS), January 2000.

[CEN 01a] CENELEC, NF EN 50128, Railway applications – communications, signalling and processing systems - software for railway control and protection systems, July 2001.

[CEN 01] CENELEC, EN 50159-1, Railway applications – communication, signalling, and processing systems. Part 1: safety-related communication in closed transmission systems, March 2001.

[CEN 01c] CENELEC, EN 50159-2, European standard, railway applications – communication, signalling and processing systems. Part 2: safety-related communication in open transmission systems, March 2001.

[CEN 02] CENELEC, NF EN 50205, Relays with forcibly guided (mechanically linked) contacts, May 2002.

[CEN 03] CENELEC, NF EN 50129, European standard, railway applications – communication, signalling and processing systems – safety-related communication in transmission systems, 2003.

[COM 06] EUROPEAN COMMISSION, ERTMS – Delivering flexible and reliable rail traffic, 2006.

[GAL 08] GALLARDO M., BOULANGER J.L., "Post de manœuvre à enclenchement informatique: démonstration de la sécurité", *CIFA, Conférence Internationale Francophone d'Automatique*, Bucarest, Romania, November 2008.

[VIL 88] VILLEMEUR A., *Sûreté de fonctionnement des systèmes* industriels, Eyrolles, Paris, 1988.

Chapter 6

Dependable Avionics Architectures: Example of a Fly-by-Wire system

6.1. Introduction

Aircraft systems support a wide range of functions. A set of functions is related to the conduct of flight and propulsion: everything that connects the pilot to the control surfaces, brakes, propulsion. These functions are supported by computers, sensors, but also power actuators. Other functions are related to flight management, navigation, ground/flight communication, all that can present information to the crew. These functions involve several very different technologies (radiofrequency, display, etc.). The level of criticality of these systems is close to that of flight control systems. The functions related to the cabin and cargo are generally less critical. In practice, they include functions with minimal safety impact, but whose unavailability is strongly felt by the passengers, and functions, such as pressurization or control of the doors, that are critical. All these systems are supported by systems of production and distribution of energy or by means of communication that are common resources and whose criticality is that of supported systems, taking into account the fact that these are common to several functions.

The flight controls have the advantage and burden of having all kinds of constraints: safety, availability, reliability (see Figure 6.1). The description of those of the Airbus aircraft will address the various threats against dependability in the

Chapter written by Pascal TRAVERSE, Christine BEZARD, Jean-Michel CAMUS, Isabelle LACAZE, Hervé LEBERRE, Patrick RINGEARD and Jean SOUYRIS.

field of avionics and associated issues. An overview of the architectures of other aircraft will have many similarities, as they are induced by very similar regulatory constraints.

Figure 6.1. *Safety, availability and reliability triptych*

6.1.1. *Background and statutory obligation*

Safety is the top priority in aviation for the obvious reason that it involves human lives. This concern appears in many aspects, like the mindset of people, the company charter, or current regulations. Almost everything is regulated in aviation, management of airspace, the age of the captain, processing of problems encountered in service, among others. We will focus on the regulation relating to embedded systems on board civil transport aircraft.

First, it is worth noting the high level of standardization between countries. Boeing and Airbus are designed on the basis of the same regulation. This body is evolving. Essentially, it takes into account technological developments and the unfortunate events that occur, in order to prevent their reoccurrence. Compliance of an aircraft to that regulation is demonstrated by the manufacturer and verified by organizations authorized by countries, the "official services": the EASA in Europe, the FAA in the United States, and others.

The starting document [FAR/CS 25] expresses the requirements and a first level of interpretation. Added to this is a set of regulatory documents produced by various bodies (EUROCAE, ARINC, SAE, and others) that provide the necessary logistics for working groups, bringing together official agencies, industry, and sometimes, other organizations, such as pilot unions. For the record, the first of these working groups was international and met in Paris in 1910.

A major objective of the regulation (expressed in paragraph 25.1309 of the [FAR/CS 25]) is that a "catastrophic" event must be "extremely improbable". A first level of interpretation is given by that same regulation: a catastrophic event is a "Failure Condition which would result in multiple fatalities, usually with the loss of the airplane". This is partly explained for example, if the available roll rate is higher than $3°$/second, then the situation is not catastrophic; if the aircraft is below the threshold, the criticality is evaluated by pilots and accepted, or not, by official services.

An interpretation of "extreme improbability" is also given. First, by a "magic" number: 10^{-9}. This is a probability of failure averaged per hour of flight.

This quantitative approach is entirely valid for designing the architecture of a system, a level of redundancy and monitoring. Such reasoning is based on the multiplication of elementary probabilities, and thus on an assumption of independence between components. This independence must be verified, mainly by a qualitative judgment. Also, a safeguard is associated with this probability calculation: a simple failure (one), regardless of the probability of its occurrence, must not lead to catastrophic consequences.

This whole process of safety analysis is regulated by the ARP 4761. Identification of safety objectives is given by a functional approach, documented in a functional hazard analysis; demonstrating compliance with these objectives is achieved by identifying the combinations of failures, and this is documented in the System Safety Assessment (SSA).

A set of "common causes of failures", i.e. "specific risks", also need to be covered. These are events, such as a localized fire or explosion of a turbine, to which it is difficult to assign a probability. Such an event could be a single event capable of affecting several components, thus putting into question the independence assumption made by the SSA, when failures are combined. All these risks are extensively analyzed and tested. In addition, the final aircraft is inspected by experts to ensure that the installation rules have been followed, to verify whether the rules of separation between components expressed by the designers are well respected, and to identify whether any additional risks are likely to occur. All this is largely governed by the ARP 4761.

Design errors are covered by other practices, recommended in the ARP 4754 for the design of complex systems (all components such as flight controls), the DO178 for the software design and the DO254 for complex hardware components. It should be added that the DO160 defines the means of demonstrating the resistance of equipment to its environment: test conditions in temperature, vibration, etc.

The DO178 inspired the ARP 4754 and DO254. Essentially, this is a classic approach of process assurance: planning development activities (design, validation and verification, configuration management, as well as safety) to a certain quality standard and demonstrating that the process and the product meet the requirements stated in these documents.

6.1.2. *History*

Before fly-by-wire, the crew controls were transmitted mechanically to the control surface actuators (see Figure 6.1). Some computers were already present for the autopilot and increased stability functions.

The first electrical flight-control system (Fly-by-Wire: FBW) for civilian aircraft was designed by Aérospatiale and installed on Concorde. It was a full authority analog system for all control surfaces, surface position being the sum of the pilot controllers position and of some stabilization orders. A mechanical backup system was available on all three axes.

The first generation of digital FBW systems emerged in the early 1980s on several civil aircraft, including the Airbus A310. These systems commanded the slats, flaps, and spoilers. These systems are subject to very strict safety requirements (in the sense that the inadvertent movement of the control surfaces is generally classified as "catastrophic" and, therefore, should remain "extremely improbable"). However, loss of function is allowed, the only consequence being a tolerable increase in the crew's workload.

The Airbus A320 was certified and put into service in the first quarter of 1988. It is the first example of a second-generation FBW civilian aircraft, which now forms part of a real family (A318, A319, A320, A321, A330, A340 and A380). The striking feature of these devices is that the pilot sets objectives and not directly a control surface position, the electrical transmission (see Figure 6.2) replaces the mechanical transmission, control columns are replaced by side-sticks and the system is designed to be available in all circumstances.

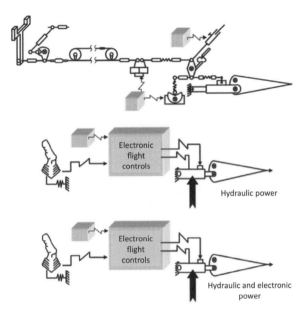

Figure 6.2. *History of flight controls*

This aircraft family has accumulated a vast and rich experience in service, with over 4,000 aircraft in operation and more than 80 million hours flown. However, the system architecture is constantly challenged to take advantage of technological advances and service experience. It is a fact that the A340-600 constitutes a major evolution compared with the A340 [BRI 93], and the A380, A350 and A400M even more so.

The A340-600 is the first significant evolution from the A320/A330/A340 standard. It entered service in mid-2002, by introducing a structural mode control, a 100% electrical rudder control, and integration of the inner loop autopilot to manual control laws. The 100% electrical rudder is now part of the definition of all A330 and A340.

The A380 is the first aircraft in use (since late 2007) to have electrically actuated control surfaces (Power-by-Wire concept, see Figure 6.3), as do the Airbus A400M and A350. In addition, new avionics principles are applied together with a fully integrated autopilot and manual control [TRA 04].

Other architectures are possible [IFI 04]. The family of architectures we have designed has the merit of having been developed step by step, in light of our experience in operation and development.

6.1.3. *Fly-by-wire principles*

On a conventional aircraft, the pilot commands are transmitted to the actuators by a set of mechanical elements. In addition, computers change the pilots feel on the commands and the autopilot computers are able to control the servomechanisms moving the entire chain of mechanical control (see Figure 6.2).

Since the discontinuation of the A300 and A310 in 2007, all Airbuses have fly-by-wire systems, all with electronically controlled surfaces, hydraulically or electrically operated.

The side-sticks are used to operate the aircraft. The pilot inputs are interpreted by the computers that cause the movement of the surfaces (through actuators) in order to get the desired flight trajectory modifications. When the autopilot is engaged, the flight-control computers take their orders from the autopilot computers. Under this aspect, the flight controls consist of five to seven computers and the autopilot of two.

Very briefly, a flight-control system supports four main functions:

– acquisition and monitoring of crew requests, through bodies such as the side-sticks and associated sensors;

– acquisition and monitoring of aircraft response;

– piloting the aircraft, via control laws that move the aircraft so that it achieves the objectives set by the crew;

– control of actuators, so that the control surfaces position appropriately changes the aircraft position.

6.1.4. *Failures and dependability*

FBW systems are built according to very strict requirements of dependability both in terms of safety (the system must not produce erroneous output signals) and availability. Most of these requirements come directly from official services (FAA, EASA, etc. [FAR/CS 25]).

The rest of the article is structured around the threats to safety and system availability, namely [AVI 01]:

– breakdowns due to physical failures, such as short-circuit or mechanical breakdown;

– errors in design and production;

– specific risks, such as engine explosion;

– human-machine interface problems.

It is interesting to note that the defenses against such threats are a useful protection against malicious attacks, in addition to more traditional measures.

For each threat, we find a summary of the applicable airworthiness requirements and a description of methods used on FBW Airbus, as well as the challenges and future trends.

6.2. System breakdowns due to physical failures

FAR/CS 25.1309 requires the demonstration that any combination of failures with catastrophic consequences is extremely improbable. "Extremely improbable" is translated into quality requirements (see sections 6.3 to 6.5, [TRA 08]) and by a 10^{-9} probability per hour of flight.

Particularly regarding the flight controls, paragraph 25.671 of [FAR 25] demands that a single failure or the combination of a single failure with a hidden failure (unless there be very strict maintenance requirements for this failure) or control surface or pilot command jamming do not have catastrophic consequences. This qualitative requirement is in addition to the estimated probability and is sometimes more stringent.

To address the problem of safety (the system should not produce an erroneous signal), the basic element is the command (COM) and monitoring (MON) failsafe computer. These computers are subjected to draconian safety requirements and are functionally composed of a command channel and a monitoring channel.

To ensure a sufficient level of availability, the system incorporates a high level of redundancy.

6.2.1. *Command and monitoring computers*

6.2.1.1. *Computer architecture*

Functionally, the computers have a command channel and a monitoring channel. The command channel ensures the function allocated to the computer (for example, command of a control surface). The monitoring channel ensures the proper functioning of the command channel [GOU 07]. This type of computer has already been used for the autopilot computers of the Concorde and Airbus (see Figure 6.3).

These computers can be considered as two different and independent computers placed side by side (either together in the same box or in two different boxes, this being the case of the PRIM A380/A400M). These two (sub) computers have different functions and software, and are placed close to each other only to facilitate maintenance. Both command and monitoring channels of a computer are simultaneously active or pending the move from a stand-by state to an active state. In stand-by mode, the computers are powered so as to activate potential dormant failures and isolate them. The monitoring process also affects the associated actuator: when deselecting the command order, the solenoid valve of the actuator is disabled and goes into stand-by mode (see Figure 6.4).

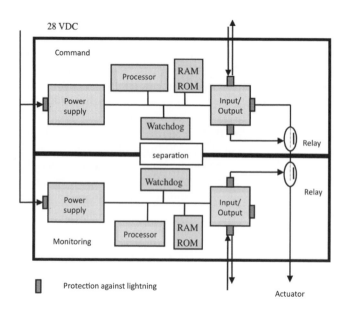

Figure 6.3. *Command and monitoring computer*

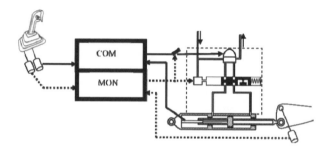

Figure 6.4. *Monitoring principle*

Two types of computers are used in the A320 FBW system: the ELAC (ELevator and Aileron Computers) and the SEC (Spoiler and Elevator Computers). Each computer includes a command channel and a monitoring channel. Thus, four different entities coexist: ELAC command channel, ELAC monitoring channel, SEC command channel, and SEC monitoring channel. This leads to four different types of software.

Two types of computers are also used on the other FBW Airbus, under a different name: they are the PRIM (primary computers) and SEC (secondary computers). Although these computers are different, the basic safety principles are similar and described below.

In addition to the ELAC and SEC of the A320, two computers are used for rudder control (FAC). They are not redundant in relation to the ELACs and SECs. On the other Airbus, the rudder control functions are integrated in the PRIMs and SECs.

6.2.1.2. *Channel architecture*

Each channel (command or monitoring) includes one or more processors, associated memories, input/output circuitry, power supply and specific software. When the results of one of these two channels diverge significantly, the channel(s) that detected the failure cuts the connection between the computer and the outside. The system is designed so that the computer outputs are in a safe state (signal interrupt via the relay). The failure detection is mainly achieved by comparing the difference between the command and monitoring orders with regards to a given threshold. This scheme allows the detection of the consequences of a computer component failure and prevents the spread of the resultant error outside of the computer. This detection method is supplemented by monitoring the correct execution of the program (sequencing) and the encoding of memories.

Flight control computers must be particularly robust. They are protected against overvoltage, under-voltage, electromagnetic attacks, the indirect effects of lightning, various vibrations, shocks, etc. The computers are cooled by a ventilation system, but can operate correctly even in case of loss of ventilation.

6.2.1.3. *Redundancy*

The redundancy aspect is managed at the system level. This section addresses only the constraints of the computer rendering system reconfiguration possible. The system functions are divided among all the computers so that each is constantly active on at least a subset of its functions. For a given function, a computer is active, others are on stand-by (hot spares). As soon as the active computer interrupts its functioning, one of the computers in stand-by passes almost instantly into active mode without jolting, or with a small jolt to the control surfaces. These computers are designed to continuously transmit a signal of good health, and when a failure is detected, the signal is discontinued at the same time as the "functional" outputs (to an actuator, for example).

6.2.1.4. *Failure detection*

Certain failures may remain hidden long after their creation. Therefore, a monitoring channel failure highlighted when the monitored channel itself breaks down is a typical case that should be avoided. Tests are made periodically so that the probability of occurrence of an adverse event remains low enough (i.e. in order to meet the quantitative requirements of FAR/CS 25.1309). Generally, a computer performs self-tests and tests its peripherals when powering up the aircraft or during each flight, and therefore, at least once a day.

6.2.2. *Component redundancy*

6.2.2.1. *Power sources*

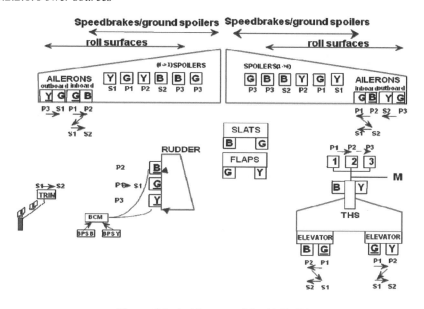

Figure 6.5. *Architecture of the A340-600*

The primary power comes from the engine for pressurizing the hydraulic circuits and electrical generation. An auxiliary generator, batteries, and the Ram Air Turbine (RAT) are also available. If all engines stop, this type of wind turbine (RAT) is deployed automatically. It provides pressurization of a hydraulic circuit, which leads to a third electric generator. The computers are connected to at least two sources of electrical energy. The aircraft has three hydraulic circuits (identified by color, green, blue and yellow for the A340-600, see Figure 6.5), one of which is sufficient to control the aircraft.

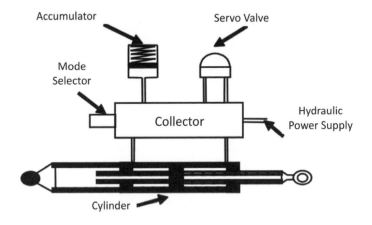

Figure 6.6. *Servo command with hydraulic power*

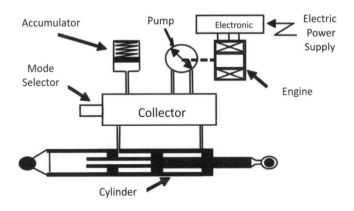

Figure 6.7. *Actuator with electric power*

This is done on the A380, A350, and A400M. The three hydraulic sources are replaced by four circuits, two hydraulic and two electric (see Figure 6.8). The wind turbine (RAT) provides electric power directly. This leads to gains in both weight and cost, as well as increased redundancy and survivability, which was the main reason for introducing this technology.

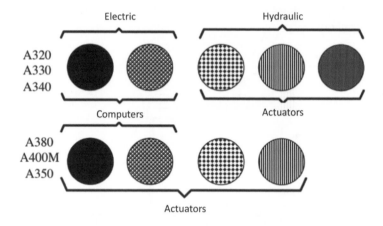

Figure 6.8. *Diversified power architecture*

6.2.2.2. *Computers*

Computers and actuators are also redundant. This is illustrated by a typical control architecture (see Figure 6.9).

Four command and monitoring computers are used, one being sufficient to control the aircraft. In normal operation, one of the computers (PRIM1) provides control of the surface, with a servo command pressurized by the green circuit for example. The other computers control the other control surfaces. If PRIM1 or one of the actuators that it controls fails, PRIM2 picks up the relay (with the servo command pressurized by the blue circuit for example). Following the same type of failure, PRIM2 can pass on the task to SEC1, and then eventually SEC2. It is noteworthy that three computers would be sufficient to meet safety requirements. The additional computer is fully justified by operational constraints: it is desirable to be able to tolerate takeoff with a computer failure. This defines the Minimum Equipment List (MEL).

In addition to ensuring a certain level of availability through redundancy, the system is capable of self-diagnosis. The electrical flight control system uses sensors throughout the aircraft and inside the actuators due to safety constraints. This results in a rapid detection of most system failures with an accurate diagnosis. Consequently, hundreds of specific maintenance messages are available to target the replaceable element concerned. Assistance to the sequence of control operations to be performed is also available on a dedicated screen.

All this helps, in case of failure, to aid decision-making by the crew before takeoff (in case of takeoff under MEL) or during flight or by the maintenance team in other cases.

Figure 6.9. *Control surface command type*

6.2.2.3. *Reconfiguration of control laws and flight envelope protections*

It is noteworthy that the laws are robust due to their design incorporating a sufficient margin of stability [DUP 04; FAR 89; FAV 94; KUB 95; LAV 05; LIV 95]. In addition, if the input vector of the system is largely outside the certified maximum flight envelope, only a simple law, using the position of the controller and of the control surfaces, is enabled (this law is similar to the type of command available on a conventional aircraft).

Laws must be reconfigured in case of loss of some sensors (especially the ADIRU). The crew is made clearly aware of the status of the control law. If the three ADIRU are available (normal case), the pilot has full authority within a safe flight envelope. This flight envelope is provided by the protections built into the control laws, by adding levels of protection to the pilot orders. The flight mode is then in a load factor mode.

If only one ADIRU is available, it is partly monitored by comparison with other independent sources of information (in particular, rate-gyro or accelerometer). In this case, the safety of the flight envelope is provided by alarms, as in conventional aircraft. The pilot is still in load factor mode. In case of loss of all ADIRU, the protections of the flight envelope are also lost, and the control law finds itself in degraded mode: direct mode. This law has gains, which depend on the aircraft configuration (the position of the slats and flaps), and allows piloting similar to that of a conventional aircraft.

6.2.3. *Alternatives*

6.2.3.1. *Computer architecture*

The more or less "intelligent" use of actuators, and therefore, of a digital network between them and the computers, is a strong alternative architecture. Boeing made a move in that direction starting with the B777. The heart of the debate is the "actuator control" function.

This function can be:

– in the same computer as the "aircraft control function"; this was the Airbus approach until A380/A400M;

– in a separate computer, as in the B777/B787;

– associated to the actuator itself, as in the A350.

A first element of decision is the level of complexity. In terms of redundancy, the basic Airbus architecture is simple. Whatever the failure (computer or actuator), the whole channel is disconnected. Separately inhibiting the resources intrinsically offers more availability, but is somewhat more complicated to manage. One advantage of separating the two functions is to place them closer to the interfaces. This is evident for the control of the actuators; the control of the aircraft depends mainly on the pilot controllers (side-sticks) and aircraft sensors that are usually under the cockpit. Placing this function at the front reduces the overall volume of wiring. Closely controlling the actuator generally reduces the volume of cables and primarily avoids intrusion into the low impedance fuselage bonds, which are sensitive to the electromagnetic environment. This is not a concern with a metal fuselage, but it is a strong constraint with composite fuselages, such as in the B787 and A350. The A350 will have an electrical control near the actuator. Communication with the main computers will use "1553" buses, not a very innovative technology, but a robust one.

In the Airbus architecture, only the "acquisition of aircraft movement" function is of the "voter" type; the other three are of the "doubled/monitored" type (command and monitoring). The B777/B787 mainly use the voter. The key of the debate is the design of the control surface. Voting with actuators means having them continuously active; if one of the actuators inadvertently moves, it is countered by the other two. Important mechanical efforts are therefore made on the control surface. On an

Airbus, only one actuator is active, the other is on hold and generates almost no effort. If the active actuator inadvertently moves, the monitoring channel must detect it and quickly make it passive. However, the control surface does not have to endure antagonistic efforts (force fighting). Either a particularly resistant and therefore heavy control surface structure is deployed or the complexity of monitoring is increased. Each manufacturer has made a choice. This being done, the "aircraft control function" follows quite naturally. What is remarkable about this debate is that the decision is not made on computer considerations or compared reliability of architectures, but rather of the final controlled object.

6.2.3.2. *Actuator architecture*

Electric power actuators are likely to evolve. The actuators used on Airbus use a hydraulic power transmission (internal to the actuator), between an electric motor and the cylinder (see Figure 6.7). Mechanical internal direct transmission is another option. Boeing uses it on some spoilers on the B787, in a not very critical function. Indeed, certain modes of failure (mechanical blocks) seem more likely than with an internal hydraulic transmission; therefore, this technology should be used with caution, although it is promising in terms of cost and weight [TOD 10].

A major change could occur with the emergence of fuel cells. Currently, all electrical and hydraulic power is taken from the engines, or from a backup generator (which uses jet fuel) or a wind turbine (RAT). A fuel cell could advantageously replace the wind turbine and the auxiliary generator. The expected benefit is directly in the weight of the aircraft, but also in a reduction of air pollution at the airport and noise when the aircraft is stationary.

6.2.3.3. *Integrated modular avionics*

Since the A380, the concept of integrated modular avionics has appeared. This concept reduces development costs for the manufacturer and operating costs for companies by communalizing the hardware resources of certain computers. Systems performing different functions use and share the same hardware resources (see Figure 6.10). This enables maximization of the utilization rate of these shared resources via the optimum installation of different systems on the resources. This is beneficial in terms of mass, volume and interface (for sharing of multiplexed interfaces such as digital buses between multiple systems).

However, by their common nature, these resources are of a limited number of types, which leads to reduced development costs and the number of changes to be provisioned thereby minimizing the cost of aircraft operation. Some critical systems already use these shared, common hardware resources to support the architecture of their control function, such as balance management and associated transfers of fuel or management of wheel brakes on the A380. This new avionics appeared on the Boeing B777 and Airbus A380, with varying degrees of standardization and scope.

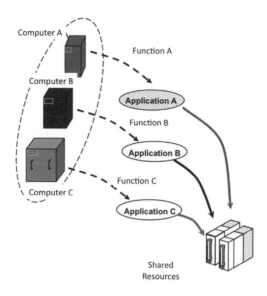

Figure 6.10. *Diversified power supply architecture*

Until the A350, flight controls did not use common hardware and software resources. However, it is possible to integrate some functions of FBW computers if the principles of safety and availability described above are met.

In terms of safety and particularly integrity, the architecture of flight control computers is based on a command channel and a monitoring channel, with a requirement of dissimilarity between these two channels. Currently, this dissimilarity is demonstrated by the dissimilarity of the command channel software and of the monitoring channel software. Therefore, it seems possible, based on this software dissimilarity, to use identical hardware resources of integrated modular avionics to meet the required safety level.

In terms of availability, FBW architecture is based on a high level of redundancy. The introduction of common hardware resources of integrated modular avionics induces the *de facto* presence of common elements in the system. In the knowledge that regulation insists that a simple failure should not have catastrophic effects, it would be necessary for certain system functions (or sub-functions such as of ultimate rescue type) not to use these hardware resources or that the integrated modular avionics resources provide dissimilar platforms. The concept of decentralizing the electronics control from the actuators (section 6.3.1) to bring the two as close as possible fits well with the concept of integrated modular avionics. Indeed, control of the electronics actuator can be used for ultimate redundancy in case of loss of more sophisticated functions, these being supported by the integrated modular avionics.

6.3. Manufacturing and design errors

These errors are dealt with in paragraph 25.1309 of [FAR 25] which requires completion of a rigorous development process based on the following guidelines:

– [ARP 4754] for the development of aircraft systems;

– [DO 178] for software development;

– [DO 254] for hardware development.

There is no clear requirement that a design be fault tolerant, unless the applicant wishes to reduce his effort in development assurance.

On the FBW Airbus, both approaches are used: prevention of errors through a rigorous development process and also error tolerance.

6.3.1. *Error prevention*

The aviation guidelines are applied, with the highest level of development assurance (level A). It is probable that the FBW A340-600 system is the first to be certified according to the ARP 4754 level A.

6.3.1.1. *Functional computer specification*

The specification of a computer includes, on the one hand, a technical specification for the "development of equipment and software" used to design the hardware and, in part, the software, and on the other hand, a "functional computer specification", which precisely specifies the functions implemented by software.

This functional specification is a key element in the FBW development process. It is designed by qualified engineers in the fields of automation and embedded aircraft systems, and used by software engineers. Although the system and software specialists are knowledgeable of each other's domain and work in the same company with a common goal, it is mandatory that the functional specification is unambiguous for each discipline. The specification is established using a graphical method assisted by computer. The specification language is SCADE [POL 05], a derivative of the old SAO. All computer functions are specified using this method: control laws, data monitoring, control of surfaces, reconfigurations, etc.

The real-time operation of these functions is very simple. The sequencing of operations is fixed and takes place continuously over a fixed period. One advantage of this method is that each symbol has a formal definition with strict rules governing its interconnections. The specification is under the control of a configuration management tool and its syntax is partially checked automatically.

The activities of validation and verification (V&V) are discussed in this article under three aspects: architecture and system integration, functional computer specification, and computer software.

The use of automatic programming tools in the translation of the functional specification of the software has become widespread. This trend occurred with the A320, and since the A340-600 a significant part of PRIMs and SECs have been automatically programmed.

The input of such a tool uses the functional board specification and a library of software components, one for each type of symbol. The automatic programming tool produces the software by assembling software components according to the interconnections of the specification symbols.

The use of such tools has a positive impact on dependability. An automated tool ensures that changes to the specification will be encoded without stress even if the change needs to be implemented rapidly (situation encountered during the flight test, for example). The automatic programming, through the use of a formal specification language, also allows the use of the embedded code from one aircraft program to another.

It should be noted that functional specification validation tools (simulators) use an automatic programming tool. This tool has common parts with the automatic programming tool used for FBW computer code generation. This increases the validation power of simulations.

6.3.1.2. *V&V architecture and system integration*

V&V of a system is divided into different phases:

– evaluation review of specifications and of their justification. This in the light of lessons learned from the meticulous examination of operational incidents;

– analysis, in particular, of the system safety, which, for a given failure condition, verifies that the monitoring and reconfiguration logic allows upkeep of the quantitative and qualitative objective, but also, analysis of system performance, and integration to the aircraft structure;

– tests with simulated systems, taking advantage of automatic encoding of the functional specification, coupled to an aircraft model;

– test of the equipment on a partial bench, with simulation of input and observation of internal variables (for computers);

– tests on Iron Bird and flight simulators. The Iron Bird is a test bench on which is mounted all system equipment and whose operation is the same as on the aircraft. The flight simulator is another test bench comprising an aircraft cockpit and flight control computers, coupled to an aircraft model. The Iron Bird and the flight simulator are coupled for certain tests;

– flight tests, using up to four aircraft, fitted with heavy flight test installations. Over 10,000 flight control parameters are monitored and recorded continuously.

The test method is twofold. It uses a deterministic method, based on a test program, with response by test report. In addition, the daily use of these test facilities for work on other systems may be beneficial. If the behavior of the system is not satisfactory, an anomaly report will be issued and recorded and the problem will be investigated.

6.3.1.3. *V&V of functional specifications*

Some functional specification verifications are performed on computer tools. For example, the syntax of the specification can be automatically controlled. A management configuration tool is also available and used.

The specification is validated primarily by backreading (especially during the safety analysis), by analyzing and testing on the ground or in flight (see section 6.3.1.2). The analysis is more or less assisted by tools and covers topics such as the propagation of uncertainties and timing for robustness. The objective is obtaining validation as soon as possible. For this, various simulation tools exist, the reason being that the specifications were written in a formal language, making the specification executable.

This enables the simulation of the entire flight control system: computers, actuators, sensors, and aircraft feedback (OCASIME tool - Common Virtual Bird). With this tool, it is also possible to inject some stimuli on data that could not be done on the real computer. The signals observed can be chosen arbitrarily and are not limited to input/output of a specification board. The scenarios thus generated can be saved and rerun later on the next version of the specification, for example. A test of overall non-regression is in place, allowing for each new computer specification standard to compare the test results of the previous version with the new version. This comparison can detect errors during modifications.

The specification part describing the control laws can be simulated in real-time (same OCASIME tool) accepting input from a real controller (in fact, simpler than an aircraft's controller), and other aircraft commands. The results are displayed on a primary flight display (PFD) of the simulated aircraft for global acceptance, and in a more detailed form for an in-depth analysis.

The OCASIME tool is coupled with an aircraft aerodynamic model.

The test scenarios are defined based on the functional goals of the specification, including testing of limits and robustness. Some formal, albeit very limited, verifications are also conducted.

6.3.1.4. Software

The software is produced with the essential constraint of having to be verified and validated. It must also meet the toughest civil aviation standards in the world (in this case software level A of DO 178B). The functional specification acts as an interface between the world of the manufacturer and that of the software developer. Most of the software for flight control is generated automatically from the functional specification, formalized in SAO or SCADE (see section 6.3.1.1). This avoids creating errors in the translation of functional specification to software specification. For this "functional" part of the software, validation is not necessary as it is covered by the work done on the functional specification, provided that the "automatic encoding" tool is qualified under the DO178. This "qualification" minimizes the risk of bugs in the automatic transfer of the functional specification software.

Overall, the software is divided into five programs plus a library. These programs are: the functional part (which was just mentioned); self-tests, in charge on power up, of verifying the proper functioning of the computer electronics; the initialization program and the sequencing tasks of the functional part; the download function; the input/output software. The library contains software components that implement the graphical symbols of SCADE formalism – or SAO – (OR, AND, FILT, etc.), the building block of the functional specification.

Validation is not done at the software level but during the functional specification. The different tasks must have time to run and in an orderly fashion. In fact, to facilitate verification of the software, various tasks are linked according to a predetermined order with periodic input sweeps. Only the clock can generate interrupts used to control task sequencing. This sequencing is deterministic. Part of the validation of the task sequencer consists of the methodical evaluation of the margin between the maximum execution time for each task (worst case) and the time allocated to this task.

Let us now focus on the portions of non-functional software. Their development (called life cycle following DO178B) requires successively: specification, design, and encoding. Verification techniques used to maintain confidence in the results of each activity and of the entire program are traditionally based on tests, backreading and intellectual analysis plus now formal techniques, also called "program proof" or "static analysis by abstract interpretation".

Take, for example, one of the most important software verifications: the unitary verification used to demonstrate that the software components (such as functions of C language), once encoded, conform to their definition ("low-level requirements" within the meaning of DO178B), as issued during the design phase.

The main criterion of a verification activity is its *functional coverage*. During unitary verification, the satisfaction of this criterion is to ensure that all lower level requirements (DO178B terminology) are covered by the verifications performed.

When the verification technique is *the test*, the activity of running the program – or part of the program – and of verifying that the results obtained are the results expected, these low-level requirements are verified by applying the method of "equivalence class". This method provides good *functional coverage* of the low-level requirements based on a guided choice of the test scenarios of those requirements. This requires the identification of the range of variation of input values of a component to be tested within which some characteristic values (range, medium) are selected for testing. This method of selecting a relevant subset of test cases comes close to a complete functional coverage, hence the expression "good functional coverage" as used above, but only ever approaching it. The implementation of all possible executions in order to verify compliance with (low-level) requirements is impossible in practice.

When using an automatic formal technique (proof tool) to verify low-level requirements [RAN 99], we obtain a more direct and complete *functional coverage*. Indeed, from the formalization of low-level requirements (during design), formal verification consists of using an evidence tool to demonstrate that all possible executions of a component code meets its low-level formal requirements.

When the verification technique is *the test*, an additional criterion must be satisfied: *the structural coverage*. For each software component, this consists of ensuring that 100% of the instructions, 100% of the decisions, and 100% of the conditions that are modified are analyzed during testing. These structural coverage criteria are specified by the DO178B.

Beyond unitary verification, the following verification activities now benefit from equipped formal techniques (automated): calculation of a guaranteed upper bound of the amount of memory used for the program stack and calculation of a guaranteed upper bound of all execution time for each functional task. This type of automatic demonstration shows that the whole program is dependable.

Verification techniques, such as those mentioned above, and any additional verification effort, have the approval of the various parties involved (manufacturer, supplier, official services, designers, quality control).

The basic rule to remember is that the software is created in the best possible way. This has been recognized by several experts in the software industry and also by the authorities. Dissimilarity (see section 6.3.2) is an extra precaution that is not used to reduce the effort in terms of software quality.

6.3.1.5. *Alternatives*

In practice, there is no alternative! The electrical flight controls for Boeing as for Airbus are developed in "A" level: system, software, hardware. Some components (hardware or software) can be developed at lower levels because they are partitioned, dissimilar, heavily monitored, etc. This remains minor. However, methodological developments do occur.

Regarding the prevention of errors, we face the challenge of getting the system right the first time. This increasingly leads to moving the V&V upstream and partially automating it. The level of formalism of the functional specification language is also an opportunity [BOC 09]. This should allow more flexibility to formally prove the properties of the system; ensure safety processes have better integration and design [AKE 06]; and measuring the structural coverage of tests undertaken.

When applied to software verification, this leads to widespread use of formal verification (assisted verification methods, static analysis). As indicated in section 6.3.1.4, a first set of verification techniques has been introduced in the verification workshop.

These early applications cover a small sub-set of the full software verification objectives, while underlying theoretical frameworks, as well as the theory of abstract interpretation [COU 00], in the future, allow other applications (automatic tools) such as verification of the absence of runtime error [BLA 03] to be obtained; the quality analysis of floating-point computation [GOU 02]; verification of properties issued from the specification on parts of the program larger than the component, that is to say, beyond unitary proof.

In addition, we will be more confident about the system earlier in the development process by using formal verification tools to prove the dependability properties by analysis of the formal functional specification.

The objective is the effective implementation of the product-based assurance concept in which confidence in the program is not only based on the quality of its development (assurance-based process) but also on its properties as a product.

6.3.2. *Error tolerance*

6.3.2.1. *Dissimilarity*

The flight control system has been subjected to a very strict process of design and manufacture and we can reasonably estimate that its safety level is consistent with its objectives. Protection has nonetheless been provided, which involves the use of two different types of computers: for example, the ELAC A320 is based on microprocessors 68010 and the SEC on 80186; the PRIM A340 on 80386, and the SEC on 80286; the PRIM A380/A400M are based on Power PC and the SEC on Sharc processors. The automatic encoding tools are also different.

The functional specification and, therefore, the software are also different: the ELAC and PRIM execute complex functions, while the SEC is simpler (fewer functions, such as flight envelope protection, autopilot on A380/A400M, passenger comfort requirements are less stringent) and, therefore, more robust.

Within a single computer, COM and MON hardware have the same basic design but with different software.

We therefore have two different design and manufacturing teams with different microprocessors (and associated circuits), different computer architectures and different functional specifications (ELAC *versus* SEC on the A320; PRIM *versus* SEC on the others). At the software level, the system architecture leads to the use of four software (ELAC/COM, ELAC/MON, SEC/COM, SEC/MON), while functionally, only one would suffice. This is even applicable to PRIM and SEC A330/A340/A380/A350. The A400M is somewhat special (see in section 6.4 the problem of ultimate back-up).

6.3.2.2. *Data diversity*

As part of the struggle against the common causes of failure, the system is loosely synchronized. The computers synchronize their data both internally (command/monitoring) and between themselves (PRIM1, PRIM2, etc.), but not their clocks. Consequently, for a given piece of information, computers use different data, sampled at different times. This is seen as an additional margin of robustness.

6.3.2.3. *Service experience and evolution*

A challenge for error tolerance is represented by reducing the number of suppliers of electronic components. It is increasingly likely that if two design teams (one for PRIM, one for the SEC) independently choose their components, they ultimately have some in common. In fact, we went from this type of "random" dissimilarity to a managed dissimilarity, so that the two design teams decide together to take different components.

Service experience has shown that the PRIM/SEC dissimilarity was fully justified. Two cases showed that the dissimilarity constituted an advantage for system availability. During an A320 flight, the two ELACs were lost following an air conditioning failure and the abnormal temperature rise that followed. It transpired that a batch of these computers had been using a component with a temperature range of operation that did not match the specified range. During an A340 flight, a very specific failure of one component temporarily trapped the logic of three PRIMs (reset was effective).

The EHA also provides an opportunity to obtain dissimilar sources of power: the A380 is able to tolerate a complete loss of hydraulic generation. The A400M and A350 will be too.

6.3.2.4. *Alternatives*

Some interesting differences emerge between Airbus and Boeing; however, let us remember that these represent safety margins. The regulation states that a level A development provides adequate safety. Factually, the two major aircraft manufacturers have made margins. If we take as a reference the Boeing 777, which is well documented [YEH 04], Boeing wanted to cover the failure of a batch of microprocessors that generated the same, identical erroneous data (vote system on three channels, each with different microprocessors), but not affect the Airbus (command and monitoring architecture, microprocessors are identical). However, the source software is identical to the three channels on the B777, while the PRIM and SEC software on Airbus are different. Here the margin is on the Airbus side. Both manufacturers compensate for the loss of all supported functions by digital computers and software. It should be noted that Airbus and Boeing have, therefore, assumed margins beyond regulatory requirements. However, it is likely that these margins will become mandatory in the future, therefore, irremovable and binding to other manufacturers.

6.4. Specific risks

6.4.1. *Segregation*

Electrical installation, in particular, the many electrical connections, is a common risk. Risks can be avoided by extensive segregation: in normal operation, two electrical generation systems exist without a single common point. The computers are divided into two sets associated with these two power generation systems. Inter-computer links are limited; the links used for monitoring are not routed with those used for command. Therefore there are at least four different electrical routes: electrical system COM 1, electrical system MON 1, electrical system COM 2, and electrical system MON 2. This proved useful when an electric arc (arc tracking) occurred and spread: every cable of a single bundle was destroyed, but the others, located elsewhere, were sufficient to ensure a continuous safe flight and landing, with margin.

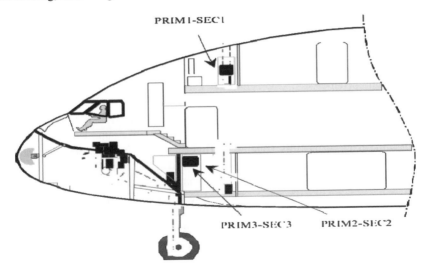

Figure 6.11. *Front sector of the A380*

The destruction of part of the aircraft is also taken into account: the computers are placed at three different locations, some connections to the actuators journeying beneath the floor, others in the ceiling, and others in the cargo hold (see Figure 6.11). The power sources are also segregated. It is interesting to note the interest of the EHA, the fact that electric power cables are easier to install and that it is possible to obtain more space between power transmission lines (electric cables and hydraulic pipes).

6.4.2. *Ultimate back-up*

Despite all these precautions, a mechanical redundancy has been retained on the A320 to A340. This mechanical system is connected to the horizontal stabilizer, which allows pitch control and to the rudder resulting in direct yaw control and indirect roll control.

The A340-600 requires precise surface control for damping of structural vibrations. This is difficult to achieve with a mechanical control when it is aging, and subject to limits and margins. Therefore, the rudder control of the A340-600 is 100% electric (like an elevator or an aileron on the A320 or the basic A340). Therefore, a new ultimate back-up has been designed; it is a redundant electric generator with independent power (hydraulic → electricity), totally independent of the basic system of PRIMs and SECs, and incorporating a gyrometer, pedal sensors, and a feedback loop from the rudder.

On the A380 and the subsequent aircraft, the final stage was reached: the mechanical connection between the controller and the PHR cylinder is removed. The ultimate rescue redundancy is similar to that of the A340-600, but it ensures the control of the rudder, a pair of elevators, and a pair of ailerons, on the basis of yoke side-stick and pedal orders. The technology is now analog.

The safety objectives for the FBW part of the system (PRIM plus SEC) have been defined without benefiting from this ultimate back-up. However, on the A400M, the back-up is fully capable of flight and safe landing, and this must be demonstrated for military qualification. This results in a decreased need for dissimilarity between PRIM and SEC; they share a common type of hardware (but different functions and software). Tolerance to a design or hardware manufacturing error is ensured by the functional dissimilarity between PRIM and SEC on the one hand, and the total hardware dissimilarity between PRIM/SEC and the ultimate rescue redundancy, on the other.

6.4.3. *Alternatives*

Few differences are evident between Boeing and Airbus. The main difference is the use of electric power actuators in addition to hydraulic power actuators on Airbus, but not on Boeing. With regards to regulatory requirements, it is not an asset in itself; it can be seen as a margin of resilience. Note that electric actuators appear on the B787, but marginally (spoilers and horizontal stabilizers).

6.5. Human factors in the development of flight controls

Human factors have been identified as a significant contributing factor in accidents and incidents [REA 90], the flight control system of the Airbus takes this into account in its development process.

This is covered extensively by the aviation regulations regarding stability and aircraft control and related topics (alarms, piloting assistance). Maintainability is also considered.

The flight control system of the Airbus offers the pilot aids, such as flight envelope protection, some of which are available on non-FBW aircraft, whereas others are specific, as well as assistive devices for maintainability. Note that the errors introduced by the designers are covered in section 6.3.

6.5.1. *Human factors in design*

Automation in the FBW Airbus system contributes to improved safety by reducing crew workload, fatigue, and providing situational awareness and better survivability in extreme situations, not to mention a better robustness against crew errors by reinforcing all the safety barriers (see Figure 6.12). Some of these barriers are described below.

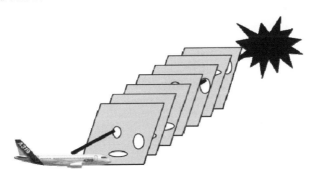

Figure 6.12. *Principle safety barriers*

6.5.1.1. *Comfort*

One of the constraints for the optimization of the control laws is the comfort of the passengers and crew in order to avoid too many fluctuations or variations [DUP 04; FAR 89; FAV 94; KUB 95; LAV 05; LIV 95] of excessive load factors. This optimization helps to reduce crew fatigue [LAC 02].

6.5.1.2. *Situation consciousness*

The Airbus flight control system provides information to the crew in order to ensure situational awareness at an appropriate level. In addition to this information and to manage situations of detected failure at their level or to prevent pilot errors, aircraft systems can trigger alarms in the form of audio/visual warnings, or implement a semi-automatic command (see section 6.1.4).

The information displayed (such as engaged Auto-Pilot mode, or indication of the stall speed on the speed scale, or flight control state on the ECAM page) provides the crew with tools to interpret the situation and maintain the control loop (the crew has full control over the aircraft and possesses all the elements to judge the situation and respond appropriately).

Alarms (visual and/or audio) presented to the crew are associated with failures or events detected by the system and help to ensure a second barrier of safety.

For example, tests and alarms T.O. CONFIG allow verification of the correct configuration of the aircraft before take-off (spoilers in, slats and flaps in takeoff configuration, etc.).

Several pieces of avionics equipment, already dedicated to the flight envelope protection, enhance situational awareness of the crew through:

– audio warning of the Traffic Collision Avoidance System (TCAS) in case of risk of collision with another aircraft, and of the Terrain Avoidance Warning System (TAWS) in case of risk of collision with the ground but also in cases of an excessive descent rate;

– display of stormy areas on the navigation display.

6.5.1.3. *Reconfiguration*

Self-diagnosis of failure and the automatic reconfiguration after failure (see section 6.1.4) helps to reduce crew workload.

For example, in cases of loss of control of an actuator, the failure is automatically detected by monitoring the divergence between the return loop and the command loop (see section 6.2.2). Then, the servo redundancy of the impacted surface picks up the relay of the faulty servo, with full transparency for the crew (but the information is available on request from the crew).

6.5.1.4. *Specific protection of the flight envelope*

The protection afforded by the flight envelope is an extra layer of safety and may be semi-automatic or fully automated.

The fly-by-wire system helps to improve the safety of the aircraft through a set of protective measures [CHA 94; FAV 94], becoming an integral part of control laws. For example, protection against large angle of attack prevents stalling of the aircraft. During flight, the crew permanently remains in a safe area, the normal and peripheral fields, as shown in Figure 6.13. The effects of atmospheric disturbances are contained in an even smaller flight envelope to the normal flight envelope (see Figure 6.11). Structural protection is provided during normal flight (extreme load factor, excessive speed).

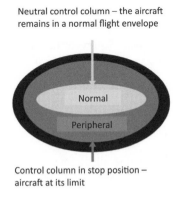

Figure 6.13. *Principles of protection of the flight envelope*

The air brakes are retracted when the pilot commands the full thrust of the engines or in case of great impact flight.

These protection measures reduce the workload of the crew, especially during evasive maneuvers of an obstacle (near miss) or in case of wind shear. A pilot who must avoid another aircraft can concentrate on the path to follow without worrying about structural limitations of the aircraft or a possible stall.

The improvement process is ongoing. On the next aircraft, a specific autopilot mode will be introduced that will automatically undertake necessary evasive action if there is risk of collision with another aircraft [AVE 06].

6.5.2. *Human factors in certification*

Aviation regulations (particularly the FAR/CS 25.1302) were reviewed for the A380 in order to minimize the risk (potentiality and impact) associated with human error.

Through this new regulation, it is necessary to demonstrate that the design of flight controls (and other systems) is appropriate in relation to the effects of crew errors, to the workload, and provides an adequate return to the crew in an aircraft situation.

This means that the design of flight controls, the interface with the crew, procedures in case of failure (Flight Crew Operating Manual – FCOM) and training guarantee:

– an acceptable crew workload;

– legibility and non-ambiguous information and procedures;

– availability of safety barriers to prevent human error from having any non-acceptable implications, during failure and outside of a failure;

– the establishment of mechanisms for detecting and recovering errors.

6.5.3. *Challenges and trends*

One challenge has been to refine all the mechanisms of failure detection. One basic choice for the FBW Airbus system was an immediate failure detection system by online monitoring instead of delayed testing during scheduled maintenance operations. This reduces the level of hidden failures during operation of the aircraft. Unfortunately, this can be a burden on the operator when the monitoring is too "talkative". The challenge is to ensure all monitoring is fully established during the commissioning of the aircraft.

There is a tendency towards strong integration of the system, in order to have more interaction between the avionics systems and all monitoring systems. For example, a study of flight controls that could automatically react to a risk of collision or improved ground control [DUP 04].

The current research focuses on approach and landing, flight phases during which the crew's workload is very important: the ability to alert the crew that an approach has a certain risk. The typical risks comprise high-powered approach (with the risk of outrunning the runway) or excessive activity in roll and pitch [CON 07a; CON 07b].

In terms of certification, working groups on human factors have also proposed recommendations on airworthiness regulations FAR/CS 25.1301 and 25.1302, particularly on:

– error tolerance: the objective being to explicitly address pilot errors that could be led by the design of the aircraft, making errors detectable and reversible. The effects of errors must be apparent to the crew;

– prevention of errors: these regulations deal formally with design features leading or contributing to errors. For example, logic control systems for crew tasks must be provided accessibly, usably and unambiguously, and should minimize the risk of pilot error. The integration within systems must also be addressed.

The Airbus cockpits are already designed this way; the new regulation only formalizes the exercise.

6.5.4. *Alternatives*

The fundamental difference is the use of the side-sticks on the Airbus, with regards to the conventional control column of the Boeing.

6.6. Conclusion

Experience has shown that the FBW Airbus system is safe, with margins. Research has also shown that new technologies can be profitable while providing additional dependability margins. These technical improvements, once established, are incorporated into the design of the aircraft, like the EHA on the A380 and following aircraft.

	A320 family	A330/A340	A380
Entry into service	1988	1992	2007
Delivered A/C	4200	1050	25
Accrued flight hours	85 million	30 million	100 thousand
Accrued take-off	50 million	6 million	10 thousand

Table 6.1. *A summary by airplane type (performed at the beginning of 2010)*

6.7. Bibliography

[AKE 06] AKERLUND O. *et al.*, "ISAAC, a framework for integrated safety analysis of functional, geometrical and human aspects", *Proceedings of 3rd European Real-Time Software Congress - ERTS*, Toulouse, January 2006.

[ARP 4754] "Certification considerations for highly-integrated or complex systems", published by SAE, no. ARP4754, and by EUROCAE, no. ED79, 1996.

[ARP 4761] "Guidelines and methods for conducting the safety assessment process on civil airborne systems", SAE, no. ARP4761, EUROCAE, no. 135, 1996.

[AVE 06] AVERSENG D., "Automatic guidance for traffic avoidance", *Proceedings of ICAS2006*, Hamburg, Germany, 2006.

[AVI 01] AVIZIENIS A., LAPRIE J.C., RANDELL B., Fundamental concepts of dependability, LAAS report n° 01-145, 2001.

[BLA 03] BLANCHEt B., COUSOT P., COUSOT R., FERET J., MAUBORGNE L., MINÉ A., MONNIAUX D., RIVAL X., "A static analyzer for large safety-critical software", *Proceedings of PLDI 2003 – ACM SIGPLAN SIGSOFT Conference on Programming Language Design and Implementation, Federated Computing Research Conference*, San Diego, California, USA, pp. 196-207, 2003.

[BOC 09] BOCHOT T., "Vérification par Model-Checking des commandes de vol : application industrielle de contre-exemples", thesis ONERA, Toulouse, 2009

[BRI 93] BRIERE D., TRAVERSE P., "Airbus A320/A330/A340 electrical flight controls – a family of fault-tolerant systems", *Proceedings of 23rd IEEE Int. Symp. on Fault-Tolerant Computing* (FTCS-23), Toulouse, pp. 616-623, 1993.

[CHA 94] CHATRENET D., "Les qualités de vol des avions de transport civil à commandes de vol électriques", *Proceedings of AGARD Conference on Active Control Technology*, Turin, Italy, AGARD-CP-560, no. 28, 1994.

[CON 07a] CONSTANS F., Méthodologie de conception d'un système d'assistance au pilotage, application à l'aéronautique civile: sécurisation des phases d'approche et d'atterrissage, thesis, ONERA Toulouse, 2007.

[CON 07b] CONSTANS F., JOUHAUD F., CHAUDRON L., LACAZE I., "Energy monitoring assistance system for large civil aircraft in the approach phase", *2007 ACC – American Control Conference*, New York, USA, July 2007.

[COU 00] COUSOT P., "Interprétation abstraite", in *Technique et Science Informatique*, vol. 19, nos 1-2-3, Hermes, Paris, pp. 155-164, 2000.

[DO 160] "Environmental conditions and test procedures for airborne equipment", published by RTCA, no. DO 160, and by EUROCAE, no. ED14, edition E, 2005.

[DO 178] "Software considerations in airborne systems and equipment certification", ARINC, no. DO 178B, EUROCAE, no. ED12, edition B, 1992.

[DO 254] "Design assurance guidance for airborne electronic hardware", ARINC, no. DO254, EUROCAE, no. ED80, 2000.

[DUP 04] DUPREZ J., MORA-CAMINO F., VILLAUME F., "Robust control of the aircraft on ground lateral motion", *Proceedings of ICAS "24th International Congress"*, Yokohama, Japan, September 2004.

[FAR/CS 25] "Airworthiness standards: transport category airplane", title 14, part 25, FAA, "Certification specifications for large aeroplanes", EASA (ex JAA), CS-25.

[FAR 89] FARINEAU J., "Lateral electric flight control laws of a civil aircraft based upon eigen structure assignment technique", *Proceedings of AIAA Guidance, Navigation and Control Conference*, Boston, MA, USA, 1989.

[FAV 94] FAVRE C., "Fly-by-wire for commercial aircraft: the Airbus experience", *International Journal of Control*, vol. 59, no. 1, pp.139-157, 1994.

[GOU 02] GOUBAULT E., MARTEL M., PUTOT S., "Asserting the precision of floating-point computations: a simple abstract interpreter" (Demo Paper), ESOP'2002, *Lecture Notes in Computer Science*, 2002.

[GOU 07] GOUPIL P., "Oscillatory failure case detection in A380 electrical flight control system by analytical redundancy", *17th IFAC Symposium on Automatic Control in Aerospace*, Toulouse, 2007.

[KUB 95] KUBICA F., LIVET T., LE TRON X., BUCHARLES A., "Parameter-robust flight control system for a flexible aircraft", *Control Engineering Practice*, vol. 3, n° 9, pp. 1209-1215, 1995.

[LAC 02] LACAZE I., Prise en compte du confort vibratoire dans la conception, note, University of Paris V, 2002.

[LAV 05] LAVERGNE F., VILLAUME F., JEANNEAU M., TARBOURIECH S., GARCIA G., "Non linear robust auto-land", *AIAA Guidance Navigation and Guidance conference*, San Francisco, United States, August 2005.

[LIV 95] LIVET T., FATH D., KUBICA F., "Robust autopilot design for a highly flexible aircraft", *Proceedings of the 13th IFAC World Congress*, vol. P, San Francisco, CA, United States, p. 279-284, 1995.

[POL 05] POLCHI J.F., "Développement système. Un exemple avec l'outil SCADE: les commandes de vol Airbus", *AFIS/Journée outils de l'ingénierie système*, Toulouse, 2005.

[RAN 99] RANDIMBIVOLOLONA F., SOUYRIS J., BAUDIN P., PACALET A., RAGUIDEAU J., SCHOEN D., "Applying formal proof techniques to avionics software: a pragmatic approach", *FM99, Lecture Notes in Computer Science*, 1709, vol. 2, 1999.

[REA 90] REASON J., *Human Error*, Cambridge University Press, Cambridge, United Kingdom, 1990.

[THE 03] THESING S., SOUYRIS J., HECKMANN R., RANDIMBIVOLOLONA F., LANGENBACH M., WILHELM R., FERDINAND C., "An abstract interpretation-based timing validation of hard real-time avionics", *Proceedings of the International Performance and Dependability Symposium (IPDS)*, June 2003.

[TOD 07] TODESCHI M., "A380 flight control actuation – lessons learned on EHAs design", *Recent Advances in Aerospace Actuation Systems and Components Conference*, Toulouse, June 2007.

[TOD 10] TODESCHI M., "Airbus - EMA for flight controls actuation system – perspectives", *Recent Advances in Aerospace Actuation Systems and Components Conference*, Toulouse, May 2010.

[TRA 04] TRAVERSE P., LACAZE I., SOUYRIS J., "Airbus fly-by-wire: a total approach to dependability", *18th IFIP World Computer Congress*, Toulouse, p. 191-212, 2004.

[TRA 08] TRAVERSE P., "System safety in a few nutshells", *4th European Congress ERTS Embedded Real Time Software*, Toulouse, January 2008.

[VAN 04] VAN DEN BOSSCHE D., "More electric control surface actuation", *Royal Aeronautical Society, JD North Memorial Lecture*, London, UK, April 2004.

[YEH 04] YEH Y.C., "Unique dependability issues for commercial airplane fly-by-wire systems", *IFIP World Computer Congress*, Toulouse, August 2004.

Chapter 7

Space Applications

7.1. Introduction

In this chapter, we focus on the solutions implemented in space systems, in terms of onboard computer (OBC) system architecture regarding the needs and constraints of dependability. After presenting the background and the different types of systems involved, we clarify the regulatory framework and the needs and constraints of dependability. We then describe architectural solutions covering three main areas of space systems (launchers, satellites, and orbital transport vehicles). Finally, we propose a summary of the different system types, needs and solutions.

7.2. Space system

A space system is a system whose mission is based on the use of at least one artificial element in space (that is, by widely accepted definition, at an altitude of at least 100 kilometers). Space missions are very diverse: acquisition of scientific knowledge, communication, geolocation, observation of the Earth, surveillance, space transport, etc. Each mission has different dependability needs, and defines, in particular, the nature of the element(s) necessary in space. This nature (service type, characteristics, trajectory, etc.) influences the capabilities and constraints to be considered in order to meet these dependability needs, particularly regarding elements in space.

Chapter written by Jean-Paul BLANQUART and Philippe MIRAMONT.

In a space system, we distinguish that which we call the "ground segment" and the "space segment".

7.2.1. *Ground segment*

The ground segment includes all the facilities on Earth necessary for the mission (during commissioning and operation. We will not discuss here the preparatory phases of definition, construction, validation, and transport to the launch site). The ground segment includes the facilities necessary for the command and control of the space segment, and its use. In practice, we distinguish the ground command and control system, the ground mission management system, and, if relevant, the elements related to the users.

The distinction between the command and control system and the mission management system comes from the distinction (technical or organizational) between services specifically related to the mission (pictures to be acquired, for example) and the overall generic services that can be found on most space elements (element position and orientation, solar panel orientation, managing battery charge and discharge, thermal equilibrium, monitoring of onboard equipment, on board-ground links, data management computer system). This distribution existing in onboard space elements (platform and payload) is found, at least conceptually, on the ground with a control system and a mission system, even if, for practical reasons, these systems are located in the same place. Note, however, that for space transport missions (launchers, transport to an orbital structure, for example), the mission is inseparable from the management of the vehicle and its trajectory, and management on the ground is therefore unique. This also applies most often to remote exploration missions due to the strong coupling between the mission needs and the state of the platform.

Finally the services of some space systems are directly accessible to the users (without having to go through a mission system that centralizes and redistributes the service). This is, for example, the case of broadcasting or geolocation systems. The terminal equipment, allowing the reception of signals from the space segment and the processing needed to provide service to the user, can then be considered part of the ground segment of the space system.

7.2.2. *Space segment*

The space segment is the part of the space system consisting of all the artificial elements in space. This set is usually reduced to one element, sometimes several (constellations, flight formation), this element being a satellite or what might be more generally called a spacecraft.

A satellite is an element (artificial in our present case) in orbit around another body (usually the Earth). "Useful" orbits are very varied, depending on the type of mission:

– low earth orbit (LEO): generally between an altitude of 300 and 800 kilometers, such an orbit is only used when the objective is to move away from the Earth's surface to make observations (e.g. astronomical) outside of atmospheric disturbances, or simply to be in orbit (circular), a steady state for conducting "micro-gravity" experiments. Because of the relatively short distance, such an orbit also enables observations of the Earth, monitoring (military but also civilian, e.g. fires, natural disasters etc.), or scientific missions (study of the atmosphere, of the magnetic or gravitational field, etc.); these orbits are characterized by an orbital period of about 90 to 100 minutes with the advantage of being able to scan the entire surface (up to the limit of the inclination of the orbit, hence the interest of "polar" orbits) of the Earth fairly quickly, but the disadvantage of limiting the visibility of control and mission systems to a succession of short periods;

– medium earth orbit (MEO): typically an altitude of 10,000 to 25,000 kilometers. In the same way as on LEOs, MEO satellites have a relative movement with respect to the Earth's surface covering, at least in longitude, of all of the Earth's surface, but with a much slower movement, facilitating ground reception; typically the orbital period is 10 hours; geolocation systems use such orbits (20,000 to 22,000 kilometers);

– geosynchronous earth orbit (GEO): the equatorial circular orbit at an altitude of about 35,800 kilometers is characterized by an orbital period equal to the duration of the rotation of the Earth on itself; traveling in the same direction. Consequently, it allows a satellite traveling from west to east to have apparently no motion because it is fixed with regards to the Earth's surface, making it very useful for space telecommunications systems;

– highly elliptic orbit (HEO): most orbits used by space systems have circular orbits or those with very low eccentricity. A highly elliptical orbit, however, presents the advantage of combining a low movement speed above a certain area (not necessarily directly above the equator, hence the interest for high latitude countries) with a low orbital period (for a faster return over the selected area).

Trajectories are sometimes a little more complicated than simple orbits. Besides the classic case of orbit adjustment, there are different types of trajectories of what is generally referred to as spacecraft:

– interplanetary exploration probes whose trajectories combine orbital phases (around planets or around the sun) and propelled phases allowing them to change orbit.[1] The orbital part may correspond to a "destination" where the probe instruments are used to acquire information (there may be several destinations during an exploration mission) or to part of the voyage towards these destinations;

– spacecraft intended to land (more or less violently) on a space body other than Earth, to conduct observations, or move around on its surface or take off;

– orbital transport vehicles whose mission it is to transport people or equipment to or from another space element, e.g. an orbital structure, such as the International Space Station;

– spacecraft whose mission, or the final part of the mission, is to return to Earth. Some (Progress, ATV) are responsible for the waste of an orbital structure and are intended for destructive re-entry into the atmosphere and uninhabited maritime areas. Others transport people and land on the ground (or at sea) after a descent slowed by parachutes (Soyuz, Shenzhou) or in the manner of an aircraft, or alternatively, a glider (Shuttle);

– a particular case, both in importance and number, is made up of launchers whose mission is to transport one or several other space elements from the ground and inject them into the Earth's orbit;

– in many cases the same element can come into several of the above categories (e.g. the American "Shuttle" is used as a launcher, a transport spacecraft, a re-entry spacecraft, even as a satellite for some of its missions); in such cases the spacecraft must meet all dependability requirements and all constraints corresponding to each category.

Therefore, a space mission involves many factors, and even several distinct space systems. Indeed for a given mission, the space segment must first be launched and installed into space, which requires an initial space system with a launcher and its command and control center (even though a launcher, as discussed later in this chapter, is a largely autonomous vehicle). The satellite(s) once launched must be installed in the correct position as per its mission, deployed, and verified. This is done using a ground command and control system dedicated to this in-orbit installation phase. Finally the mission may begin, with the corresponding space and ground segments; this may include interactions with other space systems, for example, using data relays.

---

1. An extreme case of exploration probe is formed by the Voyager 1 and Voyager 2 probes, which are now (still active for more than 30 years after their launch in 1977 for an initially planned 5 year mission) on an escape trajectory from the solar system.

7.3. Context and statutory obligation

Initially, we describe the structure and purpose of the regulatory framework, which identifies three main objectives of regulation (protection of space, protection of persons and assets, and protection of the space system and its mission) that we address in the following sections, before proposing a summary of the regulations on dependability.

7.3.1. *Structure and purpose of the regulatory framework*

The regulatory framework consists of:

– regulations, imposed by institutional national or international[2] authorities, on those involved in the space sector industries (contractors, owners, customers, operators, users);

– additional norms and standards, as well as contract terms specific to each program, adopted by those involved in the mission to extend, clarify, or supplement the applicable regulations.

In general, the goal is to meet the needs of protection against hazards caused by systems or activities. The regulatory framework strictly focuses on protection "against the system". Note that in the space sector such protection incorporates the protection of space itself, alongside the need to protect people, assets, and the environment. This protection "against the system" broadly refers to the concept of safety, while other aspects of dependability (reliability, availability) are treated by complementary norms and standards, and when necessary by contractual clauses specific to each space program.

In the space sector, national or international space agencies (such as the European Space Agency (ESA)) have a very important role as they relay international regulation with specific norms and standards. They also develop and propose international regulations or guidelines to clarify or facilitate their implementation.

Note that the space sector is subject to a series of other regulations, such as export or access to services provided by a space system considered sensitive. However important, these regulations are not addressed further in this chapter as

2. The international dimension, which almost always leads to difficulties in terms of regulation, is especially important in the space sector. Not only can the protagonists (owners, operators, users, manufacturers) be multinationals, or national entities in several countries, but the trajectories of launchers and satellites cannot confine their potential impacts to a single country.

their impact on implementing dependability solutions (non-safety related) is relatively low or at least not specific to space.

7.3.2. *Protection of space*

The need to protect space stems from the realization that space should be regarded as a limited resource that is both useful and fragile (despite appearances). This was decided in 1958, barely a year after the first satellite launch, by the constitution of the United Nations Committee on the Peaceful Uses of Outer Space (COPUOS). In particular, it was established that no one may appropriate all or part of space and everyone can explore and benefit from its resources for peaceful purposes (Treaty on principles governing the activities of States in the exploration of outer space, including the Moon and other celestial bodies, January 27, 1967).

This treaty, with its amendments and additional texts of the UN Committee on the Peaceful Uses of Outer Space, specifies the responsibilities, rights and obligations of states in the matter of damage to persons and assets (see next section) due to launch activities or re-entry of artificial space objects on Earth, but also in the sharing of orbital positions and frequencies (allocated by the International Telecommunication Union) or the rescue of astronauts and finally space pollution.

This latter point covers both the contamination of extraterrestrial space bodies (e.g. requiring the sterilization of exploration probes)[3] and the increasingly important issue of space debris.

It is estimated (2008) that there are about 17,000 artificial space objects larger than 10 centimeters[4] in orbit around the Earth (only 10% are satellites, of which about half, 900, are in operation or intact orbital stages). The rest are fragments resulting from destruction by explosion or collision, or even rubbish deliberately thrown by astronauts during spacewalk activities.

The UN Committee on the Peaceful Uses of Outer Space has appointed an inter-agency coordination committee to develop proposals on space debris, IADC: Inter Agency Space Debris Coordination Committee, involving the space agencies of

---

3. Extraterrestrial elements collected and returned by exploration missions are also subject to procedures to prevent their spread on Earth (they must of course also be protected from any "contamination" by terrestrial elements in order to conduct scientific analysis but this is more a matter of mission requirements, not of regulation).

4. This is the size limit for identifying and cataloging, and then monitoring objects in space. Approximately 13,000 of these 17,000 objects are currently cataloged. The smaller objects are not harmless and are even more numerous: there are hundreds of thousands of objects greater than 1 centimeter, and millions greater than 1 millimeter.

Germany, Canada, China, USA, France, India, Italy, Japan, UK, Russia and Ukraine, and the ESA.

Among the methods to reduce risks related to space debris it should be noted, in addition to methods of monitoring and alerting, the existence of recommendations for "passivate" space objects that are reaching the end of their lifespan (i.e. limiting the risks of explosion due to residual fuel and combustive materials), and to remove these objects from useful and crowded areas in space. In practice, for an orbital stage launcher or a satellite in low orbit, the solution advocated is deorbiting and atmospheric re-entry, while for reasons of technical feasibility and economy, a satellite in high orbit will be "over-orbited", for example, by at least 200 kilometers for a satellite in geosynchronous orbit. Such "graveyard" orbits are very stable and do not pose risks for active spacecraft operating in their own orbit.

These techniques have limitations, however, related to dependability. In fact, end-of-life satellites are either satellites approaching the end of their reserves (fuel for orbit control for example) or satellites that have experienced a major failure preventing their further use. For the first case, regulations may require operators to reserve the last part of the resources to conduct end-of-life operations according to a plan developed and approved before launch. However, for the second case, by definition there is no solution other than improving dependability to further reduce the probability of major failure before the scheduled start of end-of-life operations, or to improve the probability of retaining the ability to conduct end-of-life operations after failure.

7.3.3. *Protection of people, assets, and the environment*

Launch and preparation are dangerous operations for the manned flight crew; personnel and facilities on the launch pad; and potentially, for the public and private or public property in a zone along the first part of the launcher's trajectory. The same goes for the re-entry of spacecraft.

The UN Committee on the Peaceful Uses of Outer Space has established the principle of States' responsibility for the consequences of launches. To meet this responsibility, the major space powers have put in place structures and regulations to control the risks associated with space launches and re-entry. In the USA for example, three sectors have been defined depending on whether the launch is military, civilian, institutional or commercial. Responsibility for regulating each of these sectors is assigned to the Air Force (USAF), the Space Agency (NASA: National Aeronautics and Space Administration), and the Federal Aviation Authority (FAA) of the USA, respectively. In France this responsibility rests with the French Space Agency (CNES: *Centre National d'Etudes Spatiales*) under the authority of which the French launch is placed (the Guiana Space Center in Kourou), whatever the nature of the launch site. The CNES has established rules on the Kourou launch base, entitled "safeguard regulations".

Manned flights are currently covered by the general regulations on the launches and re-entry of spacecraft, supplemented by specific rules established by the organizations directly responsible for these missions. Until now these were still institutional organizations, space agencies, engaged in scientific or technological missions with mostly professional crews. However, the situation changed with the recent emergence of what is often called "space tourism".

Space tourism is a recent phenomenon (2001) so far comprising (late 2008) of only six fee-paying, "non-professional astronauts" who travelled with professional crews on "real" space missions. To our knowledge, the safety of participants was treated in the same way as the professional astronauts, and in any case not covered by any terms of regulation. However, this form of private space travel should remain marginal because of the limited number of manned institutional space missions that can accommodate additional participants. In parallel, a growing number of companies are preparing spacecraft specially designed to offer passenger trips into space.[5] In the USA, these activities logically fall within the jurisdiction assigned to the FAA, which the US Congress confirmed in December 2004. The FAA issued regulations in 2006 allowing the licensing of such activities. To our knowledge, in Europe there are no specific regulations for this type of activity, but in 2006 the ESA established an initiative to promote them.

Finally, space systems are not only dangerous due to the objects they are composed of, but also because of the services they provide (or rather the failure of their services), particularly space services used by other systems to provide a critical service (e.g. geo-location in support of air traffic control and aircraft landing). In such situations this adds to the regulatory standards already applicable to space systems in all matters concerning the establishment and justification of the dependability properties of the rendered service.

---

5. This concerns flights into space, i.e. flights above the generally accepted limit of 100 kilometers. However, this most often concerns suborbital flights in which the spacecraft, generally after being launched by an aircraft carrier at an altitude of about a dozen kilometers, follows a natural parabolic flight after a boosted flight phase before returning to land in a similar way to an airplane after about 10 minutes. Another example is the US company, Bigelow, which is already experimenting in space with its second orbital structure, "Genesis", with the objective of proposing, in the long run, a structure for orbital stays.

7.3.4. *Protection of the space system and the mission*

We are not dealing here with protection from the "outside" against the risks incurred by a space system, but with the protection of the space system itself (apart from protection against hazards induced by other space systems, where the system in question becomes part of this "outside" and its protection is addressed in the previous sections).

As indicated in section 7.3.1 on the structure of the regulatory context, this aspect of protection is not addressed by legislation in the strict sense[6], but by additional elements (norms, standards, contractual clauses) for which space agencies play a particularly important role.

In Europe, the ESA, with the support of national space agencies of Member States, has established a reference set of standards called the ECSS (European Cooperation for Space Standardization), to which the European industrial sector also contributes. This set of standards is structured along three axes (management, engineering, quality) and three levels:

– a set of standards covering the various topics of the axis;

– additional handbooks and technical documents with no prescriptive element, but which are intended to identify, propose, and discuss ways to meet the standards to which they are attached.

In terms of dependability, the most important ECSS standards are the second level standards (in the "Quality" axis) ECSS-Q-ST-30 entitled "Dependability" and ECSS-Q-ST-40 entitled "Safety"[7], and for software, ECSS-Q-ST-80 ("Software Product Assurance").

7.3.5. *Summary of the regulatory context*

The regulatory environment in the space sector is well structured with a hierarchy of regulations from major international treaties down to specific standards, themselves organized into a coherent structure like those of the ECSS European space sector, and defined with the maximum consistency *vis-à-vis* the higher level rules of this hierarchy.

---

6. Except where the mission is to provide a service to another system itself critical in terms of protecting people, assets, and the environment, see section 7.3.3.

7. In the space sector, the usual practice and a certain number of reasons lead to a separate consideration of safety to include not only the consequences of system failures, but also those due simply to the systems presence (e.g. risk of injury to astronauts on cutting or hot parts of the equipment).

The regulatory environment and its implementation are still complicated mainly because of the multiple parties involved and the importance of strategic and economic stakes. There is also a growing criticality of the services expected of space systems whereby regulations are also derived from the relevant regulations in the areas of service utilization.

With regards to dependability[8], space regulations are mainly prescriptive regarding goals rather than means and technical solutions. However these are sometimes the subject of proposals (or recommendations), but as supporting, non-binding standards, at least with respect to the European reference ECSS. The ECSS also provides additional flexibility by providing an explicit process of tailoring, albeit limited and organized, for its implementation in each program.

It should be noted that the regulatory environment can also have a strong and direct impact on the subject of this chapter, the solutions implemented in terms of architecture to meet the dependability needs. In this particular case, this regulatory context generally introduces, in a conventional manner, a classification of feared events on a previously defined scale of severity of consequences. In some cases the objectives of maximum probability of occurrence are defined, but without prescribing the means to achieve them. However, requirements regarding the minimum number of faults that could lead to a feared event of a particular category are often introduced, which has a direct impact on architecture (degree of redundancy, diversification). Thus:

– the "Safety Regulations of the Guiana Space Center" impose the criterion of single failure with critical risks (serious injury to persons, damage to assets, including to the environment) and of double failure, i.e. no double failure could have catastrophic consequences (loss of human life); in this context "multiple failures" must be understood in terms of combination of independent faults, including physical faults, human errors etc.;

– these same safety regulations explicitly impose a "safety" system comprising ground elements monitoring the launches in flight procedures, and responsibilities, but also an onboard element, the whole allowing the safety service to "neutralize" (i.e. "destroy") the launcher in flight in case of violation of safety criteria; this solution is imposed (in Kourou) to any launch vehicle for which without this device it can not be demonstrated that it meets the regulation requirements (including criteria for single and double failure and the quantitative targets which, allowing

8. Generally, regulations and standards do not deal only with dependability. Much of the ECSS standard is, for example, devoted to the definition of industrial organization, to processes and management, and to examinations of key issues in lifecycle. This promotes the implementation of a trustworthy system, but also has the important objective of improving the efficiency of industrial organization and control.

values of up to 10^{-7} per launch, seem difficult enough to demonstrate for the one launcher);

– the ECSS standard on safety adopts the same principle of classification of feared events and a similar requirement on the minimum multiplicity of combinations that can lead to them; note that in the latest version (issued on March 6, 2009), the total loss of mission is explicitly listed as a critical event (second level after catastrophic), systematically inheriting the "single-failure" criterion, as mentioned above, on the same level as feared critical events, in terms of safety.

7.4. Specific needs

We present the dependability needs and constraints of space systems through a review of the main properties of dependability, which are reliability, availability, maintainability, and safety. We analyze these properties for each of the main types of space systems in relation to the specific constraints that apply to them.

7.4.1. *Reliability*

Reliability refers to the ability of a system to deliver its service correctly for a given period.

In practice in the space sector the term "reliability" characterizes what might be called the "success of the mission", which is not necessarily, nor even usually, synonymous of continuous operation without failure. This concept is expressed differently depending on the nature of the mission.

7.4.1.1. *Launchers*

For a launcher, the success of a mission is an essentially binary concept (the mission is successful or not).[9] In addition, the piloting constraints impose an almost continuous operation of the command and control system for which the reliability requirements of the launcher will translate directly into a requirement of continuous operation, or with very short recovery (typically in a time corresponding to the tenth of a second), until the end of the mission. The mission duration varies with regards to the launchers and missions, from about 10 minutes to 10 hours (for the launch itself, to which must, however, be added a passivation duration of the orbital stage(s) according to the rules on space debris). Therefore, it is not the length of the mission

---

9. This is a simplified view. In reality the launch will be successful or somewhat degraded by the gap between the injection parameters (altitude, speed) achieved with regards to the objectives. This can be exploited, for example, by setting up degraded steering modes in some cases of anomaly.

which makes it difficult to achieve the reliability objectives, but the difficult conditions under which it occurs (vibration, acceleration, shock, thermal constraints, radiation, etc.).

The reliability objectives of launchers are rarely published. When they are, values ranging from 95% to 98% or even 99% are provided. Of course these correspond to the overall objectives for the entire launcher leading to higher values allocated to each of its sub-systems, usually expressed as a maximum rate of occurrence of fatal failure, e.g. 10^{-3}/hour.

To the quantitative reliability objectives can be added quality requirements. Thus the command and control system of the launcher is generally required to be tolerant to at least one fault.

7.4.1.2. Satellites

The success of the mission of a satellite is assessed most often by a combination of the quality of service it provides and the period during which it is provided. In practice, temporary service interruptions[10] are not considered and the reliability goal of a satellite is expressed by a characterization of duration before the definitive loss, either of the nominal service or, if any, from the most degraded services considered acceptable.

This objective will be given most often as a minimum limit on the probability of reaching a given duration. The probability values are rarely published, but when they are, they vary from quite modest values (around 60%) to much more constraining values of the order of 90%, for example, with allocation of values even higher for sub-systems and equipment. These values are assessed in relation to the associated duration, which may be only a few months for some missions in a very difficult environment, but are most commonly in the range of 5 to 7 years in low Earth orbit, and up to values of 15 to 20 years for telecommunications satellites in geosynchronous orbit for example.

The main constraint on the reliability of satellites and, in particular, of their computer system, is a consequence of considered duration in harsh environments (thermal constraints, radiation, etc.) and with strong limitations on available resources and redundancies (volume, mass, consumption, opportunities for intervention after launch, etc.). In particular, the identification and appropriate processing of temporary faults, whose rate of occurrence may be very high in space

---

10. Temporary service interruptions are taken into account in the availability objectives (see section 7.4.3.3 below). Note, however, that too frequent or too long interruptions are a degradation of service and as such could interfere with the reliability objectives, although in practice they are rarely expressed in such detail.

(radiation), must be provided. It is usually very difficult, and less efficient, to achieve the reliability goals without being able to re-use an element after it has been affected by a non-permanent fault.

As for launchers, qualitative requirements are often added to the quantitative reliability objectives. It is thus generally requested that no single fault can lead to the total and definitive loss of the mission.

7.4.1.3. *Exploration probes*

Space exploration probes have characteristics and needs similar to those of satellites, but are also generally characterized by the existence of a first part of the mission which is to reach the intended destination. The ratio between the duration of the observation mission and the journey is in some cases very low (for example, over 10 years of travel before an observation mission scheduled for about 2 years, such as Rosetta mission). In such cases a failure at 80% of the total planned duration will result in a mission success close to zero, which is very different from, for example, a communications satellite that would have worked correctly for 80% of the expected lifespan.

Compared with the case of the satellite, the main additional constraint is therefore the first phase, the success of which determines the following phase, the success of which must obey the reliability targets similar to those of a satellite (often over shorter periods, for example from 2 to 5 years, but with a system that already had the opportunity to fail and lose some redundancy in an environment often more aggressive than in the Earth's orbit, and with the constraints of mass, consumption and ground-onboard liaisons often stronger than in the Earth's orbit). The difficulties of the additional transport phase, besides the abovementioned constraints, come from the fact that there are often periods with very strong requirements for instantaneous availability (see section 7.4.2 below), for example, maneuvers for gravitational attraction or orbit insertion.

7.4.1.4. *Orbital transport*

A spacecraft whose mission is to deliver equipment or astronauts from the injection point (by the launcher, even if it is sometimes the same vehicle) to a satellite in the Earth's orbit[11], including docking to the satellite, is called an "orbital transport vehicle".

---

11. In practice, the destination satellite is usually a relatively large orbital structure (the International Space Station, for example). Objectively it is indeed a satellite, even if this term is usually restricted to smaller components, launched once, neither manned nor visitable by aastronauts.

For these spacecraft, the mission success is mainly binary, without reference to a period during which service is provided. The situation is similar to the first phase (transport or travel) of exploration probes. The constraints set for the probe voyage (section 7.4.1.3: mass, consumption, ground-onboard liaison, trajectory, critical periods) are weaker for an orbital transport vehicle for which the reliability constraints namely come from the precision required for approach and docking and from appended safety objectives (see section 7.4.4).

7.4.2. *Availability*

Availability refers to the ability of a system to be ready for use. This concept can be assessed in different ways depending on the system or service that users expect. Generally, two types exist: instantaneous availability and average availability (over a given period, over the lifespan (planned or actual) of the system). These concepts are expressed differently depending on the nature of the mission.

7.4.2.1. *Launchers*

For a launcher, there is no availability requirement in the flight phase, the corresponding need being covered by the reliability objective, which expects continuous operation (almost continuous with very short outages, e.g. less than about 0.2 seconds for Ariane 5).

However, an availability need is usually expressed by the probability of not resulting in a launch postponement. This is a notion of instantaneous availability, but it is important to note that it does not affect the availability of the service provided by the system, but the actual availability of each element with at least a degree of redundancy as determined to meet reliability objectives. The main constraint on the availability of a launcher is therefore that, in relation to the reliability objectives, there are still more elements whose failure must be considered, and over a much longer period. However, the ground environment is more favorable (and therefore the failure rates are lower).

You might think that the objectives of the launch at the predicted date are not as high as those of a successful launch. In practice, at least in cases where we know these figures, they are of the same order of magnitude. In fact a launch postponement is not only expensive, but also disadvantageous, in terms of reliability by increasing the probability of the presence of dormant faults (not revealed by the test procedures before launch).

7.4.2.2. *Satellites*

Availability requirements of a satellite can be expressed most often in terms of average availability or, for telecommunications satellites, in terms of the maximum duration of a service interruption (and the maximum cumulative duration, which is equivalent to an average availability). For telecommunications satellites, availability requirements are very stringent, inherited from the usual values in this field (unavailability of several minutes or dozens of minutes per year).

The main constraint on the availability of a satellite comes from the method of handling faults, while respecting the reliability objectives. A full automatic processing allows continuation of the service or restart after a very brief interruption, but this is more risky than a process limited to shifting to a safe mode, thereby stopping the mission, until diagnosis and recovery by operators on the ground is effected.

7.4.2.3. *Exploration probes*

Exploration probes add a preliminary travel phase to the scientific mission phase.

The scientific mission phase is subject to availability needs similar to those of a scientific satellite in Earth's orbit, with even more severe constraints of mass, consumption, and characteristics of ground-onboard liaisons.

The voyage corresponds to a discontinuous operation of the system limited to brief periods, some of which are critical in the sense that a failure of the trajectory control leads almost inevitably to the definitive loss of the mission. Consequently, there is a strong need for instantaneous availability at critical moments (known in advance). In general, this instantaneous availability need does not form an explicit requirement, but is covered and induced by the need of mission success (reliability).

7.4.2.4. *Orbital transport*

Similar to the voyage of an exploration probe, an orbital transport vehicle is not characterized by a service for a certain period, but by an objective, which requires the operation of the command and control system at certain moments. These moments are less critical than for an exploration probe in the sense that, in general, if a failure occurs, other additional attempts can be undertaken. There is no strong need for availability for orbital transport vehicles, at least in terms of the mission (depending on the solutions adopted, the dependability goals of the mission, mainly reliability and safety, can naturally lead to the availability requirements on some sub-systems).

7.4.3. *Maintainability*

Maintainability is the ability of a system to be repaired. Contrary to what might be thought, this concept has meaning and importance for spacecraft. We must first clarify that we mean "maintainability" and "maintenance" activities here aimed at the preservation or restoration of a service, excluding automatic actions taken by elements of the spacecraft. The latter are functions of the spacecraft, introduced in response to the objectives of reliability or availability.

However, automatic actions generally do not cover all cases and additional actions, usually remote controlled from the control center on the ground, may or must be implemented to make the best use of the state of the resources with a view of the restoration and the continuation of the mission. These are the actions that the maintainability objectives aim to facilitate.

In the general case of a satellite or exploration probe, or of an orbital transport vehicle, the maintainability objectives are mainly qualitative, in the form of rules covering:

– the vehicle's capacity to achieve a safe state ("survival mode") and hold it for a given minimum duration;

– observability, allowing operators to obtain as much information as possible about the condition of the vehicle and its components as well as information about events that preceded and accompanied the occurrence of the anomaly and its autonomous original process to achieve the safe state;

– controllability, allowing operators to exploit the resources available onboard to form a whole capable of rendering the best possible service; this includes the configuration and organization of material elements, adaptation of the operation by using programmable parameters, and the possibility of re-programming the software.

The main constraints on maintainability are:

– the definition of survival states and of (automatic) procedures to safely reach them, even though by definition the current state is abnormal. This difficulty is compounded when an increase in the autonomy of the spacecraft is required with complex procedures for processing anomalies: outside of their coverage, they risk increasing the duration in which the situation deteriorates, reducing the likelihood of success of the ultimate procedure to switch to survival mode;

– for observability, the limitations of mass, consumption and ground-onboard liaison capacity, as well as difficulties in diagnosing elements of which some are functioning, with the important task of maintaining the survival mode, and others are redundant, with normally the least active connections possible to avoid the propagation of faults;

– for controllability, in addition to the limitations specified above for observability, a difficulty arises from the ability to control and validate the actual impact of proposed changes, even though in principle the possibilities should not be limited.

Besides this general case[12], maintainability also concerns, but differently, launchers. For a launcher, maintenance actions are strictly limited to the launch preparation phase. They are no less important, given the impact of delays in launching. Maintainability is consequently expressed and processed in a conventional manner by satisfactorily facilitating the replacement operations of faulty elements. However, the difficulties increase with the progress of the launch operations (because some parts become inaccessible when other parts are progressively mounted). This aspect of maintainability is also equally applicable to other types of spacecraft during their launch preparation phase.

7.4.4. *Safety*

Safety is the ability of a system not to lead to certain given feared events, generally corresponding to events with serious consequences on people, goods and the environment, including outer space itself and other space systems.

7.4.4.1. *Launchers*

Launchers constitute by far the majority of spacecraft needing to meet safety requirements, according to a strict regulatory framework (see section 7.2.3) motivated by the risks incurred to populations, launch pad personnel, facilities and the environment in case of launch failure.

There are usually several safety objectives, which are set in consideration of the possible consequences of considered events (e.g. 10^{-7} and 10^{-4} per launch for damage to people and facilities, respectively, under the rules applicable to the Guiana Space Center). To these quantitative objectives are added qualitative requirements on the number of tolerated faults (2 and 1, respectively).

The main constraint for the safety of the launcher comes from the objectives themselves. If it is not possible to demonstrate the objectives for the launcher itself

---

12. We are not talking about cases that are rare (and expensive) regarding maintenance operations in space by astronauts (not only the maintenance of their spacecraft or orbital structure hosting them) or by automatic spacecraft.

(concept of an "intrinsically secure launcher" in the regulation terminology of the Guiana Space Center), then that same legislation imposes a solution. It consists of a "safety" organization and devices that would activate an embedded self-destruct mechanism in the launcher in the event of identified risk. The set, consisting of the launcher and the safety system, must of course meet the same quantitative and qualitative safety objectives.

7.4.4.2. *Satellites*

Satellites are only potentially dangerous as space debris at end of their life, as discussed in section 7.4.4.5, and during launch preparation and the launch phase itself (see section 7.4.4.1). They are not otherwise subject to specific safety needs.

However, some projects involve space systems whose services are critical in the sense that their failure could pose risks to people and assets. One example is the future case of the European geo-location system, Galileo, for which the objectives of precision and non-alteration (integrity) and availability of information are consistent with the requirements allowing use for critical applications in terms of human lives (e.g. air traffic control and landing assistance). Therefore, the corresponding safety requirements must be allocated to the elements contributing to the service (or at least to its failures). In the case of Galileo, the constraint induced on the satellite is relatively moderate thanks to an overall system architecture where the integrity and availability of information are essentially based on the multiplicity of satellites and on the presence of dedicated ground equipment.

7.4.4.3. *Exploration probes*

Exploration probes present an additional potential hazard concerning the protection of natural celestial bodies. In addition to sterilization procedures, these needs have sometimes resulted in trajectory requirements with a slight curvature so that in case of failure during the journey, the probe avoids its natural destination to avoid crashing into its surface. This is obviously not a generality and several other exploration missions have consisted of deliberately crashing an object on the surface of a celestial body. This precaution, however, seems legitimate particularly for probes equipped with a device for generating electricity based on nuclear power (necessary for the destinations too far from the sun for photovoltaic devices to provide enough energy).

7.4.4.4. *Orbital transport*

Orbital transport vehicles must meet safety requirements regarding risks *vis-à-vis* the crew (if any), the risk of collision with the orbital destination object, and the risks to people and assets during re-entry. The latter are subject to regulations on launch and re-entry activities (see section 7.3.3). In principle this is the case for the protection of the crew, even though current regulations do not always state precisely whether applicable objectives are identical to those concerning the population. It may be noted that at least there are exceptions, considering that NASA conducts Shuttle missions with a risk to the crew estimated at just over 1% per mission[13], which is several orders of magnitude above the regulatory objectives *vis-à-vis* the population.

The main constraints regarding the safety of orbital transport vehicles come from an "active safety" that requires the availability of a significant set of functions and components, for the return to Earth of the crew, but also, to a lesser extent, for a collision avoidance maneuver.

7.4.4.5. *Protection of space: space debris*

Considering safety broadly in terms of consequences outside of the affected system and beyond the failure of the expected service, the protection of space must be encompassed, and in particular, any space object must meet the requirements for the protection of space in terms of management of space debris (see section 7.3.2). In the absence of, or at least pending, legislation in the strict sense, recommendations and good practice guidelines are developed, more often than not relayed in the form of contractual provisions relating to the development and operation of spacecraft. These provisions are expressed in terms of "end-of-life" mechanisms and procedures (passivation, deorbit, over-orbit, etc.; see section 7.3.2), without being accompanied by precise objectives regarding efficiency or probability of success.

7.4.5. *Summary*

The dependability objectives of spacecraft cover a wide variety of needs (reliability, availability, maintainability, safety). The constraints incurred come from the combination of objectives and their application where (almost) everything must be planned before the launch, but where not all can be fully tested before launch. A

---

13. The published figure for current missions (2008) is 1/80. To our knowledge it is a projected estimation based on calculations of reliability. It happens to be consistent with the simple observation that there were two catastrophic accidents in 124 missions (up until end of 2008). This information is provided as a simple observation. Both quantities are difficult to compare because the causes of these accidents have been resolved or significantly reduced since then, and because they were probably not included, or not appropriately considered in the estimates of 1986 and 2003 when these two accidents occurred. Note finally that there have been two catastrophic accidents in a total (up until end of 2008) of 97 manned Soyuz missions.

difficult environment is added to the strong limitations of mass, consumption, and ground-onboard liaisons (speed, time, periods of invisibility, etc.).

The analysis of these needs identifies the main categories of the following missions and spacecraft:

– launchers: launchers have short missions where a virtually continuous operation is required; the main objectives concern reliability (mission success) and safety, plus instantaneous availability objectives (covering all redundancy necessary to ensure not only service but also its properties of reliability and safety);

– satellites, exploration probes: satellites have a mission consisting of the provision of a service for a certain period, usually a long period, with the objectives of reliability (lifespan) and service availability during this lifespan. Probes add a phase the success of which determines the existence of expected returns and, therefore, have high objectives of success probability with a not necessarily continuous operation, but with availability at certain critical moments;

– orbital transport vehicles: the missions are significantly shorter than for a satellite and their success does not impose very high availability constraints; however these vehicles must comply with high safety needs, involving the availability of a significant set of functions and elements.

However, these categories are schematic and simplistic; they do not cover all types of spacecraft (e.g. spacecraft that can land or move on a celestial body, or an orbital structure, such as the International Space Station, whose size and inhabited character allow implementation of different solutions). Also, some spacecraft can cover several categories (e.g. the American "Space Shuttle" is both a launcher and an orbital transport (and re-entry) vehicle, and is sometimes used as an (inhabited) satellite). These categories are nevertheless useful to identify the main classes of needs and constraints, and to describe the main solutions, which is the subject of the following sections of this chapter.

7.5. Launchers: the Ariane 5 example

7.5.1. *Introduction*

In a meeting in The Hague (Netherlands), November 1987, ministers responsible for the space affairs of the ESA Member States agreed and voted to develop a new rocket, Ariane 5. Ariane 5 is an ESA program, which delegated project management to the CNES (*Center National d'Etudes Spatiales*). As such, the CNES Directorate of Launchers has been responsible for the developments of Ariane 5.

The Ariane 5 launcher was qualified in October 1998 (flight L503). Since the initial version of the Ariane 5 launcher, several versions of the Ariane 5 launcher (A5/ECA, A5/GS, A5/ES-ATV, etc.) have been developed and qualified. Whatever the configuration and versions of Ariane, the general avionics architecture did not undergo significant changes since the first version of the launcher.

7.5.2. *Constraints*

The choice of avionics architecture of the Ariane 5 launcher is the result of a large number of tests that were conducted, taking into account, reliability, availability, and safety requirements applicable to the launch system (ground and onboard) and to the Ariane 5 launcher, and also the experience gained on previous versions of Ariane (Ariane 1 to Ariane 4).

Figure 7.1. *Ariane 5 launcher at takeoff*

The main objectives and constraints applied can be summarized as follows:

– in terms of safety, two risks are identified:

- a risk of aggression on populations (identified risk 0A) of the highest level of criticality. The objective associated with this risk in terms of occurrence is 10^{-7}/hour. Furthermore, a FS/FS (Fail Safe/Fail Safe) criterion is associated, which explicitly states that in case of double failure, the system must nevertheless remain safe, in other words, any type of double failure shall not lead to a feared event affecting the safety of people. The original objectives and criteria associated with that risk come from the safeguard regulations involving the responsibility of the state *vis-à-vis* the launch site,

- a risk of destruction of ground facilities (identified risk 0B). The objective associated with this risk in terms of occurrence is 10^{-4}/hour. A FS criterion is associated with this risk, explicitly stating that any single failure must not lead to the feared event "destruction of Guiana Space Center facilities";

– in terms of launcher reliability:

- the quantitative objective required for the reliability of the launcher is set at 10^{-2}/hour with a FO (Fail Operational) criterion stating that any single failure must not lead to the feared event "loss of mission",

- by declination and considering that the reliability objective associated with the avionics must be an order of magnitude lower than that allocated to the launcher, the reliability objective associated with the onboard avionics is set in the range 10^{-3} to 10^{-4}/hour with the same FO criterion;

– in terms of launcher availability:

- the required objective *vis-à-vis* the launcher availability is determined by a ground failure criterion causing a delay of the launch outside of the launch window with an associated objective set at 10^{-2} for a postponement beyond 24 hours,

- besides the main objectives of safety, reliability and availability mentioned above, the launcher characteristics have been taken into account in developing the avionics architecture of the Ariane launcher and especially for the FDIR (Fault Detection Isolation and Recovery) management onboard the launcher.

Indeed, the main characteristics of a launcher such as Ariane 5 can be summarized as follows:

– fully automatic flight conduct (localization, guiding, piloting, etc.) without any external intervention;

– no overall test at level 1 before the first flight;

– a mission duration of less than an hour (GTO mission) to several hours for specific missions;

– a harsh environment in terms of vibratory and thermal atmosphere, shock levels, but also in terms of a natural radiation environment (protons, heavy ions);

– a low-speed industrial production, but which must be assured over a long period;

– a natural separation between the different stages of the launcher;

– a cost control of development and production, in so much as the launcher is consumable, that is to say that a new launcher model is built for each mission.

7.5.3. *Object of the avionics launcher*

The main objective of the avionics of the Ariane 5 launcher is to independently, despite disruptions, manage all onboard functions that ultimately allow injecting payloads on the requested orbit in the desired direction, with the required accuracy.

The avionics of the launcher is operational at the ground phase (implementation, monitoring, synchronized sequence, etc.) until the end of the mission, including the release of payloads up until the passivation of the upper stage.

The avionics of a launcher consists of two main entities:

– electrical and electronic means (components, equipment, cables, connectors, etc.);

– embedded software (and associated data).

This avionics is involved in the general system functions that can be summarized as follows:

– guiding and piloting the launcher;

– inform the ground of the launcher state through telemetry;

– release the stages;

– control the behavior of the payload during release;

– release the payloads;

– neutralize the launcher if necessary (backup constraint);

– respect the orbital environment by de-orbiting or passivation of the upper stages.

7.5.4. *Choice of onboard architecture*

The reliability objective associated with the onboard avionics has been set in the range of 10^{-3} to 10^{-4}/hour. In addition, a more qualitative approach set by the FO criterion requires that a single failure of an avionics element must not lead to the feared event "loss of mission".

Although the reliability objectives required for onboard avionics of the Ariane 5 launcher do not require a redundant architecture, a duplex architecture was retained to answer without risk to the qualitative FO criterion. This choice was essentially to guard against failures that may occur on electronic components, wiring, and associated connectors, etc., which may be faulty due to manufacturing defects in so far as all electrical components operate in a severe dynamic, thermal, and radiation environment.

In contrast, although a duplex avionics architecture was chosen for the Ariane 5 launcher, this approach does not require dual conception, either at the hardware level (electrical, etc.), or at the software level, as the reliability objectives set can be achieved without this dual design. Indeed, it was not to protect against design defects but only against manufacturing and production defects.

The choice of redundancy mechanisms identified in this duplex architecture was guided by a function-by-function approach, analysis at the system level taking into account the chain, the association between electrical equipment and sensors in a global function, with the objective that this function be fulfilled even in case of failure of a function component.

Thus, initially, the functional avionics architecture of the Ariane 5 launcher was divided into four main functions summarized as follows:

– SSCV (*Sous-Système Contrôle de Vol*): flight control sub-system ensuring the steering of the different level nozzles, the start and extinguishing of motors, separation of stages, etc.;

– SSPE (*Sous-Système Puissance Electrique*): electric power sub-system providing power generation and distribution onboard, and particularly to electrical equipment;

– SSTM (*Sous-Système TéléMesure*): telemetry sub-system providing on board acquisition of all information (various and multiple sensors, equipment, software, etc.), which is formatted digitally and broadcast in real-time to the ground;

– SSSA (*Sous-Système SAuvegarde*): backup sub-system supporting onboard backup aspects with the aim to receive orders to destroy the launcher from the ground if necessary (trajectory deviation, etc.) and to detect any inadvertent separation of stages, which will automatically cause the destruction of the launcher.

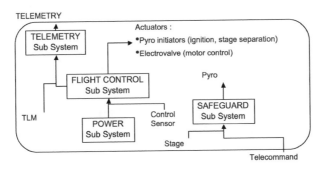

Figure 7.2. *Sub-system breakdown of Ariane 5 avionics*

This functional breakdown of the avionics aboard Ariane 5 in sub-systems can thus be represented as in Figure 7.2.

Note that if the duplex redundancy retained applies to all functional channels, the backup sub-system is independent of the functional launcher channels.

Following these studies and analysis carried out upstream on the avionics architecture onboard Ariane 5, two main rules were adopted:

– if electrical equipment is found defective for the function to which it contributes, then an irreversible switching to the redundant equipment is performed. Therefore, rehabilitation of the electrical equipment in the functional channels is not envisaged, except for the particular case of functional measures;

– when a device is found to be faulty, specific mechanisms are used to limit the spread of the failure this includes on the redundant channel.

7.5.5. *General description of avionics architecture*

According to the preliminary choices made, the avionics architecture of the Ariane 5 launcher retains a duplex system, based on two electric channels, physically and geographically independent and segregated.

The duplex architecture is centralized around the mission computer (OBC – OBC) itself redundant, and is based on two independent channels, each connected to both OBCs by a MIL-STD-1553B [MIL 78] bus. Each electrical channel is independent of the other channel and connected to a single MIL-STD-1553B bus.

Furthermore, each of the nominal and redundant OBCs is connected to two 1553 buses. The OBC master, unique at any given moment, simultaneously manages both the electrical channel buses, and thus the related equipment for both channels.

The redundant architecture is centralized around the OBC, manager of the two 1553 buses that, based on acquisitions made on both channels, then identifies the failing equipment – via word of their condition or of inconsistent data received – and causes their retirement if necessary.

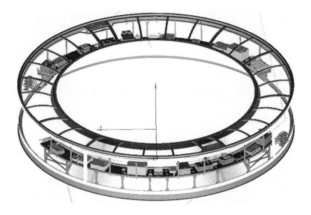

Figure 7.3. *Implantation and geographic segregation of equipment in the equipment bay*

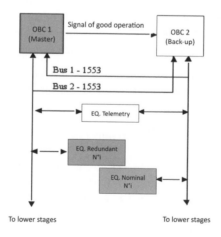

Figure 7.4. *Duplex avionics architecture of the Ariane 5 launcher*

In terms of OBCs, redundancy is organized in warm duplex: the nominal computer manages the flight while the redundant computer observes the bus traffic and performs the algorithms needed to maintain the context of the mission. Indeed the execution of the flight control algorithms by the redundant OBC is necessary so that it can keep its context up to date (in particular the attitude of the launcher). This is necessary because there is no dialog between the nominal and the redundant OBCs, in order to avoid fault propagation between them.

Figure 7.5. *Onboard computer of the Ariane 5 launcher*

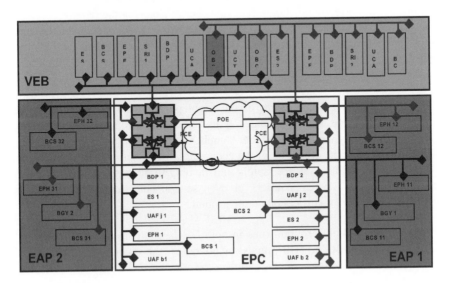

Figure 7.6. *Topology of the avionics of the Ariane 5 launcher*

During a failure auto-detection on the nominal OBC (with a coverage rate of around 90%), the latter self-inhibits itself and transmits a signal of good operation (SBF: *signal de bon fonctionnement*) to the redundant computer ensuring the resumption and continuation of onboard management and therefore the mission. The OBC switch time is always less than 220 milliseconds (worst case) in accordance with the piloting requirements in the atmospheric phase. Furthermore, the OBC synchronization is explicit and conducted by observing a 1553 joint transfer in all phases of flight and issued on the two buses.

Most of the equipment is located in the "equipment bay" of the Ariane launcher, but equipment is distributed at various stages of the launcher. The topology of the avionics of the launcher can thus be represented.

Note the presence of repeaters in the cryotechnic main stage (EPC: *étage principal cryotechnique*) which provide total system integrity of the onboard 1553 network during the separation of various solid rocket boosters (EAP: *étages d'accélération à poudre*) and EPC stages.

7.5.6. *Flight program*

Whatever the configuration of the considered launcher, the Ariane 5 flight program (PVOL; *programme de vol*) is the software embedded in the OBC which is responsible for correctly positioning the launcher payloads in the required orbit, in a totally automatic manner and despite the disturbances or failures encountered during flight. Its development is governed by the general specifications and software management developed by the National Center for Space Studies (CNES), which ultimately decides the qualification and airworthiness of this software.

The main technical challenges of the flight program are: a complex problem (management of the launcher stages with redundant electrical channels, flight control of an aerodynamically unstable launcher, diversity of targeted orbits, etc.), a high level of reliability (function of the economic aspects and preservation of goods and people), an ability to adapt rapidly and flexibly to all missions of the launcher (each flight has a different dataset), or even several launcher configurations, and finally an exhaustive qualification on the ground.

The Ariane 5 flight program runs in both OBCs, nominal and redundant. After loading in the OBC to H0 minus 6 hours to the launch, it performs the implementation functions of the application managed by the ground, which transmits the various parameters, such as time (Universal Time) and countdown before H0, to the onboard software. The implementation of the OBCs ends when the ground, following an exchange protocol ground/onboard via the communication system, gives the nominal OBC stewardship of the bus at H0 minus 3 seconds. Therefore, the PVOL launches the onboard frame distributed on the two Mil-Std-1553B buses of the embedded avionics and is then the only master onboard to manage the mission entrusted to it.

The launcher then determines its position and the optimal trajectory to meet the position criteria and desired speed for placing satellites in orbit. The conservation of structural integrity of the launcher is an obvious prerequisite for proper functioning. Thus, it is necessary to limit incidence, i.e. the angle between the longitudinal axis of the launcher and the direction of its velocity. This is achieved by turning the engine nozzles, determined according to the angular velocity measured at any moment.

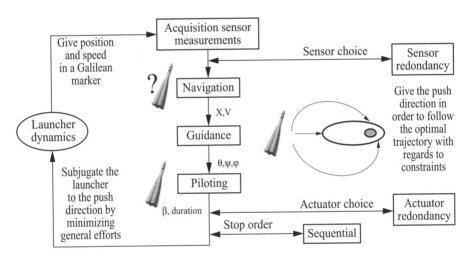

Figure 7.7. *Flight control function (adapted from CNES, 2007)*

Stopping the propulsion of a stage triggers its separation from the remaining composite. This cessation of propulsion, either detected on depletion of propellant, or decided when certain position criteria are obtained, is achieved by a succession of electronic orders. The stage separation is carried out in turn by pyrotechnic systems. In case of significant deviation from the trajectory that could endanger populations potentially in the flight path, it is possible to cause the destruction of the launcher by remote commands from the ground. Similarly, in case of loss of structural integrity of the launcher, the automatic systems provide self-destruction to avoid any further danger.

Localization of the launcher is carried by the inertial reference system (IRS). The measured accelerations are then integrated to determine the position of the launcher, and the angular velocity measured by the gyrometers to determine the attitude of the launcher.

This navigation is then used by the guidance that optimizes the trajectory at all times to reach the targeted orbit as effectively as possible. The guidance instructions (created by mathematical equations of the OBC) are transmitted to the piloting function that calculates the deflection to be applied to the nozzles of the different engines.

The flight sequential, consistent with the algorithms of flight control (navigation, guidance, piloting) implements:

– ignition of engines (and extinction) by a sequence of electronic orders temporally highly constrained (1 ms accuracy required);

– management of the release of different stages of the launcher by pyrotechnic orders;

– changing the frames of the communication 1553 bus for each flight phases;

– management of redundant electrical equipment;

– sending telemetry information to the ground;

– releasing payloads.

The flight program is classified as critical embedded software, because of the consequences caused by a malfunction. In terms of criticality, depending on the classification defined in the general specification of Ariane 5 software, the PVOL is classified functional category 1 (CF1: *Catégorie Fonctionnelle 1*). This level of criticality is roughly equivalent to Level B of the DO 178B [ARI 92] used in avionics.

7.5.6.1. *The static architecture of A5 PVOL*

From the beginning of the Ariane 5 program, the choice of a high-level language (Ada 83 [83 ANS]) was selected for the Ariane 5 flight program. The recognized advantages of this language are, namely:

– code readability and maintainability;

– the precision and consistency of its syntax and its semantics;

– precise typing of data secured by automatic controls;

– a precise and controlled definition of the interfaces between programming entities;

– information masking: external view (specification)/internal view (body);

– the hierarchical structure of the source code allows the definition of levels of abstraction appropriate to the stages of development;

– compulsory certification of development environments ensuring a good performance of the compilers and a good portability of the developed source code.

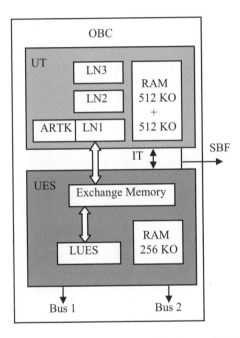

Figure 7.8. *Static architecture of the Ariane 5 PVOL*

The majority of software products which we will review are written in this language. More precisely, the static architecture of this PVOL can be broken down into several software products as shown in Figure 7.8.

The I/O software unit (LUES: *Logiciel Unité Entrées/Sorties*), running on the UES card that manages the 1553 transfer of the frame and aperiodic transfers (immediate or dated), is an automaton based on the Aonix SMART executive. It manages the frame distributed on the two 1553 buses from information provided in the tables programmed in advance and placed in the exchange memory UT/UES.

The flight software, executed on the UT card, can be broken down into several levels:

– LN1 (software level 1), which provides time management, interrupt and exchange services between the UT and LUES through the exchange memory;

– LN2 (software level 2), which is a set of services for the activation and control of the electrical system;

– LN3 (software level 3), which is the PVOL application, integrating the launcher management functions (dynamic management of ignition, pressurization, extinction and separation of stages, etc.) and the flight control (cyclic management of navigation functions, guidance, piloting and redundant functions of sensors and actuators);

– "Ada runtime" with the real-time kernel, ARTK, and associated executive, ARTE. The real-time services and management of tasks are grouped in "Ada runtime", the basic services are in "Ada libraries", and the mathematical functions in a specific library.

The choice to use a commercial operating system required significant work on qualification before being used for the Ariane 5 PVOL launcher. However, a multitasking architecture built on this real-time kernel, enabled, by its flexibility, the generic A5 PVOL to be changeed towards a PVOL corresponding to new versions and missions of the Ariane 5 launcher without questioning the real-time architecture initially chosen.

The static breakdown of the PVOL into several independent software products allows for great flexibility enabling functional changes to the LN3 application without changing the LSSI (LN1 & LUES) and LN2. Indeed, the LSSI (LN1+LUES) and LN2 change only if the definition of the electrical system of the launcher is modified.

In addition, in order to better adapt the Ariane 5 PVOL to the different missions of Ariane 5, the PVOL dedicated to a mission is "missionized" and constitutes the missionized flight program (PVM: *programme de vol missionisé*), which consists of the invariant flight program (IPV: *invariant programme de vol*) and specific data (which are the subjects of the missionization).

The IPV consists of the code (and constants data) of the different software products making it up (LN1, LN2 and LN3). The data missionized by LN2 and LN3 of the IPV to develop the PVM are classified into different categories:

– "mission" data derived from mission analysis (mass, inertia and centering of payloads, orbital set parameters, launch azimuth, etc.);

– "family" data specific to a launch family and dependent on the geometrical configuration of the launcher (short cap and SPELTRA, long cap, etc.);

– SEL configuration data;

– data that depend solely on the launcher as implemented (mostly sensor calibration).

The process of mission analysis and data development implemented for the PVOL missionization is covered upstream of the PVM production, and is the object of important study work (mission analysis) and simulation, as well as rigorous and complex management of the functional data. Following the development of this data, a specific missionization software tool (OML: *outil de missionisation des logiciels*) developed under the Ariane 5 project can compile such data in the form of Ada packages usable by PVOL and generate the executable of the missionized flight program.

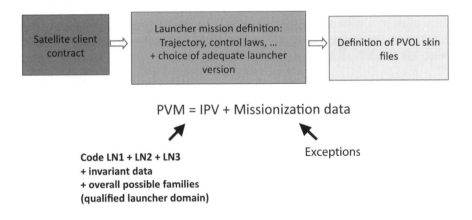

Figure 7.9. *Missionization of Ariane 5 PVOL*

7.5.6.2. *Dynamic architecture of A5 PVOL*

The A5 PVOL must meet the requirements for responsiveness to asynchronous events (orders for pyrotechnic command for stage separation, order for opening valves for engine ignition, redundancy management, etc.) and also for numerical accuracy and computing power for complex and cyclic algorithms, such as those of robust piloting H°° and guidance (explicit guidance outside atmosphere).

These constraints obviously apply in a real-time embedded environment limiting the computing power and memory space available. To handle events of a cyclic and acyclic nature, and to manage priorities between different events, while respecting the constraint of available computing power, it was decided to build the A5 PVOL on a real-time multitasking architecture.

The PVOL dynamic architecture (and specifically LN3) thus rests on six tasks identified below according to decreasing priorities:

– "Executive", which addresses the critical pilot and synchronization with the frame generated on the 1553 buses;

– "Acyclic2", which executes aperiodic sequences of the PVOL, executed and dated, either predefined or calculated by the LN3 algorithms. A sequence of this task is particularly used (for purposes of preemption) when the Vulcan engine stops during the ignition sequence on the ground;

– "Acyclic1", which focuses on the ignition sequence of the Vulcan engine;

– "Cyclic", which deals with the short-term processing and less critical cyclical functions, the activation of sequences, cyclic transfer exchanges on the frame and individual transfers of the cyclic type;

– "Guidance", which deals with long-term processing functions, guidance outside atmosphere;

– "Main", which is the background task.

These Ada tasks are managed by a preemptive-type executive which by definition affects the resources of the processor of the highest priority "ready" task.

The "Executive" task (cyclical of the highest priority) is awakened by an IT issued upon receipt by the LUES of the inter-OBC synchronization 1553 message. The "Executive" task then paces all the onboard cyclic task processes.

Aperiodic processes are performed in flight by the Acyclic task (ACYCLIC2) of the PVOL. The engine ignition sequence, stage separation, etc. constitute aperiodic sequences of the PVOL. Each aperiodic sequence is made up of a series of orders (and controls) linked to a chronogram whose relative time in relation to a key event in the sequence must be respected. The activation mechanism of aperiodic sequences implemented in the PVOL is linked to Cyclic algorithms (guidance, etc.) or to the expiry date of a mission in the flight sequential.

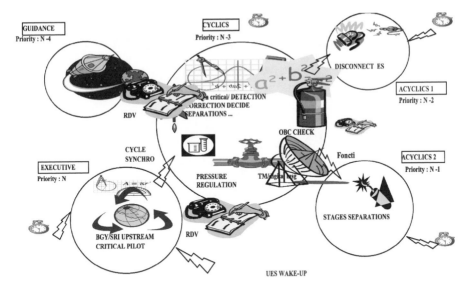

Figure 7.10. *Dynamic architecture of the Ariane 5 PVOL*

Another aspect of the dynamic architecture of A5 PVOL is the synchronization between the PVOL and LUES software, which do not run on the same electronic OBC card and are thus not synchronized. A specific mechanism is, therefore, implemented so that the functional groups that run the Cyclic and Executive tasks are synchronized with the sequence of functional messages corresponding to the frame.

These so-called functional groups are separated temporally by set deadlines so they can synchronize the frame with the LN 3 processes. Finally, the timing margins are set so that in the worst case (failure of electrical equipment followed by equipment switch, etc.) the UT/UES synchronization delays are guaranteed.

Thus it provides an explicit synchronization between the functional processes of the PVOL and those performed independently by the LUES. This synchronization, though it requires perfect knowledge of the execution times of functional groups doing cyclical tasks as well as transfer periods on the frame, makes it possible to ensure that deflection orders sent to the steering nozzles were undertaken prior to their emission to the affected equipment and that, conversely, the information processed by the PVOL have been correctly recorded.

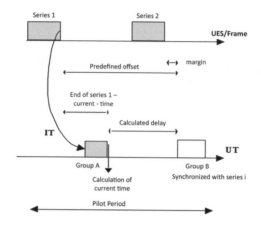

Figure 7.11. *UT/UES Synchronization*

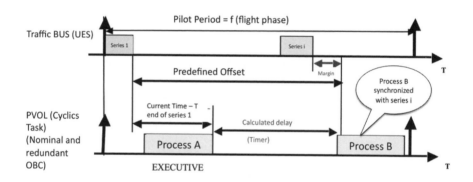

Figure 7.12. *Synchronization of functional processes of the PVOL and the frame*

The LUES of the OBC, which manages the 1553 frame on the two buses, is an automaton that independently runs the cyclical 1553 frame from its definition established in UT/UES exchange memory. This cyclical frame is different in terms of message and timing for each phase of flight. For example, the periodicity of the frame is fixed to 72 milliseconds in the EAP frame to 288 milliseconds in the EPC phase. Each frame consists of series, themselves formed of 1553 transfers. By definition of the frame, the messages that pass through the series frame are cyclical in nature. The PVOL, depending on the progress of the flight sequential, commands to the LUES, *via* the exchange memory, the orders for frame changes. For punctual transfers corresponding to specific events (order of stage separation, etc.), the concept of individual transfer has been implemented. These individual transfers fit into the time slots left voluntarily and *a priori* between each series of each frame. These individual transfers may be immediate (inserted as soon as possible in the frame) or dated. Managing the integration of these individual transfers within the frame is ensured by the LUES.

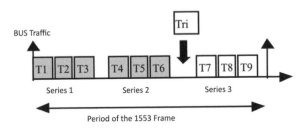

Figure 7.13. *Insertion of individual transfers*

Given the warm duplex architecture and design of the PVOL, certain principles of redundancy have been defined. The UT of the redundant OBC has the same PVOL code and the same data as the nominal OBC. Indeed, it observes (LUES observer mode in the redundant OBC) the cyclical data of the 1553 bus (BGY measures, SRI measures, LOX, LH2 level measurements, etc.). From these observations, the redundant OBC performs the same cyclical processing as the nominal OBC and, in particular, calculates the same mission time, which serves as the basis for guidance and sequential. This is very important because the piloting algorithms in the atmospheric phase are intrinsically different if they are not sealed off by the dynamics of the launcher. Therefore, it was essential that the redundant OBC strictly processes the same algorithms with the same input data, otherwise after a few dozen seconds there would be no possibility of functional recovery by the redundant OBC.

Both OBCs, being synchronous and managing the mission together, simultaneously decide the phase changes (separation, release, etc.) without it being necessary to exchange information between them.

However, the execution of aperiodic sequences (motor ignition, stage separation, etc.) is only done by the nominal OBC. Not performing these controls, therefore not knowing the context of the electrical and software system (SEL: *système électrique et logiciel*), the redundant OBC must acquire it after switching.

If there is a switch from the nominal OBC to the redundant OBC, the redundant OBC triggers the following actions:

– verification of the status of the communication system;

– restoration of the context of the electrical system;

– revitalization of the cyclical 1553 frame;

– resumption of the last aperiodic sequence.

During this algorithm recovery time by the redundant OBC, it is necessary to add a detection time of the nominal OBC failure, which may vary depending on the active detection mechanism (cyclical self-test, watchdog, dead-lock detection time, etc.).

The redundant OBC, then manager of the 1553 bus, must determine the last aperiodic sequence if this one is not finished. For all aperiodic sequences triggered in flight, the recovery mechanism in case of OBC switch is based solely on knowledge of the mission time in the redundant OBC. The recovery consists of rerunning the last unfinished sequence at the beginning or from a known recovery point.

7.5.6.3. *Onboard management of FDIR*

Due to the centralized architecture around both OBCs, all FDIR (fault detection isolation and recovery) mechanisms are grouped in the flight program (PVOL) executed within the managing OBC, and by the redundant OBC when the latter takes charge of the mission. The management of the centralized redundancies can be separated into two categories:

– mechanisms introduced to detect the failure of the nominal OBC and manage the switch of the OBCs in "warm" redundancy. The mechanisms for fault detection are voluntarily inhibited in the redundant OBC, which must continue the mission to the best of its ability, regardless of the fault;

– algorithms dedicated to the PVOL, which deal with redundant electrical equipment in "hot" (or occasionally cool) redundancy.

7.5.6.3.1. Failure detection on the OBC

Although the management of redundant equipment has been considered within a function of the launcher, analysis and mechanisms in the FDIR management of the OBCs were treated at the avionics level. The only system constraint that applies to this OBC commutation (during which deflection orders on the nozzles cannot be applied) is that this switch is fast enough so that the launcher is not subject to too much impact that would be fatal in the atmospheric phase. Thus, only three piloting cycles are tolerated to detect a failure of the OBC and transmit information to the redundant OBC, which must then be reconfigured to switch between subscriber to manager mode, so that the latter can take control of the launcher, both at the level of flight control and launcher management functions.

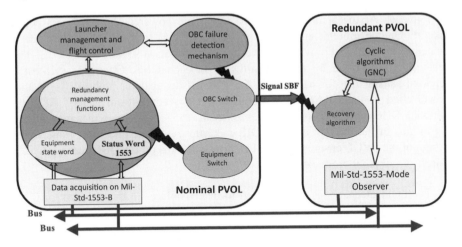

Figure 7.14. *Redundancy management of Ariane 5 avionics*

The FDIR strategy applied to the management of both OBCs is based on the following rules. It is possible that the redundant OBC detects a failure of the nominal OBC and thereby independently takes control of the mission. Conversely, if the nominal OBC independently detects a failure and through its own fault detection mechanisms it engages the switch to the redundant OBC, without knowing the status of this latter OBC to which it commutes.

These principles involve:

– only reconfiguration criteria based on autodetection of failure of the nominal OBC;

– the nominal OBC must provide a good level of failure autodetection;

– the nominal OBC must automatically passivate itself after switching to the redundant OBC;

– the redundant OBC must always be capable (except failure on his part) of regaining control of the flight at the request of the nominal OBC;

– the redundant OBC must always continue the mission as best as it can (strategy of the last survivor) ignoring its own faults (inhibition of the internal fault detection).

Thus, the FDIR management of the OBCs is different on the nominal OBC and the recovery OBC.

For each Ariane 5 mission, the two OBCs are powered about 6 hours before takeoff. On the ground, an internal self-test (AT 95) of the OBC is initiated at power-up of OBC and provides a coverage rate of at least 95% for each OBC. This self-test is performed by resident software in each OBC. Once this self-test is reported satisfactory for each OBC, the PVOL (identical for both OBCs) is then downloaded into the RAM of both OBCs. At 3 seconds from takeoff (H0), the nominal OBC becomes the manager of both 1553 buses and manages all the algorithms of the mission and all FDIR mechanisms of the onboard avionics. The design of the PVOL ensures that the FDIR mechanisms on the OBC are managed in priority to all other processes.

The main mechanisms implemented to detect failures in the nominal OBC are the following:

– an EDAC (error detection and correction) is active on all RAM memory of the OBC with the aim of detecting any failure or radiation aggression (proton, heavy ion) on this memory. Indeed, bit errors in the memory can come from a SEU (single event upset) or MEU (multiple event upset) caused by the radiation environment or after a memory failure. For example, the effect of a proton on memory may be the reverse of a bit value (0/1). The implemented EDAC detects the erroneous bit on one memory cell (Hamming code), corrects the erroneous memory cell, and transmits the correctly fixed value to the flight program. However, this corrector detects but does not correct multiple errors occurring on a memory cell. Thus, a double error detected on a memory cell used in the UT (processing unit) or the UES (input/output unit) is reported to the flight program, which then triggers the OBC switch. On the redundant OBC, and in response to the principles adopted initially, if a double error is detected, the latter is ignored and the PVOL continues its mission as best it can with this double error on a memory word ("last survivor" strategy) which may or may not have adverse consequences on the mission in light of the impacted word. That said, the probability of having to switch OBC (whatever the cause) and a double bit error in the memory of the redundant OBC (irrespective of the type of mission, i.e. GTO, GEO, SSO, etc.) is very low compared with the reliability objectives allocated to the onboard avionics. Therefore this state is quite acceptable;

– in contrast, regarding fault detection on the OBC, no "scrubbing" mechanism of the RAM memory has been implemented for fear of failure that such a mechanism could generate. Indeed, such a mechanism, which cyclically scans the memory, could detect an anomaly in the latter in an area that is widely used in the PVOL, which would then induce an undesirable switch as this erroneous memory area would have not had any impact on the conduct of PVOL within the OBC. Thus, and for example, in the ballistic phase, all data and algorithms used in the propulsion phase (EAP and EPC) are no longer used and a memory error detected on these data should not cause an OBC switch;

– the RAM memory located in the PVOL code is write-protected so that if the PVOL of the nominal OBC had to write in this area, which would then translate into a serious dysfunction of the latter, an OBC switch would take place;

– the coprocessor periodically calculates predefined trigonometric functions and if the result cyclically calculated in real-time is different than the one pre-computed and available within the OBC, the nominal OBC is detected as faulty and an OBC switch ensues;

– a classic Watchdog mechanism, based on a "timer" hardware reset cyclically by the PVOL is implemented to detect any unwanted cessation of the software;

– regarding the exceptions, any exception lifted from within the PVOL of the nominal OBC generates a proper functioning signal directly to the redundant OBC and generates an OBC switch;

– any power outage (power supply tension, etc.), which is monitored on the nominal OBC also results in an OBC switch.

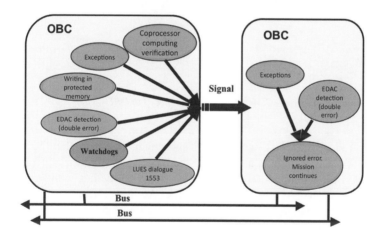

Figure 7.15. *Fault detection on the nominal OBC*

These OBC fault detection mechanisms are only located and active within the nominal OBC. The outbreak of one of them results in an OBC switch, while these mechanisms are inhibited in the redundant OBC (last survivor strategy). All these mechanisms, which are running in real-time in flight, allow a coverage rate of 90% on the nominal OBC during flight.

7.5.6.3.2. Switching the OBC

If one of the fault detection mechanisms described above identifies a defect in the nominal OBC, a good functioning signal (SBF: *signal de bon fonctionnement*) is immediately transmitted to the redundant OBC to signify that it should resume management of the mission. However, and beforehand, any dialog on the 1553 bus from the nominal OBC is inhibited (cutting off 1553 bus heads) and it is verified that, for a period of 20 milliseconds, no exchange takes place on the 1553 bus in order to ensure that no other entity takes over the management of the 1553 bus.

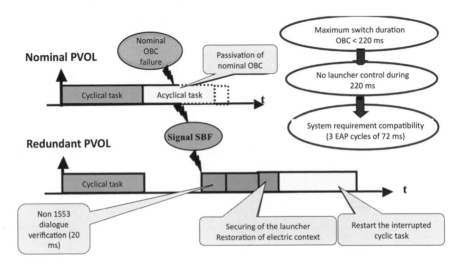

Figure 7.16. *Mechanisms engaged in OBC switch*

In the redundant OBC, which is in subscriber mode on the 1553 bus until reception of the SBF signal, a switch to the mode managing the 1553 bus is then initiated, and the redundant OBC restarts the frame on the bus with an accuracy of synchronization of less than a millisecond. At the software level, the cyclic algorithms are synchronized with the frame and the state of the avionics failures onboard (equipment failures) is then reconstituted. Emergency safety actions are engaged. Indeed, the redundant OBC is in subscriber mode until the switch is not managing any acyclic sequence (stage separation, ignition/extinction of engine) and therefore no pyrotechnic sequence. Initially, it should inhibit any preparation of pyrotechnic order onboard to secure the launcher. Moreover, if the OBC switch occurred during a sequence (stage separation, engine ignition, etc.) then the same sequence is interrupted, then resumed from the beginning by the redundant OBC.

7.5.6.3.3. Management of redundant equipment onboard

The nominal OBC manages two 1553 buses and, therefore, the two channels of redundant equipment (Figure 7.4). The PVOL managing the OBC ensures the detection of equipment failures and decides the switch to the redundant equipment. Let us recall the generally accepted principle that when onboard equipment is found to be defective by the PVOL, then this equipment is permanently abandoned for the mission.

Managing redundancy of onboard equipment is based on two principles that are applied depending on the nature of the function that implements the equipment involved:

– "hot" redundancy: the two redundant pieces of equipment of each channel are used simultaneously by the flight program. If a fault occurs on one, the PVOL continues to provide the required function with the redundant equipment;

– "cold" redundancy: only one of the two available equipment is used by the PVOL. In case of failure of this equipment, then only the redundant equipment is used.

Generally, on Ariane 5, the onboard electrical equipment is managed in hot redundancy.

Fault detection of onboard equipment is done through (Figure 7.14):

– 1553 dialog: if the equipment does not respond (via its "status word") to queries initiated by the PVOL on the bus, then it is declared faulty and is definitely not used any more;

– the status word of the equipment provided on the 1553 bus to the PVOL. Each piece of equipment has internal self-monitoring mechanisms with a coverage rate above 90%, which provide information about the status word of the equipment sent to the PVOL;

– algorithms for external redundancy (to the equipment) that run within the PVOL and detect failure on the function implementing the equipment concerned. For each function, independent algorithms specific to the function provided are implemented.

We provide below some (non-exhaustive) examples of FDIR algorithms said to be external (to the equipment) implemented in the Ariane 5 PVOL.

SRI case

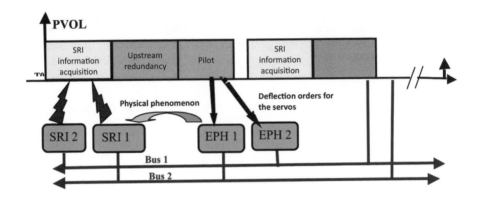

Figure 7.17. *Upstream and downstream SRI redundancy*

Two inertial reference systems (SRI: *système de référence inertiel*) are available in the avionics of Ariane 5. Each SRI is connected to a 1553 bus and the SRI No. 2 is considered as the nominal SRI by the flight program, which deals, inter alia, with GNC algorithms (navigation, guidance, piloting) and associated FDIR functions. To increase SRI fault detection, the transverse axis of the SRIs are physically shifted by 135° through the location of each SRI device in the equipment bay. The external FDIR algorithms *vis-à-vis* the SRI located in the PVOL provide a failure coverage rate above 95% with a detection rate of false failure of less than 5%. These algorithms run in both OBCs and are divided into two main parts, upstream redundancy and downstream redundancy:

– upstream redundancy algorithms deal primarily with the main outputs provided by the SRIs to provide, at the earliest, valid inertial data (attitudes) for the piloting algorithm. Indeed, the pilot preparing the deflection orders for the nozzles from attitudes provided by the SRIs, must develop these orders and make them available to the 1553 bus a few milliseconds after the acquisition of SRI attitudes. These upstream redundancy algorithms firstly analyze the status word of the two SRI equipment and their cycle counters transmitted by the SRI, as well as the 1553 dialog between the OBC and the SRI. Secondly, they test the consistency of attitudes coming from both SRIs. If the 1553 dialog between the OBC and the SRI is reported twice consecutively to be in error or if the status word shows an SRI failure, then a final inhibition of the defaulting SRI is engaged. In this case, the flight program deals only with the valid date from the inertial central system. *Vis-à-vis* the consistency of attitudes between the two SRIs, if they are consistent then the attitudes from the nominal SRI are transmitted to the pilot. In case of inconsistency between the attitudes provided by both SRIs, the attitudes predicted by the pilot serve to select the attitude to be transmitted to the pilot;

– the downstream redundancy algorithms are designed to detect failures on the gyrometers and accelerometers in order to provide validated information to the GNC algorithms (excluding critical pilot). Tests on the status words and the 1553 dialog are identical to those made on the downstream redundancy. Furthermore, specific algorithms test the accelerometer and gyrometer information, tests that eliminate, where appropriate, a defaulting SRI and provides reliable information to the GNC algorithms.

Where both SRIs would be declared inoperative (in degraded mode because of double equipment failure) following these redundancy algorithms, the GNC algorithms working by interpolation of the preset tables and sequential orders (stage separation, engine shutdown, etc.), managed by the GNC algorithms are those *a priori* predefined.

BGY case (gyrometric block)

Two gyrometric blocks (BGY: *bloc gyrométrique*) are available within the avionics of Ariane 5. They are positioned respectively on the EAP (stage booster) and provide information on speed pitch and yaw used by the EAP pilot phase, which corresponds to the atmospheric phase of the flight.

The implemented redundancy algorithms in the flight program are designed to detect more than 95% of BGY failures and have a false detection rate of less than 5%. Each BGY is composed of four gyrometers and provides two redundant angular velocities for each pitch and yaw axis. The redundancy algorithms test the 1553 dialog, the status word of the equipment (called reference voltage), and check the consistency between redundant data supplied by the same BGY and between information of the same nature provided by both BGY. The average of the measures declared to be valid is established on each axis (pitch and yaw) and this information is transmitted to the pilot in critical EAP phase.

7.5.6.3.4. Electronic hydraulic steering case (EPH: *électronique de pilotage hydraulique*)

For each EPC stage, detection/correction algorithms, which run in the flight program, verify if the EPH (electronic steering) that commands the nozzle (small loop) around the instruction transmitted by the pilot (large loop) is faulty or not.

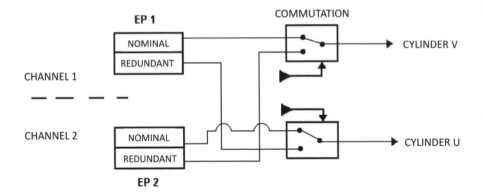

Figure 7.18. *Servo-cylinder redundancy*

Each of the two redundant EPHs is connected to a 1553 bus and each nozzle is controlled by two cylinders, along the two axes, U and V. Each EPH can pilot the two axes U and V of each cylinder. In nominal configuration, and for each nozzle, the U axis is piloted by the EPH No. 2 and the V axis by the EPH No. 1.

For each axis (U,V), the detection/correction algorithm uses the values of angular deflection of the nozzles controlled by the pilot, the measured position of the trays distributing each cylinder and provides the estimated position of each distributing tray of each controlled cylinder.

The estimated position is compared to the measured position through a preset threshold. If this threshold is exceeded, the comparison operation is repeated with new measurements.

If the overflow of the threshold is confirmed, a servo valve switching order is sent to the EPH, which does not command the axis cylinder incriminated by this exceeded threshold. The hydraulic power is transferred to the redundant channel and the servo valve in question is permanently eliminated.

Such switching can also be engaged if an EPH does not respond on the 1553 bus or if a status word shows an equipment failure. Thus, following such a switch, a single EPH commands the two cylinders and therefore the two axes U and V of each nozzle.

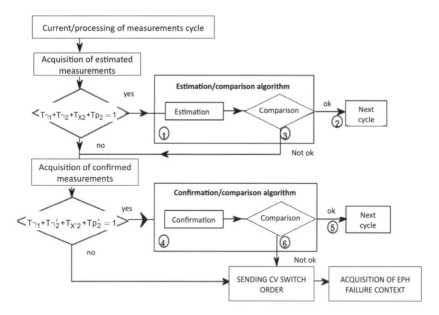

Figure 7.19. *EPC detection algorithm*

Conditioning and functional acquisition units case (UCAF: unités de conditionnement et d'acquisition fonctionnelles)

The so-called functional measures are used to regulate pressure within the various tanks, and the controls and verifications carried out during the ignition of the Vulcan engine on the ground before takeoff, etc. These functional measurements are acquired by the flight program through the UCAF (conditioning and functional acquisition unit), redundant and connected to the MIL-STD-1553B. To avoid unique failure modes, a sensor is connected to a single UCAF. The redundant measurement is performed by another sensor attached to the redundant UCAF. A measurement is declared valid if the UCAF status word and the associated refresh counter are valid and if the measured value is included in the predefined likelihood thresholds. These measurements are all acquired by the flight program and processes that use these measurements in developing "1oo2", "2oo4" logics, or conducting majority votes. These algorithms for acquisition and measurement processing authorize a functional UCAF failure, detected in each cycle, without permanently inhibiting a UCAF and without switching to the UCAF declared as the only one valid. Simply, if a measure is not declared valid on a cycle and regardless of origin, it is not used (for the cycle in question) by the processing algorithm concerned.

Solenoid valve case (EV: électrovannes)

The solenoid valves (EV) are used on the launcher for ignition and extinction of motors, the control of tank pressurization valves, etc. Several types of valves are used, with one or two coils. Each EV is connected to a sequential electronic (ES: *électronique séquentielle*) that is controlled and commanded by the flight program through the 1553 bus.

These valves, depending on the case, can be ordered several ways:

– in hot redundancy when the activation commands from the flight program are simultaneously applied to the coils on the two redundant ES;

– in cold redundancy when the controls are *a priori* applied beforehand to a single ES and the command addressed to the redundant ES is only effective in the event of a failure recorded on the nominal ES.

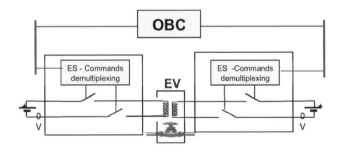

Figure 7.20. *Double coil monostable EV command*

The activation of each EV is obtained by the presence of current in one coil that provides protection against "failure delay". However, two transfers issued by the flight program on the 1553 are required on each ES, which provides protection against a "failure ahead". Measuring the voltage in response to an EV command can detect the non-inclusion of the command.

Conversely, disabling the EVs requires that no current be present in any of the coils. Thus, disabling commands transmitted by the flight program to the two redundant ESs is necessary. However, only one transfer is necessary for each of the ES, which is sufficient to open the power circuit. The effective execution of these deactivation orders is done by verification of non-error in the 1553 transfers, of the terminal voltage measurement of the affected coils. In case of detected failure, the flight program then asks a disconnection of the ES by sending an order dedicated to the electric power distribution organ, which then inhibits the ES and, in fact, removes any current in the connected EV. The flight program double-checks the disconnection of the ES and, if the order is unsuccessful, sends a command to the redundant ES (CAE command) so that it opens the power switch of the affected EV coil. These fault management algorithms, which command the opening and closing of the EVs, are managed by the layers LN2 and LN3 of the flight program. The reliability requirement *vis-à-vis* the control of these valves is set at 10^{-9} (inadvertent activation of an EV without command order and non-activation of an EV when there is an actual activation order).

7.5.7. Conclusion

The duplex architecture of the Ariane 5 avionics is the same on all versions (A5/ECA, A/ES, etc.) of the Ariane 5 launcher. FDIR mechanisms implemented have not changed since the initial design and that after 10 years of operational use of the Ariane 5 launcher, currently totaling about 40 flights.

The FDIR mechanisms implemented were initially useful, and furthermore, consistent with expectations, namely guarding against the failure of electrical equipment due to manufacturing problems on the ground and in-flight, and not allowing hardware or software failures, at the expected level of design.

The intention for the future of Ariane 5 is not to challenge or to develop these FDIR principles and mechanisms that have proven themselves. This is because the principles originally chosen *vis-à-vis* the FDIR are not questioned, even though technologies are evolving (FPGA technology, ASIC, and SOC are increasingly used).

7.6. Satellite architecture

7.6.1. *Overview*

As stated in the introduction to this chapter, artificial satellites are a very diverse family in terms of missions and physical characteristics (from a few centimeters to over 10 meters, from a kilogram to about 10 tons). We will discuss here the "classic" satellites, which are larger than what are usually called mini-satellites or micro-satellites, or even nano-satellites.

Although still quite diverse in terms of mission and constraints and in terms of size (and cost), the architectural and dependability solutions implemented in conventional satellites are often quite similar.

There are generally two different subsets in a satellite:

– the payload, which includes specific elements of a mission;

– the platform, which provides basic services necessary to accomplish the mission.

In the following section, we briefly describe payload and the principles of dependability, before focusing primarily on the platform, which is more generic with operating principles that are also more generally used for the dependability of the payload.

7.6.2. Payload

The payload of a satellite depends on its mission. We can mainly distinguish satellites' scientifics on observation and telecommunications satellites.

Scientific or observation satellites include one or more instruments (cameras, telescopes, spectrometers, etc.) with associated electronic systems for power, control, or direction of the instruments, and preliminary data processing (e.g., compression). Given their size and cost, instruments are usually provided without spares on board as there is no redundancy at that level. In contrast the electrical elements and associated electronics usually are redundant. Most often a cold redundancy of two degrees (one active element and an available backup) is set up with a switch (telecommanded from the ground).

The payload of the telecommunications satellites is different in nature, consisting of a set of electronic processing and signal amplification systems. The desired dependability properties are obtained not by "one-for-one" redundancy of the elements but by a few additional elements kept in reserve (not powered, in cold redundancy) to replace faulty elements during the mission. The replacement is done using connection matrices to establish the desired paths. When there are no more resources available in reserve, the continuation of the mission is possible in degraded operation (number of channels below the nominal specification) until the capacity of the satellite is considered inadequate in terms of its operating costs and the use of orbital position.

However, the management of faults on the payload does not remain limited to these "local" solutions due to interactions with the rest of the satellite:

– the payload directly uses the resources and services provided by the platform (electric power, thermal control, memory resources, computing, ground-onboard communications), of which any eventual failures have consequences, temporary or permanent, on the payload; in the case of permanent degradation, the mission team will be required to prepare and upload specific operational procedures, allowing them to exploit the remaining resources and capabilities;

– the payload also uses the resources of the platform as defined, for example, by the attitude, the orbit, and the precision with which the necessary parameters are maintained; platform faults leading to anomalies in pointing to vibrations have consequences on the quality of service provided by the payload;

– alternatively, payload faults can also propagate to the platform, a short circuit resulting in excessive consumption and reducing the power available for other elements of the mission or for the vital functions performed by the platform; generally, the procedures for handling faults on the platform (see section 7.6.3), at least partially, protect the platform against the propagation of faults from the payload; elsewhere, as described in section 7.6.3, above a certain level of degradation and gravity, the procedures for handling faults on the platform include an shutdown of all or part of the payload (the shutdown of a part consuming more than specified, like a circuit breaker, or a partial shutdown to preserve the most important parts of the mission, or a complete shutdown of the mission to focus on safeguarding the platform in order to wait for a subsequent recovery).

7.6.3. *Platform*

7.6.3.1. *Functional architecture*

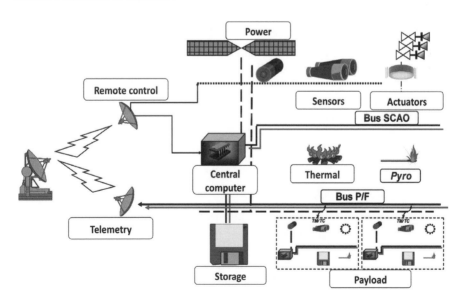

Figure 7.21. *Satellite platform: functional architecture*

The main functions of the platform of a satellite are:

– telecommands, telemetry: they provide the critical liaison function with the ground to send information on the status of the satellite and to receive the orders for the execution of the mission or the management of the platform;

– power: the functional subset regroups the energy sources (usually solar panels) and their associated mechanisms (guidance engines, sensors directed towards the sun), as well as storage devices (batteries) and electric distribution (regulators, converters, safeguards);

– attitude and orbit control system (AOCS) with sensors (inertial sensors (gyroscopes), star sensors, magnetometers) and actuators (chemical or electric thrusters, reaction wheels, magneto-couplers);

– thermal: temperature regulation is very important in spacecraft, maintaining equipment in an acceptable temperature range despite the presence (or absence) of a local or external heat source depending on the location relative to the sides illuminated by the sun; temperature regulation can be only passive, but must often be supplemented by active regulatory mechanisms with heating lines associated with temperature sensors;

– pyrotechnics: all devices allowing the deployment of different satellite elements during its installation in orbit: solar panels, antennas, etc.;

– computer, storage: the heart of computer management system of the satellite platform, which often includes all or part of the IT management of the payload, which does not always dispose of dedicated memories and computers;

– bus: these are the internal communication means between the various electronic components of the satellite; there is usually at least one avionics bus (connecting the various elements of the platform), otherwise, a bus for communication between different elements of the subset of attitude control and orbit, and a bus for communication between the various elements of the payload.

In the following sections we will detail the principles of architecture and redundancy for each platform subset.

7.6.3.2. Telecommand, telemetry

This function covers analog and digital electronic elements necessary for a radio link with the ground via antennas.

The "telecommand" function is particularly important because its loss generally leads in the short-term to total loss of the satellite. It is therefore subject to an architecture in hot redundancy (first degree). Telecommands are received, processed and transmitted to the computer by two independent entities. However, this is not a voting system, there is no comparison and the system can process all correct orders received on one or the other channel (there is an error-detection code and counters (for refusing a command out of sequence but also for not processing the same command twice) and, in general, verification of acceptability of the command based on the current state of the spacecraft).

Another aspect linked to dependability regarding telecommand is the need to process some critical telecommands (switching the equipment on and off, for example) even in case of failure, especially in the on-board computer system. For that, the telecommand system is broken down into two parts, one of which can send commands directly to the devices through dedicated links, bypassing the computer system.

However, telemetry linked to the status of the satellite is less critical and can tolerate a loss or delay of certain data. We then use the most classic pattern of redundancy in space systems, namely an active element and an element in cold redundancy that is activated, instead of the nominal element in case of failure.

7.6.3.3. Electric power

The electric power system includes electrical elements management, elements of production and power storage capacity, and a general distribution organization.

The organization of the electrical distribution is adapted to the satellite redundancy. This is usually a second-degree redundancy, therefore the electric power system is also organized to store, manage, and distribute electric power in two channels, which are as independent as possible, so that for each element of the satellite, the nominal and redundant units are powered separately.

The production (solar panels) and storage (batteries) elements have two particularities compared to most electronics avionics:

– they are sensitive to aging, leading to a gradual deterioration of their performance;

– they have some complex failure modes, but are interesting in that they do not necessarily lose all but only part of their function (a section of a panel, a cell of a battery).

In response to these two phenomena, and in addition to a specific architecture, such as panels promoting segregation between sections, oversizing can improve the likelihood of compliance, at the end of life, of the specifications despite the gradual deterioration due to aging and certain failures. In addition, specific operational procedures adapt the mission to degraded performance and preserve and extend the degraded electrical system, for example, by adjusting the cycles of battery charge and discharge and minimum or maximum values of current, voltage and load.

For those specific to a power supply channel, the electronic elements of the power system are redundant because of channel redundancy, and those common to both channels are provided with their own redundancy (generally first-degree cold redundancy).

7.6.3.4. *Attitude and orbit control system*

The sensors and actuators of the attitude and orbit control system generally have the particularity of measurements or actions on an axis, and they must be combined to cover all possible directions.

Some satellites use triplets (gyroscope, reaction wheels, thrusters), with a redundancy scheme of "1oo2", i.e. an active triplet and another as a backup (usually in cold redundancy given that some of these elements are susceptible to wear and tear). This solution has the advantage of simplicity but requires having six elements in order to be tolerant to any single fault. One will most often use sets of four elements, on four non-coplanar axes, which can also tolerate one fault, but with two fewer redundant elements. However, the steering and failure identification algorithms are a bit more complicated.

The electronic command and control elements are classically redundant, generally in cold redundancy.

Finally, note that the attitude and orbit control system is actually richer and more complex than this description might suggest. Indeed the performance requirements (accuracy, agility) lead to many additional elements of control or command. These are not redundant in the strict sense, as they are considered necessary to the nominal operation as specified, but may nevertheless provide solutions to partially tolerate at least some failures. Thus, several cases of satellites originally planned to operate with three gyroscopes were able to continue their mission (well beyond the period initially planned) under acceptable conditions with two, then one and even no gyroscope, thanks to modified control algorithms to exploit the complementary information on position from star sensors for example.

7.6.3.5. *Thermal control*

The thermal control system is treated with a conventional first-degree cold redundancy, with the exception of some unreliable sensors (e.g. thermistors) often mounted in majority vote.

7.6.3.6. *Computer, communication bus*

Avionics computers of satellite platforms and their communication bus are most often treated with the classical first-degree redundancy. However, there are satellites with computers in cold redundancy and also satellites with computers in hot or warm redundancy.

The former is used whenever the mission permits, because it offers the best performance in lifespan, given that the failure rate of a non-powered electronic element is much lower than when powered. In particular this is the solution for most observation satellites (observation of the Earth, scientific missions in Earth's orbit, etc.).

However a number of tasks impose strong constraints of availability and duration of service interruption. This is particularly the case for telecommunications satellites. The use of computers in hot redundancy, or at least warm[14], then reduces the recovery time in case of failure. Note that even in hot redundancy, a selective redundancy scheme is adopted (one unit is master and actually sends the commands). Error detection is based on the same techniques as in cold or warm redundancy, without comparing outputs of redundant units.

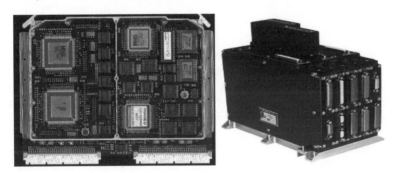

Figure 7.22. *Satellite computers*

7.6.3.7. *Information storage (memory)*

Memory covers three entities:

– the memory directly associated with the computer, to store the program and data; this memory consists of read-only memory (from where the original program is

_____

14. In "warm" redundancy, the redundant unit is powered but does not perform nominal processing. It may still update its context (and further accelerate the recovery time with regards to a cold redundancy) and undertake testing procedures, reducing dormant faults.

reloaded in case of reset, and from where the program specific to the survival mode is executed), of electrically erasable permanent memory (which stores the programs updated during the life of the satellite), and of volatile memory where the program (nominal, excluding survival) is loaded and executed and where the execution data are stored. These memories are redundant in the sense that a set is associated with each redundant computer;

– the safeguard memory, used when computers are in cold redundancy, to safeguard the context necessary for recovery; the safeguard memory is in hot redundancy;

– the mass memory, used increasingly on satellites requiring significant information storage capacities (observation, scientific missions); the mass memory, when it exists, is often located (functionally) at the interface between the platform and the payload, serving to store mission data before transmitting it to the ground and storing additional information on the status of the platform; the mass memory generally has redundancy in the form of an initial capacity in excess of its needs, plus a classic redundancy 1oo2 in the memory management circuits.

7.6.4. *Implementation*

7.6.4.1. *Physical architecture*

The physical architecture of the avionics of a satellite comes from the principles described in the preceding sections. It is organized mainly around two avionics buses, each controlled by a computer, with key elements in redundancy, each unit being connected redundantly to each of the two buses, and other elements connected to the buses (and therefore to the computers) via a key element.

In a satellite, the interconnection scheme chosen is as comprehensive as possible. Indeed, the need to tolerate any single fault (loss of equipment) requires providing redundancy for each device. When the probability of losing more than one equipment is low over the duration of the mission (for example, the case of a launcher, see section 7.5), we will seek to minimize the possibility of interconnection to reduce the complexity and risks of propagation of faults. In contrast, for a long-life satellite, in principle, thanks to a richer interconnection we can establish a complete functional set, even in case of multiple faults, as long as not all redundancies of a given element are lost. The interconnection scheme of a satellite provides the connection of each computer to each redundant element of the telemetry and telecommand set, and the connection of each redundant element of all other sets to the two buses. However, it is not necessary to connect each computer to each bus[15]. Even if it would cover more cases of faults (bus loss), the advantage is weak against the additional risk of fault propagation (e.g. loss of a bus because of the failure of a computer that commands it).

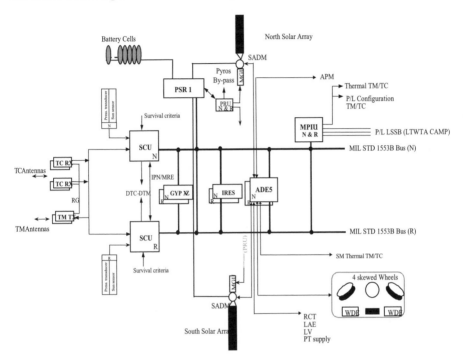

Figure 7.23. *Avionic architecture – example of a telecommunications satellite*

7.6.4.2. *Fault management (FDIR)*

Fault management corresponds to a set of procedures called FDIR in the space domain (failure detection, isolation and recovery).

The FDIR covers all procedures for handling faults and errors, from detection to recovery or reconfiguration, through the "isolation", which covers both the location (within the meaning of diagnosis) and passivation designed especially to prevent the propagation of the fault.

---

15. Unlike Ariane (see section 7.5) where the double connection is necessary as the redundant elements are connected to only one bus (even if only for layout reasons, each Ariane bus covering half of the bay where redundant elements are distributed for reasons of physical segregation).

The detection of faults is based on a monitoring set:

– technologic monitoring: voltage, current, temperature, etc.;

– functional monitoring, related to the monitored function: pump flow, thruster effect on the attitude, etc.;

– software monitoring: durations of tasks, memory access, validity or freshness of data, etc.;

– global or system monitoring: directed towards the Earth or Sun, battery under- or overload.

By employing the automatic procedures onboard, the FDIR exploits the possibilities offered by the architecture for achieving the dependability goals. The definition of FDIR is a compromise between the needs for autonomy and availability, and the requirements for reliability (lifespan) and safety, even though these safety requirements are low for satellites.

To achieve this, FDIR is organized as follows:

– a first local level handling some faults, with low or no impact on the mission, for example, by a simple re-testing or re-initialization;

– a second level reconfigures the redundant unit in the case of an anomaly localized, after "filtering",[16] to a particular unit for which a redundant unit is available; this is generally done without impact on the current mode and mission or with minor impact (temporary interruption of service);

– one or more additional levels for processing anomalies, either detected but not localized to a specific element, or when processing of previous levels has failed. These levels correspond to degraded modes with degradation or even partial or total loss of the mission. The last level is in satellite ultimate survival mode in which minimum resources are used according to simple and robust procedures for maintaining the vital functions (directed towards the sun to recharge the batteries, keeping the ground-onboard liaison, and required thermal control).

Generally, automatic procedures on-board are in charge of switching to a degraded mode when an anomaly is detected, but not of switching back to a less degraded mode after further analysis into solving a problem as this is left to the operators on the ground after further investigation. This imposes strong constraints of observability and controllability, both on the redundant components and those used for the current mode. This also imposes the need to record and transmit to the

---

16. This term is used to describe the principle that a detected anomaly must first be confirmed over one or more cycles before being processed, thereby limiting the impact of false alarms and temporary faults. This of course depends on the severity of the anomaly.

ground as much information as possible not only on the automatic operations performed by FDIR but also on the failures and the context in which they occurred.

FDIR is implemented by a combination of hardware elements and software procedures on the avionics computers. This requires a special device to deal with failures of computers and their reconfigurations. To this end, avionics architecture has an element called the "reconfiguration module" that is either explicit and separate, or attached to each computer, as in the following figure, the MRE (monitoring and reconfigurative equipment) entity appearing in the detail of the avionics platform computer described previously.

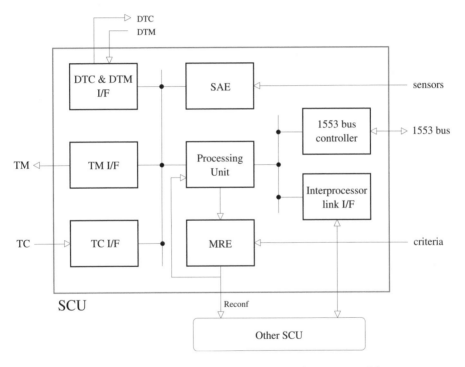

Figure 7.24. *Avionics computer and its reconfiguration module*

The reconfiguration module, either external to the two computers (and redundant) or in duplicate (and therefore also redundant) each attached to each computer, is specifically responsible for detecting failures of the active computer (technologic monitoring, a watchdog that is not rearmed upon software detection, system monitoring) and engage the necessary reinitialization or reconfiguration procedures.

7.6.5. *Exploration probes*

Although the missions and their constraints are different from those of satellites, the architectural solutions are often very similar, even if the architecture is typically more integrated with a weaker distinction between a specific platform part and a specific payload part (even if only because of stronger interactions between the mission or the management of the instruments and functions such as attitude and orbit control).

Often this consists of a dual architecture around the bus and the computers. However, some variations can meet the needs and specific constraints of such missions such as the complexity of navigation and the criticality of certain phases. For example, the European probes Mars Express, Venus Express and Rosetta[17] have two computers in each channel. In principle one is dedicated to data management and the other to the navigation and attitude and orbit control system, but the architecture enables the use of any subset of all four computers, even the four in hot redundancy, for critical phases depending on the phases of the mission. In addition, there are four reconfiguration modules, which can be used in different secondary schemes, up to four hot redundant (in vote two out of four in the sense that a reconfiguration is done when it is decided by at least two modules).

7.7. Orbital transport: ATV example

The category of orbital transport vehicles is illustrated here by the European vehicle ATV (automated transfer vehicle), developed by an industrial consortium under the responsibility of Astrium on behalf of the ESA.

7.7.1. *General information*

ATV is a vehicle (unmanned, not reusable) used to provide services to the International Space Station (ISS) and its crew; for example, ATVs can transport equipment, provide a visitable, even habitable area once docked, contribute to control maneuvers of the ISS orbit, evacuate and destruct used equipment, etc. Five ATV models are anticipated, with launches every 18 months, with options for two additional models and project developments. The first model, called ATV-1 Jules Verne, has successfully completed the inaugural mission of March 8 to September 29, 2008.

---

17. These three spacecraft, although having different mission objectives, have been designed to share the most elements possible.

Figure 7.25. *Jules Verne approaching the ISS (artist depiction, ESA)*

7.7.1.1. Mission

The ATV's mission is broken down into several phases:

– *approach and docking*: after injection into orbit (circular altitude of 260 kilometers by a specific version of the European launcher Ariane 5), the ATV adjusts its orbit to perform approach, rendezvous and docking (to the ISS, orbiting nominally at an altitude of 350 kilometers); this phase is actually divided into stages separated by key-points (defined relative to the ISS) where the ATV waits pending the approval of the ground to initiate the next step; this phase lasts a few days (except for the inaugural mission in which a period of 25 days was planned to conduct a thorough verification);

– *docked phase*: while the ATV is docked to the ISS, its capabilities are exploited (under the control of the ISS computer system and the ISS crew, and the ground control center and operators); in particular, its fuel and thrusters are exploited to assist in the control operations of the ISS orbit (typically every 10 to 45 days, with orbital lifts of a few kilometers); in addition, during this phase, the ATV must provide access to its pressurized zone, and maintain the required vital conditions (and even comfort); the docked phase can last up to 6 months;

– *departure and destruction*: the ATV unberths on command and autonomously performs the removal operation from the ISS until receipt of a command to begin deorbit and atmospheric re-entry operations, where it is consumed in large part with any remaining debris falling in an uninhabited chosen area (in the Pacific Ocean); the latter phase typically lasts a few hours.

7.7.1.2. *Key numbers*

– Mass:

- at launch: up to 20,750 kg,

- cargo capacity (towards ISS): up to 7,700 kg,

- return cargo capacity (for destruction): up to 6,400 kg;

– dimensions:

- length: 10 m,

- diameter: 4.5 m (22 m with the solar panels),

- pressurized zone: 48 m^3;

– electric power: four solar panels providing on average 4,800 W;

– propulsion: four main engines (490 N) and 28 smaller engines (220 N) for orbital control, organized in four channels (redundancy).

7.7.1.3. *Dependability history*

The history is currently limited to a single mission, which met all its objectives and which was particularly extensive with a large number of tests and demonstrations in orbit, including capabilities in degraded mode (simulated). Only three minor anomalies can be reported:

– on March 9, 2008 during the first operations after injection into orbit, a difference of pressure in the fuel and combustive was detected, leading to an automatic reconfiguration with deactivation of the dubious propulsion channel and replacement by a redundant channel; complementary operations controlled from the ground control center were then used to verify each channel and restore the nominal configuration with all the available redundancies. It is likely that the anomaly was due to special conditions during the start up of the fuel circuits and did not really need reconfiguration. That said, the detection thresholds were probably a little too strict; however, the reconfiguration was a success with automatic detection and recovery within the time specified; the choice of strict detection thresholds during the first moments of the first mission is more reasonable with regards to the fact that the impact of an unnecessary reconfiguration is extremely low;

– on March 29, 2008, the first day of demonstration, the objectives were to test the approach procedure based on differential GPS (using a relative position calculated by the computer system of the ATV from its own GPS and the information that the ISS computer system transmits to it from the ISS GPS), the bidirectional data link between ATV and ISS, and the "escape" maneuver (a degraded safe mode before the final mode reached after the collision avoidance maneuver); all operations took place successfully, despite the occurrence of an automatic reconfiguration, once again on a propulsion channel, but this time on a temperature threshold. Here again the analysis indicates that the reconfiguration was probably unnecessary, but it does not invalidate the conservative approach adopted;

– finally, a local and limited detachment of the outer layer of thermal protection of the vehicle was observed and assigned, after analysis, to the likely effect of depressurization during launch; the event is considered minor and stakeholders of the program have noted with satisfaction that the sensitivity of temperature control algorithms identified, by telemetry, a slight deviation from the predictions of thermal behavior (before directly seeing blanket positioning anomaly on the images) and that the margins of the thermal control system allowed it to fulfill its function nominally without requiring any intervention.

7.7.2. Dependability requirements

7.7.2.1. Safety

Although unmanned, the ATV must meet safety requirements:

– approach and docking: risk of collision and damage to the ISS, with potentially catastrophic consequences for its crew;

– docked phase: risk to life or health of astronauts living on the ISS or visiting the pressurized part of the ATV if the appropriate conditions of habitability are not assured (temperature, pressure, air composition);

– re-entry: risk *vis-à-vis* the people and assets in case of poor control of the deorbit and re-entry trajectory.

The preservation of living conditions is primarily based on the absence of leaks (and of course on the correct operation of air purification equipment, thermal control, and detection and treatment of fire, as well as in other parts of the ISS). In fact, during the docked phase, the ATV avionics are essentially in dormant mode; the control of the ATV equipment is transferred to the ISS systems. For re-entry, as for the launch, the ATV is subject to the regulations for launches and re-entry, which sets an objective of 10^{-7} per mission of the maximum probability of catastrophic damage to the population.

7.7.2.2. Reliability, availability

The "reliability" objective (or rather the success of the mission) is fixed at 95% for the entire mission, with an interim target of 99% for (successful) docking. As indicated in section 7.4.1, although called "reliability", this mission success goal does not necessarily correspond to continuous operation without interruption of service.

For the ATV, there are nevertheless constraints of continuity of service, which apply mainly to two short periods: during the final approach and docking (beyond the point where an avoidance maneuver can no longer be undertaken), and for re-entry; during these periods, the service must be provided without any interruption of more than 300 milliseconds. Outside these periods, longer outage has little or no impact on the overall success of the mission.

Regarding availability, the needs relate mainly to the instantaneous availability at the time of undertaking the two critical phases that are the final approach and docking, and deorbiting. As for the launcher (section 7.4.2.1), availability is defined here as not just the availability of the service provided by the avionics, but also of all the redundant elements that are necessary to fulfill the objectives of mission success and safety, at least in these critical phases. Outside these critical periods, the availability property relevant to the ATV mission could be characterized by the number of interruptions or of non-functioning on solicitation, which does not jeopardize the success of the mission but can lead to degradation (ground activities, delays). These ATV availability needs are not, however, subject to specific requirements, at least quantitatively (see below: the qualitative requirement of maintaining the operational capability in case of a single fault supports both reliability and availability).

7.7.2.3. *Qualitative requirements*

The avionics of the ATV must remain operational after all simple hardware faults and preserve the safety properties after all simple software faults (even preceded by a simple hardware fault) or from any combination of simple faults (hardware fault or operator error).

7.7.3. *ATV avionic architecture*

7.7.3.1. *Functional architecture*

The functional architecture of the ATV avionics is a hierarchical modular organization of entities classified as:

– functional units (FU): with some functions performed in hardware;

– software units (SU): functions conducted solely in software.

For each functional unit, a functional unit manager (FUM) provides the unit software services and is responsible for the configuration of the functional unit.

The avionics software thus includes software units and functional unit managers. The mission and vehicle manager (MVM) has a particularly important role. It is itself divided into:

– mission manager (MM), performing automatic sequences of operations;

– vehicle configuration manager (VCM), configuring the vehicle and managing its operating modes;

– faults manager and managing, in part, detecting and processing faults (FDIR).

The organization of MM, VCM and FDIR in the MVM and their links to other software units and functional unit managers are detailed in section 7.7.4.

7.7.3.2. Avionics implementation

The avionics of the ATV are located in a slightly conical section called the "Avionics Bay", 1.36 m in height and up to 4.5 m in diameter, inserted between the "cargo" bay and the propulsion module.

Figure 7.26. *The ATV avionics bay (photograph courtesy of the ESA)*

7.7.3.3. *Avionics architecture: dependability*

The architecture chosen to meet the dependability needs consists of two sets:

– a set in charge of nominal avionics functions, i.e. all functions related to the mission, outside circumstances preventing the pursuit of the mission in accordance with the safety requirements;

– a set in charge of monitoring and maintaining safety (MSU: monitoring and safety unit).

The nominal set consists of the elements necessary for nominal operation (propulsion, navigation, electrical power (solar panels, batteries), management of the exchange of measurements and commands with the ground and the international station, thermal control, equipment monitoring), connected by a set of avionics buses to a group of computers.

The presence of an independent safety system can limit the dependability needs of the nominal set to the requirements relative to the mission (tolerance to one fault, a goal of 99% for docking and 95% for the entire mission). Thus each piece of avionics equipment is organized in a conventional redundancy scheme (a unit in cold redundancy except for critical elements, fallible, or with long recovery time). However, unlike traditional solutions in satellites, given the objectives of continuity of service, a set of three computers in hot redundancy is used with comparison and voters distributed in each computer (to avoid failure on loss of a single centralized voter), in addition to mechanisms of error detection within each computer.

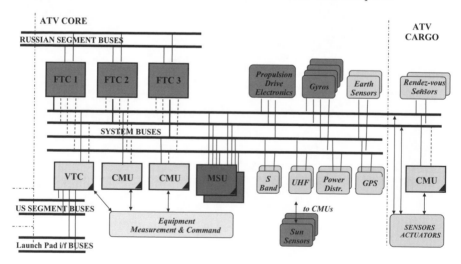

Figure 7.27. *ATV avionic architecture*

The MSU safety system of the ATV is organized according to principles of strong segregation *vis-à-vis* the nominal system, to minimize common faults (separate resources) and the propagation from the nominal system to the safety system. The safety system monitors the health of the nominal system, and the preservation of safety properties. If necessary, it is responsible for undertaking and implementing safety maneuvers using dedicated sensors and actuators (thrusters), independent of the nominal function.

The computer safety system consists of two units in hot redundancy, but without voter, and organized in a selective active redundancy scheme: the two computers are powered, receive and process inputs, but only one actually provides a single output.

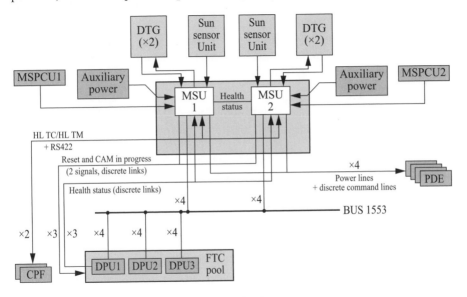

Figure 7.28. *ATV safety system*

7.7.4. *Management of ATV dependability*

Dependability is based on a hardware architecture and procedures that exploit the capabilities offered by this architecture. These procedures are what are known in space systems as FDIR.

7.7.4.1. *Safety set*

Procedures for dependability of the safety set concern:

– management of the safety function itself, i.e. the function in charge of maintaining the ATV safety properties;

– management of complementary FDIR functions for accomplishing the (safety) function according to requirements, in case of faults in the safety set.

The safety function itself corresponds primarily to the function called PFS (proximity flight safety), which is treated here as part of the overall ATV FDIR. This function corresponds to the detection, isolation, and recovery in cases of faults affecting the safety of the approach and docking phase:

– detection: the proximity safety function monitors a global property consisting of a maximum relative speed of approach based on distance to the station, a set of indicators on the good condition of the nominal system (life signal from the computers, traffic coherence on the bus), and commands from the ground or from the space station;

– isolation: isolation is limited to a total re-initialization of all computers of the nominal system; by design this results in a reboot of each computer in passive mode, with none commanding the avionics bus;

– recovery: recovery consists of the execution of the collision avoidance maneuver, which ends with the installation of the ATV in survival mode, awaiting commands from the ground.

The FDIR complementary function consists here of addressing the faults affecting the safety set. A set of detection mechanisms on the active computer (temperature monitoring, voltage, temporal monitoring), combined with software monitoring (plausibility of values, scheduling), leads to the periodical activation of a health signal. In its absence, the redundant computer takes over the function.

7.7.4.2. *Nominal set*

Dependability procedures of the nominal set are organized as indicated in Figure 7.29.

The ATV FDIR (nominal part) is not completely centralized (although this figure includes a unique element called FDIR), but in reality a hierarchical organization of partially decentralized sub-functions:

– detection: detection is performed at the lowest level (functional or software unit); when the anomaly is confirmed (multiple occurrences on a predetermined number of successive cycles), a signal is sent to the FDIR function (alarm corresponding to a group of anomalies);

– isolation: in case of an anomaly that is clearly localized and presents risks of damage to an element or propagation, isolation is performed automatically and directly on the element. In other cases, isolation is under the responsibility of the central FDIR function;

– recovery: recovery actions are decided by the central FDIR function and issued in the form of requests to the MM or VCM as appropriate.

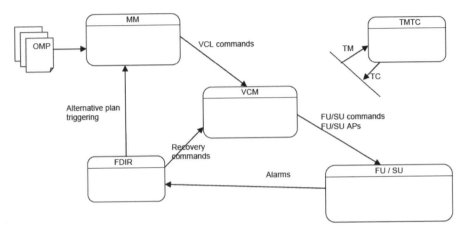

Figure 7.29. *ATV FDIR organization (nominal system)*

The FDIR function, implemented as an onboard software application, is executed cyclically and processes any eventual alarms (if applicable according to priority; one alarm is processed at a time). Several gradual recovery actions exist, from the selection of a rescue mission plan to the reconfiguration of the avionics elements, up to the engagement of the procedure survival procedure where the nominal system is re-initialized, which automatically results in a passive mode with recovery by the safety system.

7.7.4.3. *Specific case of the nominal computers*

The management of computer redundancy is always a special case in systems where fault tolerance is generally managed by a function that essentially consists of software running on these precise computers.

The nominal system of the ATV avionics has three computers with their own mechanisms for fault tolerance, organized into three levels:

– each computer has mechanisms for monitoring and detecting its own faults (temperature monitoring, voltage, watchdog, task scheduling, plausibility of values, memory access errors, detecting and correcting codes for memory error); these mechanisms lead the concerned computer to a self-reset, which places it in a standby mode where it no longer controls any bus nor sends outputs;

– computers exchange and cyclically compare their results (two-round algorithm tolerating an arbitrary fault); a faulty computer is identified by the other two (single fault case), which send it a signal to reset (leading, as indicated above, to a stand-by state without bus control); the remaining computers will take control of the bus previously controlled by the faulty computer, according to a predefined schema, and continue to perform the functions (fault masking), now organized in hot duplex self-detection and comparison. This allows detection of any other simple fault, and even to tolerate some (if the self-detection mechanisms can identify the faulty computer). Note that after a second localized fault, the remaining computer can continue to operate the nominal function with the ability to detect a simple fault (coverage by self-detection mechanisms) and safety protection provided by the MSU;

– as indicated in the preceding sections, certain anomalies detected at higher levels, by the FDIR function or by the MSU safety system, lead those entities to send a global reinitialization signal to all nominal computers, even if the self-detection and comparison mechanisms of these computers have not detected any anomaly; this signal leads each of the computers to a stand-by state, the nominal function not being ensured anymore; the absence of life signals of the nominal computers leads the safety system (even if it is not at the origin of the re-initialization) to take control of the vehicle and initiate necessary safeguard procedures.

7.8. Summary and conclusions

We conclude this chapter on spacecraft with a summary of the key points characterizing solutions and justifications for their dependability.

7.8.1. *Reliability, availability, and continuity of service*

In space systems, "traditional" dependability requirements, outside of safety, are usually achieved by selective redundancy architectures, that is to say architectures where only nominal elements provide their outputs.

The degree of redundancy depends on the criticality and the fallibility of the elements, but more often one degree is enough. It may even be the case when several elements are needed to ensure the nominal function, for example, of three gyroscopes (or reaction wheels or thrusters) in three non-coplanar axes: a fourth element on a linearly independent axis preserves a useable triplet after the loss of any element.

A redundancy of one degree is the minimum necessary to achieve the objective often required for not losing the mission on a single fault. Experience confirms that it is sufficient to achieve the lifespan objectives, even over periods as long as 15 to 18 years for telecommunications satellites (except of course for some fallible elements (sensors) or limited lifetime (batteries, components with moving mechanical parts) for which a larger number of additional elements must be provided). Note that the reliability achieved by these first-degree redundant architectures is due to the frequent use of specific components, whose reliability is further improved by conservative rules of use (derating).

In many cases, the cold redundancy solution is also used, reducing electricity consumption but also promoting lifespan because electronic components have a much lower failure rate when unpowered. This solution requires the use of other detection mechanisms than a comparison between two units.

Depending on the time constraints of recovery and continuity of service or availability needs, a solution of either warm or hot redundancy can be adopted. Hot redundancy allows a very short recovery time, consistent with the needs of a launcher, such as Ariane 5. On a satellite, a longer recovery time can be considered without any perceptible impact on the service. A warm redundancy solution will reduce latency by test programs on the redundant unit. In both cases, warm or hot redundancy will enable the mission context to be managed independently on each unit, limiting the potential propagation of faults.

Majority vote architectures are infrequently used, apart from some launchers (but the example of Ariane 5 confirms that selective redundancy architecture also meets the need, including in terms of continuity of service) and orbital transport vehicles. Their main disadvantage, at least for satellites or exploration probes, is the increase of mass and energy consumption compared to a selective architecture. Moreover, these architectures do not detect and tolerate common mode faults (that is why in the ATV the conventional detection mechanisms on each unit are kept in addition to the comparison mechanism).

The cost and duration of space missions and, in general, the impossibility of physically intervening on the vehicle after launch, lead to highly connected architectures, which limit the connections and reconfiguration capabilities as little as possible; the ideal being to continue to operate not only after having lost an element, but as long as it retains a sufficient number of each kind. These multiple connections increase, however, the possibilities of propagation of faults. In a launcher where the probability of multiple faults (independent) is low given the length of mission, the independence of channels and the simplicity of the reconfiguration are more important than the multiple possibilities of interconnection. For a satellite or exploration probe, the reconfiguration possibilities are as broad as possible, even if it complicates the validation. However, when feasible, the capacity of the vehicle will not usually be overly increased so that all the possible reconfigurations can be operated autonomously; thus a safe stable condition is achieved and maintained, with additional investigations and ground operation undertaken by operators.

7.8.2. *Safety*

The fundamental principle to meet the safety needs in a spacecraft is the segregation between a simple safety system and the nominal system.

This principle applies to safety in the strict sense, applicable to launchers, inhabited flights, and orbital transport. This corresponds to, for example, the safety system intended to destroy a launcher in case of incorrect and dangerous flight profile, or a safety system responsible for monitoring the docking of the ATV and performing the collision avoidance maneuver.

This principle also applies to the very important survival mode concept. Although it is generally not safety-related in the sense of the protection of persons and assets, it is still a similar concept in that it decides to abort the mission in order to avoid more serious consequences (i.e. definitive loss, partial or total, of the mission). The survival mode requires resources to maintain vital functions (electrical power, which assumes control of the orientation of solar panels, and a minimum battery management; communications with the ground, etc.).

Regarding safety, the management of a survival mode is based on the definition of procedures that are as simple as possible, and the choice of the smallest possible set of resources, with minimal dependencies on resources used for the mission, at least for the suspected resources after the failure that led to the decision to engage the survival mode. For example, the redundant unit may be used for every element necessary for survival that was used before the failure (but this is not always the best solution because of dormant faults in the inactive units).

7.9. Bibliography

[ANS 83] ANSI, Standard ANSI/MIL-STD-1815A-1983, Ada programming language, 1983.

[ARI 92] ARINC, "Software considerations in airborne systems and equipment certification", ARINC, no. DO 178B, EUROCAE, no. ED12, edition B, 1992.

[BRE 06] BRETON D., ROSSIGNOL A., *EUROSTAR E3000 On-board Software: Development of a Product Line Towards Multiple System Needs*, ERTS-2006, Toulouse, January 25-27 2006.

[DUR 02] DUROU O., GODET V., MANGANE L., PERARNAUD D., ROQUES R., "Hierarchical fault detection, isolation and recovery applied to COF and ATV avionics", *Acta Astronautica*, vol. 50, no. 9, 2002, pp.547-566.

[CSG-SR] *CSG Safety Regulations*, Issue 5 CSG-RS-09ACN, November 2006.

[ECSS-Q-ST-30C] *Space Product Assurance – Dependability*, European Coordination for Space Standardisation, March 6, 2009.

[ECSS-Q-ST-40C] *Space Product Assurance – Safety*, European Coordination for Space Standardisation, March 6, 2009.

[ECSS-Q-ST-80C] *Space Product Assurance – Software Product Assurance*, European Coordination for Space Standardisation, March 6, 2009.

[MIL 78] Military Standard, MIL-STD-1553B "Aircraft internal time division command/ response multiplex data bus", version B, 21 September 1978.

[OST] United Nations Committee on the Peaceful Uses of Outer Space, *Treaty on Principles Governing the Activities of States in the Exploration and Use of Outer Space, including the Moon and Other Celestial Bodies*, COPUOS, January 27, 2007. www.oosa.unvienna.org/oosa/en/SpaceLaw/outerspt.html, accessed May 3, 2010.

Chapter 8

Methods and Calculations Relative to "Safety Instrumented Systems" at TOTAL

8.1. Introduction

In the context of protection of its facilities, TOTAL follows the conventional standards and practices of the oil industry for the design of safety equipment. Regarding the control of risk related to overpressure, overheating, excessive flow, corrosive fluids, etc., the standards require the establishment of safe equipment capable of withstanding the worst conditions of production and protection systems consistent with international standards (e.g. ISO 10418) or sectoral (e.g. API RP 14C) recommendations which synthesize the know-how accumulated over time in this profession to keep risks at a level acceptable to the personnel, the public, and the environment.

When, for reasons of design, size, weight, cost, etc., the conventional protection systems cannot be installed, designers of hydrocarbon production systems then turn to safety instrumented systems (SISs) to replace them. To highlight that they replace conventional protection systems proven by use, they are then called high integrity protection systems (HIPS). Conventional systems are known to reduce risks to an acceptable level, the HIPS must therefore have a good probability of working at least equivalent to the systems they replace.

Chapter written by Yassine CHAABI and Jean-Pierre SIGNORET.

Since the 1970s, TOTAL has developed and implemented a very powerful range of methods and tools based on traditional approaches. They are used on a daily basis to perform our reliability analysis. However, in recent years international standards such as the IEC 61508 [IEC 00] and IEC 61511 [IEC 03] have proposed a new concept of safety integrity level (SIL) required to achieve a level of acceptable risk. They are progressively imposed on the design of SISs and as their scope naturally concern HIPS, their implementation cannot be ignored. Much work was necessary to establish links between these two approaches and identify their similarities and differences.

We note that with regards to convergence, for example, two types of functions identified by these standards are actually found in the oil industry: the "reactive" or "curative" HIPS (e.g. rapid closure of a valve in case of overpressure) operating at *low demand* and the "preventive" HIPS (e.g. maintaining a closed valve if the upstream is under pressure) operating in *continuous mode*.

We note that with regards to divergence, for example, the systematic alignment to a "safe" state in case of detected failure is generally irrelevant for HIPS whose inadvertent failures can cause other safety issues (risk at restart, water hammer, demands on other safety systems, human error, etc.) excluding production losses, which can be considerable. It follows that beyond the SIL, the probability of a spurious failure is also an important design criterion.

These are the issues that will be discussed in the following sections.

8.2. Specific problems to be taken into account

8.2.1. *Link between classic parameters and standards' parameters*

Generally, a *reactive* or *curative* HIPS is a periodically tested stand-by safety system. For such a system, it does not matter whether it was faulty or not before a demand occurs, if it has been repaired in the meantime. It suffices that it be "available" at time t when the demand arises. The classical probabilistic parameter of interest is therefore its *availability A(t)*. Conversely, the probability of failure of interest is its *unavailability U(t)*.

Generally, a preventive HIPS is a safety system operating continuously. For such a system, an incident occurs as soon as there is a failure completely inhibiting its safety function. It must operate without interruption during the period when it is exposed to the demand. The classical probabilistic parameter of interest is its *reliability* R(t). Conversely the probability of failure of interest is its *unreliability* F(t).

Unfortunately the standards have chosen to use the concepts of PFDavg (average probability of failure on demand) and PFH (probability of failure per hour) instead of those of unavailability and unreliability to characterize the SIL. It follows that the first task is to establish the link between the traditional rigorous notions and those of the standards.

Note first that for the traditional reliability analysis, the term PFD, is reserved for failures caused by the demand itself (denoted g) and not for the failures occurring in a pending period.

This is not the case for standards, which completely ignore pure failures on demand, bringing their share of the growing confusion on the definitions of the reliability area where polysemy is all the rage. In fact, PFDavg, as defined by IEC 61508 [IEC 00] and IEC 61511 [IEC 03], is simply the average unavailability of a safety instrumented system.

Regarding the PFH, the link is more difficult to make because it corresponds to a parameter rarely used in the conventional approach. Contrary to what a superficial mathematical analysis might induce, even though in some cases the comparison is valid, it is neither the failure rate, nor the average failure rate, or even the equivalent failure rate (conditional failure intensity or Vesely rate) but rather the average of the unconditional failure intensity $w(t)$ of the SIS considered. Physically, this parameter corresponds to the average frequency of failure.

8.2.2. Problems linked to sawtooth waves

PFDavg and PFH are both average values of time-dependent parameters: $U(t)$ for PFDavg and $w(t)$ for the PFH. When the SIS components are tested periodically, $U(t)$ and $w(t)$ take the shape of typical sawtooth curves that increase gradually, peaking just before the tests and falling to low values just after the tests.

It follows that an SIS can be SIL_i in view of its PFDavg or its PFH, while $U(t)$ or $w(t)$ have significant excursions in the SIL_{i-1} area (see Figure 8.1). *Vis-à-vis* the operating personnel, the risk may be unacceptable just prior to testing, whereas overall, the average is best. The concept of SIL appears as a necessary requirement for refining the SIS design but not sufficient to deal with the risk taken by operators in the facilities.

The first idea is to limit the acceptable *maxima* values of $U(t)$ or $w(t)$ but this is not enough because we can accept them too high for short periods (during testing for example) if particular precautions are implemented. The second idea is to limit (e.g. 10%) the cumulative time spent above the upper limit of the announced SIL. This results in the concept of a *"permanent SIL"* used by our company for HIPS, of which an operating failure would have the gravest consequences.

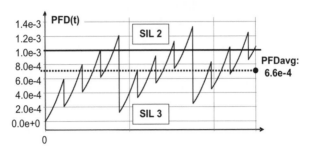

Figure 8.1. *Typical sawtooth curve*

8.2.3. *Definition*

We have already seen above the problems of confusion related to the use of the terms PFD and PFH. There are others in the definitions of types of failures which Figure 8.2 attempts to classify.

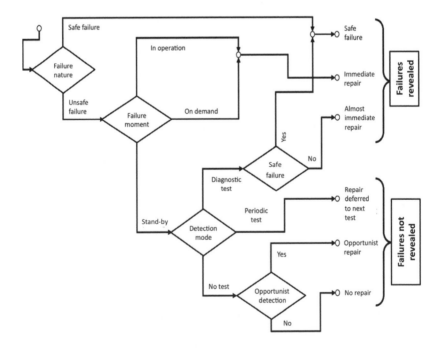

Figure 8.2. *A classification of failures*

Figure 8.2 addresses both individual components and the complete SIS. Depending on whether they impede or facilitate the safety action, the failure modes are divided into two classes with diametrically opposite effects:

– *unsafe failures*: that tend to inhibit the safety action and, ultimately, prevent it from operating when requested;

– *safe failures*: that tend to anticipate the safety action and, ultimately, trigger it unintentionally.

Note that some unsafe failures can be transformed more or less rapidly and more or less automatically into safe failures after being detected. The IEC standards divide the failures into four classes (see Figure 8.3):

– safe detected (SD) failures by a diagnostic;

– safe undetected (SU) failures by a diagnostic, but revealed after a functional test;

– dangerous detected (DD) failures by a diagnostics;

– dangerous undetected (DU) failures by a diagnostic, but revealed after a functional test.

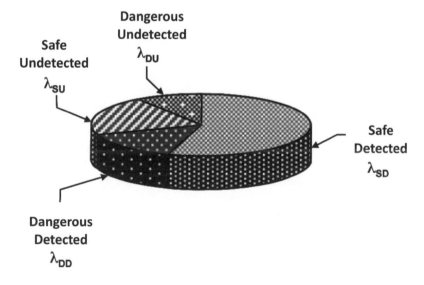

Figure 8.3. *Different types of failures according to the IEC standard*

If *dangerous failures* of IEC standards match the *unsafe failures* above, this is not the case for *safe failures*. Indeed, in their current editions, any *non-dangerous* failure is considered *safe*. This allows the supplier to consider safe any kind of failure (e.g. SU failure) without any relationship to the safety function in question and to announce the SFF (*safe failure fraction*, i.e. proportion) to be much higher than in reality.

Beyond the safe/unsafe partition, two major classifications of failures occur:

– operating/on-demand/on stand-by;

– revealed/not revealed.

Even if failures in operating are most often *revealed*, and failure on stand-by failures *unrevealed*, they are different concepts that should not be confused. A (too) fast reading of standards often leads to an assimilation of *revealed failure* ≡ *safe failure*, which of course is true only after an action has been successfully undertaken to complete the transformation.

It should be noted that genuine on-demand failures (that is, to due to the demand itself say because of the request) cannot be tested while revealed failures can undertake prompt corrective action (shutdown and/or repair of the protected unit).

All these types of failures appear during the HIPS analysis and require specifically adapted modeling and mathematical processing.

8.2.4. *Reliability data*

Before describing the models dealing with HIPS, we must address the evaluation of reliability parameters of their basic components. This is most often a major weak point of reliability approaches, but in the oil sector, we have the chance of participating in a reliability database common to most oil majors for over 25 years: OREDA (Offshore Reliability Data).

OREDA was launched in 1982 with the following objectives:

– improve the safety of installations by providing feedback and data on risks;

– improve the reliability and availability of facilities through the use of reliability data to select the most reliable equipment and configurations;

– improve the efficiency of maintenance by using failure data to define maintenance strategies;

– improve the reputation of the industry by demonstrating a high degree of understanding of performance and equipment characteristics.

OREDA enables the accumulation and exchanging of operating experience in a common format, serving as the basis for the publication of the ISO 14224 standard for data collection in the oil and gas industry.

As part of this project, we have access to the entire updated database but less detailed data are available to the public through a publication issued every 4 to 5 years. These data provide a solid basis for our analysis of dependability and safety.

From the OREDA data, supplemented by other more specific instrumented system data (PDS, EIXIDA), we selected the "preferred" reliability data that we use routinely in our SIL calculations.

Other industries, such as nuclear power, for example, have established this kind of data collection, but in general, and as mentioned above, reliability data are the weak point of probabilistic calculations. The IEC standards are trying to compensate for this problem by adding deterministic constraints subject to caution (e.g. architectural constraints based on the concept of "safe failure fraction", SFF) while the solution lies in the organization of better feedback data collection from users of components. It is illusory to believe that the feedback can be completely replaced by the analysis and constraints applied more or less blindly. Therefore, we can only encourage other industries to follow the example of the oil and gas or nuclear sector and organize and establish collective databases.

8.2.5. *Common mode failure and systemic incidences*

When the safety of a facility is assured by several cascading protective systems, the IEC standards propose to evaluate the risk reduction factors necessary for each of them so that the overall risk reduction achieved meets the criteria of acceptable risk. Thus the sequencing of two layers of protection, each bringing a risk reduction of 100 (SIL 2), seems to provide a risk reduction of $100 \times 100 = 10,000$ (SIL 4).

Even if the simplistic calculation above is commonly done, it is nonetheless non-conservative because it ignores two very important issues:

– common mode failure between layers of protection;

– systemic incidences between layers.

The first problem is identified by the IEC standards, which require that safety systems operating in sequence are completely independent. This is almost never realized in the processes domain as this would put many final elements in series (e.g. two valves for emergency shutdown plus two HIPS valves). In reality the final elements are often shared and that entails a significant incidence on reducing risk.

The second problem is much more subtle. It is because the average probabilities cannot be manipulated like pure numbers. Consider two independent and identical protection layers with the same dangerous undetected failure rate λ_{DU} and tested periodically with an interval τ:

– the basic calculation gives each one a PFDavg of $\lambda_{DU}.\tau/2$ and a risk reduction factor of RRF=1/PFDavg= $2/(\lambda_{DU}.\tau)$;

– risk reduction for both operating systems in sequence seems to be $RRF^2 = 4/(\lambda_{DU}.\tau)^2$;

– the problem is that the PFDavg of the two identical systems in parallel is $(\lambda_{DU}.\tau)^2/3$;

– the risk reduction is only of $3/(\lambda_{DU}.\tau)^2$ and the simplistic calculation is non-conservative.

Viewed differently, the first system provides a reduced risk of $2/(\lambda_{DU}.\tau)$ when the second provides only $3/(2.\lambda_{DU}.\tau)$ which is only 75% of the expected risk reduction for a system off the shelf! This problem, the ransom of the convolution product replacement by ordinary products, worsens when the redundancy and the number of safety layers increases. This is a systemic incidence that cannot be properly understood solely by the separate analysis of each layer of protection.

Therefore, the more we aim for a higher SIL, the more the simplistic calculations are non-conservative. Only a systemic approach can correctly interpret these difficulties and, therefore, we have developed methods and tools to cope with this issue.

At the level of an individual SIS, common mode failures are also considered when redundancy is implemented. The IEC standards propose the use of the classical β factor method and this method is effective when the number of identical elements is about two or three. In the oil and gas industry occasionally there are a much larger number of elements involved – for example, if the facility stops, dozens of wells must be closed under penalty of sending the ignited liquid through the flare. In this case, instead of the β factor, we prefer the *shock method* to manage the problem.

8.2.6. *Other parameters of interest*

The simplistic PFDavg calculations above neglect the impact of duration of testing and maintenance. They are strictly valid only when the unit protected by the safety function is stopped during testing and repairs which, of course, is not the case most of the time.

In addition, many other parameters can be identified with a negative impact, that is more or less important, on the probability of a SIS failure:

– the duration of the test;

– state (available or not for the function) during the test;

– the duration of the first interval between tests (to stagger tests with similar components);

– probability of failure because of the test;

– non-detection of existing failure (human error);

– non-reconfiguration after test (human error);

– etc.

For example, if the element tested is isolated to do the test, it can make a strong contribution to its average unavailability (PFDavg) and increase the likelihood of human error.

All these parameters must be analyzed and treated correctly during probabilistic studies concerning HIPS or risk obtaining non-conservative results.

8.2.7. *Analysis of tests and maintenance*

8.2.7.1. *Tests*

HIPS components are subjected to periodic tests to detect unrevealed failures occurring during a pending period and taking into account the policy applied during testing, which is an important element in SIL calculations.

Two cases arise regarding the occurrence of a demand during the period when a test is performed:

– either the protected unit is stopped and the *threat* is *suspended* during testing. In this case the risk no longer exists and there is no need to take the test duration into consideration for the SIL calculation: for example, some underwater HIPS need to be isolated and production shut down in order to perform tests;

– or the protected unit continues to function normally and the *threat* is *maintained* during testing. In this case the test duration is particularly sensitive and needs to be carefully taken into account: for example, many redundant components of HIPS installed on the topside are tested during normal operation of the facility.

In the second case, three different situations are considered *vis-à-vis* the safety function fulfilled by the component tested:

– either it is still "*active*" and the component continues to ensure its safety function during the test. Example: testing closing of a valve, which must close if requested;

– or it is "*forced*" and everything happens as if the component were tested in safe failure. Example: output forced to 0 for a sensor operating in de-energize to trip configuration;

– or it is "*inhibited*" and the component is unavailable during testing. Example: the component is isolated during testing.

We find ourselves facing many different circumstances:

– in case 1, there is no need to model the test period;

– in case 2a) the failure rate may be higher during the test and the situation slightly degraded;

– in case 2b) the situation is more secure than in the nominal case, therefore, do not take into account the period of test if it is conservative;

– in case 2c) the situation is less secure than in the nominal case and taking into account the test period is unavoidable.

The safety function can be perfect, improved, degraded, or completely inhibited during testing. It is particularly important to identify potential cases of type 2c) because even if the test time is short, the impact on the SIL can be significant and constitute a key factor for high SILs.

Similar to the diagnostic tests introduced in the IEC standards that have a diagnostic coverage (DC), periodic tests are not necessarily able to identify all modes of failures occurring while being on stand-by. When analyzing tests, it is, therefore, necessary to identify failure modes that are actually covered. For a valve participating to a HIPS function, we can thus identify the following types of tests:

– *full stroking* tests testing closure and sealing;

– *partial* stroking tests not testing leakages;

– periodic disassembly in the workshop for revealing cracks in mechanical equipment in order to avoid failures during potential demands.

So far we have mostly discussed the beneficial aspect of tests but there are detrimental aspects that must also be carefully analyzed and modeled. For a valve participating in a HIPS function, we can thus identify the following effects:

– provocation of *on demand failures* due to the tests themselves (e.g. breaking of the axis of a valve, electrical failure, etc.);

– potential *human errors*:

    - failure to put it back online after a test,

    - non-total reopening after a test (the valve whistles and loses its sealing),

    - reassembly error after complete disassembly;

– *financial losses*: production losses, cost of testing, etc.

The above aspects strongly depend on the components considered and the policy of the adopted tests.

8.2.7.2. *Maintenance*

For HIPS, the failures revealed or detected during testing are usually repaired as quickly as possible to restore the nominal situation *vis-à-vis* safety and the two cases identified for the tests remain relevant: it is necessary to take maintenance into account if the threat persists while it is being done.

Maintenance policies may be very different and more or less complex:

– *individual* maintenance of a failed component;

– *collective* maintenance of several components (e.g. standard exchange of a block of several components);

– *opportunistic* maintenance of failures unrelated to the safety function concerned;

– *periodical change* of components subject to aging;

– *logic change* at the first failure and repair at the second failure (e.g. a change from 2oo3 to 1oo2 at the first failure);

– etc.

It is noteworthy that the exchange or disassembly/reassembly of a component can be used to repair failures that were not detected by tests.

Conversely, maintenance may also involve the mobilization of personnel, tools or specific intervention means that should be identified and modeled.

8.2.7.3. *Effect of testing and maintenance on the PFD of an elementary component: the multiphase Markovian approach*

If the Markovian approach is difficult to implement rigorously for complete SIS because of the many states to consider, it is particularly effective in treating individual components.

We will use this section to demonstrate the allure of instantaneous unavailability, PFD(t), of individual components with regards to the parameters of interest. In each case we find on the right-hand side of Figures 8.5 to 8.9 the detail of what happens around zero or close to a test.

The revealed failures are shown in Figure 8.4 where the PFD(t) quickly converges to an asymptotic value equal to λ/μ.

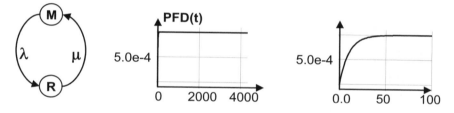

Figure 8.4. *Revealed failure, quickly repaired*

When the component is tested periodically, the implementation of a multiphase Markovian modeling is necessary. This is shown in Figure 8.5. Between two tests the system can be subject to a dangerous undetected failure (DU, see the Markov graph on the left).

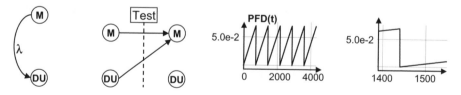

Figure 8.5. *Failure detected by a test and immediately repaired*

It then remains in this state until the next test where the failure is immediately detected and repaired (see test matrix). Thus the probability of working is reset to 1 after each test.

When the repair has to be taken into account, the Markov graph contains an additional state (repair). In addition to the previous case, it may return to work between two tests by a repair initiated after a test.

As shown in the test matrix, the state of failure becomes a state of repair immediately after the test. The probabilities of working, failure, and repair just before a test are used to calculate the initial probabilities of the Markov process just after a test.

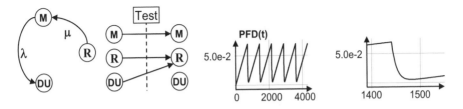

Figure 8.6. *Failure detected by a test, not immediately repaired*

When the test itself is the source of a failure, the operating condition just before a test can lead either to an operating condition after the test (probability 1-γ), or to a state of repair (probability γ). This is modeled by the test matrix.

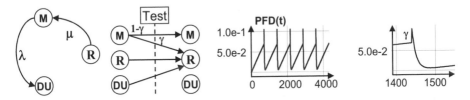

Figure 8.7. *Failure detected by a test, failure due to a test, not immediately repaired*

When the test duration must be taken into account, a supplementary phase is interposed between the periods between tests. In the model below a failure due to the test is detected immediately, but the DU failure is detected only after the test. During the test, the component remains available for the safety function but it may fail with a different and higher failure rate (λ') than when on stand-by.

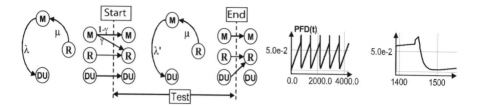

Figure 8.8. *Failure detected by a test, failure due to a test, not immediately repaired, test duration not negligible, available during the test*

When the component is taken offline during the test, it is unavailable to ensure its safety function. The model is the same as Figure 8.8 except that the operating state does not exist during the test. We noted state DD (dangerous detected) in Figure 8.9. As the rest is similar to the previous figure, we have not shown it again.

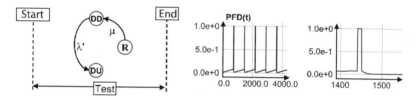

Figure 8.9. *Failure detected by a test, failure due to a test, not immediately repaired, test duration not negligible, not available during the test*

The exercise could be continued indefinitely, but the goal is to show the great variety of behaviors encountered and the flexibility of the Markovian approach to understanding them, so we will conclude there.

The above models are small enough to allow us to develop corresponding analytical formulas, as has been done in the ARALIA [RAU 06] software in order to be able to perform calculations presented in the chapter on fault trees.

As soon as we grapple with complete real HIPS, the combinatorial explosion in the number of states makes it difficult to rigorously apply the Markovian approach, which is hardly possible without tools to automatically generate Markov graphs from the corresponding models based, for example, on the AltaRica Data Flow [ARN 00; RAU 98]. But even then, only very small systems can be treated rigorously. Therefore, we more readily implement the approach by stochastic Petri nets as described later in this chapter.

8.2.8. *General approach*

To address the safety and dependability of HIPS, we use the following approach based on classic stages:

– identification of unwanted events and initiating events;

– identification of safety barriers to be taken into account and whose failure causes the demand on the analyzed HIPS;

– analysis of component failures and their impact on the safety function;

– analysis of common mode or common cause failures;

– modeling with regards to the parameters to be calculated (PFD, PFH, spurious failure frequency) and the nature of the concerned HIPS (topside or subsea);

– probability calculations;

– identification of weak points;

– improving the HIPS architecture, development of the testing procedure and maintenance to be applied to achieve the objectives (safety and production availability);

– verification that the SIL is "permanent" and return to phase 8 if this is not the case;

– eventual verification that given the uncertainties about the data, the SIL objective is obtained with more than 90 chances out of 100 and a return to phase 8 if this is not the case;

– systematic modeling of all safety barriers (including HIPS) to assess the overall probability of an accident.

Since the early 1980s, we have developed and improved the range of methods and tools to meet our dependability studies: reliability, availability, production availability, and now SIL. As previously mentioned, the three main approaches [CRA 02; SIG 06] used are:

– fault trees [RAU 06; SIG 08b];

– Markov processes [RAU 04; SIG 04];

– stochastic Petri nets and Monte Carlo simulation [DUT 03; SIG 98; SIG 08a].

The fault trees require a slight adjustment in order to be readily applied and are very effective in treating curative HIPS whose components are "reasonably" independent, such as those installed on the topside parts of our facilities. For underwater HIPS, where maintenance is much more complex, the multiphase

Markovian approach can be used but, given the combinatorial explosion that occurs when the number of components exceeds a few units, approaches using Petri nets and Monte Carlo simulation are more effective.

For preventive HIPS or the evaluation of the frequency of spurious failures, the fault tree can also be used when the components are "reasonably" independent but important mathematical knowledge is needed to understand the exact meaning of the calculations realized. It follows that in this case, the approach of Petri nets and Monte Carlo simulation is also the easiest to implement because it is very easy to understand.

It should be noted that with current personal computers, the evaluation of SIL 4 is no longer a problem of computing time when using an effective stochastic simulator, such as the MOCA-RP [RAU 04], which is the software we use and which has been distributed these past 25 years.

The following sections are devoted to the illustration of the calculations mentioned above with examples.

8.3. Example 1: system in 2/3 modeled by fault trees

Example 1 is deliberately simplified in order to present the principle of calculation by fault trees. We will show how common causes of failures are very easily modeled and how the staggering of tests and the test policy can be taken into account.

8.3.1. *Modeling without CCF*

Let us consider the system with three sensors, periodically tested and presented on the reliability block diagram in Figure 8.10.

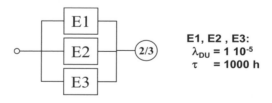

Figure 8.10. *Three sensors in 2oo3 without CCF*

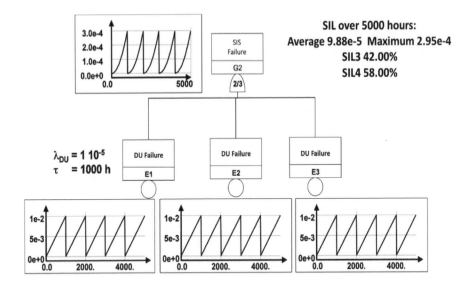

Figure 8.11. *Failure without CCF*

The fault tree modeling the system failure and the results are presented in Figure 8.11.

This system meets SIL 4 even though it only spends 58% of its time here. For 42% of the time it is in the SIL 3 area with a push to 3×10^{-4} just before testing.

8.3.2. *Introduction of the CCF by factor β*

Let us now introduce CCF on the sensors. The reliability block diagram is modified in the following manner (see Figure 8.12).

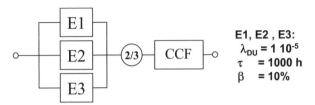

Figure 8.12. *Three sensors in 2oo3 with CCF*

The fault tree modeling the system failure and the results are presented in Figure 8.13. The impact of common cause failures is important and the system now meets the SIL 3 requirements where it spends 71% of its time. However, it is now SIL 2 for 20% of the time with a push to 1.3×10^{-3}. Just prior to testing, the risk to the operator was multiplied by about five.

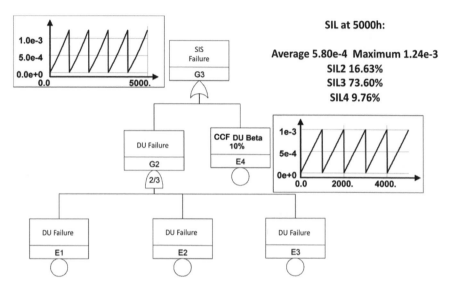

Figure 8.13. *Failure with CCF*

8.3.3. *Influence of test staggering*

8.3.3.1. *Synchronized tests*

Let us take the example above with an interval between tests increased to 3 months (2,190 hours) and a β factor of 5% only. The results are shown in Figure 8.14. The system went to SIL 2, but it spends 47% of its time in SIL 1 with a push to 2.35×10^{-3}.

Besides the sawtooth curve on the PFD(t) at the top of the fault tree, we also show the PFD(t) of each component and the CCF in this figure. As the tests were all performed at the same time, the curves are identical for the components and the CCF is also tested every 3 months.

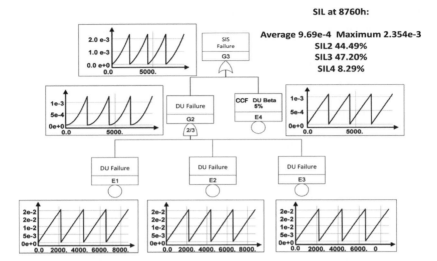

Figure 8.14. *PFD calculations with non-staggered tests*

8.3.3.2. *Staggering of tests without impact on CCF*

Now let us look at what happens when, all things being equal, we stagger to one third the interval of tests of all three components. It follows a shift $\theta_{C3} = 730$ (1 month) for component 3, $\theta_{C2} = 1,460$ (2 months) for component 2, and $\theta_{C1} = 2,190$ (3 months, i.e. no shift).

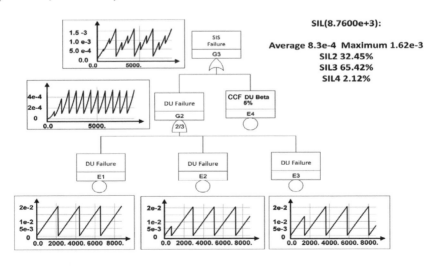

Figure 8.15. *Calculations of PFD with staggered tests without impact on the result*

Note that the staggering of tests not only improves system availability (SIL 3 for 62% of the time instead of 47%) but also decreases the maximum value.

8.3.3.3. *Staggering of tests with impact on CCF*

However, in the above calculation we found that CCFs were separately tested in the components every 3 months. In fact, in reality (and provided that the ad *hoc* procedure is in place), CCF can be detected during testing of the components themselves. So each test component is also a test of CCF and for our system, when the test components are shifted the frequency of testing of CCF is multiplied by three. This leads us to Figure 8.16.

In this case, the impact on the SIL and the maximum value is even greater than before. The staggering of tests is, therefore, an essential element to be taken into account in calculating the availability of HIPS and is a very effective way of achieving or improving the level of SIL desired. The implementation of this operation can be cumbersome, a little education may be required from the operators to explain all the ins and outs!

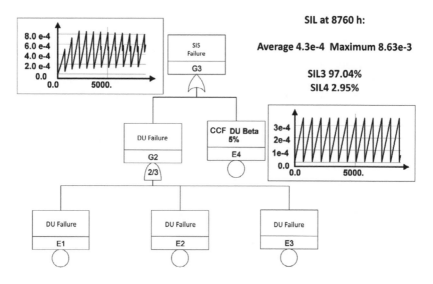

Figure 8.16. *PFD calculation with staggered tests and impact on the result*

8.3.4. *Elements for the calculation of PFH*

The fault tree above can also be used to calculate the PFH of the modeled system. As the calculations are similar, we will only give some indications on the calculations of PFH by fault tree.

Figure 8.17 shows the evolution of the unconditional failure intensity w(t) and the equivalent average failure rate $\Lambda_{average}(t)$ corresponding to the fault tree in Figure 8.17.

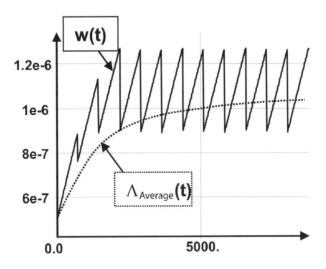

Figure 8.17. *w(t) and $\Lambda_{average}(t)$ typical of a SIS periodically tested*

The PFH of this system corresponds to the average of the wave *w(t)* above, a failure rate of about 1.5×10^{-6}/year (1.7×10^{-10}/hour) and this system is SIL 4 according to the standard. This result is more optimistic than the one previously found using the PFDavg. When redundancy is present, the results given by the PFDavg and the PFH are not necessarily identical. Caution must be applied when using these concepts.

We see that the equivalent average failure rate converges very slowly towards this asymptotic value. Using it as an estimate of the PFH is not conservative in this case.

The above results are typical of SIS including components tested periodically but the behavior is very different when the system contains only safe failures, revealed and repaired quickly. With the fault tree above but with revealed failures ($\lambda_{SD} = 10^{-4}$/hour, $\mu = 0.1$/hour) and a factor β of 5% we can find the results shown in Figure 8.18.

We note that here *w(t)* converges rapidly (two to three times the MTTR) to an asymptotic value, which is the PFH one. The equivalent average failure rate also converges towards the same asymptote but much more slowly (20 to 30 times the MTTR). It therefore provides a non-conservative estimate in the short term.

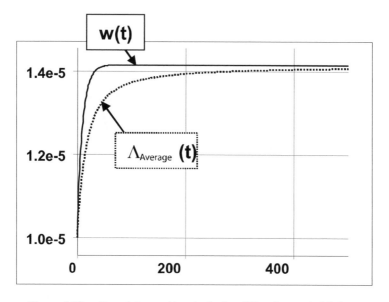

Figure 8.18. *w(t) and $\Lambda_{Average}(t)$ typical of an SIS with revealed failures*

8.4. Example 2: 2/3 system modeled by the stochastic Petri net

If the fault tree is very effective for dealing with HIPS that have reasonably independent components, its results are unreliable when this constraint is not respected. We must then implement a method to compensate for this deficiency. The method selected is based on a representation of the behavior of HIPS by stochastic Petri nets (PN) and a calculation by Monte Carlo simulation.

Figure 8.19 shows the behavior of a single component periodically tested and repaired when a failure is detected.

In this figure the circles represent the potential states of the component (stand-by, hidden failure, and repair) and the rectangles the transitions (that is to say events) that may occur. The token (small black circle) indicates the actual state of the component and which transitions are valid (i.e. corresponding to events that may occur) at every moment. When a transition is fired one token is removed from the places upstream, and a token is added in each of the downstream places and assertions (represented by "!!") are updated.

Thus, in the PN below, the component fails with a failure rate of 9.5×10^{-6}/hour (exponential law) which is detected by a periodic test every 3 months (IFA 2190, 0 law). When the fault has been detected, it is repaired with a repair rate 0.1/hour (Exp 0.1 law) before being restored to its stand-by state. The message (!!C1) is used to indicate whether the component is working (!!C1 = true) or failed (!!C1 = false).

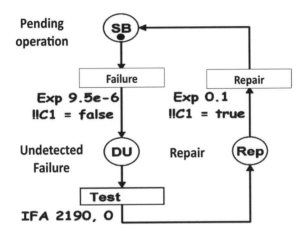

Figure 8.19. *Simple component periodically tested*

The simple component of Figure 8.19 can model (see Figure 8.20) the system in two out of three with the CCF and staggering of tests, which we have already studied through fault trees. Note in Figure 8.20:

– the structure deliberately recalling a reliability block diagram;

– the firing law of "instants fixed in advance" (example: IFA 2190, 730) whose first parameter corresponds to the interval between tests and the second to the duration of the first interval;

– the common cause of failure modeled by a component C4;

– the formula Out1 = (@(2) (C1, C2, C3)), which makes Out1 true when two messages out of C1, C2 and C3 are true;

– the formula Out = Out1 & C4, which indicates that the system works when there is no failure present at the entrance of C4 and that C4 is in good working order. This Out message is used to calculate the instantaneous availability and average availability of the system;

– the small PN at the top and on the right allows detection of the first failure in order to perform the reliability calculations (the dotted arc is an inhibitor arc that prohibits a second firing).

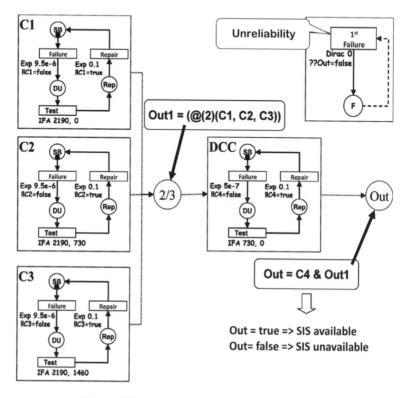

Figure 8.20. *2oo3 system with CCF modeled by PN*

The results obtained and presented in Figure 8.21 are very similar to those found previously by the fault tree. Of course they are less accurate than analytical calculations but this precision is easily controlled thanks to the confidence interval provided by the Monte Carlo simulation and which we have drawn on the PFD(t) and F(t) curves.

These results were obtained with 10^6 simulations of 8,760 hours in a few dozen seconds on an ordinary PC:

– PFDavg was directly calculated from statistics on the OUT message;

– PFDmax was read on the curve;

– F(8760) was obtained by the firing frequency of the "1st failure" transition.

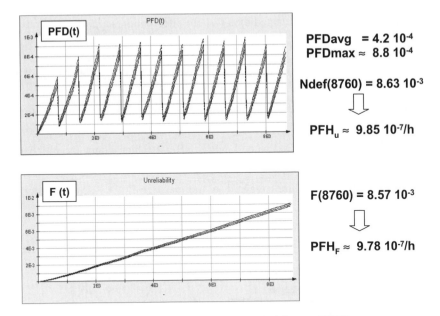

PFDavg = $4.2\ 10^{-4}$
PFDmax ≈ $8.8\ 10^{-4}$

Ndef(8760) = $8.63\ 10^{-3}$

⇩

PFH_u ≈ $9.85\ 10^{-7}$/h

F(8760) = $8.57\ 10^{-3}$

⇩

PFH_F ≈ $9.78\ 10^{-7}$/h

Figure 8.21. *PFD(t), PFDavg, reliability, and PFH obtained using Monte Carlo simulation*

Regarding the PFH, two cases are considered:

– this system is the last barrier intervening before an accident and the PFH should be calculated from the reliability model: $PFH_F = F(8760)/8760$;

– this system is not the last barrier intervening before an accident and the PFH should be calculated from the number of failures Ndef(8760) observed in the availability model: $PFH_U = Ndef(8760)/8760$.

As expected, PFH_U exceeds PFH_F but as the probability of failure is very low, these two parameters are substantially equal. The interest of this example is to show that the same model can handle two cases at once.

Note also that the spurious failures are modeled in exactly the same way and are calculated from the number of failures Ndef(T) observed on the simulated period of duration T.

Of course, these calculations are useful for comparison purposes only and the PN are reserved for cases where fault trees cannot be used as in the example given below where, if a failure is detected by a test, an intervention support (Rig) must be mobilized to perform repair.

The PN on the left is obtained by slightly modifying the one that served as the basis until now (the part in thick lines). It should be noted:

– instead of the DU place representing the potential state where failure is detected but pending intervention support;

– assertions !! NbD=NbD+1 and !! NBD=NBD-1 which count the number of failing components at a given time;

– the common mode failure triggered by the message ?? CCF from another PN not shown here.

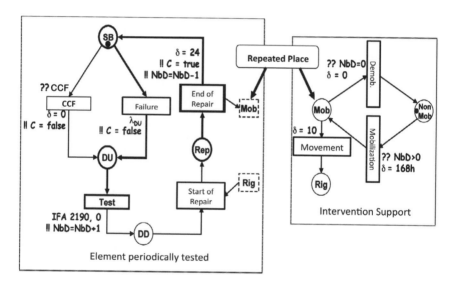

Figure 8.22. *Component requiring mobilization of the intervention support*

The PN on the right represents the mobilization of the intervention support:

– it is triggered when NbD becomes positive (predicate ?? NbD > 0);

– after 1 week (168 hours) the support is mobilized;

– it then heads to the place of repair and arrives there after 10 hours;

– repair can begin (note the "repeated" place Rig on the left PN;

– after 24 hours the repair is complete (transition "end of repair") and the intervention support is released;

– it is then demobilized (NbD = 0) or goes to the following repair;

– etc.

The use of the message !! C = true when the element is functioning and !! C = false when it is failing allows use of this model in exactly the same way as has been described earlier in this section.

The CCF mechanisms or of mobilization above do not present any difficulty for being taken into account by the PN but could not be modeled correctly by the fault tree. They correspond to the problems we encounter when studying subsea HIPS for which the PN modeling is particularly effective.

In addition to mobilization of intervention supports, they take into account:

– management of spare parts;

– change of logic (i.e. 2oo3 transferred to 1oo2 when a failure is detected);

– repair at the second failure;

– repair of several failures at a time;

– etc.

8.5. Other considerations regarding HIPS

8.5.1. *SIL objectives*

As stated in the introduction, a HIPS is a SIS used to replace a conventional protection barrier test proven by use and must, therefore, have a probability of good operation at least equivalent to the system it replaces. For our company the preferred solution is always conventional protection and the installation of a HIPS is still the subject of an ongoing debate. Therefore, a "HIPS committee", independent of projects, has been established to monitor the cases investigated by the involved projects, accept them or not, define objectives to be achieved, and validate the studies undertaken to demonstrate that those objectives have been achieved. This is also why a third, independent body is responsible for certification [CHA 08].

As the conventional protections installed to protect against incidents/accidents with significant impact have equivalent SILs ranging from SIL 2 to SIL 3 and analysis and calculation never provide a confidence as great as the feedback, it is necessary to have a safety margin for the HIPS objectives. Therefore, starting with conventional protection as a basis, we aim for objectives ranging from SIL 3 to SIL 4: SIL 3 when the consequences are significant without endangering life (soft HIPS) and SIL 4 when the consequences affect human life or where environmental or economic consequences are very important (hard HIPS).

These objectives can be relaxed to "permanent" SIL 2 or SIL 3 when they are too difficult to achieve and the probability of a demand is low and/or compensatory measures are implemented. These relaxations are the responsibility of the "HIPS committee" which accept them or not depending on the results of studies.

This margin, serving to compensate the various uncertainties encountered (reliability of the data used, analysis of incompleteness, inaccuracy of the models, approximate calculations, etc.) is not huge, and therefore, it is necessary to perform analysis and probabilistic calculations with the greatest possible rigor, the best available data, and models close to actual physical systems.

The modeling techniques used depend on the mode of operation (reactive or preventive HIPS) and location (surface installations or underwater) of the HIPS concerned. The following sections are intended to briefly give some additions and illustrations to the problems mentioned above.

8.5.2. HIPS on topside facilities

Figure 8.23 shows a typical HIPS installed between two units of triphasic separation (oil, gas, and water) and protecting the downstream separator (DS2) against overpressure (see Figure 8.23) coming from the upstream separator (DS1) when the latter fills with gas. This event, called gas blow-by, may be the result of unintentional and complete opening of the control valve CV (operational error, reception of an erroneous opening signal, mechanical failure of the valve).

The conventional protection against such accidents is the safety loop process (PSD) and valves (PSV) installed on the separator DS2. However, the latter protection is not 100% effective because the BP torch network is not sized to evacuate the flow caused by the gas blow-by. In case of demand, if it works properly, it will lessen the violence of the accident. As it is not possible to change the flare network, the conventional PSV protection must be replaced by an instrumented system, which is precisely the HIPS shown in Figure 8.23.

Seeing the potentially important consequences (human, environmental and economic) of the accident, this HIPS is qualified as hard, which, with regards to our rule, defines a SIL 4 objective.

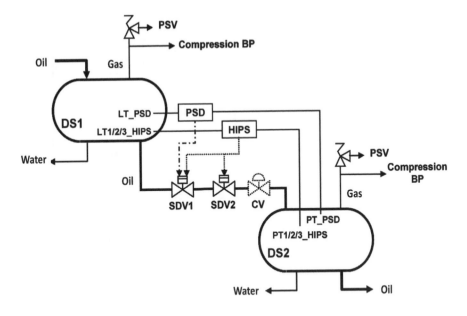

Figure 8.23. *Typical safety barriers*

The safety system against the blow-by gas therefore comprises:

– PSD barrier (level sensor on DS1, pressure sensor on DS2, process calculation automaton and safety valve SDV1);

– HIPS (three level sensors organized in 2oo3 on DS1, three pressure sensors arranged in 2oo3 on DS2, an automatic calculation of SIL 4 calculation automaton in wired status logic, two safety valves (SDV1 and SDV2)).

PSD and HIPS share the same SDV1 valve but use dedicated solenoid valves to control it.

The assessment of the probability of accidental opening of the control valve CV can be estimated from the feedback compiled in reliability databases (e.g. OREDA) and/or the expertise of operators exploiting production facilities. In this case, there is a probability of accidental opening of the control valve CV of about 0.1 per year. It follows that the PSD and HIPS barriers are requested less than once per year and, according to the IEC, they operate at low demand mode. As explained in previous chapters, it therefore requires calculations of the PFD type.

The reliability data used to carry out the calculations are presented in Figures 8.24 and 8.25.

Parameters / Components	Failure Mode	λ_{DU} (h-1)	DC	Interval between tests	Date 1st test	β (DCC) %
PT	Non emission of signal	4.47e-7	0	2190	2190	
LT	Non emission of signal	7.00e-7	0	2190	2190	10
SDV1	Valve blocked open	2.66e-6	0	2190	2190	
SDV2	Valve blocked open	2.66e-6	0	2190	2190	10
SDV1	Incomplete valve closure	8.90e-7	0	8760	8760	
SDV2	Incomplete valve closure	8.90e-7	0	8760	4380	10
SOV1	Non transmission of signal	8.80e-7	0	2190	2190	
SOV2	Non transmission of signal	8.80e-7	0	2190	2190	10
HIPS automaton	PFDavg = 5e-5					
PSD automaton	PFDavg = 5e-4					

Figure 8.24. *Reliability data*

Parameters / Components	MTTR (h)	Test duration (h)	Available during tests	Probability error reconfiguration
PL, LT	1	1	No	1.00e-3
SDV	0	0	Yes	0.00
SV	1	1	No	1.00e-3

Figure 8.25. *Test and maintenance parameters*

Being located in the topside part of the installation, the components are easily accessible and quickly repaired. Therefore, they are relatively independent in terms of maintenance (they have maintenance priority and the probability of simultaneous failure of several priority components is low). So the approach by fault tree is the most appropriate to treat the problem.

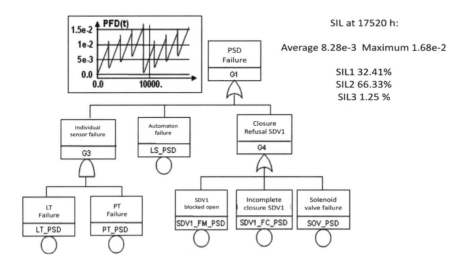

Figure 8.26. *Failure of PSD barrier*

The fault tree shown in Figure 8.24 corresponds to the PSD. It is relatively simple and requires few comments except for the failure modes of the valve separated into two classes according to whether they are detected by a quarterly test of partial stroking or detected by an annual test of full stroking. The quarterly testing is incomplete, and the probability of failure does not return to zero, which gives the PFD(t) curve its unique shape.

According to the results shown in Figure 8.24, the system spends approximately two-thirds of the time in SIL 2 zone and one-third of the time in the SIL 1 zone. The risk reduction according to the IEC standard is RRF1 = $1/8.28 \times 10^{-3}$ = 120.1.

With this single barrier in place (and without regard to a possible common mode) the probability of a gas blow-by is of the order of 10^{-4}/year. According to our rules and given the consequences of the accident, this probability is too high and a further barrier is necessary. The HIPS, whose existence is already justified by the ineffectiveness of the PSV barrier, will play this role.

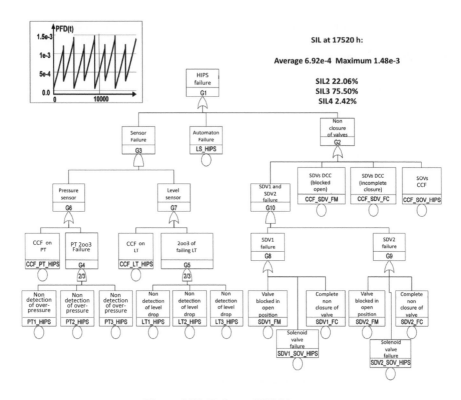

Figure 8.27. *Failure of HIPS barrier*

The following calculations are carried out according to the general procedure described in section 8.2.8 and include, in particular, the following steps:

– step 1: modeling and PFD calculation of individual HIPS;

– step 2: modeling and PFD calculations of all PSD + HIPS;

– step 3: evaluation of the residual accident probability;

– step 4: assessment of the frequency of spurious valve closures SDV1 or SDV2.

The first step will check if the SIL objective of the HIPS is reached. Here, as the request frequency is very low (10^{-4}/year), the objective may be relaxed and set, for example, to SIL 3. It requires the realization of the fault tree shown in Figure 8.27, which is the same type as that conducted for the PSD.

The full stroking test of the valves of the HIPS are staggered by 6 months and it doubles the frequency of testing common cause failures.

The results show that the system spends three quarters of the time in SIL 3 and a quarter of the time in SIL 2 and that the risk reduction is RRF2 = $1/6.92 \times 10^{-4}$ = 1445.1.

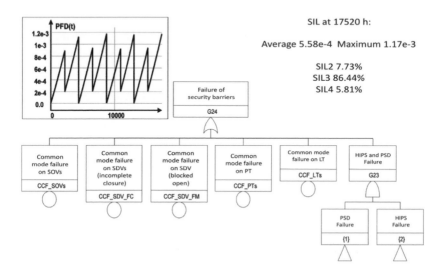

Figure 8.28. *PSD and HIPS failure*

Step 2 is required by the CCF and the "systemic incidences" (see section 8.6.2.5) which involve the creation of a global model ("systemic" or "holistic") to understand the real risk reduction provided by the two barriers acting in concert. It requires the realization of a fault tree (see Figure 8.28) grouping the trees made for the DSP and HIPS.

The system formed by the two barriers spends 86% of the time in SIL 3 and 8% of the time in SIL 2 and brings a total risk reduction RRFt = 1792.1.

If now we compare the reduction of total risk calculated by considering that the two are completely independent barriers we find: RRFt'=120.1×1445.1=173556.5. The gap between RRFt and RRFt' is 96.8! The traditional calculation commonly performed by the analysts is optimistic by a factor of about 100 compared to that fully accounting for dependencies (common events, systemic incidences). This clearly illustrates the danger that exists in combining SILs in Lego-type approaches or risk reduction factors by simple multiplication and without using a global (systemic) model of all barriers.

Step 3 evaluates the most important interest parameter. Given a frequency of demand of about 0.1/year we deduce from the above result (probability of average failure 5.58×10^{-4} per demand) that the estimated probability of gas blow-by is of the order of 6×10^{-5}/year.

Step 4 verifies that the additional safety provided by the HIPS is not at the expense of spurious failures, which themselves pose even more problems related to the safety and productivity of the facility. It requires the creation of specific fault trees and calculations of the PFH type.

This last step implements the techniques previously described and so we will not go into further detail.

8.5.3. Subsea HIPS

The consequences of underwater HIPS failures do not concern human aspects but rather the environmental and economic aspects (e.g. availability of production).

Spurious actions have a far more important impact and maintenance is much more difficult than for HIPS installed on the surface because the mobilization of intervention support (e.g. a dynamically positioned vessel) causes significant delays. Therefore, degraded modes of operation can be tolerated for some time (to repair the second failure of redundant systems) or the logic of sensors can be changed when a failure is detected (2oo3 changed to 1oo2) instead of proceeding to the repair itself.

It follows that the fault tree is inappropriate for the probability calculations and a dynamic model becomes necessary. As the Markovian approach is very quickly limited, behavioral modeling using stochastic Petri nets and the Monte Carlo simulation are used for modeling and calculations of subsea HIPS.

A simplified example of subsea HIPS is shown in Figure 8.25. It is intended to protect the production system in case of overpressure in the production pipeline.

The pipeline upstream from the valves is sized to hold the pressure while the downstream pipeline is not: when the pressure increases beyond a certain threshold, the sensors send signals to the processing automaton, which then generates the order to close the valves.

Here the number of sensors is increased to six because, for the actual system studied, it is equally important that the HIPS functions when needed (risk of destruction of the expedition pipeline) and that it has no spurious failures (risk of not being able to restart the facility once stopped).

Two criteria are therefore necessary: a high level of safety integrity (SIL 3) and a minimum acceptable spurious failure frequency.

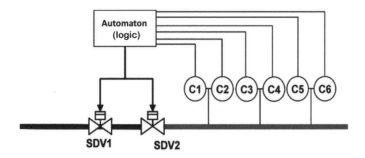

Figure 8.29. *Example of subsea HIPS architecture*

As these criteria are conflicting, it is important to determine which sensor logic is the best compromise to satisfy them. Different logics have thus been analyzed and the results obtained on the sensor part from reliability data of components and selected test policy are presented in the table in Figure 8.30.

Architecture	Signal forced to 0 after detection	PFDavg (test every 6 months)	Spurious failure probability over 2 yrs	
2oo3 of 1oo2	No	1.34 E-5	2.19 E-2	
	Yes	6.46 E-6	2.21 E-2	Best compromise
1oo2 of 2oo3	No	9.95 E-6	6.28 E-3	
	Yes	9.29 E-6	2.38 E-2	
2oo3 of 2oo2	No	6.22 E-4	4.55 E-3	
	Yes	1.87 E-4	1.83 E-4	
2oo3 of 1oo1	No	2.02 E-4	7.47 E-3	
	Yes	6.41 E-5	1.21 E-2	
2oo3 of 1oo2 Cold redundancy	No	7.07 E-5	3.62 E-3	

Figure 8.30. *Choice of sensor architecture*

We note that for both the PFDavg and the spurious failures, the results vary by a factor of 1,000 between the best and the worst configuration. Of course the best configuration for a parameter is the worst for the other and ultimately, the best compromise satisfying both the SIL and the spurious failure objectives is obtained for the 1oo2 of 2oo3 architecture (that is to say sensor architectures 2 sensors out of

3 whose outputs are organized in 1 out of 2). These results clearly show the impact of the architecture and the interest of this detailed analysis in order to draw the right conclusions.

8.6. Conclusion

The application of IEC 61508 and IEC 61511 for the design of HIPS pose some difficulties. However, most can be resolved by returning to the definitions, analysis methods and tools of classical calculations developed over the last 50 years and which form the state-of-the-art field of reliability.

This performs studies that are more relevant, coherent and comprehensive than what is described in these standards and, in particular, to replace the "Lego" analysis with real systemic analysis and to conduct rigorous and conservative calculations using available powerful algorithms in place of simplistic formulations that might induce the uninitiated to believe that the indiscriminate application of certain magical formulas is enough to understand calculation problems. The problem is particularly evident in the calculations of the risk reduction factors that may be vastly overvalued.

Disseminated among our major subcontractors and implemented daily in our HIPS studies, the methods and tools described in this chapter have demonstrated their operational character on industrial size systems with dozens of components. Note that the same methods and tools are also very efficient for performing the classic reliability/availability studies and beyond, of the production availability.

We finish by highlighting one of the basic concepts of the IEC standard which consists of imposing a minimum value to the proportion of safe failures (SFF). This concept is to be treated with the utmost restraint because it systematically leads to building up safety at the expense of production. In addition to significant production losses that its application would result in, it may, in many cases, prove dangerous. This is the case in the industry of processes where there are no really completely safe states but rather states that are less dangerous than others and where all restart phases (after an spurious shutdown) are often more dangerous. We therefore consider this criterion (SFF) as irrelevant and we look for HIPS architectures that are the best compromise between the probability of not functioning in case of need and the probability of spurious failure. This allows both a high level of safety and minimization of production losses thus *ensuring safe production*, a fundamental objective of our company.

The bibliographical elements attached, and in particular [DUT 04] and namely [INN 08], complement this chapter.

8.7. Bibliography

[ARN 00] ARNOLD A., GRIFFAULT A., RAUZY A., POINT G., "The AltaRica language and its semantics", *Fundamenta Informaticae*, vol. 34, p. 109, 2000.

[CHA 08] CHAABI Y., SIGNORET J.P., TIENNOT R., GRENOUILLOUX C., BERTHO P., NICOLAS B., "Etude et certification d'un système instrumenté de sécurité sous-marin", *Congrès Lambda Mu*, 16, Avignon, 2008.

[CRA 02] CRAYE E., NIEL E., *Maîtrise des risques et sûreté de fonctionnement des systèmes de production*, collection IC2, Hermes, Paris, 2002.

[DUT 03] DUTUIT Y., SIGNORET J.P., "Tutorial on dynamic system modeling by using stochastic Petri nets and Monte Carlo simulation", *Congrès Konbin03*, Gdansk, Poland and *ESREL 2003*, Maastricht, Netherlands, 2003.

[DUT 06] DUTUIT Y., INNAL F., RAUZY A., SIGNORET J.P., "An attempt to understand better and apply some recommendations of IEC 61508 standard", *ESReDA Seminar*, Trondheim, Norway, 2006.

[IEC 00] IEC 61508, Functional safety of electric/electronic/programmable electronic safety-related systems, Parts 1-7, 1998, 2000.

[IEC 03] IEC 61511, Functional safety. Safety instrumented systems for the process sector, Parts 1-3, 2003.

[INN 08] INNAL F., Contribution à la modélisation des systèmes instrumentés de sécurité et évaluation de leurs performances – analyse critique de la norme CEI 61508, PhD thesis, University of Bordeaux 1, 2008.

[LAG 99] LAGRANGE X., GODLEWSKI P., TABBANE S., *Réseaux GSM-DCS*, 4th edition, Hermes, Paris, 1999.

[RAU 98] RAUZY A., SIGNORET J.P., *et al.*, "The Altarica Language", *Proceedings of the ESREL '98 Congress*, Balkema, Rotterdam, Holland, 1998.

[RAU 04] RAUZY A., "An experimental study on six algorithms to compute transient solutions of large markov systems", *Reliability Engineering and System Safety*, vol. 86, p. 105-115, 2004.

[RAU 06] RAUZY A., DUTUIT Y., SIGNORET J.P., "Assessment of safety integrity levels with fault trees", *ESREL 2006*, Estoril, Portugal, 2006.

[SIG 98] SIGNORET J.P., "Modeling the behavior of complex industrial systems with stochastic Petri nets", *ESREL 98*, Trondheim, Norway, 1998.

[SIG 04] SIGNORET J.P., "Analyse des risques des systèmes dynamiques: approche markovienne", [SE 4 071], *Techniques de l'ingénieur. Sécurité et gestion des risques*, 2004.

[SIG 06] SIGNORET J.P., "Managing risks in HIPS by making SIL calculations effective", *IQPC 2006*, Aberdeen, UK, 2006.

[SIG 08a] SIGNORET J.P., "Analyse des risques des systèmes dynamiques: réseaux de Petri", [SE 4 072 and SE 4 073], *Techniques de l'ingénieur. Sécurité et gestion des risques*, 2008.

[SIG 08b] SIGNORET J.P., "Arbres de défaillance, concept et limites", *Séminaire sur les arbres de défaillances*, *IMdR*, Paris, 2008.

Chapter 9

Securing Automobile Architectures

9.1. Context

Electronic systems, critical from a safety viewpoint, have become commonplace in the automotive field. Examples of publicly known features are ABS/ESP and speed control. Customer requirements and European regulations limiting pollutant emissions via the Euro 4, 5 and 6 standards have made electronics indispensable. In an effort to make vehicles more environmentally friendly, the move to hybrid solutions and electric vehicles cannot be done without electronics.

To better manage the increasing complexity of embedded systems, an international association consisting of automotive manufacturers, suppliers, and companies specializing in electronics and information technology emerged in 2003: AUTOSAR[1] (automotive open system architecture). Their goal is to develop and establish a standardized software architecture open to vehicles.

As regards safety, each manufacturer is required to place only safe products on the market "[...] any product which, under normal or reasonably foreseeable use, [...] does not present any risk or only risks reduced to a low level compatible with the use of the product and considered acceptable with respect to a high level of protection of the health and safety of people [...]". But what is the state of the art? Or the state of technical knowledge and industry?

Chapter written by David LIAIGRE.
1. For more information, see www.autosar.org.

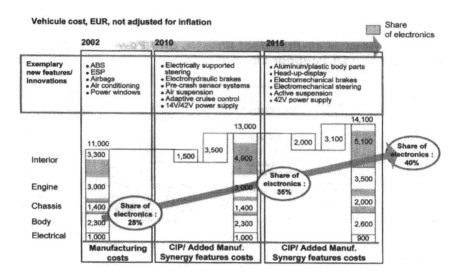

Figure 9.1. *Evolution of the cost of vehicles, with kind permission of PSA*

To answer this question, the automobile world is in the process of developing a suitable standard taken from IEC 61508 [IEC 98]: ISO 26262 [ISO 08], which will define the state of the art regarding the safety of automotive electronic systems.

The specific constraints (see Figure 9.2) of the automotive field have led engineers to find optimized solutions. The available space in a vehicle is limited and one cannot double the size of a car to ensure safe operation. Automobiles affect the general public, which does not allow these problems to be solved through restrictive maintenance operations. Price and design time impact this issue.

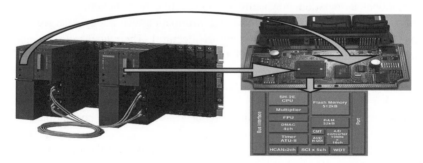

Figure 9.2. *Height, weight and consumption problems*

Taking into account these various constraints has resulted in safety solutions for automotive electronic architectures that are very specific to this domain.

9.2. More environmentally-friendly vehicles involving more embedded electronics

The European regulatory environment imposes the levels of CO_2 emissions: 120 g CO_2/km in 2012 and 95 g in 2020. This is equivalent, for a gasoline engine, to 5 l/100 km and 4 l/100 km.

The political and social context also requires vehicles to become greener. We can see emerging urban use rates like in London, bonus/penalty systems depending on the level of CO_2 production and an environmental summit in France. Moreover urban mobility is evolving to become greener, we see emerging opportunities to cycle in urban areas (Vélib' in Paris).

This global context has forced automobile manufacturers to equip vehicles with "micro-hybrid" systems (example: stop and start, the engine is stopped when it is not necessary), full hybrids (mixed operation of the vehicle with conventional thermal and/or electric propulsion), or even purely electric. In the near future, the use of hydrogen is also being considered.

Currently, alternative propulsion remains marginal so the medium-term challenge remains the reduction of consumption/emission of gasoline and diesel. The gain in consumption/emission may be increased as shown in Figure 9.3.

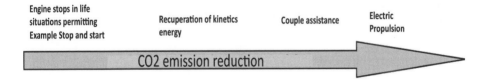

Figure 9.3. *Gain in consumption/emission*

All this significantly impacts the use of embedded electronic systems and increases their complexity. This growing complexity must therefore be mastered.

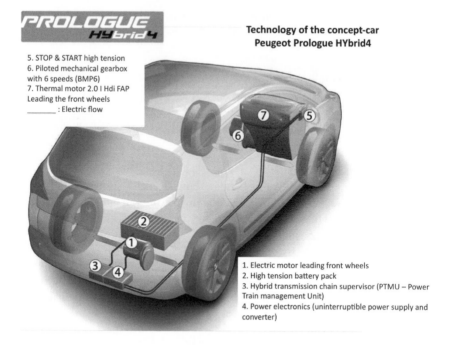

PROLOGUE
HYbrid4

Technology of the concept-car
Peugeot Prologue HYbrid4

5. STOP & START high tension
6. Piloted mechanical gearbox
with 6 speeds (BMP6)
7. Thermal motor 2.0 l Hdi FAP
Leading the front wheels
_____ : Electric flow

1. Electric motor leading front wheels
2. High tension battery pack
3. Hybrid transmission chain supervisor (PTMU – Power
Train management Unit)
4. Power electronics (uninterruptible power supply and
converter)

Figure 9.4. *Example of new vehicle architecture*

9.3. Mastering the complexity of electronic systems

One way to master the complexity of electronic systems in the automotive field is the use of the AUTOSAR standard.

The objectives of the AUTOSAR [FEN 06] association are:

– master the growing complexity of electronic features;

– improve the quality and reliability of electronic systems;

– make the adaptation and evolution of electronic features more flexible;

– ensure the adaptation of software modules on different vehicle platforms;

– master development errors.

For this, AUTOSAR developed a structure facilitating the integration of software modules, regardless of the hardware host structure. The AUTOSAR software modules are reusable on any AUTOSAR structure.

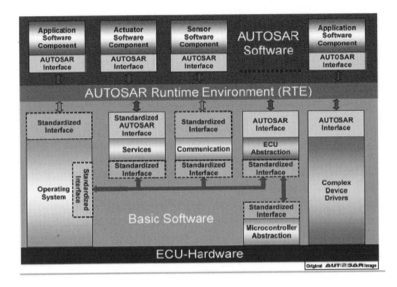

Figure 9.5. *Example of AUTOSAR-based architecture*

Figures 9.5 and 9.6 show that the AUTOSAR application layer is made independent of the hardware and the basic software thanks to the RTE layer (AUTOSAR RunTime Environment).

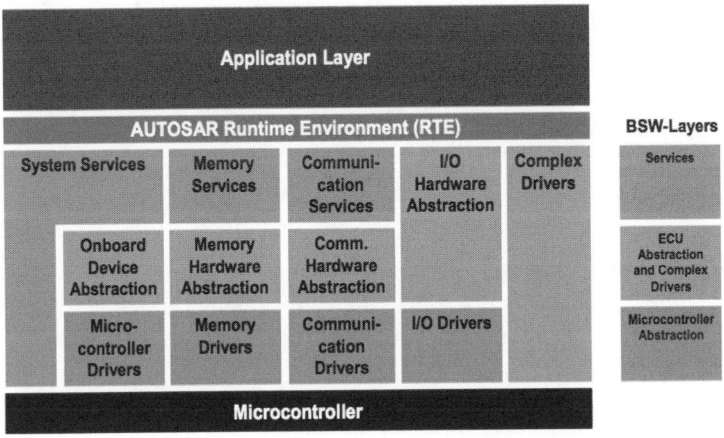

Figure 9.6. *Layered architecture*

Communication between software components of the application layer and the basic software is done via the RTE. RTE is a kind of virtual bus. The APIs

(Application Program Interfaces) are standardized for this purpose, the software modules are encapsulated and their interfaces standardized.

The AUTOSAR standard is thus a means to address the growing complexity of electronic systems for the automotive industry by offering the opportunity to make modular software architectures, portable and reusable applications on electronic host structures predisposed to this effect.

These hardware and software architectures are involved in the safety of automobile products. They must be designed to ensure the safety of people.

9.4. Safety concepts in the automotive field

At the calculator level, the target is a probability of failure of the order of 10^{-9}/hour for maximum safety levels.

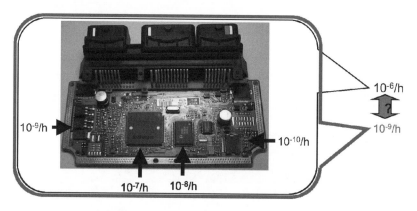

Figure 9.7. *Layered architecture*

However, looking more closely at the example of the automotive calculator in Figure 9.1, the conclusion is that all possible critical faults are rather of the order of 10^{-6}/hour, hence the need for safety concepts to control all critical faults.

9.4.1. *Ensure minimum safety without redundancy*

The first safety concept existing in the automotive field, used for low-level safety, is based on a simple and non-redundant electronic platform with principles of simple safety.

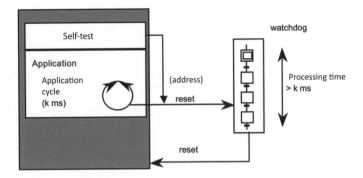

Figure 9.8. *Example of non-redundant architecture*

The processing unit (see Figure 9.8) is secured by self-tests. To limit the number of common modes between the primary function and safety functionalities, it is possible to link the self-test results to the address calculation of the watchdog or remain stuck in an infinite software loop. The watchdog will preferably be an external watchdog to demonstrate a minimum independence for securing the system.

The level of application safety is then based, in part, on the effectiveness of the embedded self-tests, or rather their coverage rate. These self-tests should cover all the faults concerning memory (RAM (random access memory), ROM (read-only memory), EEPROM (electrically erasable programmable ROM), etc.) and the instructions and addressing modes. We can for example use a 16 bit CRC to verify the integrity of the ROM, a reading/writing test of the AAh/55h type for the RAM and a BIST (built-in self-test) supplied by the micro-vendor for the instruction set. The test interval must be defined to ensure detection of faults before they lead to a critical failure.

An important point will also be setting up an acceptable safe state. Typically, the reset is used. This will compel a set of complete self-tests during initialization of the microcontroller to ensure error detection and remain in permanent reset without restarting the application in case of permanent fault.

For the rest of the system, sensors and actuators, the principles are to detect critical faults via electrical diagnostics or a simple consistency check. The design is intended to ensure that the most likely failures are non-dangerous. For example, we will wisely choose the transfer functions of a sensor, its mode of acquisition (pull-up or pull-down) and the hardware and software filtering to be applied in order to ensure that the bundle problems and electrical connectors of the short-circuit to ground or the open circuit type are not critical from a safety standpoint.

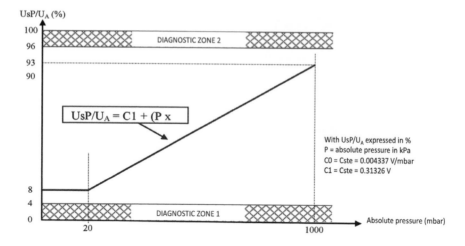

Figure 9.9. *Transfer function of a pressure sensor*

For example, take the pressure sensor supplied with Ua and delivering the output voltage UsP, with the transfer function of Figure 9.9. Figure 9.10 describes the acquisition of the sensor.

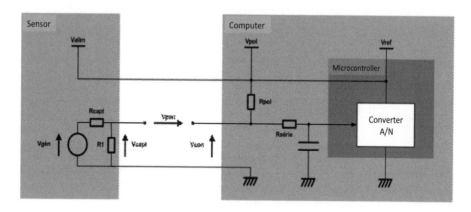

Figure 9.10. *Means of acquisition of a pressure sensor*

In this case, the bundle problem of a short circuit to ground and open circuit type will be directly diagnosed using the diagnostic zones 1 and 2, as shown in Figures 9.11 and 9.12.

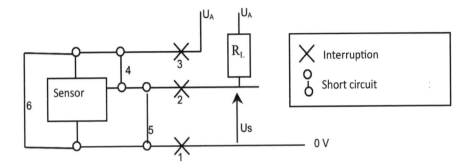

Figure 9.11. *Example*

Moreover, the transfer function of this sensor is studied so that the increase of line resistance of the bundles and connectors, with their aging, will tend to provide decreasing pressure information.

This sensor and its mode of acquisition are therefore suitable for applications where erroneous values are lower in the actual pressure are not critical.

Defect	Diagnostic zone	Defect	Diagnostic zone
1	Diagnostic zone 2	4	Diagnostic zone 2
2	Diagnostic zone 2	5	Diagnostic zone 1
3	Diagnostic zone 1 or 2	6	Diagnostic zone 1 or 2

Table 9.1. *List of faults*

9.4.2. *Hardware redundancy to increase coverage of dangerous failures*

To gain in safety level, the coverage rate of critical faults must be increased.

At the level of the processing unit, we primarily seek to limit the number of possible common modes using a diversified redundancy of the processing unit. The self-test results are exchanged between processing units (see Figure 9.12).

The two processing units have the possibility to put the system in a safe state via two independent (distinct) channels.

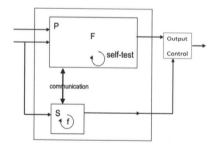

Figure 9.12. *Dissymmetric redundancy without functional redundancy*

Regarding self-tests, the most common are:

– for instructions and addressing modes (ALU):

    - self-tests provided by the manufacturers of the components directly verifying different hardware channels, generally called BIST,

    - more functional self-tests, such as verifying the results of an operation by injecting test values;

– for volatile memories:

    - reading/writing tests in memory zones of the 55h/AAh type that can flip (from 0 to 1 and from 1 to 0) all the bits but requires interrupting access to the memory for the duration of the test. These tests are usually performed over several application cycles and place a heavy load on the central processing unit (CPU),

    - comparison of duplicate data in memory. The duplicated data can also be diversified, for example, by complementing them to one;

– for non-volatile memories:

    - use of "checksum" usually encoded in 16 bits,

    - or "CRC" coded in 16 bits.

It is important for this type of safety based on self-tests, to have an application that is as robust as possible regarding transient faults that are not covered by periodic self-tests. This is the case for the majority of current automotive applications. For example, data stored in memory are refreshed before their impact becomes critical.

The test intervals on the main unit must be defined to allow the second processing unit to put the system in safe condition before the spread of a defect has become critical.

The test intervals of the second processing unit (called redundant) are defined to ensure that it will be able to detect and respond as appropriate. They are less restrictive because they must cover latent system failures. Usually in the automotive field, latent failure tests are performed at least once by running (e.g. initialization or termination by power latch of the calculator).

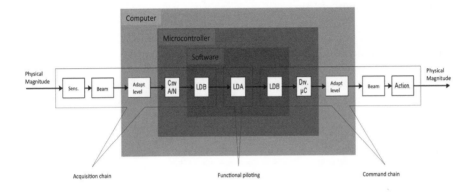

Figure 9.13. *Processing chain*

Failure modes of **analog** signals

1/ CC+12V, CC+5V	→	High diagnostic
2/ CC mass	→	Low diagnostic
3/ Open circuit	→	High OR low diagnostic
4/ Upper erroneous	→	Consistency diagnostic
5/ Lower erroneous	→	Consistency diagnostic

High diagnostic

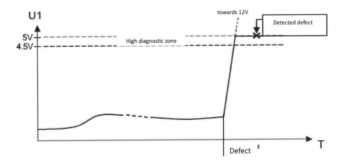

Figure 9.14. *Analog signals*

For the rest of the system, we will, in addition to the above principles, also increase the coverage rate using PWM type technology, in power latch analog acquisitions (ADC) using more important consistency checks of input and output data, or even of the overall behavior of the system.

All the processing channels must be taken into consideration in order to make the best choices (see Figure 9.13).

The choice of sensor technology is based on the ability to diagnose using "electrical" or "functional" diagnostics.

For example, Figures 9.14, 9.15 and 9.16 describe the diagnostic probabilities said to be "electrical" in relation to the sensor technology retained.

Failure modes of **PWM** signals

1/ CC+12V, CC+5V	⟶	Frequency diagnostic
2/ CC mass	⟶	Frequency diagnostic
3/ Open circuit	⟶	Frequency diagnostic
4/ Upper erroneous	⟶	Consistency diagnostic
5/ Lower erroneous	⟶	Consistency diagnostic

Low diagnostic

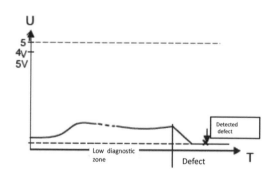

Figure 9.15. *PWM signals*

The choice of mode of acquisition is also done with regard to the failure modes that one wants to cover. Indeed some signal errors are difficult to detect in a simple manner.

Failure modes of **TOR** signals

1/ CC+12V, CC+5V	⟶	No diagnostic possible
2/ CC mass	⟶	No diagnostic possible
3/ Open circuit	⟶	No diagnostic possible
4/ Upper erroneous	⟶	No diagnostic possible
5/ Lower erroneous	⟶	No diagnostic possible

Consistency diagnostic

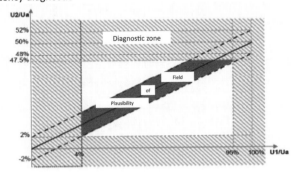

Figure 9.16. *TOR signals*

For example, Figures 9.17 and 9.18 show the behavior of a signal with regards to certain failures following their mode of acquisition.

Protection against micro-interruptions: pull-up problematic

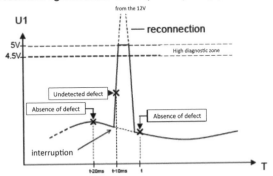

Figure 9.17. *Processing of micro-interruptions*

Therefore, the influence of the levels of input acquisition is important, as shown in Figure 9.18.

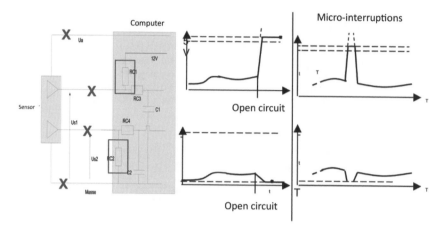

Figure 9.18. *Influence of acquisition faults*

The figures thus show that previous acquisitions of the pull-down type are more appropriate in case of micro-interruptions and open circuits, whereas erroneous information superior to the actual state is critical from a safety point of view.

But caution is required because the influence of increased line impedance (aging process) has the opposite effect. This means clearly defining what faults must be covered in order to make the right choice and therefore the complete processing chain must be carefully studied and the faults that require treatment identified in light of their impact on the system and the diagnostic possibilities available.

It is important to note that studies on the subject must take into account the final impact of a defect, but also the behavior during the transition phase.

9.4.3. *Hardware and functional redundancy*

Finally, in order to achieve high levels of safety, the principles of diversified hardware and functional redundancy will be used on a larger scale and will be optimized (see Figures 9.19 to 9.24).

For example, Figure 9.19 shows that the elements measuring the physical magnitude (Sx) are redundant and acquired by two microcontrollers before releasing information on a network (here CAN).

Both sets of information thus calculated via the two microcontrollers can then be compared. If they are different, then the transmission on the network can be interrupted by the two microcontrollers.

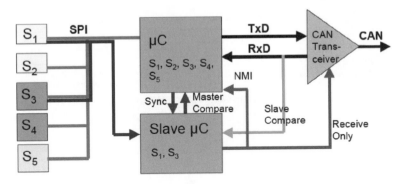

Figure 9.19. *Acquisition of physical phenomenon*

The time intervals and coverage rate of self-tests of the two processing units are then less binding because they remain mainly to cover latent or hidden faults in the system.

The concept of hardware and functional redundancy can be optimized. Let us start off from the basic safety principle, which is to make the function fully redundant and to compare the results of these functions in order to determine their proper implementation. The optimization process is described in the context of Figure 9.20 taken from [DUF 05].

The safety concept, the last step, can be represented in a more structured fashion as shown in Figure 9.21.

The application is divided into three layers:

– level 1: functional aspect, performing functions, acquisition of inputs, generation of outputs and inputs/outputs diagnostics;

– level 2: monitoring functional process and execution control. It aims to detect faults in level 1 processing and control reactions in case of error detection on level 1;

– level 3: monitoring control and testing of hardware integrity. This level is independent of level 2 and suggests a "different" verification based on a question/answer set.

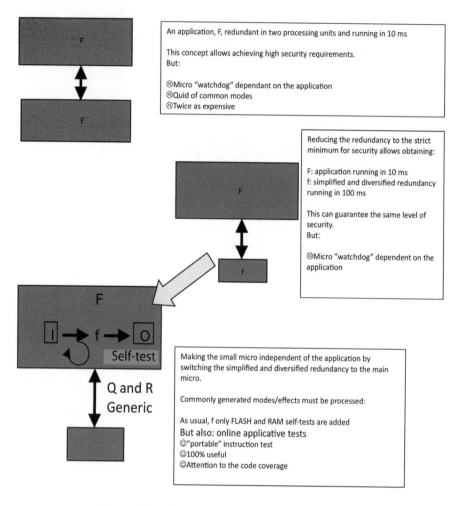

Figure 9.20. *Optimization process of the architecture*

Of course, the optimization process of redundancy solutions does not always go all the way through when it is not necessary considering the simplicity of the features associated with component production volumes.

Moreover, this optimization will inevitably reduce the overall level of safety that the system can aspire to (common mode hardware and code coverage) but maintains a generally satisfactory level.

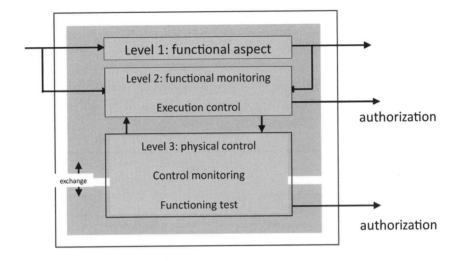

Figure 9.21. *Dissymmetric architecture*

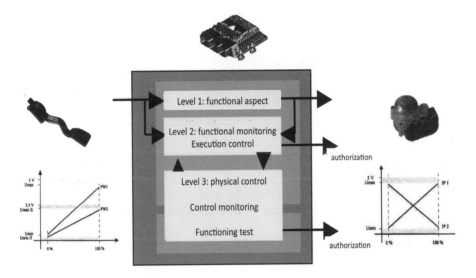

Figure 9.22. *Implementation of dissymmetric architecture*

An example of architecture may be the one in Figure 9.22, taking into account the complete processing chain.

It includes the redundant and diversified acquisition of information, such as stepping down on the accelerator pedal, which is processed in a safe calculator in order to control the motorized throttle monitored by redundant and diversified signals.

An important point to note is that the simpler the functional diversified redundancy, the higher the level of safety that will be ensured. Indeed, it is easier to safely develop and validate something that is simple.

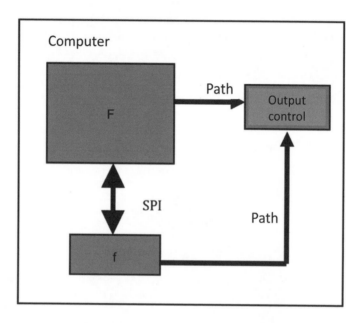

Figure 9.23. *The architecture forms a whole*

Of course, there are two possibilities for implementing these architectures based on hardware and functional redundancy (see Figures 9.23 and 9.24):

– embedded in the equipment (redundant microcontrollers, etc.):

    - more compelling at the hardware level for the organs,

    - more restrictive in relation to the development process of the system and organs,

    - simplified and more reliable architecture,

    - ease of aftermarket diagnosis;

– using the vehicle architecture (using different calculators, etc.):

    - less restrictive on the majority of organs,

    - less restrictive on the majority of organ development,

    - more complex and less reliable architecture,

    - requires substantial work on aftermarket ability to diagnose (risk of unjustified removal).

In the case of a distributed safety on the vehicle architecture, special attention must be allocated to the time needed to detect faults and put the system in a safe state, as well as for the synchronization of the two functions F and f.

The constraints of networked and wired media must be taken into account. For example, the information transmission time on the CAN is not guaranteed, it is necessary to provide margins: a frame issued every 10 milliseconds typically transmits information with a possible lag of 20 milliseconds, with regards to the provision of information to the CAN protocol manager of the Issuer, and the impact of a data frame issued every 10 milliseconds is important for the load of a vehicle network of the CAN (500 Kb/s) type.

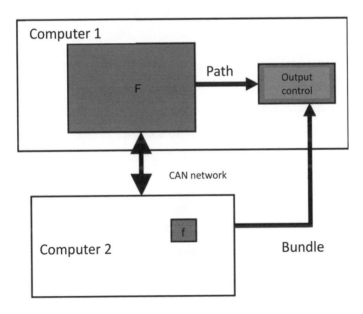

Figure 9.24. *The architecture is distributed*

9.5. Which safety concepts for which safety levels of the ISO 26262 standard?

9.5.1. *The constraints of the ISO 26262 standard*

The ISO 26262 [ISO 08] standard is the variation of the IEC 61508 [IEC 98] standard of the automotive industry. Levels SIL 1 to SIL 3 are adjusted on a scale known as ASIL (automotive safety integrity level) described below with the impacting key points for the safety concepts.

This structure allows refining of the level of effort applied in the design to ensure system safety (see [LIA 08]).

The ISO 26262 standard defines the following four safety levels, in order of decreasing importance.

ASIL D:

– probabilistic target: 10^{-9}/hour;

– management of directly dangerous failures: *single point fault metrics* > 99%;

– management of latent failures: *latent fault metrics* > 90%;

– avoidance of systematic errors at ASIL D level: use of semi-formal methods and important validation effort.

ASIL C:

– probabilistic target: 10^{-8}/hour;

– management of directly dangerous failures: *single point fault metrics* > 97%;

– management of latent failures: *latent fault metrics* > 80%;

– avoidance of systematic errors at ASIL C level: use of semi-formal methods and important validation effort.

ASIL B:

– management of directly dangerous failures: *single point fault metrics* > 90%;

– management of latent failures: *latent fault metrics* > 60%;

– avoidance of systematic errors by a definition specific to safety concepts and design and validation traceability.

ASIL A:

– management of directly dangerous failures: *single point fault metrics* > 60%;

– avoidance of systematic errors by a definition specific to safety concepts and design and validation traceability.

Therefore, the standard provides tools for:

– avoiding systematic faults, which will constrain the process, methods and development tools;

– limiting the occurrence and extent of random faults, which will constrain the material, effectiveness and time of detection of faults.

Constraining architectural metrics, to cover faults, are defined as single point fault metrics and latent fault metrics, their definition being:

$$\text{Single Point Fault metric} = 1 - \frac{\sum\limits_{\text{Safety related HW elements}} (\lambda_{SPF} + \lambda_{RF})}{\sum\limits_{\text{Safety related HW elements}} \lambda} = \frac{\sum\limits_{\text{Safety related HW elements}} (\lambda_{MPF} + \lambda_S)}{\sum\limits_{\text{Safety related HW elements}} \lambda}$$

The single point fault metrics can be seen as the capacity of a system to be non-dangerous or to control dangerous failures:

$$\text{Latent Fault metric} = 1 - \frac{\sum\limits_{\text{safety related HW elements}} (\lambda_{MPF\,Latent})}{\sum\limits_{\text{safety related HW elements}} (\lambda - \lambda_{SPF} - \lambda_{RF})} = \frac{\sum\limits_{\text{safety related HW elements}} (\lambda_{MPF\,perceived} + \lambda_S)}{\sum\limits_{\text{safety related HW elements}} (\lambda - \lambda_{SPF} - \lambda_{RF})}$$

The latent fault metrics can be seen as the capacity of a system to control latent or hidden failures.

With a failure rate λ of each element relative to safety, it can be broken down in the following way:

– rate of directly dangerous failures: λ_{SPF} ;

– rate of residual dangerous failures: λ_{RF} ;

– rate of indirectly dangerous failures, latent: λ_{MPF} ;

– rate of latent detectable and controllable failures: $\lambda_{MPF\ P}$;

– rate of latent undetectable failures: $\lambda_{MPF\ L}$;

– rate of non-dangerous failures: λ_S ;

– with: $\lambda = \lambda_{SPF} + \lambda_{RF} + \lambda_{MPF} + \lambda_S$ and $\lambda_{MPF} = \lambda_{MPF\ P} + \lambda_{MPF\ L}$.

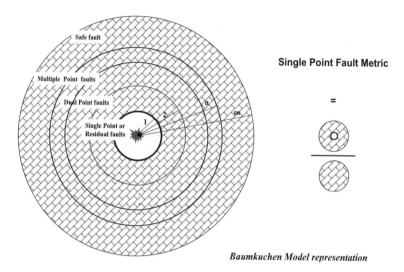

Baumkuchen Model representation

Figure 9.25. *Single point fault metric*

Therefore, it is important to understand that the application of the standard will define the constraints for the processing of random hardware faults (with the metric in terms of probabilistic targets and coverage rate of dangerous or latent failures) and the processing of systematic faults (with rigorous and adapted design and validation processes).

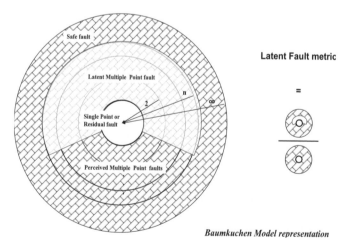

Baumkuchen Model representation

Figure 9.26. *Latent fault metrics*

The metrics, in terms of probabilistic targets, are already known and applied in the automotive field.

Conversely, with regards to metrics on the coverage of dangerous or latent failures, they are a novelty.

The process of constraint allocation is an important point in the automotive field where developments are divided between manufacturers and suppliers, but also internally between these groups.

These metrics do not allocate themselves easily because:

$$\frac{\sum_i \lambda_i}{\sum_i \lambda_{ti}} \neq \frac{\lambda_1}{\lambda_{t1}} + ... + \frac{\lambda_n}{\lambda_{tn}}$$

In fact, the relation is:

$$\frac{\sum_i \lambda_i}{\sum_i \lambda_{ti}} = \alpha \frac{\lambda_1}{\lambda_{t1}} + ... + \omega \frac{\lambda_i}{\lambda_{ti}} = \frac{\lambda_{t1}}{\sum_i \lambda_{ti}} \frac{\lambda_1}{\lambda_{t1}} + ... + \frac{\lambda_{tn}}{\sum_i \lambda_{ti}} \frac{\lambda_n}{\lambda_{ti}}$$

In addition, these safety mechanisms are not embedded in the components themselves but more often externally.

Taking into account these considerations have led to the following formulas, which allocate, to the different components of a system, metrics having the same definition as those described in the standard:

$$SPFM_{system} = \sum_i \left[\frac{\sum_j \lambda_{component\,i,j}}{\sum_i \left(\sum_j \lambda_{component\,i,j} \right)} \times \left(\frac{\sum_j \left(\lambda_{MPF\,i,j} + \lambda_{S\,i,j} \right)}{\sum_j \lambda_{component\,i,j}} + ExternalCoverage_i \right) \right]$$

For a system containing i elements of j components with:

− $\sum_j \lambda_{component\,j}$, corresponding to the global failure rate of component j;

− $\dfrac{\sum_j \left(\lambda_{MPF\,j} + \lambda_{S\,j} \right)}{\sum_j \lambda_{component\,j}}$, corresponding to the *single point fault metric* of component j.

The same principle can be applied to the latent fault metric. It is possible to allocate the various metrics to the different components of a system.

Regarding the eradication of systematic failures, the hardware and software design process, the methods and the tools will be constrained by the standard:

– planification (planning using set goals, strategies and schedules);

– traceability of requirements and reviews;

– specification methods in natural language up until semi-formal methods;

– structured design and modularity;

– simulation;

– verification activities, which can become important;

– qualification of the tools;

– etc.

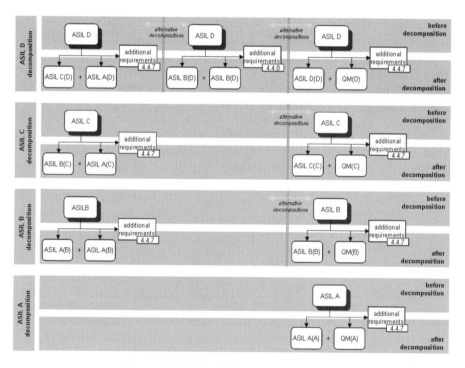

Figure 9.27. *ASIL and decomposition criteria*

The constraints are based on the ASIL level; therefore the ASIL level determines the effort to be applied. However, rules of level decomposition are given subject to adequate independence justifications (see Figure 9.27) or studies of criticality (see Tables 9.2 and 9.3).

Criticality category	Description
CC3	Designates an element that can directly generate or indirectly violate a safety requirement.
CC2	Designates an element that can generate the violation of a safety requirement by combination with the failure of another element that is not interfering with the considered element.
CC1	Designates an element that cannot contribute to the violation of a safety requirement.

Table 9.2. *Criticality category*

		Criticality of the element		
		CC1	CC2	CC3
Initial ASIL of the element	ASIL A	QM	Resulting ASIL: ASIL A (recommended)	Resulting ASIL: ASIL A (required)
	ASIL B	QM	Resulting ASIL: ASIL A (required)	Resulting ASIL: ASIL B (required)
	ASIL C	QM	Resulting ASIL: ASIL B (required)	Resulting ASIL: ASIL C (required)
	ASIL D	QM	Resulting ASIL: ASIL C (required)	Resulting ASIL: ASIL D (required)

Table 9.3. *Resulting ASIL of criticality*

9.5.1.1. *Example of allocation*

Let us take the example of the distributed architecture seen earlier and imagine it hosting an electronic locking feature for the steering column (see Figure 9.28).

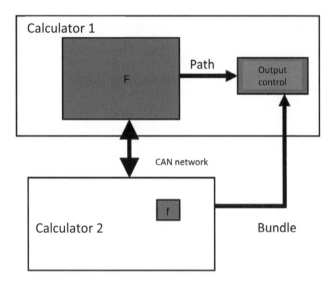

Figure 9.28. *Distributed dissymmetric architecture*

There is a risk of unintentional locking of the column in a life situation where it is moving; therefore, we are dealing with ASIL D.

The design of the system must accommodate the following requirements in relation to the inadvertent locking of the steering column while moving:

– probability of failure $<10^{-8}$/hour;

– acceptable residual of directly dangerous failures: 1%;

– acceptable residual of latent failures: 10%;

– state of emergency (safe state): inhibiting locking of column;

– time to detect faults and to switch to safe state: 200 milliseconds (related to the dynamics of the actuator);

– rehabilitation conditions: during the next run if the defect disappears.

The idea is to secure, on the basis of information from the moving vehicle, allowing:

– the operation of the locking module only at standstill;

– AND/OR allowing the locking element when stopped.

Thus, in addition to powering calculator 1 only when stopped, calculator 2 transmits over the CAN the information that the vehicle is stationary in order to allow locking and blocks the command of outputs of calculator 1 while the vehicle is stationary via wired output.

The safety constraints for the system components are for example (the list here is not exhaustive):

For calculator 2:

– wired information that the vehicle is moving and the erroneous CAN at "stopped or immobile": ASIL D (D):

  - dangerous failure metrics: 0.5%,

  - latent failure metrics: 10%,

  - failure probability: 5×10^{-9}/hour;

– safe state: signal the defect or otherwise interrupt CAN communication;

– detection time: 200 milliseconds;

– ASIL D adapted development process;

– technically, to obtain this:

  - diagnostic EE + consistency check between the four speed sensors for the wheel,

  - we will use the maximum speed of the wheel to determine whether the vehicle is running,

  - the safety concept of calculator 2 is adapted to secure the processing of internal information (example: two processing units + hardware self-tests + diversified functional redundancy),

  - securing the information transmitted via a checksum and a process counter.

For the CAN:

– use of CAN safety protocol.

For the bundles and connections:

– erroneous wired information of the moving vehicle at the "stopped or immobile" state: ASIL B (D):

   - dangerous failures: 0% (no directly dangerous failures for the system),

   - latent failures: 90%,

   - probability of failure: 10^{-7}/hour,

   - the main failure modes are short circuits to ground and open circuits, therefore in order to authorize locking, the information transmitted will be, for example, a square signal.

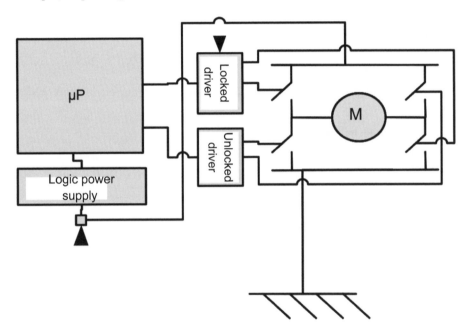

Figure 9.29. *Safety of calculator 1*

For calculator 1:

– inadvertent locking of the column: ASIL D (D):

   - dangerous failures: 1%,

   - latent failures: 10%,

   - probability of failure: 10^{-9}/hour;

– safe state: inhibition of the locking of the column;

– detection time: 200 milliseconds;

– adapted development process ASIL D;

– technically, to obtain this:

- safety concept of calculator 1 is adapted to securing the locking command (see Figure 9.29): power supplied only during stopped position and external independent hardware safety (independent of the processing unit) via the wired information "moving vehicle",

- diagnostic of the wired information "moving vehicle".

9.5.2. *The safety concepts adapted to the constraints of the ISO 26262 standard*

We can note that the effectiveness of the diagnostics (coverage rate of diagnostics) of dangerous faults is important. We must therefore consider the types of critical faults to be detected and controlled.

Moreover, the possibility of decomposition of the ASIL level using the principle of diversified redundancy is important in order to put less constraint on the process methods and tools for hardware and software design as well as validation activities.

9.5.2.1. *Ensure minimum safety without redundancy*

The use of a non-redundant channel with protection by electronic diagnostic self-tests and rules of choice of robust design against the most likely failures is currently used for low level safety applications to achieve the requirements of the 10^{-6} and 10^{-7} failures/hour of the operation type. The possibility of justification of the coverage rate is about 60% to a maximum of 90%.

This principle of a safety concept should be acceptable at the maximum for ASIL A and B levels following the diagnostics coverage rates. Transient faults are not covered so the application must be robust in itself even when the transient faults are frequent. The level of development, including for software, must be at the right level of safety.

All system elements, including software, must be developed with the maximum ASIL level.

The advantages/disadvantages of this type of safety concept are presented in Table 9.4.

ALU or instruction set	☺ Impossible to eliminate all common modes
RAM	☺ Following the type of test chosen
ROM or FLASH	☺ If *checksum* or CRC over 16 bits
EEPROM	☺ If *checksum* or CRC over 16 bits
ES	-
Robustness to fugitive faults	☹
Clock	☹ Only one clock for the calculation unit
CPU load	☹ If continuous self-tests necessary
Evolution impact	☺
Management of safe states	☺ Safe state associated with calculator reset so attention to detection times
Software	☺ Necessary to develop secure software at ASIL A or B level
Cost	☺

Table 9.4. *Characterization of non-redundant architecture*

On balance, we can say that this architecture is applicable for low safety levels: ASIL A or B maximum:

– because of limited coverage rate by the common hardware mode of the unique microcontroller: we cannot justify a coverage rate above or equal to 90%;

– transient or fugitive faults are not detected;

– special attention should be paid to the reset calculator in safe state, which requires rapidly detecting faults.

9.5.2.2. *Hardware redundancy to increase the coverage of dangerous faults*

Using a redundant channel with self-test protection, electronic diagnostics, rules of choice of robust designs against the most likely failures and consistency checks can increase the coverage rate of diagnostics by reducing the possibilities of common modes between the main features and the diagnostics.

These concepts are currently used for requirements of the 10^{-9} failures/ hour of the operation type. The ISO 26262 standard is likely to affect the ability of this concept to achieve these types of requirements for reasons that coverage rates need to be justified. In fact, as this concept is not robust enough against fugitive faults, it will be difficult to justify coverage rates above 97%. Moreover, efforts in design and validation, particularly in the software, will be constraining.

This principle of a safety concept is, therefore, possible at the maximum for levels ASIL B and C following diagnostics coverage rates. Except for very specific robust applications against a large number of faults (for example, several different models must converge to achieve the safety event), this principle of safety does not seem to have any future in the automotive field.

ALU or instruction set	☺ Following the coverage rate of the implemented test
RAM	☺
ROM or FLASH	☺
EEPROM	☺
ES	☺
Robustness to fugitive faults	☹
Clock	☺
CPU load	☹ If continuous self-tests are necessary
Evolution impact	☺
Management of safe states	☺
Software	☹ Necessary to develop secure software
Cost	☺

Table 9.5. *Characterization of redundant architecture*

On balance, we can say that this architecture is applicable for low safety levels: ASIL B or C maximum:

– if the detection time is not too constraining and the application is robust against fugitive failures, today the achievable coverage rates are of the order of 95%.

9.5.2.3. *Hardware and functional redundancy*

For high levels of safety, the safety concepts to be implemented are those using the principles of diversified hardware and functional redundancy that are the only ones able to attain a coverage rate of about 97 or 99%.

ALU or instruction set	☺
RAM	☺
ROM or FLASH	☺
EEPROM	☺
ES	☺ Attention to potential common modes (even hardware)
Robustness to fugitive faults	☺
Clock	☺
CPU load	☹
Evolution impact	☺ Following optimization of the concept
Management of safe states	☺
Software	☺ Possibility of diminishing the severity
Cost	☺ Standardization of the control unit
Validation effort	☺ Safety is assure by simplified hardware and software redundancy

Table 9.6. *Characterization of redundant architecture*

These concepts are actually capable of being robust against permanent as well as fugitive faults and limiting the common modes. These concepts are currently used for requirements of the 10^{-9} failure/hour of operation type. The principle of the safety concept is therefore possible at the maximum for ASIL levels C and D according to diagnostics coverage rate. The major issue is the use of these concepts in a manner optimized for ASIL D.

On balance, we can say that this architecture is applicable for low safety levels: ASIL C or D.

9.6. Conclusion

Electronic systems have become indispensable in the automotive field and the number of features using electronics continues to grow. Whether for reasons of environmental standards, passive or active safety or customer requirements/ expectations, the complexity is growing. This forces manufacturers and suppliers to adapt by standardizing architectures and by establishing a standard defining the state of the art with respect to safety.

Safety concepts tailored to the automotive field are consequently implemented and adapted to the level of safety that must be assured. Mostly, the main types of safety concepts applied today in the automotive field will be compatible with ISO 26262 [ISO 09].

Despite the constraints specific to the automotive field in terms of size, weight, cost, opportunities for maintenance, etc., there are many adaptable safety possibilities depending on the application.

The global targeted safety concept must be known to choose the most pertinent solution.

9.7. Bibliography

[DUF 05] DUFOUR J.L., "Automotive safety concepts: 10^{-9}/h for less than 100Euro a piece", *Automation, Assistance and Embedded Real Time Platforms for Transportation – AAET 2005*, Braunschweig, Germany, 16-17 February 2005.

[FEN 06] HELMUT F., *et al.*, Achievements and exploitation of the AUTOSAR development partnership, AUTOSAR, 2006.

[IEC 98] IEC, IEC 61508: Functional safety of electrical/electronic/programmable electronic safety-related systems, International standard, 1998.

[ISO 09] ISO, ISO/CD 26262, Road vehicles – functional safety, unpublished.

[LIA 08] LIAIGRE D., "Impact de ISO 26262 sur l'état de l'art des concepts de sécurité automobiles actuels", *LambdaMu'08*, Avignon, October 2008.

Chapter 10

SIS in Industry

10.1. Introduction

Safety system technology has been constantly changing in recent years, and new products arrive regularly on the market. The emergence of electronic safety modules or safety-Related Programmable Logic Controllers allows the establishment of new solutions. These products increase the flexibility and wiring, but the complexity of the components may pose some problems regarding the evaluation parameters of dependability.

In older facilities, safety is often realized as wired logic (electro-mechanical relay) in parallel to the operational installation system completed in wired logic or on computers, depending on the age of the facility. There are typical schematics of electro-mechanical relay systems that meet the requirements for redundancy and self-test of a safety system. The structure is described in the context of Figure 10.1.

Communication between the safety system and process control is very limited (state of the relay using auxiliary contactors).

Electronic modules called "electronic safety relay" subsequently appeared, implementing predefined-type schematics, which are easier to wire, and integrating summary diagnosis. These modules are widely used in the manufacturing sector for the management of emergency stop, zone control by immaterial barriers, or for the

---

Chapter written by Grégory BUCHHEIT and Olaf MALASSE.

protection of doors. In the process industry, the use of programmable logic controllers specific to the management of critical functions is also common. In the case of the use of electronic modules, communication is still limited, but the use of controllers specific to safety has facilitated dialog and development of the diagnosis functions of the installation (Figure 10.2).

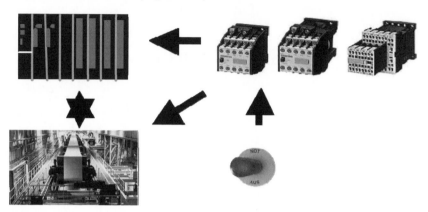

Figure 10.1. *Wired safety – electro-mechanical relay assembly with standard PLCI*[1]

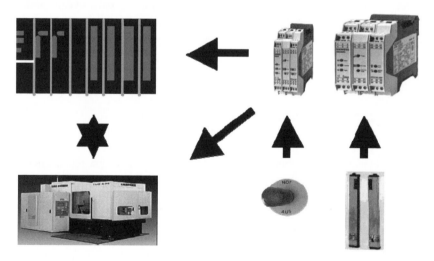

Figure 10.2. *Wired safety – electronic relay assembly with standard PLC*

---

1. Programmable Logic Controller.

Less than 10 years ago, some manufacturers developed systems enabling control management, within a single system, of both traditional and safety functions. This allows strong integration of safety through installation control and very good diagnosis capabilities. The structure is that of Figure 10.3.

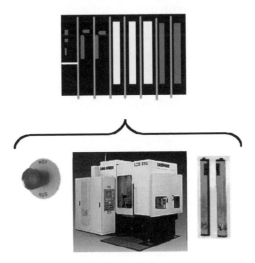

Figure 10.3. *Integrated safety – assembly with safety controller*

These technologies are increasingly implemented in facilities, despite diffident beginnings due to opposition to the concept of separation of the safety functions which previously remained independent and mainly wired. In most facilities, safety consists of cutting off the power supply of a component (motor, valve maintained, etc.) in order to put the system in a safe state. Therefore, we have gone from configuration 1 to configuration 2.

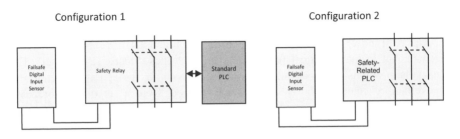

Figure 10.4. *Separation/integration of safety*

Although historically the parts relating to safety have been "separated" from the process control parts, the increasing reliability of programmable electronic components has allowed the integration of more safety functions within the control system. However, this integration also requires the inclusion of special precautions during the design, integration, operation and maintenance of systems.

Safety tends to increasingly integrate itself into command and control systems and therefore uses the same resources as the latter. Increasingly, safety fieldbuses are appearing on the market which manage safety in a distributed mode and concentrate the logic in a programmable logic controller. Thus, the design of the safety function integrated to the control system facilitates dialog with the control and monitoring unit, which naturally allows the introduction of a more sophisticated diagnosis. Figure 10.5 shows the safety loop.

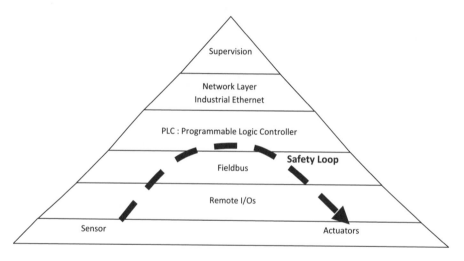

Figure 10.5. *The safety function in the automation system*

Up until now, only fully automated safety functions have been taken into account, but in many critical functions, man intervenes directly (PLC level). This raises the problem of human reliability and incorporating the operator's action into the reliability chain of the safety function. Indeed, from a set of environmental parameters or human "observable" actions, the operator is often able to identify a dangerous situation and activate a mitigation action, via a mechanical or an electronic and/or programmable feedback chain. This area of reliability of the human-machine interface is not addressed in this document.

Evolution of industrial system architecture:

– maximum use of existing hardware resources (control layer), thus sharing the PLC communication layer and the human-machine interface.

=>Additional costs associated with the implementation of hardware resources, while some are usable under a number of conditions (reaction time, maximum outflow, conflicts, etc.), must be avoided;

– we prefer to multiply the number of additional safety functions with lower levels of safety integrity level (SIL);

– more frequent use of microprocessors whose flexibility may allow the introduction of advanced functions (degraded operation, diagnosis, etc.);

– organization by layer (control/network) of the system;

– distribution of human responsibilities *vis-à-vis* the system: repair, supervision, etc. and, therefore, of decision-making positions;

– reduced development costs of suppliers by putting in place flexible and programmable systems and the use of referenced modules (off-the-shelf components);

– possibility of using components from different suppliers and of different development (distributed programmable architecture).

The problem of a spurious trip during the use of a unique safety controller (no redundancy for the availability) remains a major concern.

There are controller systems with high availability, but they are often reserved for applications in the field of the process industry because of their high cost.

The choice of solution is based on three major criteria:

– safety (probability of failure by demand + response time + fault tolerance);

– desired availability;

– size of the facility.

The establishment of a safety instrumented system (SIS) is a prevention measure, which aims to reduce the frequency of damage occurrence. Risk reduction using these SISs should not constitute the first barrier of the safety system. Thus, a risk reduction factor, ΔR, is associated with an SIS, as shown in Figure 10.7.

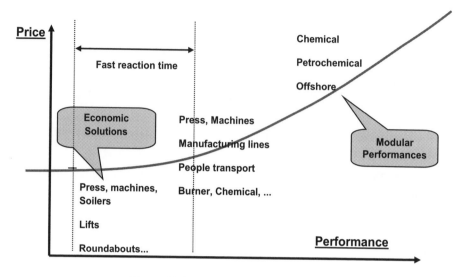

Figure 10.6. *Criteria of choice of solutions*

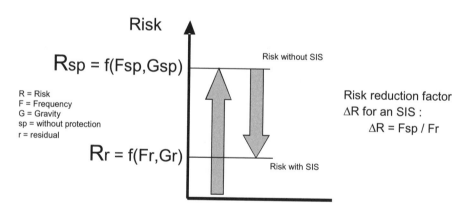

Figure 10.7. *Risk reduction by SIS*

10.2. Safety loop structure

In an automated system, it is important to differentiate the process control and safety functions (SRCF: Safety Related Control Function – IEC 62061 [IEC 05]). Safety functions must be managed by a safety system.

The functions of emergency stop of an engine, of access management, or of ESV (emergency shutoff valve) are intended to ensure the safety of the system in the presence of danger and, therefore, are crucial to prevent damage to goods and people. Risk analysis is used to indicate the safety level that can be achieved.

An example of a SRCF:

– control function: regulation of speed;

– safety function: emergency stopping of engine on request: this last function is said to be a safety function and must operate reliably in case of danger. The circulation of data between the sensor, the logical process unit, and the safety actuator therefore constitutes circulation of data relative to safety.

Thus, special attention must be paid to:

– detection;

– transmission and processing of these alarm signals to the control system;

– the reaction of the actuator in question.

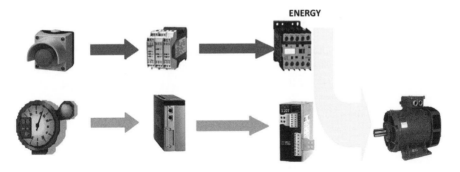

Figure 10.8. *Separation of standard and safety processing safety*

In the safety of production systems, we often work in negative logic. The sensors and actuators are in the safe default position and it is the safety data that give them the order to place themselves in an operating position (for example, closed in case of a contactor). Therefore, two things must be ensured:

– order is maintained in operating position;

–safety is ensured upon request (for safety reasons, erroneous messages or errors will result in a request for system safety).

10.2.1. *"Sensor" sub-system*

For signal acquisition, we will include the sensor and signal acquisition element (transducer, digital/analog input card).

We generally use a NC (normally closed) contact that will trigger the safety function in case the circuit opens. In the case of applications on machines, it is called a positive opening maneuver, because the separation of contacts results from the displacement of the control switch organ (contact at tearing). A detector operated by another organ in motion by direct contact is said to a positive command.

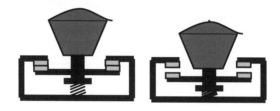

Figure 10.9. *Example of emergency stop by positive command*

There are various alternatives for establishing a redundant architecture that will depend on the controlled equipment. Thus, for sensors with digital output, a 1oo1/1oo1D structure (D for diagnosed) may result in the diagram of Figure 10.10.

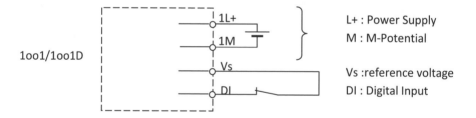

Figure 10.10. *Example of assembly in 1oo1/1oo1D*

The 1oo1 structure is not fault tolerant. If a dangerous failure occurs for the only element, then the sub-system will be unable to operate and ensure its safety function. The diagnosis function allows the online detection of some of the failures that may be encountered.

The 1oo1D structure increases the safety level of the production unit, but reduces its availability. Indeed, with a 1oo1 system, a detected fault does not necessarily result in a stop as in the case of a 1oo1D structure.

The use of 4-20 mA analog sensors in the process also allows this distinction when used with appropriate threshold functions. The use of analog sensors is recommended when the measured quantity is a continuous variable because the measured value can be directly compared with the measurements of sensors dedicated to operating the controlled equipment.

Thus redundant structures can be used that can be exploited in 1oo2/1oo2D, 2oo2/2oo2D with two contacts triggering the same physical phenomenon.

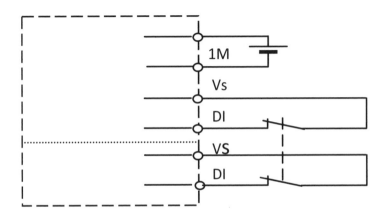

Figure 10.11. *Example of assembly in 1oo2/1oo2D or 2oo2/2oo2D*

The "1oo2" structure is composed of two elements connected in parallel so that each can perform the sub-system function. Under normal conditions of use, both channels request the safety function. A dangerous failure in both channels would result in the safety function not being processed correctly. The result of any diagnosis test does not alter the outcome of the 1oo2 majority logic. It corresponds to the operation of two channels in parallel for the transmission of safety information (e.g. two redundant pressure sensors, two closing valves in series, etc.).

On this type of installation, additional tests are possible:

– crossed short circuit by applying voltage gap to the voltage Vs;

– time discrepancy between the two channels;

– etc.

It is possible to perform other types of assembly (e.g. 2oo3, etc.), but we will limit ourselves to those discussed previously.

10.2.2. *"Actuator" sub-system*

In terms of actuators, multiple configurations are possible to increase safety or availability, any combination of these different architectures is possible. However, a maximum of three actuators is usually used because of the price of actuators of which the following configurations are representative (e.g. closing a power supply pipe with solenoid valves). Some strategies can be very advantageous in terms of SIL, but are often considered too expensive.

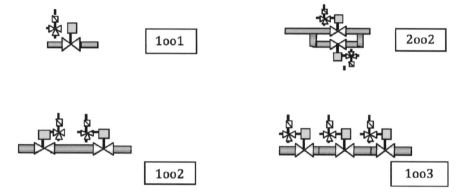

Figure 10.12. *Examples of redundant structures for actuators*

10.2.3. *Information processing*

The traditional safety functions are typically performed by electro-mechanical components, while the programmable electronic systems are suitable for more complex functions. Thus the combinatorial logic is integrated on an electronic card that is commonly called "safety relay".

It is also possible to process safety functions using a programmable logic controller (PLC), provided that it meets the following requirements:

– during development, implementation, and maintenance, various measures and procedures should be adopted to avoid systematic faults;

– the PLC must be able to control systematic failures appearing during operation;

– the PLC must be able to detect and control hardware failures appearing sporadically during operation;

– the PLC must be able to control these detected failures by reliably executing the safety function provided to this effect.

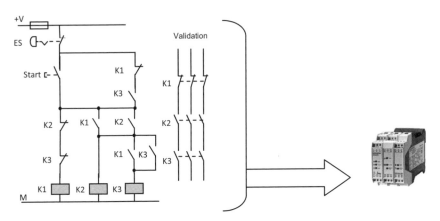

Figure 10.13. *Example of safety logic block*

10.2.3.1. *Why use a safety-related programmable logic controller?*

Standard CPU	Safety CPU
Uncertain fallback position in presence of failure	Safe fallback position in presence of failure
Limited internal test function	Additional monitoring tests Password for access to safety program
Untested program memory	Program memory cyclically tested by CRC
Program executed once per cycle	Temporal redundancy of the execution of the safety program

Table 10.1. *Comparison between standard and safety-related central processing unit safety*

Table 10.1 presents the fundamental differences between a standard and a safety-related CPU.

The arguments in favor of using a safety PLC are:

– possible use of shared hardware between control layer and safety layer;

– lower design cost (certified blocks) and series;

– flexibility;

– sale of service and function expertise;

– cost and serialization of certain components (robustness of modules against stress and isolation of critical modules);

– possible use of imported hardware and numerous sensor interfaces (complex function).

The constraints on the use of a safety PLC are:

– sharing of hardware resources (bus, memory, processor, sensors, actuators) through the control and safety layer;

– the need for a large memory buffer (for comparison of results);

– bus communication and strong timing constraints (update, organization of procedures);

– difficulty of assessing metrics by multiplying the counter-measures and strategies for degraded mode, which are both integrated and constructible by a logic block;

– low traceability of control procedures in the user blocks;

– increased difficulty of validating safety-oriented functions.

10.2.3.2. *Siemens safety integrated solution*

"Safety integrated" designates a safety automation system developed to achieve safety concepts in the field of protection of machines and people. It relies on the "distributed safety" concepts. It includes at least the following components:

– a failsafe CPU (failsafe $\rightarrow$ safety);

– failsafe signal modules (I/O) in centralized configuration.

But it is also possible to extend the architecture by using:

– failsafe signal modules in a system of decentralized peripheral (ET200);

– safety modules (motor starter in decentralized peripheral);

– safety DP slaves safety(with the use of the open protocol PROFIsafe).

The standard and safety-related programs are executed in the same CPU. Using the wiring, parameters, and appropriate programming, safety levels up to SIL 3 (see IEC 61508 [IEC 02]) can be achieved.

10.2.3.2.1. From wired logic to the safety-related PLC for management of safety functions

The need for integration is exacerbated to optimize the availability and safety of the production facility. Integration significantly saves on wiring and maintenance (ease of diagnosis and homogenous hardware).

Safety integrated makes it possible to fuse the process control part and the safety management part within a single global control system with distributed architecture.

The CPU contains the standard program and the safety-related program. The remote stations deported on the network integrate I/O standard and safety cards. The standard and safety information are transmitted on the same medium thanks to the PROFIsafe profile of the PROFIBUS.

Functional safety is primarily achieved in the failsafe program using safety functions. The safety functions are performed by the S7-300F or S7-400F/FH system in order to produce or maintain the facility in a safe state when a hazardous event occurs.

10.2.3.2.2. For the integration of safety technology, there are two safety automation systems in SIMATIC S7

Use of the automation system, S7-300F, is recommended to achieve safety for the protection of machines and people (access and doors management, emergency stop, etc.) and small safety applications in the process industry (burner, boiler, etc.).

For larger facilities, such as those belonging to the process industry (chemical, petroleum, pharmaceuticals, etc.), use of the safety automation system, S7-400F/FH, is recommended, which allows more significant management, which can be highly available. The highly available S7-400FH system presents a redundant architecture avoiding interruptions of the process in the safety system in case of error through a switching mechanism on the redundant system.

10.2.3.2.3. Principle of S7-300F safety functions

Functional safety is achieved by using safety functions primarily at the software level. The safety functions are performed by the S7-300F system to induce or maintain the facility in a safe state in case of a hazardous event. The safety functions are contained mainly in the following components:

– safety user program;

– the F-CPU;

– the safety I/O (failsafe periphery).

Failsafe periphery ensures the processing of the safety field information (emergency stop, light curtains, motor starter). It has all the hardware and software components required for safe processing in accordance with the required safety class. The user simply programs the user safety functions. The safety function for the process is achieved either by a user-based safety function, or by a fault reaction function. When the F system is no longer able to provide the user safety function in case of failure, a fault reaction function is triggered: for example, the corresponding outputs are set to 0.

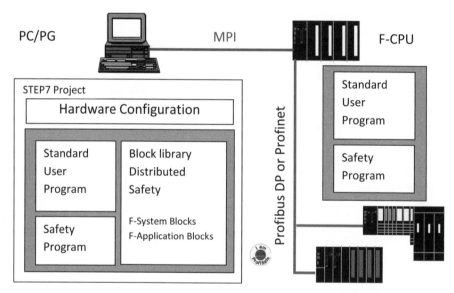

Figure 10.14. *Overview of S7-300F architecture*

The 315F-2DP CPU was designed on the basis of a standard CPU with additional protection mechanisms for the processing of safety applications added to the operating system. However, the CPU can process the standard applications without restrictions.

The design of the E/E/EP modules is addressed in the IEC 61508 [IEC 02] standard and distinguishes the main differences for this viewpoint. For the user, usage is a bit more "binding" in order to meet the safety requirements:

– LVL (limited variability language);

– identification and password;

– tracking of changes (traceability);

– very structured on-line modification;

– etc.

10.2.3.2.4. Processing at the processor level

The processing of the safety program is directed by a single processor, which from a hardware perspective is not redundant (1oo1D structure), but has specific mechanisms to ensure the correct processing of the program. These mechanisms are in fact a combination of specific measures for detecting errors in hardware, in terms of the safety function (effective against hardware and software errors) and externally by controlling the safety output modules.

The safety program data are processed redundantly. In fact, 16 redundant bits are used. Diversity is achieved through the use of controls in the telegrams and the use of additional data in data blocks and parameters. The safety parameters are therefore structured in a data element (of Boolean type) and an additional element (of word type).

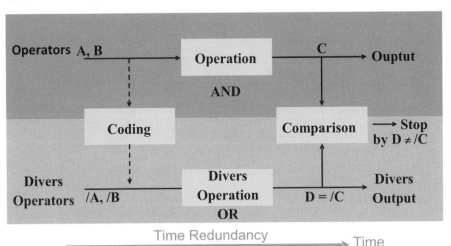

Figure 10.15. *Time redundancy of the program process*

The data elements are processed first (A,B); then the additional elements (/A,/B). Diverse operations are used to detect processing defects.

Example of processing: Boolean AND:

– Boolean data (A,B) are processed by a bit-AND operation in the arithmetic logic unit;

– coded data (/A,/B) are then processed by a word-OR operation in the ALU.

The results of the diverse calculations are then compared directly in the safety application program for a better localization of errors, but also indirectly by the receiver of the safety telegram, which also makes the comparison.

Where there is no diverent operation to realize, the process is always performed twice to detect transient errors and code violations during each cycle.

The execution of the safety program is done cyclically (time configurable by the user). The cycle time is controlled by the safety application program as well as by the receiver of the safety telegram (e.g. safety output card).

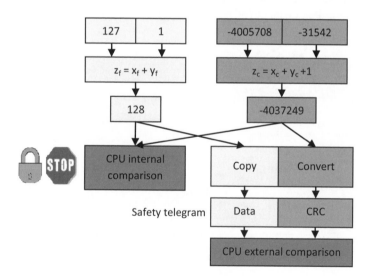

Figure 10.16. *Example of addition: 127 + 1*

The safety program is then signed by a specific procedure to validate its authenticity when it is transmitted. If the receiver of the telegram, which has also calculated this signature, detects a difference, then the CPU puts itself in a safe fallback position (STOP) and the transmission of telegrams is stopped.

This mode contrasts with other manufacturers who prefer simultaneous processing with two or three different processors. Diversity largely levels off the spread of any possible systematic failures of the single processor that could bias the output. We have here two diverse processes that are undertaken in succession.

Diverse storage with an inverted arithmetic code (AN-Code) against operand errors:

– un-coded data xf;

– coded data xc = INV(A•xf) with A = 31541.

Diverse processing with coded operations against operation errors:

– uncoded operations programmed by the user are executed with the uncoded data *xf*;

– coded operations inserted by the F compiler are executed with the coded data *xc*.

CPU internal comparison:

– in output drivers;

– fault reaction: outputs are locked and CPU stops.

External monitor and second switch-off capacity:

– by the safety telegram receiver (fail-safe output modules or other CPUs);

– fault reaction: safe substitute values and error message.

10.2.3.2.5. Safety input cards

The signal acquisition modules must also have a safe architecture so that they can be used to process safety functions. Regarding the input cards, we can consider that these modules consist of pairs of parallel channels. For each module, two microprocessors will allow periodic inspection by an input/output test on the sub-modules, of each channel in succession.

The module can be recognized as two 1oo1D sub-systems in parallel. In cases of detected hardware failure, a diagnosis bit is transmitted to the CPU. A control LED can also directly display the alarm at the module level.

We may, in this case, either use a sensor on two parallel channels or two sensors (various sources) on both channels. We will then have, by comparing the two signals acquired using a conventional comparator, a verification of the equality of the input on each of the parallel channels. If this equality is not proven by verification, we will have a diagnosis bit emission announcing the failure of the module. Therefore, it should be noted that in the case of such an alarm, both the module and sensors can be a source of failure so this must be verified.

We can represent the F modules by two 1oo1D systems in parallel, then a 1oo2 comparator in series. The emission of a diagnosis bit can occur in three cases: circuit 1 detected faulty, circuit 2 detected faulty, dissonant results of channels 1 and 2.

The cards are configurable through the programming interface of the hardware provided by the manufacturer. From a safety point of view, the following are important modifiable parameters:

– validation of the diagnostic alarm: the module brings back the diagnostic information detected by its diagnostic functions internal and external to the CPU;

– choice of safety mode:

- 1oo1 evaluation: there is one sensor and it is connected to the module via a single channel (SIL 2 max),

- $1oo2^2$ evaluation: the two input signals are compared for equivalence or non-equivalence and are combined into a channel pair (max SIL 3);

– monitoring time: if no valid communication is detected between the module and the CPU during a period greater than this time, the module goes into a safe fallback position. This time must be defined according to the application;

– sensor power supply via the module;

– with a short-circuit test: if the sensors are powered via the module, it is possible to activate a short circuit test (switching the sensor power supply off for a short period);

– type of sensor connection: two equivalent channels, two non-equivalent channels, one double channel;

– discrepancy time: maximum time interval between the switching of the two redundant channels.

2. Note that if a channel is exploited in 1oo2 mode, access to the data will be done via the low volume channel.

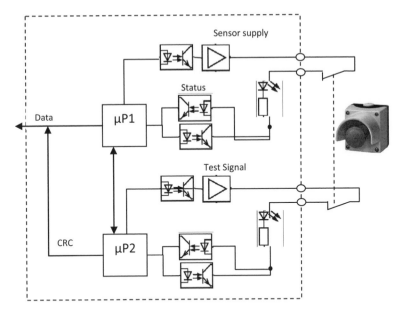

Figure 10.17. *Safety mechanisms in an input card*

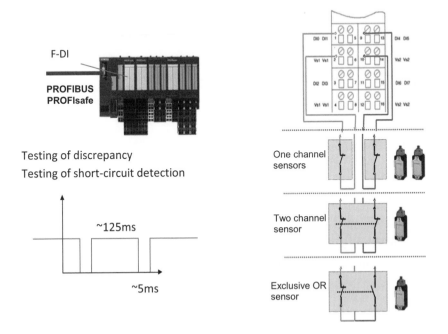

Figure 10.18. *Types of sensors and channel test*

Figure 10.19 shows some examples of sensor wiring on input cards and the level of SIL qualified by the sub-system. Typically with this type of card:

– the sensors can also be powered by an external power supply;

– the sensors must be qualified accordingly.

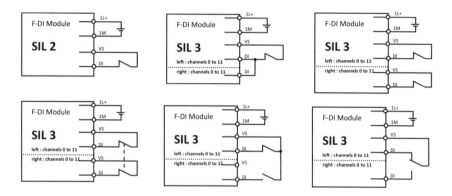

Figure 10.19. *Assembly of sensors*

10.2.3.2.6. Safety output cards

Regarding the output cards, they are equipped with two microprocessors with the following features:

– output read-back;

– integrated "signal test" function;

– diagnostic;

– means for redundant shut-off.

Features of an output card:

– validation of diagnostic alarm: the module brings back diagnostic information detected by its diagnostic functions, internal and external to the CPU;

– choice of safety mode:

- safety mode SIL 2 (no test on output),

- safety mode SIL 3 (with test on output);

– monitoring time: if no valid communication is detected between the module and the CPU for a period longer than this time, the module goes into a safe fallback position. This time must be defined according to the application;

– the signal changes at least once a day or more:

   - dark period test only (the output is switched off briefly),

   - light and dark period test (the output is switched on and off briefly);

– reaction when CPU stops: only available in standard mode (substitute value "0" on all outputs);

– apply replacement value 1, in the safety mode, the default value is always 0.

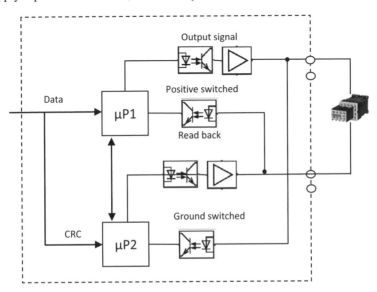

Figure 10.20. *Safety mechanism in an output card*

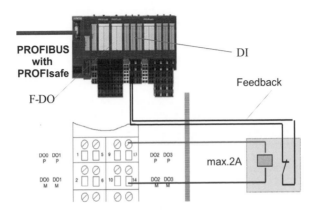

Figure 10.21. *Connection of an actuator with an output card*

Figure 10.22 shows some examples of pre-actuator wiring on output cards and the SIL level qualified by the sub-system.

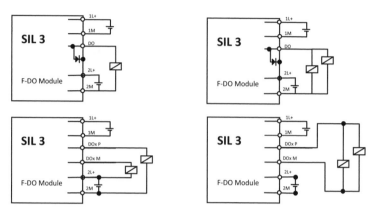

Figure 10.22. *Assembly of pre-actuators*

The S7-300F [EIS 06a] system leads to the following architecture:

– configurable input modules 1oo1D (SIL 2) or 1oo2D (SIL 3);

– controller module (1oo1D);

– output module 1oo2D.

The whole thing can claim a SIL 1 to SIL 3 level according to the parameters and assembly.

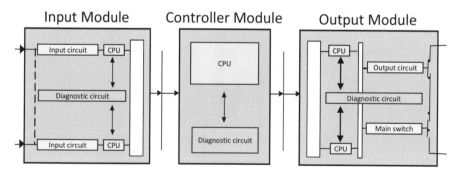

Figure 10.23. *Structure of an S7-300F architecture*

10.2.4. *Field networks*

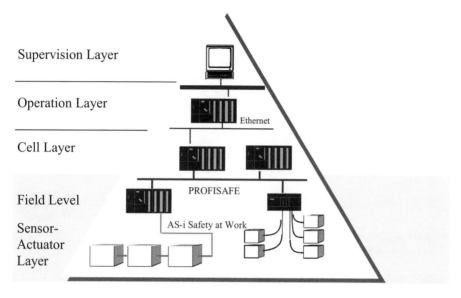

Figure 10.24. *Architecture*

Maintaining the safety function of a device or a facility incorporating several elements depends on the proper functioning of each element involved in this function. Potential hazards related to the involvement of a field network in the maintenance of a safety function can be caused by:

– an alteration of information processing;

– a delay in information processing.

Networks dedicated to safety are "components":

– *able* to meet the specifications of SIL 1, 2, or 3;

– *designed and promoted* to facilitate the scalability of equipped facilities;

– *open* to the outside world regarding *the safety application* (difficulty in controlling influences):

- by the hardware: use of a medium not dedicated to application safety,

- by the software: functional management of the facility in addition to safety functions in a single device;

– *complex* to implement (abundant documentation, difficult access to essential information, response time concept delicate to handle, etc.).

10.2.4.1. *The safety profile PROFIsafe*

The safety profile PROFIsafe defines the connection of intrinsically safe equipment (emergency stops, immaterial barriers, locks) to programmable controllers on PROFIBUS. The specific area of safety, most of whose constituents were previously connected by wire, may benefit from the multiple strengths of open communication on PROFIBUS.

Based on the DP (decentralized peripherals) profile, PROFIsafe accepts RS 485 transmissions, fiber optics or IEC 1158-2.

Equipment operating under PROFIsafe is able to function without limits in perfect harmony with standard equipment on the same cable. It is therefore a software solution that combines safe communication and standard transmission over a single channel, without any other special wiring.

PROFIsafe takes into account any errors that may sneak into the standard serial transmission (repetition, loss, insertion, sequence error, delay, masquerade, data corruption, and addressing failures). It defines additional safety mechanisms that go beyond simple detection and error correction of the PROFIBUS access management.

The combination of the different safety measures available (numbering frames, temporal monitoring with acknowledgment, source identification, destination, cyclic redundancy check and patented "SIL monitor") can achieve levels up to SIL 3.

10.2.4.2. *Bus structure*

PROFIsafe must ensure the necessary safety on a single channel communication system while offering increased availability with redundant communication channels. The aim is also to develop a solution in the form of a PROFIBUS profile, using a specific format for the useful data (Figure 10.25).

Achievable safety levels are SIL 3 (according to IEC 61508 [IEC 02]). Under this standard, we must consider safety circuits as a whole, that is to say, sensors, transmission equipment, processing units, and actuators involved in the safety function. PROFIsafe admits a probability of failure of the communication equipment of 1%.

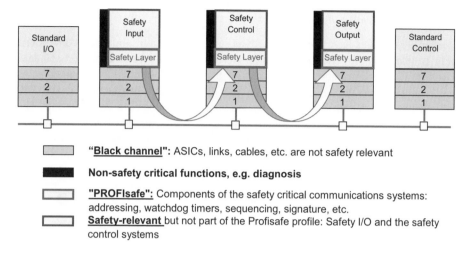

"**Black channel**": ASICs, links, cables, etc. are not safety relevant

Non-safety critical functions, e.g. diagnosis

"**PROFIsafe**": Components of the safety critical communications systems: addressing, watchdog timers, sequencing, signature, etc.

Safety-relevant but not part of the Profisafe profile: Safety I/O and the safety control systems

Figure 10.25. *Communication network*

An attractive first approach, consisting of treating the existing communication as a "black channel", of ignoring the safety devices on the bus and of consolidating all safety measures only in PROFIsafe options, quickly leads to inefficient solutions. It is necessary only to harmonize additional measures with existing ones, mobilizing only the means that are strictly necessary. In this case, the standard communication equipment is called the "gray channel". The current literature on the subject lists the faults that can occur on a communication system and the available deterministic corrective actions are well known. Indeed, messages may be lost, repeated, additionally inserted, appear in the wrong order or with a delay, and thus cause data corruption.

In the case of a safety application, an erroneous address can be added, namely a standard message that erroneously appears as safety information to a component of a safety network (masquerade). Among the many corrective actions, PROFIsafe has selected four: messages are assigned a continuous number, act as a sign of life, and useful data are secured by an appropriate CRC polynomial. Each time, it is established only between the sender and the receiver of a communication link 1:1 known to both (identification) which acts as a "password". The fourth measure is to provide for each receiver a scrutinizing period (watch dog) for the arrival of messages and acknowledgments. All these mechanisms work to ensure safety, even in the presence of unknown stations on the bus.

10.2.4.3. *Management of safe messages*

These messages have the same form as standard messages, but their content can only be interpreted by the safety master. Here we see the organization of a standard PROFIBUS message, and how we ensure that the information communicated is accurate. The message begins with a numbered reference. Then comes the start bit, followed by the length announced by the message, repeated a second time. The destination address is then communicated as is the source address (for the response). The type of message is then communicated, followed by the message itself. Finally, a test sequence is sent, followed by the end bit. This is how messages are sent on PROFIBUS.

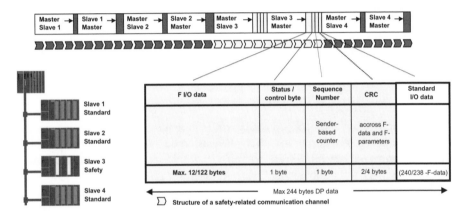

Figure 10.26. *Message exchange*

However, on PROFIBUS the system does not adequately secure the data and ensures there are no errors. Safety messages take on a form similar to standard messages, but the verification sequences of the frame and parity ensures the safety of the message.

The safety message is part of the 244 byte frame of the standard message intended for standard communication, but the message is carried out in a way so that safety is ensured. The first part contains the data for safety input/output, with a maximum of 124 bytes. The next byte is a byte of the status or control (according to the communication way) of the safety slave, then comes the byte encoding the sequence number. Thanks to this byte, we can be sure that the message received corresponds to the last request, because for each request by the master, this sequence number is incremented. Then comes the CRC2 code, it is through this code that we can certify the integrity of the safety message.

Safety is ensured by the presence of CRC2 encryption. Indeed, a standard message is not able to create a safety message with a correct CRC code and the correct consecutive number. Moreover, the addressing is guaranteed by the fact that the safety sender of the pair is considered the only one that can generate the key to the corresponding CRC, expected by the safety receiver. In this way, we ensure the authenticity of the safety sender's address, the addresses being encrypted in the CRC.

10.2.4.4. *Message tracking*

As mentioned earlier, message tracking is performed by incrementing a number contained in the safety message. For each request of the safety master, this number is incremented, the answer necessarily containing this number, and it is during this condition that the message is declared valid. If the message is delayed or is received outside of the watchdog, the message is no longer valid because the master has sent the request again with the next number, so the message received is not valid. Similarly, if there was corruption of the incremented number, which could mean that there was an insert in the message, again the message would not be valid.

10.2.4.5. *Analysis of failure modes, reaction to a malfunction*

To maintain a safety level and prevent errors from spreading, the communication service must be able to deal with all possible eventualities. For each type of error, we introduce the principle of the error, then the system response to such an event, that is to say the means of protection established by the concept (Table 10.2).

	Failure	System response
Repetition	The failure of the bus causes repetition of obsolete messages at a bad time, which could lead to the dangerous operation of a receiver (e.g. door signaled as closed when it is still open).	In the DP mode, data are transferred cyclically. Thus, the incorrect message inserted once will immediately be replaced by the correct message. The possible delay for an urgent request can be the watchdog time. Moreover, the consecutive number can identify the obsolete messages that have been repeated and these can be disregarded.
Loss of information	The failure of the bus erases the message (e.g. request to stop the safety operation).	The lost information will be recognized by the increase and monitoring of the consecutive number, as well as by the absence of response before expiration of the watchdog.

Table 10.2. *Type of failure and associated response*

	Failure	System response
Insertion	The failure of the bus inserts a message (e.g. deselection of the mode "safe stop").	The receiver will recognize the message because of the rigorous sequential expected of the consecutive number. Moreover, the inserted message must arrive at the receiver during the watchdog, and it must have the correct sender/receiver code.
Incorrect order	The failure of the bus modifies the message order (e.g. before processing a safety stop, speed must be safely reduced. Confusing these messages, the machine will continue to operate rather than stop).	The receiver will recognize all incorrect sequence as a result of the rigorous sequential expected of the consecutive number.
Corruption or alteration of message	Failure of the bus or of transmission links corrupts the messages.	The CRC2 code recognizes the data corruption between the sender and receiver. The CRC2 code is generated from the safety parameters and the safety data of the process. Thus, if the message has been altered during transmission, the CRC2 code calculated by the receiver will not be identical to the one emitted via the message.
Delay	Exchanged operational data exceeds the communication link capacity. A bus mechanism creates an overload situation by simulating incorrect messages so that the system blocks the actions associated with the messages.	The time of the watchdog in the corresponding receiver must not be surpassed (duration of the watchdog for safety communication). The duration of the watchdog is the sum of the necessary time for the creation of the message, for the calculations relative to the sending out of the message, for the transmission of the message, for the waiting time of the message processing in the receiver, for the transmission of the return message, and for its reception. Moreover, this time is a maximum that cannot be exceeded.
Standard/ safety amalgamation	The failure of the bus causes an amalgam between standard and safety telegrams.	Data result from the correct sender or go to the correct receiver. This is guaranteed by the CRC2 signature through the safety parameters, the identification between sender and receiver, and the watchdog.

Table 10.2. (continued). *Type of failure and associated response*

In the end (Table 10.3), for each type of error, one or more solutions are present for detection. For repetition of a message, the message number helps avoid the error. For message loss, the sequence number and the watchdog help avoid the error. For insertions, the two preceding components plus the identification between sender and receiver via the CRC key help avoid the error. Data corruption is eliminated by verifying data consistency. Delays are avoided by the watchdog, and masquerades, errors in message delivery, are preventable through a combination of the watchdog, the identification between sender and receiver, and verification of data consistency.

	Measure			
Errors	Sequence number	*Time out* in reception	Identification for the sender and receiver	Verification of data consistency
Repetition	X			
Deletion	X	X		
Insertion	X	X	X	
Incorrect order	X			
Data corruption				X
Delay		X		
Standard/safetysafety amalgamation		X	X	X

Table 10.3. *Synthesis*

10.3. Constraints and requirements of the application

10.3.1. *Programming*

Generally, the user program in the F-CPU consists of a standard user program and a safety program. The standard user program is created with standard programming languages (according to IEC 61131), while the safety program is programmed in F-LAD (Ladder Diagram, based on the representation of circuit diagrams) or F-FBD (Function Block Diagram, based on graphic logic symbols also known in Boolean algebra).

The coexistence of standard and safety programs in a F-CPU is possible because the safety data of the safety program are protected from unintended influences of data in the user program.

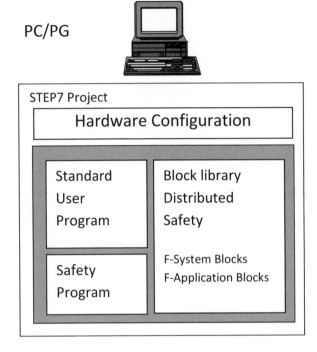

PC/PG

Figure 10.27. *Architecture of the application*

The programming language F-LAD and F-FBD is largely similar to the standard languages LAD and FBD with restrictions at the level of operation sets, data types and areas of usable operands.

F-LAD		F-FBD	
--|/|--	Normally closed contact	>=1	OR Logic operation
--( )--	Output coil	&	AND Logic operation

Table 10.4. *Characteristics of programming languages*

In the safety program, the following operations are *non-permissible*:

− counters (fail-safe counters are implemented via F-Application blocks from the d Distributed Safety F-Library);

– timers (fail-safe timers are implemented via F-Application blocks from the Distributed Safety F-Library);

– Shift and Rotate instructions (shift instructions are implemented using F-application blocks from the Distributed Safety F-library);

– Elementary data types (for example, BYTE, DWORD, DINT, REAL);

– Complex data types (for example, STRING, ARRAY, STRUCT, UDT);

– Parameter types (for example, BLOCK_FB, BLOCK_DB, ANY);

– Data blocks of the standard user program;

– Data blocks (F-DBs) using "OPN DI";

– Data blocks that were automatically added (Exception: certain data in the F-I/O DB and the F-shared DB of the safety program);

– I/O area: Inputs;

– I/O area: Outputs;

– Call standard blocks (FBs, FCs);

– CALL: Call FC/SFC without parameters;

– Call F-FBs, F-FCs conditionally (interconnection of EN and EN = 0);

– Call SFBs, SFCs.

10.3.2. *Program structure*

The launch of the safety program is done by calling a specific block (F-CALL) from the standard user program. It is recommended to call the F-CALL directly in an OB, preferably an OB alarm clock to ensure the execution frequency of the safety program (e.g. OB35).

Communication between the F-CPU (Process Image) and the F-periphery to refresh the process image is done via the particular safety protocol in accordance with PROFIsafe.

The Process-Image Input: at the beginning of each cycle (OB1), the F-CPU reads the inputs on all I/O devices (F and standard) and saves the values in the process-image input. Access to input channels of the I/O devices is possible only through reading via the units mentioned. A plausibility check specific to the processor is also required.

At the beginning of the safety execution group (F-CALL), the F-CPU reads the inputs on the F-I/O devices and saves the values in the process-image input. Access to input channels is only possible through reading.

The Process-Image Output: the safety program eventually calculates the output values of the standard I/O devices and saves them in the process-image output. At the end of OB1, the F-CPU writes the output values calculated in the output of the standard I/O devices.

Access to output channels of the standard I/O devices is possible only through writing via the units mentioned. The safety program calculates the output values of F-I/O devices and saves it in the process-image output. At the end of the safety execution group (F-CALL), the CPU F writes the output values calculated in the output of the F-I/O devices. Access to output channels is possible only in writing.

NOTE: The process-image input of F-I/O devices is refreshed not only at the beginning of the safety execution group before the processing of the F-program block but also by the standard operating system before processing the OB1. Therefore, note that during the access to the process-image input of F-I/O devices in the standard user program, you can obtain different values depending on whether you access it before or after the processing of the safety program.

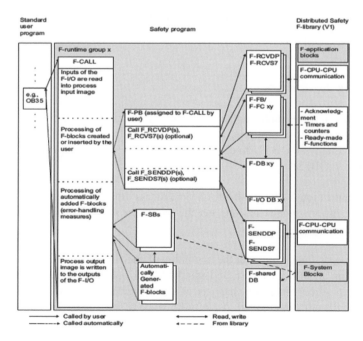

Figure 10.28. *Example of program structure*

10.3.3. *The distributed safety library*

These blocks have been validated by the TÜV (Technischer Überwachungs-Verein) and are listed in the annex of the certification report furnished by the manufacturer.

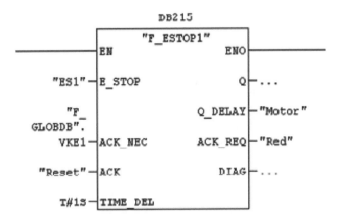

Figure 10.29. *Example of a block*

This application block (Figure 10.29) F executes an emergency stop with acknowledgement for the stop categories 0 and 1. The validation signal Q is set to 0 as soon as the input E_STOP takes the signal status 0 (stop category 0).

	Parameters	Type	Description	Default value
Input	E_STOP	BOOL	Emergency stop	0
	ACK_NEC	BOOL	1 = necessary acquittal	1
	ACK	BOOL	1= acquittal	0
	TIME_DEL	TIME	Delay time	T#0 ms
Output	Q	BOOL	1 = Validation	0
	Q_DELAY	BOOL	Late validation at fall	0
	ACK_REQ	BOOL	1 = acquittal request	0
	DIAG	BYTE	Maintenance information	B#16#0

Figure 10.30. *I/O description*

10.3.4. *Communication between the standard user program and the safety program*

The exchange of data between standard and safety programs in the F-CPU is possible by means of bit memory or by accessing the process input and output image.

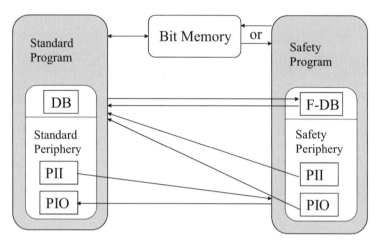

Figure 10.31. *Management of standard/safety exchanges*

Figure 10.31 shows the different types of data transfer from the safety program to the standard user program (and vice versa). The different types of transfer can be summarized as follows:

– the standard user program can read all the data from safety program:

- DB requested from F-FB,

- F-DB,

- process input and output images F-I/O devices;

– the standard user program can write in the F-DB;

– the safety user program can only read the PII of the standard program;

– the safety user program can write in the standard PIO but not in the standard DB or PII.

10.3.5. *Generation of the safety program*

When the safety program is generated, the software automatically performs safety checks and incorporates additional safety blocks for fault detection and fault reaction. Therefore, the detection of failures and faults is assured, as well as the triggering of corresponding reactions intended to maintain or bring the F-system to a safe condition.

Consistent: the collective signature of all F-blocks with F-attribute in the block container is identical to the collective signature of the safety program. F-blocks that are not called in the F-run-time group of the safety program are displayed in the "Safety Program" dialog without the F-attribute in the block symbol and are not included in the calculation of the collective signatures. When the safety program is compiled, you are notified about unused F-blocks in the block container safety.

Inconsistent: the collective signature of all F-blocks with F-attribute in the block container and the collective signature of the safety program are different, because, for example, an F-block with F-attribute has been copied, but the copied F-block with F-attribute is not called in the F-run-time group of the safety program. While unused F-blocks with F-attribute produce an executable safety program, this program cannot pass acceptance tests due to inconsistent collective signatures. Therefore, before the safety program is downloaded to the F-CPU, a warning is displayed ("The ... safety program is inconsistent").

Modified: Before the safety program is downloaded to the F-CPU, a warning is displayed ("The safety program has been changed"). You then have the option of generating (i.e. compiling) a consistent safety program.

10.4. Analysis of a safety loop

The definition of a safety function always includes:

– the specification of the function itself (e.g. stop in dangerous situations);

– the safety integrity level SIL resulting from the risk analysis.

The safety integrity level (SIL) of a function is partly defined by its probability of failure and its architectural constrains on hardware.

There are a number of techniques to analyze the safety integrity of an E/E/PE safety-related systems. The two most used techniques are reliability block diagrams and Markov models. Both methods, if properly applied, give similar results; however, for complex programmable electronic sub-systems (e.g. when a logic prioritized to multiple channels and automatic tests are used), the use of Markov models is preferable. For simplicity, the standards suggest the use of reliability diagrams.

To calculate the PFD/PFH of a safety instrumented function, we must process the sum of the PFD/PFH of each of its sub-systems (sensors, logic processing, actuators) and taking into account various parameters:

– hardware reliability:

   - failure rates,

   - level of self-diagnosis;

– architecture:

   - number of redundancies,

   - coverage rate of dangerous failures,

   - common mode failure (in case of redundancy);

– maintenance:

   - test period,

   - average repair time.

The general methodology for calculating the PFD/PFH of a safety function can be summarized as follows:

– first, identify the architecture used for each part of the SIS;

– then, list the elements involved in building the studied part by involving performance in terms of reliability (failure rate, coverage rate of diagnosis, MTTR, etc.);

– from these data, perform the calculation of the PFD/PFH associated with each part of the SIS;

– once all the PFD/PFH$_g$(i) have been determined, the PFD/PFH associated with the safety system for the concerned function is the sum of the PFD/PFH(i).

10.4.1. *Calculation elements*

For certified components, the manufacturer provides the necessary values (SIL CL and PFH); alternatively, here is a method for obtaining these values.

The sensor sub-system, like the actuator, can be assessed by two different methods:

– either we have the values given by the manufacturer;

– or we need to calculate those values.

If we perform the calculations, we must therefore know:

– B10 (number of switching cycles after which 10% of the elements being tested have failed);

– MTTF (mean time till dangerous failure);

– C (number of commutations per hour);

– T1 (expected lifetime);

– DC (diagnostics coverage: measurement of the efficiency of the diagnosis).

To then be able to estimate:

– SIL CL (claimed SIL limit);

– PFH_D (probability of dangerous failure per hour).

Here is a brief explanation of the different parameters that will be taken into account in the remaining calculations:

– the failure rate of an electro-mechanical component is calculated as follows (according to IEC 62061):

$$\lambda = 0.1 \times C/B10;$$

– the failure rate is composed of a dangerous failure rate and secure failure rate:

- $\lambda = \lambda_S + \lambda_D$,

- $\lambda_D = \lambda \times$ dangerous failure fraction of the element (in %);

– common cause failure: β (method proposed in IEC 62061);

– test intervals:

- T1: lifetime of the element,

- T2: diagnostic test interval (T2=1/C).

The maximum limit claimed of a SIL safety function can be determined by the smallest SIL CL relative to the architectural constraints of the sub-system.

10.4.2. *PFH calculation for the "detecting" sub-system*

We will consider in this example the use of an position switch sensor.

10.4.2.1. *Case of a single element*

Parameter	Value	Reason	Definition	
B10 value	$1 * 10^6$	Manufacturer's data	**Manufacturer**	
Dangerous failure fraction	0.2 (20%)	contacts do not open		
C Number of times that the device is actuated	1 / h	Assumptions: It is actuated once per hour	User	

Dangerous failure rate of the detecting sub-system element (λ_{De})

$\lambda = 0.1 \times 1/1,000,000$

$\lambda = 10^7$

$\lambda_{De} = \lambda \times$ dangerous failure fraction

$\lambda_{De} = 10^7 \times 0.2 = 2 \times 10^8$

10.4.2.2. *Case of two elements in parallel*

We place ourselves in the case where we have all the information about the architecture in which these sensors are used. Here we are only interested in a demonstration of the calculation. According to IEC 62061, we note that this is a type D architecture.

Parameter	Value	Reason	
λ_{De}	$2 * 10^{-8}$ / h	Dangerous failure rate of the sub-system element	
T1 Usage time	87,600 h	Lifetime of the position switch	
T2 Diagnostics test interval	1 h	It is actuated once every hour	
(CCF factor) Prone to failures due to a common cause	0.1 (10%)	When installing according to IEC 62061, a CCF factor of 0.1 (10%) is reached. With this value, you are on the safe side ("conservative value")	
DC Diagnostics coverage	0.99 (99%)	Crosswise comparison in F-DI	

$$\lambda_D = (1 - \beta)^2 * \lambda_{De}{}^2 \{[DC * T2] + [(1 - DC)\,T1]\} + \beta * \lambda_{De}$$

$$\lambda_D = (1 - 0.1)^2 * 2e\text{-}8^2 \{[0.99 * 1] + [(1 - 0.99)*87600]\} + 0.1*2e\text{-}8$$

$$\lambda_D = 2.0003 \times 10\text{-}9$$

$$PFH_D = \lambda_D * 1h$$

$$PFH_D = 2*10\text{-}9$$

10.4.3. *PFH calculation by "actuator" sub-system*

10.4.3.1. *Case of a single element*

Parameter	Value	Reason	Definition	
B10 value	$1 * 10^6$	Manufacturer's data	**Manufacturer**	
Dangerous failure fraction	0.75 (75%)	contacts do not open		
C Number of times that the device is actuated	1 / h	Assumptions: It is actuated once per hour	User	

Dangerous failure rate of the detecting sub-system element (λ_{De})

$$\lambda = 0.1 \times 1/1{,}000{,}000$$

$$\lambda = 10^7$$

$$\lambda_{De} = 10^{-7} \times 0.75 = 7{,}5 \times 10^{-8}$$

10.4.3.2. *Case of two elements in parallel*

As before, we put ourselves in a case we have all the information about the architecture in which these sensors are used. Here, we are only interested in a demonstration of the calculation. According to IEC 62061, we note that this is a type D architecture.

Parameter	Value	Reason	
λ_{De}	$7{,}5 * 10^{-8}$ / h	Dangerous failure rate of the sub-system element	
T1 Usage time	87600 h	Lifetime of the contactor	
T2 Diagnostics test interval	1 h	It is actuated once every hour.	

β(CCF factor) Prone to failures due to a common cause	0.1 (10%)	When installing according to IEC 62061, a CCF factor of 0.1 (10%) is reached. With this value, you are on the safe side ("conservative value")	
DC Diagnostics coverage	0.99 (99%)	Crosswise comparison in F-DO	

$$\lambda_D = (1 - \beta)^2 * \lambda_{De}^2 \{[DC * T2] + [(1 - DC)\ T1\ ]\} + \beta * \lambda_{De}$$

$$\lambda_D = (1 - 0.1)^2 * 7.5*10^{-82} \{[0.99 * 1] + [(1 - 0.99)*87600]\} + 0.1*7.5*10^{-8}$$

$$\lambda_D = 7.5*10^{-9}$$

$$PFH_D = \lambda_D * 1h$$

$$PFH_D = 7.5*10^{-9}$$

10.4.4. *PFH calculation by "logic processing" sub-system*

We place ourselves in the case where we have a F-DI card, a *Profinet* field network with PROFIsafe profile, a safety CPU, a second field network (PROFIBUS) with a PROFIsafe profile, and a safety F-DO card (the data are based on documents from manufacturers that have been certified).

Figure 10.32. *Example of architecture*

Parameter	Component	Value	SIL CL
PFH$_D$ (F-CPU)	CPU 315F-2 PN/DP	$5.43 * 10^{-10}$	3
PFH$_D$ (F I/O)	F-DI	$1 * 10^{-10}$	3
	F-DO	$1 * 10^{-10}$	3
PTE (F-communication)	F Communication: F-CPU and I/Os	$1 * 10^{-9}$	3

Table 10.5. *Characteristics of our sub-systems*

SIL CL sub-system TL <= SIL CL sub-system (weak)

SIL CL sub-system TL <= 3; 3; 3; 3;

SIL CL sub-system TL = SIL 3

$PFH_D = PFH_D\,(\text{F-CPU}) + PFH_D\,(\text{F I/O}) + P_{TE}\,(\text{F Communication})$

$PFH_D = 5.43 * 10^{-10} + 1 * 10^{-10} + 1 * 10^{-10} + 1 \times 10^{-9}$

$PFH_D = 1.743 * 10^{-9}$

10.4.5. *PFH calculation for a complete loop*

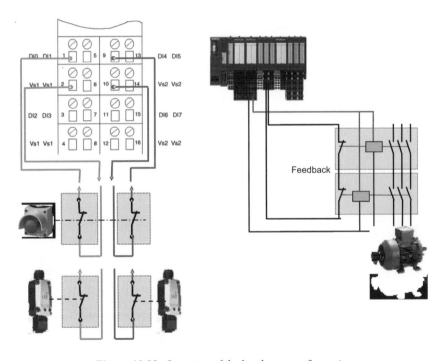

Figure 10.33. *Overview of the hardware configuration*

We will treat the example of monitoring an emergency stop control organ and a movable protector:

– a safety controller monitors the emergency stop control organ. When the emergency stop is activated, the safety controller shuts down the safety outputs on which the positive maneuver contactors are wired;

– the position of the movable protector is detected by position switches. When the movable protector is open, the reaction is the same as for the emergency stop function.

There are two safety functions:

– SF1: when the emergency stop is activated, the motor must stop;

– SF2: when the movable protector is open, the motor must stop.

10.4.5.1. Processing the safety function 1

If we take the calculations above with the following parameters for the two channel emergency stop:

Parameter	Value	Reason	Definition	
B10 value	$1 * 10^5$	Manufacturer's data	**Manufacturer**	
Dangerous failure fraction	0.2 (20%)	contacts do not open		
C Number of times that the device is actuated	$1*10^{-2}$ / h	Assumptions: it is actuated 10^{-2} times per hour	User	

Dangerous failure rate of the detecting sub-system element (λ_{De}).

Parameter	Value	Reason
λ_{De}	$2 * 10^{-9}$ / h	Dangerous failure rate of the sub-system element
T1 Usage time	87600 h	Lifetime of the position switch
T2 Diagnostics test interval	100 h	T2=1/C
β(CCF factor) Prone to failures due to a common cause	0.1 (10%)	When installing according to IEC 62061, a CCF factor of 0.1 (10%) is reached. With this value, you are on the safe side ("conservative value").
DC Diagnostics coverage	0.99 (99%)	Crosswise comparison in F-DI

$$\lambda_D = (1 - \beta)^2 * \lambda_{De}^2 \{[DC * T2] + [(1 - DC) T1]\} + \beta * \lambda_{De}$$

$$\lambda_D = (1 - 0.1)^2 * 2e^{-9}{}_2 \{[0.99 * 100] + [(1 - 0.99)*87600]\} + 0.1*2e^{-9}$$

$$\lambda_D = 2 \times 10^{-10}$$

$$PFH_D = \lambda_D * 1h$$

$$PFH_D = 2*10^{-10}$$

Safe Failure Fraction (SFF)	Hardware Fault Tolerance IEC 62061		
	0	1	2
< 60 %	Not allowed	SIL 1	SIL 2
60 % to < 90 %	SIL 1	SIL 2	SIL 3
90 % to < 99 %	SIL 2	SIL 3	SIL 3
>= 99 %	SIL 3	SIL 3	SIL 3

Table 10.6. *Architectural constraints*

Given that the emergency stop is connected to the safety input card of the controller, and that it is diagnosed, we can claim a SFF> 99% with a hardware tolerance of 1, which allows us to obtain a SIL CL 3 (according to Table 10.6).

10.4.5.2. *Processing the safety function 2*

We will take the calculations done previously (values for the switches and contactors).

Parameter	Component	PFH$_D$	SIL CL
SS1.1	Position switch	$2 * 10^{-9}$	3
SS1.2	Emergency shutdown	$2 * 10^{-10}$	3
SS2	F-DI	$1 * 10^{-10}$	3
SS3	F-CPU	$5.43 * 10^{-10}$	3
SS4	F-DO	$1 * 10^{-10}$	3
SS5	Actuators	$7.5 * 10^{-9}$	3

Table 10.7. *Characteristics of our example*

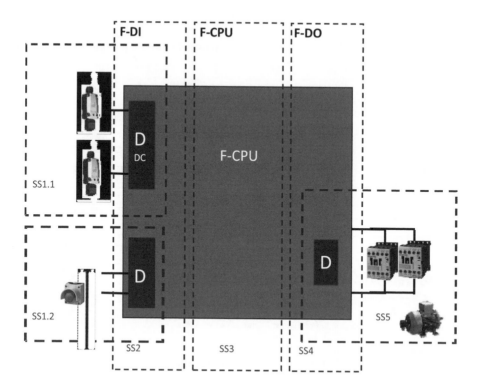

Figure 10.34. *Sub-system notion*

For the calculation of the SIL CL and the PFH_D for function SF1 (AU + F-DI + F-CPU + F-DO + Actuator):

SIL CL SYS <= (SIL CL sub-system) weak

SIL CL SYS <= 3; 3; 3; 3;

->SIL CL = SIL 3

PFH_D = PFH_D (SS1.2) + PFH_D (SS2) + PFH_D (SS3) + PFH_D (SS4) + PFH_D (SS5) < PFH_D SIL SRCF

$PFH_D = 2 * 10^{-10} + 1 * 10^{-10} + 5.43 * 10^{-10} + 1 * 10^{-10} + 7.5 * 10^{-9}$

$PFHD = 8.443 * 10^{-9}$

-> SIL 3 (according to Table 10.8)

SIL according to IEC 62061	Probability of dangerous failure per hour [1/h] (PFHD)
3	$\geq 10^{-8}$ to $<10^{-7}$
2	$\geq 10^{-7}$ to $<10^{-6}$
1	$\geq 10^{-6}$ to $<10^{-5}$

Table 10.8. *SIL equivalence and PFH$_D$*

The safety function SF1 achieved a safety integrity level of SIL3.

For the calculation of the SIL CL and the PFH$_D$ for function SF2 (Position Switch + F-DI + F-CPU + F-DO + Actuator):

SIL CL SYS <= (SIL CL sub-system) weak

SIL CL SYS <= 3; 3; 3; 3; 3

->SIL CL = SIL 3

PFHD = PFH$_D$ (SS1.1) + PFH$_D$ (SS2) + PFH$_D$ (SS3) + PFH$_D$ (SS4) + PFH$_D$ (SS5) < PFH$_D$ SIL SRCF

$PFH_D = 2 * 10^{-9} + 1 * 10^{-10} + 5.43 * 10^{-10} + 1 * 10^{-10} + 7.5 * 10^{-9}$

$PFH_D = 1.0243 * 10^{-8}$

-> SIL 3 (according to Table 10.8)

The safety function SF2 achieved a safety integrity level of SIL3.

10.5. Conclusion

This chapter has provided an opportunity to present the implementation of an SIS based on industrial controller. This type of system is subject to the regulatory constraints [IEC 05] and/or [IEC 02]. The safety of this type of system is based on the identification of safety functions (SRCF) and their management.

This chapter has shown how the techniques presented in Chapter 1 are implemented.

10.6. Bibliography

[BUC 08a] BUCHWEILER J.P., INRS: circuits de commande des machines – référentiel normatif pour conception, INRS PR 34 211, 2008.

[BUC 08b] BUCHWEILER J.P., INRS: réseaux terrain dédiés Sécurité – temps de réponse, INRS ND 2291, 2008.

[CHA 02] CHARPENTIER P., INRS: Architecture d'automatisme en sécurité des machines – étude des conditions de conception liées aux défaillances de mode commun, PhD thesis, l'INPL, 2002.

[IEC 02] IEC 61508, parts 1 to 7, IEC 61508, Functional safety of electrical/electronic/programmable electronic safety-related systems, March 2002.

[IEC 05] IEC 62061, Safety of machinery – functional safety of safety-related electrical, electronic and programmable electronic control systems, July 2005.

[MYS 08] MYSLIWIECK B., SIEMENS AG: "Coded processing in Factory and Process Automation", *TÜV 8th International Symposium*, Cologne, Germany, 2008.

[SCH 00] SCHENK A., SIEMENS AG: "Simatic S7-400F/FH: safety-related programmable logic controller", *SAFECOMP*, Rotterdam, Holland, 2000.

[SIE 06a] SIEMENS, S7-300 - modules de signaux F, 2006.

[SIE 06b] SIEMENS, Technique F S7 - manuel système, 2006.

[SIE 06c] SIEMENS, Technologie F S7 - description système, 2006.

Chapter 11

A High-Availability
Safety Computer

11.1. Introduction

The computers used for the automation of railway systems have increasingly important needs in terms of safety and availability. The operation of such a system relies on automation, with increasing use of computers and digital communications (e.g. CBTC), and ever more systems operate or can operate without drivers or supervisors onboard, and with a limited number of PCC operators. In the case of driverless operation (UTO = unattended train operation), any failure of fixed or embedded computers can have extremely serious consequences in terms of availability; the availability objectives are very high in order to avoid any shutdown of operation: we can not afford such an event on a single equipment failure.

In addition to the need for increased availability, the complexity of functions and the need for system performance increases significantly.

To meet these demanding conditions, an appropriate response must be provided: the design of computers can no longer be seen as just a pair of simple computers made redundant, but as a complete set of equipment providing a service resistant to failures.

Chapter written by Sylvain Baro.

The redundant computer DIGISAFE XME[1] is based on a redundancy management protocol that allows two coded uniprocessor computers to work as symmetrically as possible. Each computer (called units) is intrinsically safe, and the maintenance of consistency between the execution contexts of the two units allows the switching or transition to the non-redundant (isolated) unit at any time, without requiring special precautions at the application or system level. This last point is extremely important because it significantly reduces system complexity and the associated safety analysis.

We begin by presenting the architecture and safety principles of the simple computer, based on the principle of encoding (section 11.2). We then present the principles of redundancy used in the past (section 11.3). Finally, we present the integrated redundancy protocol that we currently use to provide the high availability demanded by the railway applications mentioned above (section 11.4), starting from the principles and objectives to the detailed design. We conclude with the advantages and disadvantages of our system.

Figure 11.1. *Photo of the automatic metro Roissy-CdG*

11.2. Safety computer

The safety computer DIGISAFE XME is an evolution of the DIGISAFE platform used for railway automation applications since 1989: first on SACEM systems [GEO 90; MAR 90; HEN 94], see, for example, the RER A of the Parisian

---

1. DIGISAFE is a registered trademark of Siemens Transportation Systems.

underground railway (metro), then the SAET-METEOR [LEC 96; MAT 98] (see Figure 11.2), which was put into service on line 14 of the Parisian metro and which has enabled full automatic driving since 1998.

Figure 11.2. *Photo of an automatic subway train on line 14 of the Paris metro*

The development of the safety computer is based on encoding techniques (see Chapter 2) by using a single commercial processor (Intel architecture) and a co-processor dedicated to safe redundancy calculations developed by Siemens (MSCA) and hosted in a field program gate array (FPGA). This safety setting ensures that any execution of a calculation inconsistent with the source code is detected with a very high probability (of the order of the power of the code used). In other words: either the source code is compiled, linked, loaded on the computer, and executed correctly, or the safety computer detects an anomaly and is automatically placed in a safe state.

11.2.1. *Architecture*

The DIGISAFE computer is a calculation platform that we use for CBTC (communication based train control [IEE 04]) applications, whether for embedded computers or fixed computers.

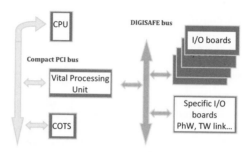

Figure 11.3. *Architecture without redundancy*

To fulfill this role, DIGISAFE secures all processing from input reading to output application, taking into account all layers of software architecture.

Applications processed on this platform are cyclical: during each cycle, the inputs are read, the calculations are made, taking into account these inputs and, of course, the internal states of the computer (variables), and determining the outputs. Finally, the outputs are applied. The inputs and outputs can be of several kinds:

– analog: binary cabled I/O;

– digital: inter-equipment I/O messages sent over the network, or radio;

– acquisition of dedicated safety sensors: odometer, transponder beacon reading, etc.

The safety analog Is/Os are acquired via dedicated safety cards, which convert the input signal into an encoded, time-stamped message, and which is then transmitted to the various software layers for processing. The acquisition and encoding of inputs are both compatible with safe level safety integrity level (SIL) 4 processing requirements with regards to the CENELEC EN 50129 [CEN 03] standard. In parallel, non-safe inputs (called "functional inputs") are acquired by other cards.

Different applications are then triggered cyclically: safety applications and the "functional" application. The functional application is used for non-safe tasks (SIL 0) in particular:

– the actual driving of trains;

– mission management;

– maintenance support;

– etc.

The safety application is in charge of safety tasks:

– control of the emergency brake;

– inhibition of traction;

– enforcing the aspect of signals;

– etc.

The inputs are used for "usual" calculations allowing the evolution of the computer application context and the production of safe and functional outputs. To ensure that these calculations are correct (compared to the source code), all safety data is encoded. Therefore, each variable is found in two separate fields: the first is the functional part, denoted X_f, containing the expected value of the variable (which can be an integer, a Boolean, or a table) and computed "normally" using the expected operations (+, ×, allocation, subscripting), the second field, called the safety part, denoted X_c, constitutes the encoded part (the redundancy) of the variable. It contains all the information necessary to safe the calculations and values, and is computed from the corresponding safety algorithms corresponding to the operator used.

This encoded part contains a static signature representative of the *occurrence* of the variable in the code, of the operations used to produce the value, a representative part of the value X_f and a time stamp to ensure the freshness of the variable (in order to be sure it has been recomputed where necessary during each loop).

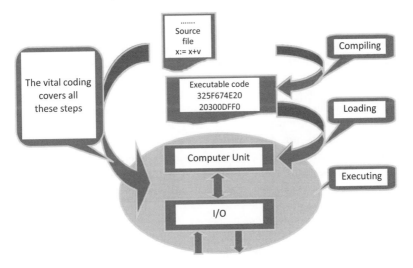

Figure 11.4. *Presentation of the generation and execution chain*

Any data, message, or equipment are called *out-of-code* when the variable (X_f, X_c) is not consistent with the code anymore; conversely, the data are said to be *in-the-code*.

Strictly speaking, it would suffice to consider that an error on a variable is propagated from variable to variable until the outputs themselves are *out-of-code*, but it is not enough if we consider an arbitrary number of errors appearing in the cycle: for each new error that can compensate for prior errors at the code level, the probability of not detecting an error would depend on the number of operations performed in the cycle! To avoid this, we use an accumulator (the tracer), which integrates the difference between the code produced and the expected code during each operation: in case of *out-of-code*, the tracer carries the indelible mark of the error and propagates it until the end of the cycle.

To facilitate the computation of coded variables, and finally, to use them as "normal" variables from an application viewpoint, we define a set of primitive operations on these types of data: elementary operations (OPEL: *opérations élémentaires*). These operations encapsulate both the computation of the functional part and the manipulation of the coded part.

To take the example of OPEL corresponding to the addition (plus assignment): $(Z_f, Z_c) = (X_f, X_c) + (Y_f, Y_c)$ produces $Z_f = X_f + Y_f$ and Z_c, which is computed from X_c and Y_c (and certainly not from Z_f!) but which is such that (Z_f, Z_c) is in the code.

In terms of *data types*, it is interesting to note that this approach also ensures a complete (and syntactic!) separation of the safety data: a safe output is necessarily encoded; any encoded variable can only depend on operations and variables, which are themselves encoded, except the use of the OPEL "ENCODE": it is sufficient to analyze the software part concerned with encoded variables to determine the safe conduct of this software.

To ensure smooth operation with regards to the source code, it is not sufficient to encode the variables: it must also be ensured that the correct OPEL is called. For this, we integrate a static signature in the encoded variables. This signature is representative of the occurrence of a variable, and is uniquely modified by the call to each OPEL. The signature computed for the outputs is always the same (up to the time stamp) and is compared to a predetermined signature. In case of divergence, the equipment is set into a safe state. In parallel to the "compilation, link edition, executable loading, execution" chain beginning with the source code, there is also a "predetermination of static signatures, loading of static signatures, calculation of signatures" chain also beginning with the source code. The predetermination is undertaken starting from the source code, by a dedicated tool, during the generation of the executable, and the final calculation is performed in the MSCA by the OPELs.

The two chains are joined at both ends: the source code on one side, and the application outputs on the other. Therefore, the slightest error (including in the production of the executable) renders the predetermined signatures and the signatures computed in real-time inconsistent.

The wired binary safety outputs are initially computed by the safety application, and then sent across the DIGISAFE bus (which allows exchanges between peripheral cards and cards containing the central processing unit (CPU) and coded processor), so as to control the safe output signal (24 V, which guarantees that any error will cause failure) through the safety output cards. The data are sent to the protected card by a code (including the state of the tracer and the static signature), the card applies voltage depending on the value of the output.

Neither the application of voltage, nor its non-application, is safely guaranteed, but a safe backreading is performed to ensure that the outputs are not wrongly *true*. If this occurs, the dynamic controller (CKD) detects an inconsistency between the backreading of the outputs and the code, and safely reduces the output power supply.

In addition to binary I/O, safe messages are exchanged between equipment, either through a wired network (e.g. Ethernet) or by radio. These messages are transmitted through *non-safe* communication layers, which are considered, from the perspective of the *safe* channel, as black boxes. However, safe messages are compacted to a specific format including, among others, an encoding allowing verification of the integrity of the message. Only safety applications are able to create or modify the code without altering it. A corrupted message (*out-of-code*) is detected at reception. Of course, a given piece of equipment is only capable of creating a message *in the code* if it is itself *in the code*! It is necessary to specify that the properties of freshness, sequence, and identity of transmitters and receivers are not processed at this protocol level, but at a higher level, in the body of the message itself.

In addition to this information, specific sensors may be used in conjunction with DIGISAFE XME. These sensors are most often used for calculations of speed and train position. There are two kinds of sensors:

– those that emit a message in standard DIGISAFE format (which behaves as separate equipment), for example, OSMES[2] (optical speed measurement), which consists of a fully-fledged computer and a device measuring displacement by comparison to "photographs" taken on the rail;

2. OSMES is a registered trademark of Siemens Transportation Systems.

– those that are wired directly to the DIGISAFE computer, such as the "safe coded odometer", an odometer measuring rotation and producing a "teeth" counter and a code corresponding to the measured displacement.

11.2.2. *Properties*

In terms of safety, this architecture has many advantages. First, the demonstration of safety does not depend on the properties of the "computerized" components of the computer (processor, memory, network, etc.), but only on the protection afforded by the code, which is sufficient to be used for SIL 4 level requirements. This principle of safety construction guarantees that any error occurring in any part of the safety application, resulting in an error in the safety output values (including messages), would lead to an *out-of-code* of both the data and the computer. This raises the interesting corollary that any data or part of the software having an impact on the outputs can only be encoded or constructed via the use of OPEL. In other words, the parts of the software that do not use the OPEL do not need to undergo safety validation.

The principles used for the time stamp of outputs have, in addition to the correct property, the fact that the code can only be consistent with the values if the outputs are applied at the right moment. This, combined with a safety clock, safely ensures the cycle timesafetysafe.

To summarize, whatever the cause leading to an error during the cycle calculation, the output will be *out-of-code*, and finally unpowered: a single DIGISAFE computer is sufficient to guarantee safety.

However, automation is becoming increasingly complicated, and now requires more than just a simple computer undertaking control/command tasks: in the most complex applications, computers can not be reset without causing a significant loss of system availability across the board.

This is particularly true for systems operating full automatic driving (UTO) where the malfunction of embedded equipment can lead to the blockage of a train in a tunnel, until manual resumption of the train by an operator.

For all these reasons, it is necessary to add one layer of redundancy to the system in order to prevent a single failure impacting the passenger service.

11.3. Applicative redundancy

Redundancy was used by our previous architecture, the DIGISAFE for the METEOR line (Paris L14). On this platform, the redundancy is given by two DIGISAFE computers (of which each is safe), in which at least one is "active" at any given time (information provided by a hardware component). Both units are able to communicate through a serial link, and unit outputs are combined by an OR gate. From the software (and system) perspective, the whole redundancy management logic is handled function by function, on a case by case basis. In any safety software, for each function, it is necessary to:

– define the behavior when the function is active;

– define the behavior when the function is passive (in order to prepare a possible redundancy switching);

– determine what data are to be exchanged between the two units (in order to prepare for a potential redundancy, and to manage inter blocking functions for which a crude OR on the output could be dangerous);

– analyze the switching scenarios in order to determine whether there is a sequence of events leading to a dangerous situation for the system.

This approach has the advantage of not requiring the development of a protocol or of redundancy management software, but the inconvenience of leading to an intertwining of functional processes and processes related to the management of redundancy, adding a layer of complexity to the software design, and making safety analysis more difficult. This increase in the overall complexity of the construction and determination of safety is unacceptable today, given the increasing complexity of the functions to be performed: the closer the software is to a simple control-command (CC) structure, the less difficult it is to add redundancy at the application level; but with increasing complexity, the functions managing the evermore rich states and the increasingly sophisticated state machines, make it virtually impossible to manage a redundancy switch leaving the system in a consistent state.

11.4. Integrated redundancy

After SAET-METEOR, another approach was investigated in order to achieve a solution with fully integrated redundancy, based on the same hardware architecture, but this time completely seamless from an application viewpoint. This approach comes from work undertaken on PADRE, a redundancy management protocol where consistency is guaranteed by a process on the execution contexts of the applications [ESS 99].

The basic principle guiding the design of the redundancy management function is the complete separation between the software application layers and the management of the redundancy itself. This leads to an encapsulation of the application in the redundancy management software (SEC_RED), as shown in the figure below. Warning: from the functional viewpoint (shown below) the SEC_RED can be seen as a unique element running "between" the two computers. In reality, there are two instances of the same software, running on each of the computers, communicating through the serial link and maintaining it a consistent state.

All inputs are supplied to SEC_RED, which is then free to modify the input according to values received by the other unit and according to its own internal state (especially in the redundancy mode).

Each application then computes its own output (as it would be without redundancy) and begins to update its own state, the only difference being that these calculations are done only if the redundancy allows: in other words, the redundancy can "freeze" all cyclical application processing. Finally, the outputs are provided by the application to SEC_RED, which decides, still according to its own state and the outputs of the redundant unit, if they can be applied as they are, or if they should be forced to a restrictive state.

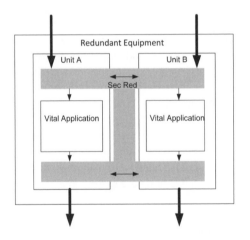

Figure 11.5. *Logical architecture of the redundancy*

11.4.1. *Goals*

The objectives of integrated redundancy are the following:

– maintain the service at 100% in case of a simple failure at any point in the chain of data processing;

– ensure that the redundancy switch between the two pieces of equipment is always secure (ensuring consistency between the states of the two units);

– separate the application processing from the redundancy management processing (application processes are the same regardless of redundancy state);

– become an "off-the-shelf solution" for managing redundancy for all our rail automation applications; and, of course

– be safe and compatible with the implementation of SIL 4 requirements on a DIGISAFE computer, and certified by an independent certification body.

11.4.2. *Overview of operation*

The behavior of the SEC_RED is controlled by the redundancy mode, which can take two values: isolated or redundant. When isolated, a single unit (e.g. the active one) runs the cyclic application process, and is authorized to implement permissive outputs. However, in redundant mode, both units (*active* and *passive*) run the application process, and apply their binary wired outputs. However (mainly to avoid an unnecessary consumption of communication resources), only the *active* unit sends messages to remote devices. In this mode, it is essential to avoid inconsistent behavior or decisions between the two units.

Moreover, whatever the mode, switching between *active* and *passive* must always be safe:

– if the current mode does not authorize switching, it should lead the equipment to a restrictive state;

– the behavior of the newly active unit must be consistent with the "commitments" made by its predecessor.

To ensure safety, the application software must be executed during every cycle (at least on one unit) with "fresh" input and a correct application context. The computed outputs must be applied to the cycle where they were computed.

11.4.3. *Assumptions*

In order for the redundancy protocol not to depend on the application behavior, certain assumptions must be made on the equipment and on the software application, especially regarding the I/O semantics. The first of these assumptions (which is strongly linked to our DIGISAFE platform) claims that the redundancy should not be concerned with increasing the level of safety.

H1: Each unit taken separately is sufficient to guarantee proper safety.

The redundancy management protocol must also be able to alter the I/O while ensuring safety. In particular, forcing a false binary input or output should always enhance safety. Similarly, to lose or reject a message (either input or output) must always be safe: not receiving a message must be considered by any equipment as "restrictive".

H2: All wired binary I/O are "directed": true being the permissive value and false being the restrictive value.

H3: Rejecting or losing an input or output message is always safe .

However, it is necessary to assume that it is always safe to reset the equipment.

H4: The behavior of the safety application must be safe at initialization.

11.4.4. *Hardware architecture*

The integrated redundancy protocol is designed to run on a hardware platform consisting of two DIGISAFE computers (as described in section 11.2). Each of these equipment sets is connected to its own wired inputs and outputs (safe and non-safe), and to a network of inter-equipment communications (used for I/O messages).

Among all the safe inputs, we distinguish two particularities:

– the first is the backreading state of the dynamic controller verifying that the unit is in the code, thus indicating to each unit if it is *out-of-code* or not;

– the second is the *active/passive* state of the unit, provided to both units by a device ensuring exclusivity of the active state (non-overlapping relay).

All other inputs are wired so that any input *i* on unit A corresponds to the acquisition of the same information as the same input on unit B.

Regarding the binary outputs, the outputs of the two units are put in OR, which means choosing, output by output, the one emitted by the more permissive unit.

Both computers are connected by a point-to-point high-speed connection, used for the exchange of administrative data related to the redundancy protocol (inter unit messages).

11.4.5. *Synchronization and time stamping*

Both computers are synchronized in an extremely precise manner ($\sim 10^{-5}$ seconds). This synchronization is not guaranteed. As far as safety is concerned, a synchronization control is performed, which is significantly less accurate, but is largely sufficient for the applications of interest to us (of the magnitude of a few milliseconds). This synchronization control causes the transition to the isolated mode in case of failure.

Furthermore, the clocks pacing the cycles of the two computers are safety clocks ensuring a relative drift below a given threshold.

This ensures a fairly good synchronization between the beginning of the cycles of the two units. To this, we add a counter on each unit called Safe Logic Clock (SLC). At initialization, the passive unit synchronizes its SLC with that of the active unit. This SLC is then used to time stamp and check the freshness of all messages exchanged inter unit.

11.4.6. *Safety inputs*

Two types of safety inputs must be processed by SEC_RED:

– binary wired inputs, which can therefore take the *true* or *false* values, used by onboard controllers, to acquire the rolling stock state (e.g. wayside train controllers) and for selected train operating modes, to be interfaced with a signaling system (e.g. position of the pints, route entry authorization, aspects of signals);

– input messages sent by other equipment, which may contain all kinds of data (e.g. the position of a sent train of the embedded equipment to the fixed equipment, or of the signal state of a computerized signal), but containing in particular a safety header used to time stamp and identify the sender or recipient.

Regarding the binary inputs, SEC_RED should be able to distinguish between redundant inputs (which are usually identical between the two equipment), from non-redundant inputs (typically the *active/passive* input or state of the dynamic controller as seen above).

No specific processing is performed on non-redundant input. In contrast, for redundant input, values acquired by the two units are exchanged via the inter unit link, and if the exchange succeeds are simply put in OR, so that on the one hand it can overcome a failure or low asynchrony in the acquisition of inputs by a unit; and on the other, it can ensure that the two units are fed with the same inputs (nevertheless not guaranteed as far as safety is concerned).

Regarding the safety message, they are simply compared in order to determine the union of all messages received in this cycle by both units, and to provide to the two units the messages they might have missed.

Of course, whether for binary inputs or messages, the process of comparison and "completion" of information can always fail (e.g. in case of a transfer error on the inter unit link). In this case, the unit uses its own input, which may cause discrepancies between the computation performed by the safety applications of the two units, which may in turn lead to an inconsistency in the units' contexts, or differences in the applied outputs.

In this case, the integrated redundancy protocol does not guarantee the absence of such discrepancies, but rather controls their safety with respect to the rest of the system. This is done by processing the emitted outputs, or eventually, if the discrepancy is sustained, by sending a *passivation* causing a return into the isolated mode. These points are detailed below in sections 11.4.8 and 11.4.9.

Therefore, it is not dangerous to introduce a divergence in the contexts, provided that there is a guarantee that the inputs supplied to both units are fresh and accurate.

11.4.7. *Application and context*

As described above, it is not dangerous to introduce an inconsistency between the states (or state variables) of both units. However, it is necessary to keep some good properties in order to determine whether a context is safe or not.

The *context* is defined as the set of the safety variables (those that are encoded) used by the safety, with which their values are associated.

It is said that the context of a unit is *well formed* at the beginning of cycle n, if one of the following conditions is true:

– it is the initial context of the safety application;

– the context was *well formed* at the beginning of cycle $n-1$, and the safety application was executed during this cycle, with fresh input;

– the considered unit is *passive*, the redundant unit is active, the context of the *active* unit is *well formed* at the beginning of cycle n, and is equal to the context of the *passive* unit at this cycle (see *safety image* further down).

To paraphrase this definition, the concept of a *good formation* of the context reflects the state which the safety application is in when it runs cycle after cycle, using the fresh input provided each time.

This leads us to consider three scenarios. At initialization, when a unit detects that it is active, it is allowed to run beginning from a state that corresponds to the variable's initialization state of the safety application. However, it is necessary to ensure that this context has never been altered. The active unit continues to run cycle after cycle, by reading its inputs and applying its output, so as to maintain its *well-formed* context.

During this time, the passive unit is frozen, and waits for the active unit to start running. Once both units are in the right state, the active unit starts a process which involves sending portions of the context (which as a whole is too large to be sent in a cycle over the inter unit link). This process usually lasts a few cycles, then it is followed by a convergence process in which the updates that have occurred since the submission of the context portion are sent. This process also takes several cycles to complete. Note that if the inter unit link is too slow compared to the number of variables changing from one cycle to another, the process may never end. This whole process is quite similar to that described in [BON 98].

This whole copy and transmission phase is not guaranteed in terms of safety. Once the transmission is complete, a "safety photograph" representative of the context is taken of each unit, during the same cycle. Once the photograph is taken, the unit goes into a passive mode where it runs its safety application, without applying the outputs (the process has not determined whether an error has occurred in the copying process).

During the few cycles that follow, the "safety photographs" are compared, as well as the outputs constructed by the two applications. If the process concludes that the "photos" are equal, the two units are allowed to switch to a redundant mode, and from that moment, the outputs are actually applied by the two units. Switching becomes possible, because it is safe. If an error is detected, the passive unit is reset and the process starts over.

It is important to note that these processes are entirely managed by the redundancy management software. The only new process integrated into the safety application is the processing of a Boolean indicating whether the application should be executed or not.

Even if the two contexts are *well formed*, it is possible that differences between the variables of one unit and another will appear. This may be due, for example, to a slight asynchrony in the acquisition of inputs that could not be compensated for by the protocol. Therefore, it is essential to supplement the process with a particular output process in order to prevent dangerous situations.

11.4.8. *Safety output*

Like safety inputs, outputs are either wired binary outputs or messages sent to remote equipment. If a unit is not authorized to issue its outputs (e.g. it is isolated and passive), they are forced to a restrictive state, and sending messages is prevented. In the final cycle, each unit sends the output computed by its safety application to the redundant unit, and a comparison process is made on both sides in order to detect differences. These differences appear mainly due to differences at the context level.

We will consider three types of events affecting outputs:

Event 1

The outputs are erroneous compared to the expected behavior.

Example

The inputs indicate that an event occurred (transgressing a speed limit), which the computer must react to by applying the emergency brake (in reality, putting the output "no emergency brake" to *false* in order to meet the I/O semantics hypothesis). However, due to inconsistencies in the contexts, the output is not ordered to be restrictive.

The feared event is prevented by the following reasons:

– the safety inputs are fresh and safe;

– either the context is *well formed*, or the unit is in a state where its outputs are forced to be restrictive;

– the execution of the safety application and application itself are deemed safe.

These three properties together ensure that if the emergency brake is not applied by one of the units, it is because it does not need to be applied! Therefore, we deduce that the unit applying the brakes applied it for a wrong reason (slight asynchrony, failure). Therefore, it is sure that the brake must not be applied, and that is the behavior that the equipment will follow thanks to the presence of the OR gate.

Event 2

The output of each unit is correct, but different; the inconsistency introduces a dangerous discrepancy.

Example

The train is stopped at the station and the doors are closed and locked. Unit A decides that the train must leave the station, and *Authorizes the Traction*. Unit B decides that the train should allow the exchange of passengers, and so *Unlocks the Doors*.

Each of these behaviors is correct and is safe in itself; however, the transition into the OR gate will unlock doors while the train is in traction!

To avoid this behavior, SEC_RED on each unit compares the outputs of the local unit with the outputs of the redundant unit (received by the inter unit link). If differences exist, the outputs of each unit are applied as is (so that if an output management card is faulty, the outputs are still applied by the equipment). However, if a difference between the outputs is detected, then for each problematic output, all transition from restrictive state to permissive state is prohibited (see Figure 11.5).

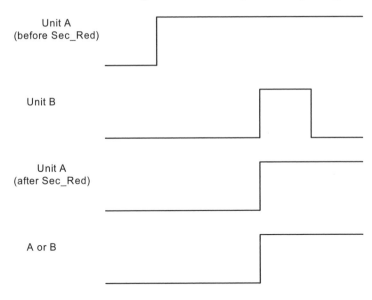

Figure 11.6. *Inconsistent binary outputs*

Thus, if unit A was permissive and remains permissive (e.g. it *authorizes the traction*), when unit B becomes restrictive, the overall output remains permissive. But if neither A nor B authorize the *Unlocking of Doors*, but B now demands unlocking, the inconsistency finally prohibits the application of the output, and this lasts until the two units are in agreement about the unlocking process.

It is relatively easy to show that this prohibition is sufficient to avoid the case of dangerous asynchrony; to exist in cycle n, it would have had to exist in cycle $n-1$, and as it did not exist at the first cycle (all outputs were restrictive), it can therefore not be.

To maintain service, it is however necessary that the situation does not last. Where the inconsistency is transitory, everything goes back to order in the next cycle (the train can then either move or open the doors). Where the problem persists, *passivation* is triggered, leading to isolated mode and the reset of the passive unit. The behavior then becomes nominal, however, this takes a little longer (~ 1 second).

Event 3

Unit B does not respect "a commitment" made by unit A.

Example

The wayside equipment sends a message (not safety guaranteed) to the onboard equipment, asking it to stop if possible before a given limit. In the onboard equipment, we consider that A is active and B is passive. Moreover, for some unknown reason (bug, failure, inconsistency in the context, etc.) B does not process the message. A takes into account the message, stores the requested breakpoint, and sends back to the wayside equipment a message (safety message) before acknowledging the stop before the considered breakpoint. Obviously, in this case B does not memorize the breakpoint and does not respond.

Receiving the acknowledgement message, the wayside itself authorizes a red aspect signal, and moves the processing through the breakpoint downstream. Before the train has begun to break, unit A fails, causing the switching and active (and isolated) passage to unit B. B not having committed itself to respect the breakpoint, the train continues on its way towards the moving point and possibly derails.

In this scenario, SEC_RED ensures safety by processing the safety output message. Of course, messages are only emitted by the active unit, but what is important is that they are issued only when the two units build an identical message. In this example, SEC_RED would have prevented unit A from responding with a confirmation message (or more accurately: A responded, but the message was destroyed), so the wayside equipment, not having received a "permissive" message would have assumed that the train was not respecting the breakpoint and, therefore, would not have moved the point.

Regarding function, it should be noted that the management function does not require additional study of the stop assurance, as the function must be robust enough to withstand the loss of a message!

As for the binary outputs, although the system remains safe in the presence of divergence between unit outputs, it is not desirable to let the problem persist, as this prevents the broadcasting of messages, and thus the smooth operation of the system. Therefore, it is necessary to go back to an isolated mode when the divergence is sustained, so that a single unit makes decisions and that it may start emitting again.

11.4.9. *Passivation*

When the divergence on the outputs lasts only a few cycles (configurable), the *passivation* process is triggered. The objective of this process is to ensure that the two units will be isolated.

Passivation must be effective as soon as possible in order to limit the number of messages that are lost during the divergence phase: if too many messages between the two equipments are lost, the receiver considers that communication is lost, and will go into a safe state.

Conversely, passivation must also allow for a possible switch, if it is necessary; in some cases, switching can take several cycles before being effective. This type of behavior can occur in cases of sudden failure of the active unit, for example.

Passivation must also ensure that whatever the occurring scenario (complete loss of communication between units, in one direction, etc.), the passive unit will be isolated before the active one. However, any lack of communication must not be sanctioned by a passivation, otherwise the system would frequently be in an isolated state, and thus sensitive to all failures.

The passivation process is triggered both by output differences, and by loss of messages on the inter unit link, used by SEC_RED to exchange I/O, but also to convey its own "administrative" commands and states.

11.5. Conclusion

SEC_RED was used for the first time in onboard and wayside equipment for the resignalization of the L underground railway (subway) line in New York into CBTC (Canarsie Line). It has since been deployed in the wayside train control of the CdGVal driverless metro of the Roissy-Charles De Gaulle airport in Paris, and in 2009 on the line 9 metro in Barcelona (driverless CBTC). SEC_RED is also being deployed in Paris under the OURAGAN program, and on line 1 for driverless operation.

Figure 11.7. *An automatic subway train in Barcelona*

This experience has convinced us that the solution developed really was "off the shelf" as it could be introduced on the new systems without too many changes to SEC_RED or to the system in question. In addition, for the New York and Paris projects, the redundant computer version has been certified for compliance with CENELEC standards by an independent certification body (TÜV Rheinland) in 2005 and again in 2008.

There remains a point where it is necessary to take special care: the processing of data from odometers. These equipment sets provide accurate and safe data on the kinematics of the train to the onboard computer (speed, displacement, acceleration). Each type of odometer has specific properties, including timing and interfacing with the computer (direct acquisition, time-stamped messages, etc.). It is also desirable to connect the odometers to the two units, but this raises the following difficulty. The odometers are accurate, but subject to complex error models. The values produced have little chance of being equal. We must therefore put in place a specific process for these data, so as to feed the two units with equal data in order to avoid creating divergent contexts.

City	Project	Wayside eq.	Onboard eq.	Comments
Paris	Paris L14 (Meteor)	7	21	
New York	NYCT Canarsie Line	10	53	
Algiers	Alger L1	2	14	
Barcelona	Barcelona L9	4	50	
Paris	Paris L3	n.a.	45	Only onboard eq.
Paris	Paris L5	17	n.a.	Only wayside eq.
Paris	Paris L1	16	49	
Budapest	Budapest L2	2	26	
Budapest	Budapest L4	N.C.	15	
Sao-Paulo	Sao-Paulo L4	3	14	
Roissy	Roissy CDGVAL (+ LISA)	18	n.a.	No onboard eq. on VAL
Helsinki	Helsinki L1	9	54	

Table 11.1. *Equipment deployed*

A second difficulty is that although the inclusion of the redundancy protocol is seamless at the system and specifications level, it is not completely the case in terms of achievement. The reintegration phase (copy and safety photograph context) is costly in terms of cycle time. A rigorous optimization was therefore necessary so that applications could run in the allocated time. Some optimizations are furthermore related to the management of context exchange: for example, it is better to avoid decrementing a large quantity of timers in each cycle, as it may prevent the convergence of contexts (see section 11.4.7). In this case, we will optimize by processing the timers from a single clock and by memorizing the time at the end of the timer.

However, this additional complexity at the software level can not be compared with the gain of simplicity that is achieved by isolating the redundancy process from functional issues.

11.6. Bibliography

[BAR 08] Baro S., "A high availability vital computer for railway applications: architecture & safety principles", *Proceedings of Embedded Real-Time Software*, (ERTS 08), 2008.

[BON 98] Bondavalli A., *et al.*, "State restoration in a COTS-based N-modular architecture", *Proceedings of Object-Oriented Real-Time Distributed Computing*, (ISORC 98), 1998.

[CEN 03] CENELEC, NF EN 50129, European standard. Railway applications – communication, signalling and processing systems – safety related electronic systems for signalling, 2003.

[ESS 99] Essamé D., Arlat J., Powell D., "PADRE: a protocol for asymmetric duplex redundancy", *DCCA-7 – Dependable Computing for Critical Applications*, 1999.

[FOR 89] Forin P., "Vital coded microprocessor principles and application for various transit systems", *IFAC - Control, Computers, Communications in Transportation*, pp. 137-142, 1989.

[FOR 96] Forin P., "Une nouvelle génération du processeur sécuritaire codé", *Revue Générale des Chemins de Fer*, n° 6, pp. 38-41, June 1996.

[GEO 90] Georges J.P., "Principes et fonctionnement du Système d'Aide à la Conduite, à l'Exploitation et à la Maintenance (SACEM). Application à la ligne A du RER", *Revue Générale des Chemins de Fer*, n° 6, June 1990.

[GUI 90] Guihot G., Hennebert C., "SACEM software validation", *ICSE*, March 26-30, 1990, pp. 186-191.

[HEN 94] Hennebert C., "Transports ferroviaires: Le SACEM et ses dérivés", *ARAGO 15, Informatique tolérante aux fautes*, Masson, Paris, 1994, pp. 141-149,

[IEE 04] IEEE, 1474.1, IEEE Standard for Communications-Based Train Control (CBTC) Performance and Functional Requirements, 2004.

[LEC 96] Lecompte P., Beaurent P.J., "Le système d'automatisation de l'exploitation des trains (SAET) de METEOR", *Revue Générale des Chemins de Fer*, n° 6, pp. 31-34, June 1996.

[MAR 90] Martin J., Wartski S., Galivel C., "Le processeur codé: un nouveau concept appliqué à la sécurité des systèmes de transports", *Revue Générale des Chemins de Fer*, n° 6, pp. 29-35, June 1990.

[MAT 98] MATRA, RATP, "Naissance d'un Métro. Sur la nouvelle ligne 14, les rames METEOR entrent en scène. PARIS découvre son premier métro automatique", *La Vie du Rail & des Transports*, n° 1076, hors-série, October 1998.

[MCD 92] McDermid J. A., Shi Q., "Safe composition of systems", *Proceedings of the Eighth Annual Computer Safety Applications Conference*, 1992

Chapter 12

Safety System for the Protection of Personnel in the CERN Large Hadron Collider

This chapter presents the operating principles of the personnel protection system *vis-à-vis* the radiological dangers involved in operating the LHC, the Large Hadron Collider.

12.1. Introduction

12.1.1. *Introduction to CERN*

CERN, the European Organization for Nuclear Research, is one of the largest and most prestigious scientific laboratories in the world. It is dedicated to the discovery of the constitution and laws of the universe. It uses the most complex scientific instruments to probe the ultimate constituents of matter: the fundamental particles. By studying what happens when these particles collide, physicists learn about the laws of nature.

Founded in 1954, CERN sits astride the Franco-Swiss border near Geneva. It was one of the first European joint venture organizations and now has 20 member states: Germany, Austria, Belgium, Bulgaria, Denmark, Spain, Finland, France, Greece, Hungary, Italy, Norway, the Netherlands, Poland, Portugal, the Czech and Slovak Republics, the UK, Sweden and Switzerland.

Chapter written by Pierre NININ, Silvia GRAU, Tomasz LADZINSKI and Francesco VALENTINI.

The instruments used at CERN are particle accelerators and detectors. The particle beams are accelerated to high energies to make them collide either with each other or with fixed targets. Detectors observe and record the results of these collisions.

Figure 12.1. *The LHC tunnel*

Figure 12.2. *One of the LHC particle detectors*

12.1.2. *Legislative and regulatory context*

On July 11, 2000, CERN and the government of the French Republic signed a convention on the safety of particle accelerator complex SPS and LHC, likening them to a basic nuclear installation. Safety systems are thus subject to the approval of the Nuclear Safety Authority (ASN: *Autorité de Sûreté Nucléaire*) after instruction of descriptive dossiers of each system by the Radioprotection and Nuclear Safety Institute (IRSN: *Institut de Radioprotection et de Sûreté Nucléaire*). Systems affected by this instruction are the safety systems related to access, protection against radiation, and those related to the environment [FAU 01].

Designing a safety system to protect personnel in a particle accelerator complex must take into account the industrial and specific nuclear risks. To this end, two standards are used [NIN 09]: IEC 61508 [IEC 00], which specifically considers the safety life cycle and risk quantification aspects; and IEC 61513 [IEC 01] on instrumentation and control of nuclear power plants.

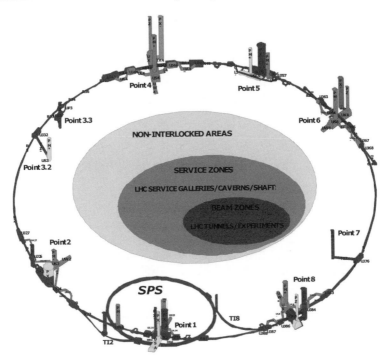

Figure 12.3. *Accessible zones of the LHC*

12.1.3. *Goal of the system*

The LHC is a large circular particle collider of 27 kilometers in circumference, located 100 meters underground, where the particles will circulate at an energy of 7 TeV [EVA 09]. In order to protect the personnel from risks of exposure to ionizing radiation in the environment of the LHC and its experiments, a specific safety system has been implemented [ROY 05].

Figure 12.3 shows the different underground works of the LHC and the different access zones.

The strategy implemented to prevent any dangerous situation for personnel has led to the provision of a safety system which, according to the mode of operation, locks physical barriers or brings the accelerator to a safe stop in order to secure the personnel.

The principle of personnel protection of the LHC is based on the implementation of two complementary systems. The systems are the LHC Access Control System (LACS) and the LHC Access Safety System (LASS).

The purpose of the LACS is to [NIN 04]:

− identify, authenticate, and control personnel access permissions;

− provide a physical barrier outside and inside the LHC perimeter by means of access equipment of the following types: personnel and equipment security doors, fences, doors, shielding walls, etc.

The purpose of LASS is to position the LHC in a safe state for personnel in all operating modes, i.e. to control the envelope and the 80 sectors of the LHC so that there are no people inside when the accelerator is in beam operation mode, and when it is stopped, to ensure that no beam can be injected or is circulating in the accelerator. This defines the interlock mechanism applied to secure the LHC.

The LASS acts on Items Important to Safety (IIS), which are either IIS Access or equipment suitable for the LHC accelerator called IIS Beams and IIS Machine, depending on the mode of operation of the LHC: Access mode or Beam mode.

12.2. LACS

The objective of LACS is to:

− provide a physical barrier around the LHC and divide it into different access sectors through doors, gates, security doors, etc. called IIS Access;

− identify the personnel, control their access permissions granted on the basis of need and followed by safety training;

− oversee and manage the IIS Access;

− ensure audio and video connections between different access points and the CERN control center (CCC).

The access control of controlled radiological areas has been strengthened by the installation of "personnel" security doors (of air-lock chamber type) replacing turnstiles used in previous installations.

Using them simultaneously ensures the uniqueness of passage and biometric identification. Indeed, each security door comprises an iris recognition system verifying the correspondence between the iris of a person located inside the security door and the user's badge.

The "equipment" security doors allow introduction and removal of the equipment in the LHC. The passage of personnel through these security doors is strictly forbidden. A human detection system using a camera verifies compliance with this safety condition.

The badge, consisting of a chip and an RF antenna, is built into the personal dosimeter, ensuring that each person entering the accelerator is in possession of their personal dosimeter.

The computer architecture of the LACS is based on an industrial access control system, including redundant central servers, front-ends providing communication with local controllers of the IIS Access. All system configuration data, permissions, and access transactions are recorded in a centralized database.

The LACS is also responsible for disseminating the operating modes "beam" or "access" of the accelerator to different access points. There are four different access modes:

– The "general" mode used for long periods of shutdown of the facilities, where each authorized person may enter the LHC without supervision by the control room.

– The "patrol" mode aims to ensure that the accelerator is empty of all personnel before restart. Only the dedicated team ensuring that mission is authorized to enter the LHC.

– The "restricted" mode used during short stops, under supervision of the control room. This mode of operation is critical because no LHC patrol will be made before restart. The system delivers to each person entering the LHC a token. The accelerator will not start until all tokens are returned.

– The "closed" mode locks IIS Access on which the mode is applied.

Figure 12.4 illustrates an LHC access point, composed of two personnel security doors and one equipment security door.

Figure 12.4. *An LHC access point*

12.3. LASS

LASS is an interlock system ensuring that no beam can circulate or be injected into the LHC during "access" operations and that any intrusion detected during the "beam" operation will result in placing the accelerator in a safe position and in a controlled manner.

12.3.1. *IIS Beams*

IIS Beams were selected among vital LHC components, for their ability to prevent the injection and circulation of beams, and this, in parallel to the beam extraction system. The elements preventing injection are mobile absorber blocks, horizontal dipole magnet chains, and injection "septa" magnets. They are located in tunnels ensuring the beam transfer between the SPS (Super Proton Synchrotron) accelerator and the LHC. In each injection tunnel, three IIS Beams define an interlock chain, named "LHC2" chain and "LHC8" chain, respectively.

Elements stopping the circulation of beams are separator magnets located in the region of the LHC collimators and beam absorber blocks. These three IIS Beams form the interlock "LHC1" chain. The interlock points for the magnets are 18 kV high-voltage cells and the power converters powering them. This choice of IIS Beams provides triple functional redundancy for each interlock chain, a geographical separation, and technological diversity.

Unlike the beam extraction system requiring permanently powered "active" magnets, the magnets used as IIS are not pulsed and do not require specific discharge and therefore, in all cases, guarantee their mission to stop the beams, even in the absence of voltage. By design, they are considered "failsafe".

Figure 12.5 shows the IIS Beams and interlock points used to stop the injection and circulation of the beams in the LHC. In case of an incident, the beams are stopped by a system called "Beam Dump". However, because of its pulsed operation, this is not an ISE.

On each IIS Beam, different interlock points are used, for example, the separator magnet D3 of the LHC3 point will see a veto (signal for beam stop) applied to its power converter and its 18 kV electric power cell.

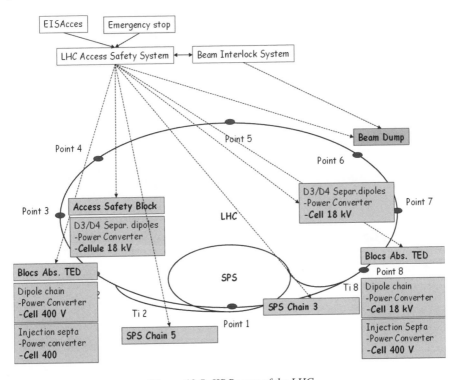

Figure 12.5. *IIS Beams of the LHC*

12.3.2. *LASS architecture*

LASS is a distributed control system whose architecture is based on safety programmable logic controllers (PLC) of the Siemens 417FH series [SIE 09].

At each point of the LHC, a redundant controller monitors the status of all IIS and calculates the site results, which will then be transmitted to a controller ensuring overall control of all sites (see Figure 12.6). The latter monitors the information from each site and triggers the safety actions, resulting in the application or removal of the IIS veto. A unidirectional gateway controller ensures the dissemination of data and alarms of the LASS to other monitoring systems.

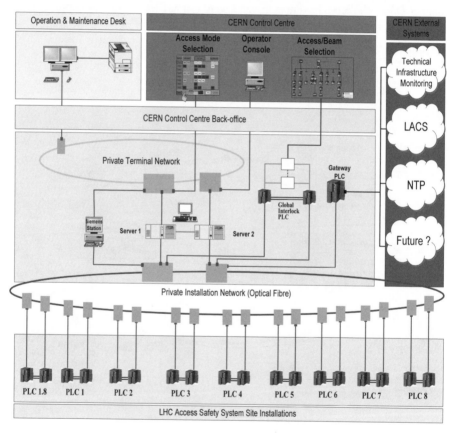

Figure 12.6. *Architecture of safety controllers*

A veto is implemented by the opening of a contact in series in the electric power supply chain of an IIS, following the fail-safe principle. A veto on an IIS Beam is a command to stop the beams. A veto on an IIS Access will lock it, preventing its use. Each local controller oversees about 50 IIS Accesses (see Figure 12.7), meaning primarily the reading of the position contacts or the emergency passage equipping each IIS Access. These digital sensors are redundant and ambivalent: a contact is normally open and the other normally closed. Contacts and actuators are connected via copper cables using different cable paths. The local controller also controls the IIS Beams located on the same site.

The controllers communicate with each other through a "self-healing" optical fiber network running through the LHC tunnel. The attenuation of an "indicative" fiber is monitored in areas of high radiation. In case of double network failure and therefore loss of communication, each controller ensures the safe positioning of all the IIS it is controlling, this fallback position prohibits the operation of access and beams. From a practical point of view, placing the safety controller's intrinsic output to zero applies vetoes on all the IIS.

Figure 12.7. *A local controller rack*

12.3.3. *Performance of safety functions*

The safety functions executed on the controllers have been exclusively implemented using the Siemens "S7 Distributed Safety Program" tools. The main advantage of this approach is the availability to the programmer of a library of functional objects tested and certified to safety integrity level (SIL) 3 (according to IEC 61508). The safety program can only be implemented by the combination of these certified functional blocks.

Two types of objects have been used to produce the LASS software: the safety matrix and the certified functional blocks.

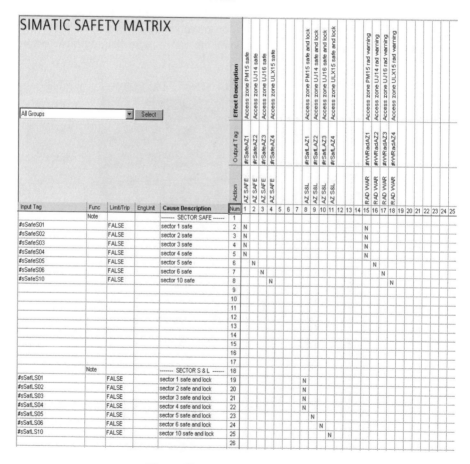

Figure 12.8. *Cause and effect matrix*

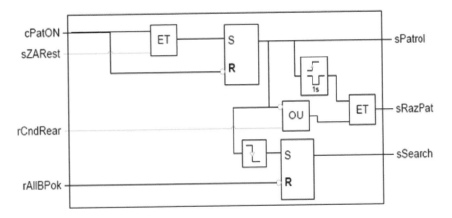

Figure 12.9. *Functional safety block*

The safety matrices are "cause and effect" matrices helping to reduce configuration time, testing and maintenance by integrating the development stages of a cause and effect matrix. The cause and effect matrix is used to define "how" and "when" actions are executed by the system. Its use requires organizing the process events into categories of causes and effects, and then connecting them. These links are called intersections, they define what effect will result from the activation of a cause. The number of tests to be performed is limited to the functional part and not to the code of the matrix as it is already certified.

The SIL 3 certified functional blocks from the S7 library are instantiated and interconnected to create new blocks, which will be used in the program. However, the interconnection logic should be exhaustively tested in order to detect interconnection or design errors that would lead to an unsafe behavior of the system. Each functional block has been tested and certified SIL 3 by the German body TÜV. This is made possible by the fact that each functional block performs simple functions, as required by an interlock system. Conversely, complex mathematical operations are not permitted or possible in this type of environment.

12.3.4. *Wired loop*

In addition to the LASS safety controller architecture, and to ensure that the response time is always controlled by the sensor-actuator chain in the event of multiple failures, a wired logic loop was introduced. A reaction time in case of network or controller failure, or a time exceeding the cycle time, can be too long, resulting in the exposure of a person to the danger of radiation in case of intrusion in beam mode.

This conservative approach and the addition of a wired loop improve the fault tolerance of the overall system.

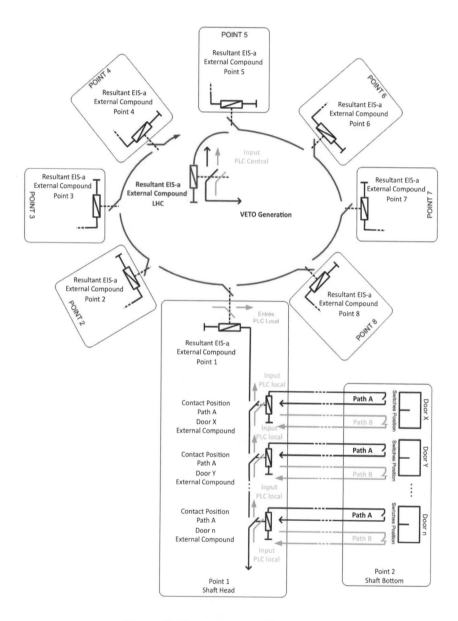

Figure 12.10. *Architecture of the wired loop*

12.4. Functional safety methodology

The technical requirements of the IEC 61513 standard and the various phases of IEC 61508 were used as a framework for the project. Regarding specific aspects of functional safety, the various phases listed in the table below have been followed.

1	Functional safety plan
2	Preliminary risk analysis
3	Specification of safety functions
4	Provisional safety study and collection of safety data
5	Definitive safety study
7	Verification and validation plan
8	Operation and maintenance plan

Table 12.1. *Stages of functional safety approach*

To these stages are added the classic stages of each IT project, namely: analysis of user requirements, definition of requirements, functional analysis, definition of external interfaces, definition and design of the architecture, development, on-site installation, functional testing, etc. A classical V cycle was followed.

12.4.1. *Functional safety plan*

The functional safety plan is intended to describe the application of the IEC 61508 standard in the context of the project; in particular, the documentation, activities, organization, and tools put in place to deal with functional safety aspects during the life cycle of system development.

12.4.2. *Preliminary risk analysis (PRA)*

Preliminary risk analysis defines the Equipment Under Control (EUC), its limits, its environment, all modes of operation, the dangers and risks associated with the equipment and its control system. An inventory of risk is established and the risks that are covered by the system are confirmed. In our case, it was initially decided that only the radiation risks were covered; other risks, such as electrical hazards, are covered by other protection barriers.

The risks involved are those related to human exposure to prompt radiation due to the circulation or injection of beams, radiation generated by radiofrequency cavities used for accelerating beams, induced or remnant radiation in equipment or in the air.

The SIL required to reduce each identified risk is equally defined at this stage.

For example, for the LHC, the risk linked to prompt radiation exposure resulting from the circulation of beams is assessed at SIL 3 in the tunnel where the beams circulate and SIL 2 in adjacent areas called service zones.

12.4.3. *Specification of safety functions*

The next step involves the specification of safety functions that are implemented to protect the personnel from risks identified in the PRA.

In order to protect the personnel from prompt radiation issued from the circulation of beams in the LHC, two safety functions are put into place:

1. maintain a safe position and lock the entrances and exits of interlocked zones (FS1);

2. detect the non-safe position of an IIS Access in an interlocked zone, stop the circulating beams in the LHC, and prevent a new beam injection through the injection tunnels (FS2).

The two functions must be guaranteed while the LHC is in the Beam operation mode or any transitory mode involving the Beam mode.

The first function locks all IIS access to avoid any intrusion (personnel and equipment security doors, LHC sector door). To close and lock these IIS, the LASS orders relay to cut off the power supply or the control of actuators opening the IIS.

The second function provides continuous monitoring of all IIS Access (personnel and equipment security doors, sector door, mobile shielding wall, end of zone door, etc.). On detection of a non-safe position of even just one of these IIS Accesses, the function stops the circulating beams, and prevents all further beam injection.

The LASS monitors all IIS Access and we consider that the function is no longer fulfilled when an IIS Access is no longer monitored. However, in many cases, given the topology of the LHC, for there to be at risk of irradiation in case of an intrusion (access to dangerous areas), it is necessary to cross several IIS Accesses. Considering that the function is not fulfilled when at least one IIS Access is not monitored is therefore very prudent in light of the actual danger.

Stopping the circulating beams is done by sending a veto command over three IIS beams in the LHC1 chain. The function fails if the three IIS beams are not placed in a safe position. Indeed, one of these IIS beams is sufficient to stop the circulating beams. A one out of three redundancy is ensured at the IIS beam level.

Preventing beam injection is done by sending a veto command over three IIS beams of LHC 2 interlock chain and over the three IIS beam of LHC 8 interlock chain. The function fails if the three IIS beams are not placed in a safe position. Again, a one out of three redundancy is provided at the IIS beam level.

These safety functions are SIL 3, although according to the manufacturer of the safety controller, a SIL 3 can be achieved by this technology alone; it was decided that two independent technological barriers should be implemented: a path based on safety controllers and another path based on an independent wired loop. This choice helps to guarantee the response time of the safety functions. Without the wired loop, the accumulation of internal timeout of the controllers or the related inter-controller communication may cause a delay greater than the acceptable limit for triggering certain safety functions.

12.4.4. *Provisional safety study*

Following the definition of safety functions, an initial system architecture is proposed. The provisional study aims to verify that this architecture achieves the levels of SIL defined in the PRA.

The study [LUS 05] begins with an analysis of the sensor-actuator chain relative to each safety function, based on the system architecture. The objective is to identify each component involved in the execution of a safety function.

The detection of a non-safe position of an IIS Access is done via two ambivalent "open door" contacts installed on each IIS Access.

A "Failure Mode and Effects Analysis" (FMEA) is performed in order to identify the failure modes of each component and the safe and non-safe failures are identified. A failure rate is associated with each mode of failure. In addition, the fault tree technique is applied to the entire architecture in order to analyze common modes and assess the SIL achieved.

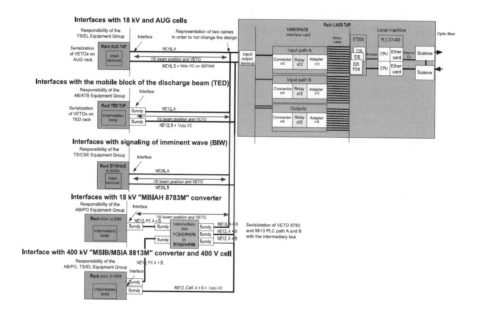

Figure 12.11. *Example of PLC-actuators chain*

12.4.4.1. *Summary of the provisional safety study for "intrusion" functions*

FS1: Maintain in safe position and lock the entries and exits of the interlocked zones.

Only undetected failures of local PLCs or the global PLC and of I/O cards involved in this function can lead directly to the loss of the function, therefore to a non-safe state for the personnel working in the LHC. Only certified SIL 3 equipment can lead to the loss of a safety function. Generally, such equipment is designed with internal redundancy. Moreover, these potential failures will be highlighted during periodic testing. In these circumstances, compliance with the single failure criterion is met.

Other components can be a source of failure leading to a degraded state of the LASS, but in this case, it is necessary to have at least a second failure for the LASS to no longer be able to perform that function. These components are systematically designed with redundancy. Physically, redundancy is achieved by two commands coming from two separate paths (different cables, different cable paths, different connecting terminals, different actuators). This principle helps to guard against common cause failures. Moreover, the safety setting is achieved by the lack of voltage, the "no voltage" common cause failure does not exist in this case.

FS2: Detect the non-safe position of an IIS Access in an interlocked zone, stop the circulating beams in the LHC and prevent all new beam injection through the injection tunnels.

This function is divided into three parts.

12.4.4.1.1. Detection of unsafe IIS Access

As for the placing of IIS Access in a safe position, the pieces of equipment that alone lead to the loss of the function are the PLC and I/O cards. The acquisition of information "IIS Access open" is done systematically by two door position contacts, the information is then sent through two cables, which are physically separated. The signals are ambivalent, to guard against common cause failures (CCF).

12.4.4.1.2. Placing IIS Circulating Beams in safe position

Due to the 1 in 3 redundancy of the IIS, it appears that only an undetected failure of the global PLC can lead to a dangerous state of the LHC. Other failures of different components or equipment involved in this function alone cannot lead to a non-safe state of the LHC.

12.4.4.1.3. Placing IIS Injected Beams in a safe position

These IIS also have a 1 in 3 redundancy. However, the local PLC, the I/O cards dedicated to the IIS and the global PLC commands appear at order 1.

In conclusion, the two functions FS1 and FS2 are complementary and contribute to the reduction of the same risk: radiation exposure during an intrusion.

The FS2 function can be regarded as a fallback position of the FS1 function. In other words, there is danger if:

– access to the LHC is not locked;

– an intrusion is not detected;

– the beams are not stopped after detection of the intrusion.

In this case, it appears that only the undetected PLC failures lead to a dangerous state of the LHC. If the architecture complies with the separation of the following I/O modules:

– no common module for the control and detection of IIS Access;

– no common module for the control and detection of IIS beams;

– no common module for the IIS Access and IIS beams,

then the I/O modules do not intervene at order 1.

12.4.4.2. *Wired loop*

The function performed by the wired loop is to detect the non-safe position of an IIS Access of the external envelope, and after detection, to place the IIS injected and circulating beams in a safe position.

To meet the requirements of the IEC 61513 standard on nuclear safety, the wired loop provides a technologically diverse redundancy for the PLC path.

Given this specification, and as shown in the FMEA, only the position sensors of the IIS Access are common to the wired loop and the PLC loop. However, the PLC loop uses a second position contact in its safetyy logic equation. Furthermore, the 48 V power supplies are separated.

The FMEA shows many simple failures leading to loss of the wired loop. This is acceptable and expected because it was not intended to provide redundancy at this path level, as it is itself a redundancy of the PLC path.

In conclusion, this loop ensures that its mission is to be the redundancy for the PLC and the I/O modules, equipment appearing at order 1 in all LASS safety functions. Thus, doubts about the compliance of the single failure criterion at the PLC and I/O module level have no reason to be on the main "intrusion" function.

12.4.4.3. *Collection of safety data*

The collection of safety data contains all the qualitative and quantitative hypotheses retained in the evaluation of the safety function levels, including:

– component failure rates;

– failure modes;

– periodicity of tests;

– SILs;

– repair time.

12.4.5. *Definitive safety study*

This study will be conducted in two phases. In the first phase, an identical approach to the provisional safety study is performed on the system as built, quantitatively demonstrating that the safety functions are achieved and the safety objectives are met.

In a second phase, the feedback is taken into account; in our case, this may result in the replacement of some electromechanical components with those that are better adapted to the environment of the accelerator. The failure rates are measured and the parameters of the new elements are updated in the collection of safety data.

12.4.6. *Verification and validation plan*

The verification and validation plan describes the documentation, activities, organization and tools put in place to ensure the proper development of the system and its proper operation. The various stages of system tests are described in detail in section 12.5.

12.4.7. *Operation and maintenance plan*

The performances of a safety system are maintained throughout its operation only if the maintenance range and periodic inspections required during the safety study are met, particularly considering the detection of dormant failures: those that appear only when the system is solicited. The frequency of systematic verification comes from the collection of safety data and is undertaken about once or twice a year for each sensor and each actuator.

Using a Computer Maintenance Management System (CMMS) ensures the periodicity of preventive maintenance and the tracking of corrective maintenance. In addition to the maintenance range and periodic inspection, the operation and maintenance plan also includes:

– procedures to document system operation and maintenance feedback and to update the collection of safety data;

– procedures for the analysis of dangerous events, the dissemination and implementation of recommendations intended to minimize the probability of recurrence;

– procedures for updating the preliminary risk analysis based on the evolution of the installation;

– procedures for making modifications to the safety system, and even to the document approval circuit.

12.5. Test strategy

12.5.1. *Detailed description of the validation process*

Validation of a safety system represents a considerable effort in terms of time, human and material resources; it must also ensure that test coverage is adequate *vis-à-vis* the level of SIL defined for the system [VAL 08]. In principle, only exhaustive testing can ensure the validation of the correct functioning of the system. However, in practice, it is often impossible to test the full theoretical coverage. This must be compensated by the quality of the development methodology used and the test strategy implemented.

12.5.2. *Architecture of the test and the simulation platform*

The core of the system validation process is done on a simulation platform faithfully reproducing the system architecture. It recreates the safety controller environment and the human-machine interfaces ensuring operation and supervision of the system. The software for each LHC site has been fully tested on this platform by activating inputs and verifying outputs at the electrical level. This form of verification and validation optimizes the final test campaigns conducted in the 27 kilometer tunnel of the LHC ring, the service zones, and the experimental adjacent zones.

The heart of the test platform consists of an emulation station, to emulate the condition of every IIS. A dedicated software program can activate all the entries and read all outputs and system states. To do this, a PC hosting the emulation software communicates via Ethernet with a programmable controller whose aim is to ensure the physical interface at the input/output level with the safety controllers.

The test platform consists of two site redundant safety controllers, a redundant global controller and a gateway controller (Figure 12.12). It can reproduce all the safety requirements and thoroughly test software for both sites of the LHC at the same time.

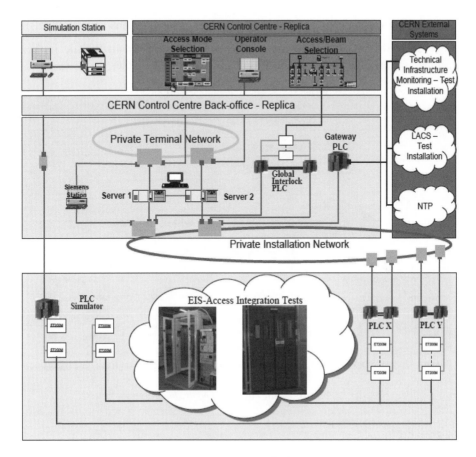

Figure 12.12. *Test platform*

12.5.3. *Organization of tests*

The complexity of the system, due to the large number of devices controlling the various operating modes and their geographical distribution around the 27 kilometer ring required the establishment of a validation strategy capable of detecting all the hardware and software errors in a short period of time.

As shown in Figure 12.13, once the software is developed, tested and integrated, the validation strategy is articulated on three axes:

– simulation test platforms allowing us to gain confidence in the controller software and to eliminate all design errors;

– physical verification of all the equipment, cables, connections, inputs-outputs;

– verification of the correct functioning of the system for all IIS and in their operating modes, in a first time site-by-site, and then on all 10 sites.

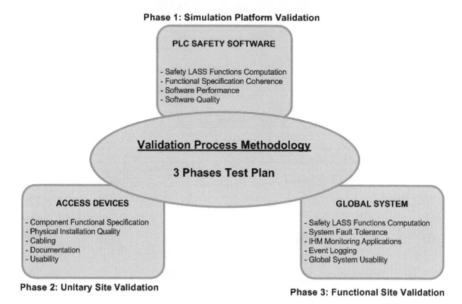

Figure 12.13. *Validation methodology*

12.5.4. *Test platforms*

Initially, the main objective is an exhaustive verification of all functional blocks, safety matrices and their interconnection.

The program consists of "safe", "certified", and "validated" software objects, and the test strategy adopted is based on the principle of "white box testing" [GAR 98]. This method produces test scenarios directly from the program structure, significantly reducing the space of possible tests. The test criterion [ZHU 97] for a function block consists of ensuring that every possible path from input to output has been activated (transition from state 0 to state 1).

All the tests necessary to solicit the function block in Figure 12.9 are given in the table below:

Inputs	Test 1	Test 2	Test 3	Test 4	Test 5	Test 6	Test 7
cPatOn	1	1	1	0	0	1	0
sZARest	0	1	1	1	1	1	1
rCndRear	0	0	1	1	1	1	1
rAllBPok	0	0	0	0	1	1	1

Table 12.2. *Tests table*

Conversely, if we cannot rely on the Siemens development methodology for safety controllers, the principle of "black box testing" should be applied. For each non-elementary functional block, this would result in a test of all possible combinations of input, in order to ensure the achievement of desired output states in all cases! In the simple case of the functional block mentioned above, the number of tests required would have been $2^4 = 16$.

Secondly, the software is tested in its entirety, in order to ensure that all program blocks are properly connected and there is no logical error in their interactions. The dynamic behavior of the IIS is also emulated.

This testing strategy is called "black box functional testing" and does not take into account the structure of the program, but it derives significant tests directly from the functional specifications. The tests are organized by category of event. Each safety function has been completely validated by the generation of at least one event on each IIS. The typical non-compliances discovered during this phase are listed in Table 12.3.

Type	Description	Occurrence
Compliance	The functionalities partially conform to specifications.	Weak
Usage	The performance of certain functions makes the system difficult to operate.	Weak
Inconsistency	Problems due to incomplete functional specifications.	Weak
Software defects	Bad association of electrical signals with their logic variable.	Weak

Table 12.3. *Synthesis of non-compliance*

12.5.5. *Unit validation on site*

The objective of unit validation conducted on the overall LHC sites is a physical verification of all the installed equipment.

In particular, this means ensuring that:

– all IIS work properly;

– all the control signals coming from the IIS are properly wired and acquired by the various safety controllers;

– the installation of each component follows the requirements of the safety study.

This validation phase is complex because of the large number of IIS installed, the large distances separating them, and the analysis of documentation certifying that everything has been done according to the rules. A dedicated system for managing non-compliances is used to ensure the necessary traceability.

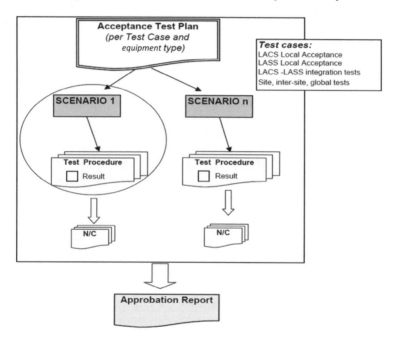

Figure 12.14. *Organization of the validation documentation*

A validation plan, consisting of procedures grouped into scenarios, has been prepared for each type of equipment. In this context, the test procedures are derived directly from the technical and functional specifications of the different components. These tests are supplemented by visual inspections, aiming to validate the qualitative aspect of equipment and their installation. The typical errors highlighted during these phases are listed in Table 12.4.

Type	Description	Occurrence
Wiring/electricity	Missing or defective wiring, defective elementary component (fuse, relay, etc.)	Average
Completion	Incomplete or not very qualitative installation	High
Functionality	Usage difficulty of certain equipment caused by poor mechanical assembly	Average
Ergonomics	Missing user signaling equipment	Average
Documentation	Missing or incomplete electrical schematics	Weak

Table 12.4. *Synthesis of site non-compliance*

12.5.6. *Functional validation on site*

The functional validation tests on site are part of the last phase of the validation process and aim at verifying the correct behavior of the system, especially considering the integration aspects of all the hardware and software components.

It is based on the two previous phases of validation verifying software safety and proper installation of all equipment.

In particular, it is necessary to validate that:

1) all LASS safety functions, simulated successfully on the test platform, correctly function on site and that information is exchanged correctly between all controllers;

2) the HMI remote monitoring systems are operating and functioning properly;

3) the system is robust and able to react independently to failures in the communication network or its power supply;

4) tools for archiving events conform and are usable;

5) the operating tools conform to the needs of operators.

The test strategy used in this phase is again one of "black box testing". All safety functions are considered and verified in their scope of application, either on a single point of the LHC, or throughout the LHC.

For site tests, each safety function is tested on each IIS by the generation of a physical event triggering the function, e.g. intrusion by activation of the emergency passage, triggering an emergency stop, etc. Comprehensive tests are conducted for each operating mode.

For the global tests, the test criterion will be the execution of each safety function on a sample of each type of IIS. The complete sensor-actuator chain is again verified. Unlike previous tests, characterized by a large number of small tests, the global test requires a large number of personnel.

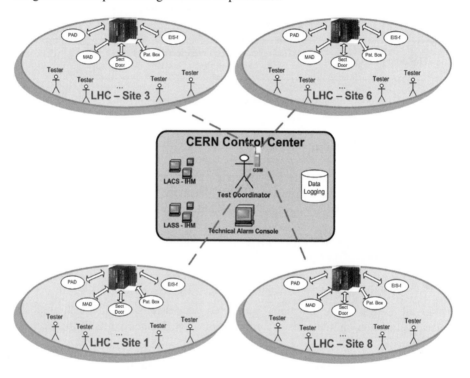

Figure 12.15. *Organization of tests*

12.6. Feedback

The system of personnel protection of the LHC has been in operation since 2007 [PET 08]. Table 12.5 shows the number of entries in the interlocked areas of the LHC during the third quarter of 2009 [LAD 09]. In total, more than 166,000 transactions were recorded over a period of 3 months. Of these, 13,153 entries have been supervised by the operators of the control room. This period of intense activity corresponds to the preparation of restarting the accelerator in 2009.

	General access	Restricted access	No rights	Total
Service area	65,777	4,657	902	71,336
Tunnel area	19,390	5,643	29	25,062
Experiment area	66,642	2,853	858	70,353
Total	151,809	13,153	1,789	**166,751**

Table 12.5. *Number of accesses in interlocked zones of the LHC during the third quarter of 2009*

Figure 12.16. *CERN control center*

Such a high number of entries requires an appropriate operation and maintenance plan. Moreover, it is not possible to perform maintenance operations during the operation of the accelerator, and during the technical stop phase, maintenance operations are very difficult to undertake because they impede the smooth functioning of the system, which is much in demand during these periods. Good coordination of activities and flexibility of the teams becomes very important.

12.7. Conclusions

Since it was commissioned, the system has been strongly solicited by the large number of users of the LHC, its experiments, and the LHC commissioning tests.

Usage statistics show that the access control system is used much more than initially planned.

During the first 2 years of operation, the safety system was not solicited by an intrusion or by an untimely safe positioning of the IIS beams, except for testing or maintenance. The initial design has proven itself, particularly in terms of stability and availability. Physical barriers and safety functions have functioned properly in securing the various modes of operation of the accelerator.

Changes targeting automation of certain access control tasks are being considered to enable operators to more efficiently manage the flow of personnel and new safety functions are provided to safe the testing phases of cryogenic magnets.

Development, verification and validation processes, and especially the implementation of a large-scale test platform, enabled the effective deployment and management of required modifications under tight deadlines, while keeping the rigor necessary for this type of system.

The working methods and standards used have established effective communication with the Nuclear Safety Authority. This will be extended for similar projects of the organization.

12.8. Bibliography

[EVA 09] EVANS L. (ed.), *The Large Hadron Collider: A Marvel of Technology*, EPFL Press, Lausanne 2009.

[FAU 01] FAUGIER A., "Operations at CERN under INB regulations", *Proceedings Workshop on Accelerator Operation*, Villars-sur-Ollon, Switzerland, Jan 28-Feb 2, 2001.

[GAR 98] GARDINER S., *Testing Safety-Related Software*, Springer, UK, 1998.

[IEC 00] IEC 61508, Functional safety of electrical/electronic/programmable electronic safety-related systems, 1998, 2000.

[IEC 01] IEC 61513, Nuclear power plants – instrumentation and control for systems important to safety – general requirements for systems, 2001-03.

[LAD 09] LADZINSKI T., *et al.*, "The LHC access system", *Proceedings 12th International Conference on Accelerator and Large Experimental Physics Control Systems, ICALEPCS '09*, Kobe, Japan, October 12-16, 2009.

[LUS 05] LUSSON B., *Dossier de Sûreté Provisoire LASS*, Rapport de Schneider Electric, October 2005.

[NIN 04] NININ P., SCIBILE L., "The LHC access control system", *9th European Particle Accelerator Conference, EPAC '04*, Lucerne, Switzerland, July 5-9, 2004.

[NIN 09] NININ P., "IEC 61508 experience for the development of the LHC functional safety systems and future perspective", *Proceedings 12th International Conference on Accelerator and Large Experimental Physics Control Systems, ICALEPCS '09*, Kobe, Japan, October 12-16, 2009.

[PET 08] PETTERSSON T., *et al.*, "LHC access system: from design to operation", *Proceedings 11th European Particle Accelerator Conference, EPAC '08*, Genoa, Italy, June 23-27, 2008.

[ROY 05] ROY G., "Access system and its impact on LHC operation", *Proceedings 2nd LHC Project Workshop*, CERN, Geneva, Switzerland, January 17-21, 2005.

[SIE 09] SIEMENS AG, *Simatic Controller - The Innovative Solution for All Automation Tasks*, Siemens Brochure, April 2009.

[VAL 08] VALENTINI F., *et al.*, "Safety testing for LHC access system", *Proceedings 11th European Particle Accelerator Conference, EPAC '08*, Genoa, Italy, June 23-27, 2008.

[ZHU 97] ZHU H., HALL P., MAY J., *Software Unit Test Coverage and Adequacy*, ACM Computing Surveys, UK, vol. 29, 1997.

Glossary

A/C	Aircraft	Chapter 6
ABS	*Antiblockiersystem*	Chapter 9
ADIRU	Air Data and Inertial Reference Units	Chapter 6
AE	Adverse Event	Chapter 3
AEFD	Deterministic Finite State Automaton *Automate à Etats Finis Déterministe*	Chapter 4
ALU (see UAL)	Arithmetic Logic Unit	Chapters 1, 9
API	Programmable Logic Controller *Automate Programmable Industriel*	Chapter 10
ASIL (see SIL)	Automotive Safety Integrity Level	Chapter 9
ASN	Nuclear Safety Authority *Autorité de Sûreté Nucléaire*	Chapter 12
ASTS	ANSALDO STS	Chapter 3
ATC	Automatic Train Control	Chapter 2
ATP	Automatic Train Protection	Chapter 3
AUTOSAR	Automotive Open System Architecture	Chapter 9
BGY	Gyrometric Block *Bloc Gyrométrique*	Chapter 7
BIST	Built-In-Self-Test	Chapter 9

BSP	Board Support Package	Chapter 3
CBTC	Communication Based Train Control	Chapter 11
CCT	Central Command Terminal	Chapter 2
CDVE	Aircraft Flight Control System *Commande De Vol Electrique*	Chapter 6
CEI (see IEC)	International Electrotechnical Commission *Commission Electrotechnique Internationale*	Chapters 2, 8, 10, 12
CENELEC	European Committee for Electrotechnical Standardization *Comité Européen de Normalisation Electrotechnique*	Chapters 2-4, 11
CCC	CERN Control Center	Chapter 12
CCF	Common Cause of Failure	Chapter 12
CDU	Unique Failure Criterion *Critère de Défaillance Unique*	Chapter 12
CES	Security Input Card *Carte d'Entrée de Sécurité*	Chapter 3
CKD	Dynamic Controller *Contrôleur Dynamique*	Chapter 3
COTS	Commercial off-the-shelf	Chapters 1, 5, 10
CPL	Coupler Software *Logiciel Coupleur*	Chapter 3
CPLD	Complex Programmable Logic Device	Chapter 5
CPU	Central Processing Unit	Chapter 5, 9, 10
CRC	Cyclic Redundancy Check *Code à Redondance Cyclique*	Chapters 1, 3, 5, 9, 10
CSD	Available Security Computer *Calculateur de Sécurité Disponible*	Chapter 3
CTRL	Channel Tunnel Rail Link	Chapter 3
DESP	Physical Input/Output Device *Dispositif d'Entrée Sortie Physique*	Chapter 3
DIVA	Dynamic Integrated Vital and Available system	Chapter 3

DS	Safety case *Dossier de Sécurité*	Chapter 5
EAP	Solid Rocket Boosters *Etage d'Accélération à Poudre*	Chapter 7
EASA	European Aviation Safety Agency	Chapter 6
ECU	Electronic Control Unit	Chapter 9
ED	Error Detection	Chapter 1
EHA	Electro Hydrostatic Actuator	Chapter 6
EIS	Important Safety Element *Elément Importants de Sûreté*	Chapter 12
EMC	Electromagnetic Compatibility	Chapter 5
EOQA	Expert or Approved and Qualified Organization *Expert ou Organisme Qualifié Agréé*	Chapter 2
EPC	Cryotechnic Main Stage *Etage Principal Cryotechnique*	Chapter 7
EPH	Hydraulic Steering Electronics *Electronique de Pilotage Hydraulique*	Chapter 7
EPSF	Railway Safety Authority *Etablissement Public de Sécurité Ferroviaire*	Chapters 2, 5
ERTMS	European Railway Traffic in Management System	Chapter 3
ESA	European Space Agency	Chapter 7
ESP	Electronic Stability Program	Chapter 9
EV	Solenoid Valve *Electrovanne*	Chapter 7
FAA	Federal Aviation Authority	Chapter 6
FDIR	Fault Detection Isolation and Recovery	Chapter 7
FO	Fail Operational	Chapter 7
FPGA	Field-Programmable Gate Array	Chapters 2, 5, 11
FMEA	Failure Mode and Effects Analysis	Chapter 12
FS	Failsafe	Chapter 7

MTTR	Mean Time To Repair	Chapter 10
NC	Normally Closed	Chapter 10
nOOm	n-out-of-m *n parmis m*	Chapter 1
OBC	On Board Computer	Chapter 7
OPEL	Elementary Operations of the Coded Uniprocessor: primitives used to manipulate coded variables *Opérations Elémentaires du monoprocesseur* *codé*	Chapters 3, 11
OREDA	Offshore Reliability Data	Chapter 8
OS	Operating System	Chapters 3, 4, 7
PADRE	Protocol for Asymmetric Duplex Redundancy	Chapter 2
PC	Personal Computer	Chapter 5
PCD	Remote Command Terminal *Poste de Commande Distant*	Chapter 4
PFH	Probability of Failure per Hour	Chapters 8, 10
PIPC	Computer-based Interlocking System *Poste Informatique à technologie PC*	Chapters 4, 5
PLC	Programmable Logic Controller	Chapter 12
PRA	Preliminary Risk Analysis	Chapter 12
PRCI	Computer-controlled Relay Interlocking System *Poste à Relais à Commande Informatique*	Chapter 5
PREDIT	Program for Coordinating Research and Innovation Policy in the area of Land Transportation *Programme de Recherche et D'Innovation dans* *les Transports terrestres*	Chapter 3
PSC	Coded Safety Processor *Processeur Sécuritaire Codé*	Chapters 1, 3
PU	Processing Unit	Chapters 3, 7
PVM	Missionized Flight Program *Programme de Vol Missionisé*	Chapter 7

PVOL	Flight Program *Programme de Vol*	Chapter 7
RAMS	Reliability Availability Maintainability and Safety	Chapter 4
RAT	Ram Air Turbine	Chapter 6
RER	Regional Express Network *Réseau Express Régional*	Chapters 1, 2
RFF	French Rail Network *Réseau Ferré de France*	Chapter 5
RTE	RunTime Environment	Chapter 9
SACEM	Driving, Operational and Maintenance Assistance System *Système d'Aide à la Conduite, à l'Exploitation et à la Maintenance*	Chapters 1-3
SAET	Automation of Operational Train Control System *Système d'Automatisation de l'Exploitation des Trains*	Chapter 2
SdF	Dependability *Sûreté de Fonctionnement*	Chapter 4
SDV	Sign of Life *Signe de Vie*	Chapter 3
SEC_RED	software managing the integrated redundancy *SECurité REDondance*	Chapter 11
SEEA	Software Error Effect Analysis	Chapter 5
SEI	System of Integrated Interlocking *Système d'Enclenchement Intégré*	Chapter 3
Security Application	The application part of the security software	Chapter 11
SIL	Safety Integrity Level	Chapters 2-5, 8, 9, 11
SIS	Safety Instrumented Systems	Chapters 8, 10
SNV	Non Validated Output *Sortie Non Validée*	Chapter 3

SPS	Super Proton Synchrotron	Chapter 12
SRCF	Safety Related Control Function	Chapter 10
SRI	Inertial Reference System *Système de Référence Inertielle*	Chapter 7
SSIL	Software Safety Integrity Level	Chapters 3-5
STRMTG	National Agency Taskforce for Ropeway and Guided Transport Safety *Service Technique des Remontées Mécaniques et des Transports Guidés*	Chapter 2
SYMEL	Modular System for Line Equipment *Système Modulaire d'Equipement des Lignes*	Chapter 4
TGV	High Speed Train *Train à Grande Vitesse*	Chapter 3
THR	Tolerable Hazard Rate	Chapter 3
TI	Injection Tunnel *Tunnel d'injection*	Chapter 12
TOR	All or Nothing Type Signal *Tout ou Rien*	Chapters 2, 5, 10, 12
TVM	Train Vital Management	Chapters 2, 3
UAL (see ALU)	Arithmetic Logic Unit *Unité Arithmétique et Logique*	Chapter 1
UES	Input / Output Unit *Unité Entrées/sorties*	Chapter 7
VAL	Automatic Light Vehicle *Véhicule Automatique Léger*	Chapter 2
VME	Versa Module Eurocard	Chapter 3
VL	Logical Path *Voie Logique*	Chapter 3

List of Authors

Marc ANTONI
SNCF
Paris
France

Sylvain BARO
SIEMENS Transportation System
France

Christine BEZARD
Airbus
Toulouse
France

Jean-Paul BLANQUART
Astrium Satellites
Toulouse
France

Jean-Louis BOULANGER
CERTIFER
Anzin
France

Grégory BUCHHEIT
ENSAM
Paris
France

Jean-Michel CAMUS
Airbus
Toulouse
France

Yassine CHAABI
Total
Pau
France

Daniel DRAGO
Thales Rail Signalling
Vélizy-Villacoublay
France

Christophe GIRARD
Ansaldo STS
Les Ulis
France

Silvia GRAU
CERN
Geneva
Switzerland

Isabelle LACAZE
Airbus
Toulouse
France

Tomasz LADZINSKI
CERN
Geneva
Switzerland

Hervé LEBERRE
Airbus
Toulouse
France

Gilles LEGOFF
Ansaldo STS
Les Ulis
France

David LIAIGRE
PSA Peugeot Citroën
La Garenne-Colombes
France

Olaf MALASSE
ENSAM
Paris
France

Philippe MIRAMONT
CNES
Courcouronnes
France

Pierre NININ
CERN
Geneva
Switzerland

Patrick RINGEARD
Airbus
Toulouse
France

Jean-Pierre SIGNORET
Total
Pau
France

Jean SOUYRIS
Airbus
Toulouse
France

Pascal TRAVERSE
Airbus
Toulouse
France

Francesco VALENTINI
CERN
Geneva
Switzerland

Index